The British in Germany, 1918–1930

David G. Williamson

This study analyses the British presence in Germany from the Armistice until the end of the Rhineland occupation in 1930. It looks at British involvement in the Rhineland, Danzig, Upper Silesia, Schleswig and East Prussia and in the inter-Allied Control Commission in Berlin. The author explores the problems facing British military and civil officials, their attitudes towards the Germans and their relations with their allies – particularly the French. In addition, he examines diplomatic activities and the question of how key decisions in London and Paris were reached. In conclusion, both the official and unofficial retrospective assessments of the first occupation of Germany during the time when the second occupation was being planned (1943–5) are discussed.

David G. Williamson is Head of History and Politics at Highgate School, London.

The British in Germany, 1918–1930

The Reluctant Occupiers

David G. Williamson

BERG

New York / Oxford

Distributed exclusively in the US and Canada by
St Martin's Press, New York

First published in 1991 by
Berg Publishers Limited
Editorial Offices:
165 Taber Avenue, Providence R.I. 02906, USA
150 Cowley Road, Oxford OX4 1JJ, UK

British Library Cataloguing in Publication Data
Williamson, D.G. (David Graham) *1940–*
  The British in Germany, 1918–30.
  1. Great Britain. Foreign relations with Germany, history
  2. Germany. Foreign relations with Great Britain, history
  I. Title
  327.41043

Library of Congress Cataloging-in-Publication Data
Williamson, D.G.
  The British in Germany, 1918–30 / David G. Williamson.
    p.   cm.
  Includes bibliographical references and index.
    1. Germany—History—Allied occupation, 1918–1930.   2. Military
  government—Germany—History—20th century.   3. Military
  government—Great Britain—History—20th century.   4. British
  Germany—History—20th century.   5. Reconstruction
  (1914–1939)—Germany.
  6. Rhineland (Germany)—History.   I. Title.
  DD238.W55   1991
  943.085—dc20   90–37546
                                                                            CIP

ISBN 0–85496–584–X

Printed in Great Britain by
Billing & Sons Ltd, Worcester

To Mary, Alexander and Antonia who have had to tolerate the researching and writing of this book for so long

Contents

Contents

Contents

Acknowledgements

Without the kindness, encouragement and ready assistance of so many archivists, librarians and relations of those who served in Germany during the period 1918–30, this book would never have been written. I am particularly grateful to the staff of the Public Records Office at Kew, of the Imperial War Museum and of the Foreign and Commonwealth Office Library where I have been a frequent and demanding visitor. They never complained and unfailingly produced the files I needed. On my shorter visits to the National Army Museum, the Liddell Hart Centre for Military Archives, the Archives of the Bank of England, the Midland Bank and Lloyds Bank, the National Library of Scotland, the House of Lords Record Office and the Royal Institute of International Affairs, I met with the same helpfulness and courtesy. I was as expertly and generously assisted by the archivists of the Bundesarchiv, Coblenz, the Historisches Archiv, Cologne, the Ministère des Affaires Etrangères, Paris and the Service historique de l'Armée de Terre, Château de Vincennes.

I also received invaluable advice, background information and generous hospitality from Dr R. Roberts of Schroders, Major H. Bingham, Mr C.J. Ball, Dr J. Fox, Major D.S. Robertson, Mr B. O'Brien, Miss W. Tower and Mr D.W.M. Long, while Dr J. Bourdillon, Lord Dunboyne, Mrs H.M. Piggott, Mr P. Quarry, Dr R. Davenport-Hines, Lord Eden of Winton, Mr C. Beaumont, Dr J.F. Mason and Lord Kilmarnock have all been patient and very helpful in answering either by post or on the telephone my frequently obscure questions. My thanks are also due to Mr R. Morelle, Mr C.H.R. Gee, Corporal C. Painter and Sergeant J. McLellan, who all served on the Rhine and whose reminiscences brought the period to life for me.

Without three generous grants from the British Academy I would never have been able to work in the French and German archives.

I would like to thank the following for granting me permission to use copyright material within their possession: Dr M. Ashby; Mr C.J. Ball; Mr C. Beaumont; Major H. Bingham; the British Library; Mr J. Carter; the Governing Body of Christ Church, Oxford; Miss J. Douglas; Mr A. Fleetwood-Wilson; Mrs A. Gedye;

Acknowledgements

Mrs P. Goodman; Earl Haig; Messrs Haldanes, Maclaren and Scott; the Editor of *History Today*; the Clerk of the Records, House of Lords Record Office; the Labour Party; the London Yearly Meeting of the Religious Society of Friends; the Trustees of the Liddell Hart Centre for Military Archives, King's College, University of London; Lloyds Bank; Midland Bank; the National Army Museum; the Editor of the *Review of International Studies*; Major D.S. Robertson; Lord Robertson of Oakridge; Lord Sackville; the Warden and Fellows of St Antony's College, Oxford; Mr H. Tiarks; Miss R.A. Vining; Mr J. Winscomb. In some cases copyright owners have been elusive, despite every effort to track them down.

I am most grateful to Mrs Paula Abbott for so professionally typing my manuscript, to Mrs Trudi Barnett for photo-copying endless pages, to Mr Alex Williamson for drawing two maps, and to Miss Antonia Williamson for helping me to check the footnotes during that hot July of 1989.

D.G.W.
London, May 1990

Note on References

The abbreviations ADM, BT, CAB, FO and WO in the footnotes refer to the Admiralty, Board of Trade, Cabinet, Foreign Office and War Office papers in the Public Record Office, Kew. For the location of all other documents quoted consult the List of Abbreviations and Bibliography.

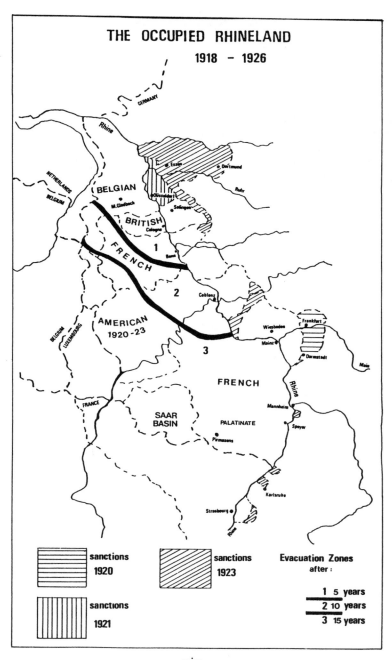

THE OCCUPIED RHINELAND
1918 – 1926

GERMANY

Rhine

NETHERLANDS

BELGIUM

BELGIAN

Essen   Dortmund

M.Gladbach   Düsseldorf   Ruhr

Solingen

BRITISH

Cologne

FRENCH   1

Bonn

2   Coblenz

AMERICAN   Wiesbaden   Frankfurt
1920-23   Mainz

BELGIUM

LUXEMBOURG   3   Darmstadt   Main

FRENCH   Rhine

FRANCE   Mannheim

SAAR   PALATINATE
BASIN   Speyer

Pirmasens

Karlsruhe

Strasbourg   Rhine

	sanctions 1920		sanctions 1923	Evacuation Zones after :

1 5 years
2 10 years
3 15 years

sanctions 1921

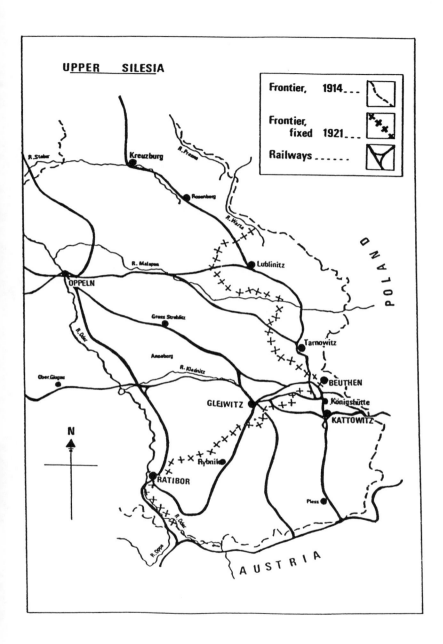

Introduction

Between December 1918 and June 1930 British officials, sometimes reinforced by troops, played a decisive role in the commissions which were set up by the Treaty of Versailles to oversee and guarantee the execution of the peace terms by Germany. British troops remained in the Rhineland until December 1929 and a British representative sat on the inter-Allied Rhineland High Commission until its dissolution in June 1930. A decade earlier the British administrative and military presence in Germany reached its peak. There was a British High Commissioner with troops in Danzig, further garrisons and officials were deployed by the inter-Allied Plebiscite Commissions in Schleswig and Allenstein, while British administrative elements sat on the Marienwerder and Silesian Commissions. In May 1921 at the time of the third Korfantry revolt a British division was sent to Silesia where it remained for over a year. British officers also played a key part on the Military, Aeronautical and Naval Commissions which were charged with the responsibility for monitoring the pace of German disarmament.

This British military and civil presence in Germany has never been the subject of a comprehensive analysis.[1] Initially the very

1. For short accounts of the British in the Cologne Zone see M-L. Recker, 'Adenauer und die englische Bestazungsmacht (1918–26)' in *Konrad Adenauer. Oberbürgermeister von Köln. Festgabe der Stadt Köln zum 100. Gerburtstag ihres Ehrenbürgers am 5.1.76*, Cologne, 1976, pp. 99–121; D.G. Williamson, 'Cologne and the British', *History Today*, vol. 27, Nov. 1977, pp. 695–702. There is some useful background material in F.L. Carsten, *Britain and the Weimar Republic*, London, 1984, and A. Kaiser, *Lord D'Abernon und die englische Deutschlandpolitik 1920–26*, Frankfurt a.M., Bern, New York and Paris, 1989. On Silesia the most useful study is by G. Bertram-Libal, 'Die britische Politik in der Oberschlesienfrage, 1919–22', *Vierteljahrshefte für Zeitgeschichte*, vol. 20, no. 2, April 1972, pp. 105–32. There is no specific study of the British role in the other plebiscite regions or in Danzig, although there is useful background information in S. Wambaugh, *Plebiscites since the World War*, 2 vols, Washington DC, 1933, and C.M. Kimmich, *The Free City: Danzig and German Foreign Policy, 1919–34*, New Haven and London, 1968. A.M. Cienciala and T. Komarnicki, *From Versailles to Locarno. Keys to Polish Foreign Policy, 1919–25*, Kansas, 1984, contains relevant material on both Upper Silesia and Danzig. There is similarly no comprehensive study of British participation in the

novelty of the occupation inspired some of the participants to write racy and often informative accounts of the British in the Rhineland.[2] By the early 1930s the occupation was seen as a 'postscript to the Western front',[3] but in 1943 when a second Allied victory over Germany seemed certain, the occupation of 1918–39 acquired a new significance, and studies of its military, civil and legal aspects were made in preparation for the post-war occupation. Brigadier-General Edmonds, the Head of the Historical Department of the War Office, compiled a detailed history[4] of the military occupation of the Rhineland based on the memories of contemporaries and on those records of the British Army of the Rhine which had escaped destruction in the Blitz. Edmonds' work found little favour with the Foreign Office, which criticized it both for neglecting the political dimension to the occupation and for its allegedly anti-French bias.[5] Consequently only a small number of copies were printed and the type was destroyed in November 1947.[6] In 1987 it was belatedly reprinted.[7] As a record of the Rhine Army it is an essential book of reference, but it lacks an analysis of the political and economic dimensions to the occupation and inevitably only touches perfunctorily on the Plebiscite and Control Commissions.

The end of the Second World War prompted a number of retrospective studies by veterans of the first occupation, studies which were, for the most part, scathingly critical of British policy in Germany in the 1920s, and which interpreted the mildly pro-German attitude of British troops and officials at that time as the consequence of 'insidious German propaganda',[8] or of an almost criminal gullibility on the part of the officers and officials con-

three Control Commissions. M. Salewski, *Entwaffnung und Militärkontrolle in Deutschland, 1919–27*, Munich, 1966 is an indispensable general survey, but the only specific study is in J.P. Fox, 'Britain and the inter-Allied Military Commission of Control, 1925–26', *Journal of Contemporary History*, vol. 4, April 1969, pp. 143–64.
2. For instance see V.R. Markham, *A Woman's Watch on The Rhine*, London, 1920 and the articles by G.E.R. Gedye in *The Bystander*, 1919–21 (Collection in IWM Gedye/12). Unfortunately no senior British officials in the Rhineland published their diaries or 'Rhineland memoirs' as did General Allen, the Commander of the American forces on the Rhine.
3. F. Tuohy, *Occupied, 1918–30: A Postscript to the Western Front*, London, 1931.
4. J.E. Edmonds, *The Occupation of the Rhineland*, HMSO, 1944, CAB 44/31.
5. See Minute by Prof. Webster, 4.11.43, and note from A.B. Acheson to J.W. Nicholls, 9.3.49, CAB 45/82.
6. Latham to Trend, 17.12.57, CAB 45/82.
7. Facsimile edition with Introduction by G.M. Bayliss (Imperial War Museum), HMSO, 1987.
8. E.R. Troughton, *It's Happening Again*, London, 1945, p. 49.

cerned.[9] Inevitably the cataclysmic consequences of Hitler's war and the almost immediate onset of the Cold War led to 'a certain narrowness of perspective amongst historians',[10] who tended to view the inter-war period as a prelude to the Second World War and the later division of Europe. More recently there have been major attempts to study the first post-war era on its own terms. Historians have begun the task of placing the diplomatic history of the 1920s within the context of contemporary economic and social developments.[11] New light has been shed on French policy in the Rhineland and Silesia,[12] the American occupation of the Coblenz zone,[13] Anglo-American financial policy in the period 1918–24[14] and on the economic and social constraints on British foreign policy,[15] but still no comprehensive monograph has emerged on the British in Germany, 1918–30. Consequently, this book is an attempt to supplement our understanding of the post-1918 reconstruction of Europe by studying in detail the British military and administrative involvement in Germany in the 1920s, where as a result of their efforts to modify the Treaty of Versailles in 1919, the British found themselves trapped in the storm centres of Central Europe: the Rhineland, Danzig and Upper Silesia, as well as being heavily committed to participating in the long drawn-out and at times bitterly contested operations of the Military, Naval and Aeronautical Control Commissions. I have drawn heavily on the

9. J.H. Morgan, *Assize of Arms*, vol. I, London, 1945.
10. K.L. Nelson, *Victors Divided*, Berkeley, 1975, p. ix.
11. For instance C.S. Maier, *Recasting Bourgeois Europe*, Princeton, 1975, and P. Krüger, *Die Außenpolitik der Republik von Weimar*, Darmstadt, 1985.
12. G.H. Soutou, 'La Politique Economique de la France en Pologne (1920–24)', *Revue Historique*, vol. 251, 1974, pp. 85–116; W.A. McDougall, *France's Rhineland Diplomacy, 1914–24*, Princeton, 1978; G.H. Soutou, 'La France et Les Marches de l'est, 1914–1919', *Revue Historique*, vol. 260, 1978, pp. 341–88; R. McCrum, 'French Rhineland Policy at the Peace Conference, 1919', *Historical Journal*, vol. 21, no. 3, 1978, pp. 623–48; D. Stevenson, *French War Aims*, Oxford, 1982.
13. Nelson, *Victors Divided*.
14. See for instance P. Abrahams, 'American Bankers and the Economic Tactics of Peace, 1919', *Journal of American History*, vol. 56, no. 3, 1969, pp. 572–83; D. Artaud, 'Le Gouvernement Américain et la question de dettes de guerre au lendemain de l'armistice de Réthondes, 1919–20', *Revue d'histoire moderne et contemporaire*, vol. 20, 1973, pp. 201–29; S.A. Schuker, *The End of French Predominance in Europe*, Chapel Hill, 1976; M. Trachtenberg, *Reparation in World Politics: France and European Diplomacy, 1916–1923*, New York, 1980.
15. G. Niedhart, 'Multipolares Gleichgewicht und weltwirtschaftliche Verflechtung: Deutschland in der britischen Appeasementpolitik 1919–33', in M. Stürmer (ed.), *Die Weimarer Republik – belagerte civitas*, Königstein, 1980, pp. 113–30; B. Porter, *Britain, Europe and the World, 1850–1982, Delusions of Grandeur*, London, 1983; L. Jaffe, *The Decision to Disarm Germany. British Policy towards Post-war German Disarmament, 1914–1919*, London and Sydney, 1985.

cable traffic between Cologne, Coblenz, Oppeln, Danzig, Berlin and London, but I have supplemented it with other material from British, French and German military and civil archives, as well as from private collections and newspapers in order to give an account, whenever possible, of the problems at local level confronting British military and civil officials in the Rhineland and Danzig and on the Plebiscite and Control Commissions and to show how the subaltern, private soldier, civilian official and their dependents lived in what were at times virtually British colonies in Germany.

A study of this first British involvement in Germany is long overdue not only because it formed an essential reservoir of experience for the second and much more complex occupation after 1945, but also because Germany was the major arena where rival Anglo–French plans for the reconstruction of Europe clashed. An analysis of the day-to-day problems of British officials on the various inter-Allied commissions and of their relations with their French colleagues, and with the Germans, enables the actual execution of Britain's post-war policy on European reconstruction to be studied. The dramatic rows, crises and diplomatic fence-mending that occurred in Coblenz, Oppeln, Danzig and on the Inter-Allied Military Control Commission (IAMCC) in Berlin is an important aspect of the history of the *Entente* in the early 1920s. It also provides a graphic illustration of the consequences of the essential weakness of British power. The British could not afford to stand aloof from Europe, but lacked the means to intervene effectively.[16] Their military presence was either non-existent, as initially was the case in Silesia in 1920, or often composed of almost token forces, which were greatly outnumbered by the French armies of occupation. The Foreign and War Offices thus sought to bridge the gap between British responsibilities and lack of resources by relying on the diplomatic skill of their representatives on the spot. Sometimes the burden was too great to be borne, especially when officials lacking experience of post-war Germany were confronted with the intractable problems caused by the fundamental clash between British and French interpretations of the Treaty of Versailles. The limits of British power were then painfully exposed. As the interpretation of the execution of the Treaty of Versailles was the main point of issue between the British and French in Germany, it is perhaps paradoxical but hardly surprising that, with some important exceptions, British officials were more concerned with the

16. C.J. Lowe and M.L. Dockrill, *The Mirage of Power*, vol. 2, pp. 375–9, London, 1972; Porter, *Britain, Europe and the World*, pp. 82–110.

French 'problem' than the German 'problem'. In British eyes it was the French, at least up to 1925, who created the German problem by threatening German unity and economic revival, which were essential prerequisites for a European economic recovery, and by constantly needling the Germans into a desire for revenge.

In the winter of 1918/19 the British army in the Cologne Zone, in marked contrast to the naval personnel who inspected the German ports after the Armistice,[17] did not share the rabid Germanophobia of the British public, which had been fuelled by wartime propaganda. It is arguable that reports of the civilized, even friendly reception given to the Second Army in the Rhineland began to modify Britain's perception of the 'Hun'. The army was quick to point out the impact on the German population of the continued blockade and the paramount importance of restoring the German economy if revolution was to be avoided. As the logic of Britain's post-war situation began to be appreciated in Britain, public opinion caught up with and even overtook the army's initially more realistic attitude towards Germany. Essentially Britain's only hope of survival as a great power was the rapid restoration of peace and the revival of world trade, in which process the German economy would have to play a leading role.[18] The City, industry and the trade unions rapidly grasped this and most junior British officials in Germany instinctively understood it. In their desire to 'play the game'[19] and to protect the German 'underdog' in the period up to 1924, they were executing their country's policy of preserving Germany as a great economic power. Inevitably, of course, there were a few officials who had a fierce loyalty to the French, and a larger number who were indifferent to the Germans and the German problem and who stayed on in Germany to enjoy the advantages of a life as a comparatively well-paid British official in a post-war Germany racked by inflation. The occupying forces and officials, with their families, represented a cross-section of British society. Their views and actions are thus revealing about British attitudes to the post-war German 'underdog' during the period 1919–24.

The turning point in the history of the British in Germany came in 1924. Up to the early spring of that year British officials were

17. See for instance E.W.C. Thring's 'Diary of Events connected with the Allied Naval Commission to Germany in December 1981', 20 Dec. 1918, IWM 71/30/1.
18. Porter, *Britain, Europe and the World*.
19. The significance of the phrase 'play the game' is explored by C. Veitch in '"Play up! Play up! and Win the War!" Football, the Nation and the First World War, 1914–15', *Journal of Contemporary History*, vol. 20, no. 3, 1985, pp. 363–76.

primarily concerned with restraining the French from exploiting the Treaty of Versailles in order to establish a permanent hegemony over Germany. After the failure of the Ruhr occupation, the adoption of the Dawes Plan in August 1924 and the subsequent Treaty of Locarno in October 1925 marked the restoration of Germany as a great European power. The Rhineland occupation now increasingly appeared as an anomaly and was subjected to mounting criticism by both the Germans and the British Labour and Liberal Parties. It became an irritant in Anglo–German relations rather than a positive factor, which it had hitherto been, as it no longer protected the local population from the French. When the Rhine Army moved to Wiesbaden in January 1926, it never established the same rapport with the local population which it had enjoyed in Cologne. Not surprisingly relations improved with the French to the point where the Germans feared a new *Entente*. In the final three years of the occupation the British led a life in the remote neo-colonial world of the Wiesbaden Zone which was not so different from that led by the Raj in India.

PART I

The Armistice and the Peace, 1919

Introduction

The difference between the genesis of the two British post-war occupations of Germany could not be more marked. In May 1945 an Allied occupation had already been decided upon in principle and meticulously planned as an essential guarantee of denazification and disarmament. The German collapse in the spring of 1945 had long been foreseen: the only surprise was that it had not come earlier. In stark contrast to this, not only in September 1918 did no British plans for an occupation exist, although preparations for feeding the population of the liberated Belgian and French territories had been drawn up,[1] but Germany still appeared a formidable and tenacious enemy, whose defeat at the very earliest could not be anticipated until the summer of 1919. Indeed the Treaty of Brest-Litovsk of March 1918 with Russia had opened up the prospect of German expansion into the Caucasus, Persia and Afghanistan and ultimately to India itself.[2]

The very nature of British war aims discouraged elaborate plans for an occupation of Germany.[3] Essentially the British wanted the destruction of German militarism by a decisive defeat, which would discredit the 'Prussian' militarists and enable peaceful democratic forces to take over. As a consequence of victory, the British government naturally intended to ensure the permanent destruction of the German fleet, the liquidation of the German Colonial Empire, and the renegotiation of the Treaty of Brest-Litovsk. But in

1. Quartermaster-General's Diary, 'Explanatory Review', Sept. 1918, Appendix IX, p. 7, WO 95/40.
2. 'Allied Plans for the Autumn of 1918 and the Year 1919', Wilson Papers, IWM 73/1/26 file 12D. V.H. Rothwell, *British War Aims and Peace Diplomacy, 1914–1918*, Oxford, 1971, p. 185.
3. For a discussion of British war aims see H.I. Nelson, *Land and Power. British and Allied Policy on Germany's Frontiers, 1916–19*, London and Toronto, 1963, pp. 3–87; and Rothwell, *British War Aims*. Also A.J.P. Taylor, 'The War Aims of the Allies in the First World War', in R. Pares and A.J.P. Taylor (eds), *Essays to Namier*, London, 1956, pp. 475–505.

no way did it envisage that the Allies themselves should re-educate the Germans or, but for the shortest of periods, occupy German territory. The logic of British war aims was that the new Germany arising out of the defeat of 'Prussian' militarism needed to be appeased and, above all, not alienated by the annexation or lengthy occupation of its territory. Britain's territorial ambitions lay in the Middle East and not in Europe. A chastened Germany would be required to play her role in a new European balance of power, especially as, in the words of a Foreign Office official, 'a new danger – no less deadly – looms up in the near future. That danger is Bolshevism with its doctrine of irreconcilable class war.'[4]

4. Lowe and Dockrill, *The Mirage of Power*, p. 321.

-1-

The Occupation of the Rhineland

The Decision to Occupy the Rhineland, October 1918

The sudden collapse of the Central Powers, accelerated by the threatened domino effect of the Bulgarian capitulation of 28 September, caught the Allies by surprise. The German High Command privately conceded defeat on 29 September and urged the Kaiser to form a constitutional government, which by its liberal nature would impress the Allies, and be more effective in negotiating an armistice with them. On 4 October, the new German Chancellor, Max von Baden, dispatched the first of his notes to Washington indicating Germany's willingness to accept a peace on the basis of the 14 Points outlined by President Wilson in his speech on American war aims in January 1918. Decoded by French Intelligence it prompted the *Entente* to draft their own armistice conditions in order to be in a position to respond quickly when informed officially by Washington of the German note.[1] The urgency of this task enabled Marshall Foch and the French Prime Minister, Clemenceau, eventually to manoeuvre Lloyd George into accepting a temporary military occupation of the Rhineland, despite the obvious opportunities this would afford the French to pursue their aim of separating the Rhineland from the Reich, which the British government had consistently opposed.[2] However, until the Armistice agreement was signed Lloyd George oscillated between advocating modest terms, which would not drive Germany into a bitter defensive campaign, and using the full weight of Allied superiority to dictate an armistice that would be practically synonymous with a German surrender. He was above all haunted by the fear that once the conscript British army stopped fighting, it would refuse to renew the struggle if the Armistice broke down.

1. Rothwell, *British War Aims*, p. 251.
2. Lloyd George, *War Memoirs*, vol. 2, London, 1938, ch. 75. See for example Balfour's statement in the Commons, 19.12.17; *Parliamentary Debates*, 5th series, col. 2017.

Back in July his foreign secretary, Balfour, had already warned him of the dangers of a German peace offensive, which by making offers sufficiently plausible to be dangerous, though not sufficiently far reaching to be acceptable, would undermine the determination of both the soldiers at the front and the civilians at home to persevere with hostilities.[3]

On 8 October Allied military and naval experts prepared terms which would in practice entail a German capitulation. The first mention of the occupation of the Rhineland appeared in a separate note Foch sent to the Allied Supreme War Council in which he suggested that the left bank of the Rhine and three bridgeheads, each of a 30 kilometre circumference, should be occupied as a guarantee for the future payment of reparations and 'administered by the Allied troops in concert with the local authorities up to the time of the signature of the peace'. Initially Lloyd George was critical of the severity of these terms, but when the text of Wilson's reply of 8 October to the German note reached Paris, he began to suspect that a German acceptance of the 14 Points, 'which were capable of any number of interpretations', might provide a smokescreen behind which the enemy would retire to regroup their forces. He consequently swung round virtually to endorse Foch's terms.[4]

On 11 October Lloyd George returned to London and for the next two weeks the Cabinet anxiously followed the exchange of notes between Washington and Berlin. Ministers, unaware of the imminent German collapse, were concerned by the growing exhaustion of the Allied armies. On 21 October when Sir Douglas Haig, the Commander of the British Expeditionary Force, stressed that the German army was still capable of fighting, opinion within the Cabinet was divided between those who sought military security in the severest possible armistice terms and those who feared that such an approach would be self-defeating by encouraging the German army to even greater tenacity. Haig opposed a Rhineland occupation and advised the Cabinet to insist merely on the evacuation of Alsace-Lorraine and a German withdrawal back across her own frontiers. His cogent arguments had a considerable impact,[5]

3. 'Notes on some of the problems which will face us if the German offensive fails', 17.7.18; HLRO, LG, F/160/1/12.
4. 'Process Verbal of a Conference held at the Quai d'Orsay on . . . 8.10.18' (IC 80), Appendix I and p. 5; ibid. 9.10.18 (IC 81), p. 4, CAB 28/5 fos 19–21 and 22–4.
5. War Cabinet, 21.10. 18 (no. 489(a)) and Appendix II, CAB 23/14, fos 178–216a. For similar advice on 19.10.18 see R. Blake, *The Private Papers of Douglas Haig*, London, 1952, pp. 332–4.

but their eventual rejection by the War Cabinet was foreshadowed when Admiral Wemyss outlined a draconian set of naval demands, which, as Haig noted later, were 'incapable of enforcement except by a land force'.[6]

An added note of urgency was given to these discussions when Wilson on 23 October at last referred the Germans to the *Entente* governments. Clemenceau immediately instructed Foch to confer with the Allied commanders-in-chief and informed him that a *sine qua non* of any armistice was a military occupation of the left bank of the Rhine. Haig, however, remained unconvinced and argued strongly that the German defensive position would be stronger behind the Rhine than if their troops were left 'astride the river holding the . . . frontier of 1870'. He suspected that 'on the whole' Foch's arguments were 'political'[7] rather than military, but at a conference at Foch's headquarters at Senlis on 25 October, he failed to convince either Pétain or the American commander, General Pershing, who both supported an occupation.[8]

The War Cabinet ultimately accepted that the participation of British troops in an occupation was necessary as a gauge 'to secure the abolition or reduction of the German fleet', even though Lloyd George was under no illusions that 'if the gauge consisted of territory west of the Rhine, France would not be in any hurry to give it up . . .'.[9] In a series of crucial meetings between 29 October and 4 November, President Wilson's representative, Colonel House, the Allied leaders and the Service Chiefs formulated the armistice conditions. The British statesmen remained uneasy at their severity. Balfour was still convinced that Germany would not accept them until she was 'beaten in the field much worse than was now the case'.[10] Lloyd George was particularly critical of Foch's plans to occupy Mannheim, Mainz and Cologne, and on 1 November persuaded the Allied leaders to reconsider Haig's arguments against an occupation, but Foch allayed some of his fears of a German counter-attack by stressing that 'the collapse of Austria, Bulgaria and Turkey would enable the Allies to concentrate all the forces released against Germany'.[11]

6. J. Terraine, *To Win a War*, London, 1978, p. 213.
7. Haig's Diary, 24.10.18, pp. 50–2, WO 256/37.
8. Terraine, *To Win a War*, pp. 216–18.
9. War Cabinet, 26.10.18 (no. 491B), CAB 23/14 fos 247–73.
10. 'Notes of a Conversation in M. Pichon's Room at the Quai d'Orsay', 29.10.18 (IC 83), p. 16, CAB 28/5 fos 30–4.
11. 'Notes of a Conversation at the Residence of Colonel House', 1.11.18 (IC 87), p. 5, CAB 28/5 fos 79–82. For an account of the Armistice negotiations with the Germans see K. Nelson, *Victors Divided*, pp. 22–3.

The armistice terms, which involved, as far as the Western Front was concerned, the immediate cession of Alsace-Lorraine to France, the withdrawal of the German army from all the invaded territories behind a line to the east of a designated neutral zone on the right bank of the Rhine, and the occupation by the Allies of the left bank and of the three bridgeheads of Mainz, Coblenz and Cologne, were finally approved by the Supreme War Council on 4 November. Three days later they were presented to the Germans at Réthondes and were signed in the early morning of 11 November after Foch had agreed to reduce the neutral zone to a width of 10 kilometres and to promise that the administrative links between occupied and unoccupied Germany would not be broken by the occupying authorities.

Right up until its signature the British government was doubtful whether the Germans would accept the armistice agreement and continued to have second thoughts about advancing into a Germany which appeared to be in the throes of a bolshevik revolution. Spreading from Kiel and Wilhelmshaven, where the ratings had mutinied against plans to launch the High Seas fleet on a suicide attack against the British navy, soviets of sailors, soldiers and workers had sprung up in many of the north German cities. On 7 November the Cologne garrison of 45,000 troops had mutinied and formed a revolutionary council. On the same day the left-wing journalist, Kurt Eisner, seized power in Munich. At a War Cabinet meeting on 10 November it was thus not surprising that Lloyd George should dramatically warn that 'marching men into Germany was marching them into a cholera area. The Germans did that in Russia and caught the virus, i.e. of Bolshevism.' Sir Henry Wilson, the Chief of the Imperial General Staff (CIGS), advised that the Rhenish provinces should be garrisoned as far as possible by American troops, while Churchill sounded a paradoxical note by warning that 'we might have to build up the German Army, as it was important to get Germany on her legs again for fear of the spread of Bolshevism'.[12] Already then, by the time of the signing of the Armistice, the 'virus of bolshevism', rather than German militarism, which was in such visible disarray, appeared to both the Cabinet and the British army to be the challenge of the future.

---

12. War Cabinet, 10.11.18 (no. 500A), CAB 23/14 fos 297–302. For a background of the events in Germany see G.A. Craig, *Germany, 1866–1945*, Oxford, 1978, pp. 396–402; E. Eyck, *Geschichte der Weimarer Republik*, vol. I, Zürich, 1956, ch. 2.

The March to the Rhine, November–December 1918

For Foch and his staff the military occupation of the left bank of the Rhine was an action of immeasurable importance, which gave France the chance to seal her victory over Germany by creating an independent French-orientated Rhineland. His aims were clearly stated in memoranda, which received the tacit support of Clemenceau and 'provided the skeletal form for the policy given official blessing until the end of March 1919'.[13] Despite their reservations about French intentions in the Rhineland, neither Haig nor Lloyd George showed much interest in the initial preparations for the occupation.

It fell to Foch, as Allied Commander-in-Chief, to draw up the detailed plans for the occupation. A preliminary allocation of zones, which was determined by the size of the occupying forces each power was ready to contribute and by the position of their armies in the field, was made on 9 November and confirmed on the 15th.[14] The French gained control of virtually half the left bank. In the south their zone included the whole of the Palatinate, the Saar, Rhenish Hesse and the Prussian Rhineland up to the Mosel, while in the north the Belgians were allotted a small strip of land running from Aachen to the Dutch frontier, but the key political and administrative centres of Coblenz and Cologne, together with their hinterland, were allocated to the United States and Britain.

Only on one issue was Haig moved to intervene. Foch had originally intended to occupy the three major bridgeheads of Cologne, Coblenz and Mainz with an inter-Allied force, but Haig, motivated more by the desire to avoid the complications of a mixed command rather than by any political foresight, insisted that a purely British and Dominion force should constitute the sole occupying army in Cologne. In retrospect Foch's agreement to this was a considerable error as British control of Cologne, which was the political and economic capital of the Rhineland, as well as the hub of the railway network in Western Germany, was to be a serious obstacle to French attempts to engineer an independent Rhineland.[15] Right up to 1926 the British stubbornly refused to

13. McDougall, *Rhineland Diplomacy*, p. 38. See Foch's Note of 28.11.18 (no. 7128) and Le Rond's 'Etude Sur Le Régime Futur Des Pays De La Rive Gauche Du Rhine', 17.11.18, Service historique de l'Armée de Terre, Château de Vincennes (hereafter Vincennes), 4N92–1.
14. Edmonds, *The Occupation*, pp. 9–32. Grant to DMO, 9.11.18 (no. 210), and 16.11.18 (no. 216), WO 158/84/Pt.5.
15. Haig's Diary, 17 and 18.11.18, NLOS Acc.3155/133 Grant to DMO, 20.11.18 (no. 220), WO 158/84/Pt.5. McDougall, *Rhineland Diplomacy*, p. 42.

evacuate Cologne even though in November 1919 they handed over the southern half of their zone to the French in order to economize on occupation personnel.

The guidelines for the occupation of the Rhineland[16] were drawn up by Foch's staff and served as the basis for the instructions issued to Plumer, the Commander of the Second Army, which was to constitute the British element of the occupying forces. They followed closely the rules formulated in the Hague Conference of 1899 on 'Military Authority over the Territory of the Hostile State'.[17] The Rhine provinces were to be placed under martial law but the local civilian authorities were to continue in office under the surveillance of Allied officers. To ensure a uniform administration, the Allied zonal commanders were ordered to send liaison officers weekly to Foch's headquarters. As Military Governor of the Zone with responsibility for the control of the civil population, Plummer appointed General Fergusson, the Commander of the XVII Corps.

Haig accepted these guidelines with an amused scepticism. He recorded approvingly in his diary the observation of one of his staff officers that 'the only possible way for a German to avoid contravening one or other of the many bye-laws will be to stay in bed' – and even then 'he will only escape provided he does not snore'. A week later, however, in his criticism of French plans to restrict the operation of the German postal system in the Rhineland, he revealed a more fundamental opposition to French policy when he confided again in his diary that 'we must not forget that it is in our interests to return to peace methods at once, to have Germany a prosperous, not an impoverished country'.[18] In November 1918 this view was not yet widely held in Britain, but over the next five years it was to become the guiding force in Britain's European policy. The War Cabinet was more concerned about the growing contradiction between the plans of its Demobilization Committee and the continuing need for troops in Western Europe, Russia and the Middle East,[19] than with the technical details of the Rhineland occupation. It was not until the informal 'Allied Conversation' of 3 December[20] that Lloyd George was given a report on the planning of the military occupation of the Rhineland, which he accepted with little comment, even though Foch assumed that the occupa-

16. Edmonds, *The Occupation*, pp. 60–83; see also Vincennes 4N92–1.
17. Edmonds, *The Occupation*, p. 60.
18. Haig's Diary, 20 and 27.11.18, NLOS Acc.3155/133.
19. War Cabinet, 21.11.18 (no. 505), CAB 23/8 fos 86–9.
20. 'Notes of a Conversation held in the Cabinet Room, 10 Downing St.', 3.12.18 (IC 100), CAB 28/5 fos 122–5.

tion would last for a year after the signature of the peace.

The Germans evacuated the occupied areas of France, Belgium and Luxemburg by 26 November. The first units of the Second Army crossed the German frontier on 2 December, and for the next two weeks a steady stream of troops poured into the Cologne Zone.[21] Although there was some fear of possible German snipers in the forests, Plumer's staff were more concerned with the dangers of socialist propaganda and the perils of fraternization with German women.[22] The British representative on the Armistice Commission, General Haking, had warned Haig that the British occupying troops possessed but the thinnest 'veneer of military training and discipline' and that 'our men have been killing Germans for four years and they think no more of killing a German than squashing a fly. We cannot expect that our troops will necessarily behave better in Germany than the Germans did in Belgium and France.'[23] In fact, despite hearing lurid tales of German atrocities in Belgium, the mood of the soldiers was for the most part one of curiosity and compassion. They crossed the border with fixed bayonets, colours flying and bands playing, but there was little desire to lord it as conquerors, although there was, of course, every intention to take advantage of the chance to obtain comfortable billets and other creature comforts. In a revealing entry in his diary a private in the Royal Engineers described how when a German civilian inadvertently walked through the marching ranks of a British infantry brigade at Malmedy, the Brigadier-General and his Aide-de-Camp

> rode round to the civilian . . . and forced him back to where he came from and told him off for it. Possibly he didn't understand, but the Brigadier said 'why don't you remove your hat when you talk to a general?' As the civilian didn't take any notice, the Brigadier snatched his hat off and flung it into the mud. And that's merely doing as their officers have done in France and Belgium.[24]

The German officials cooperated willingly with the military authorities as martial law filled the dangerous vacuum left by the retreating German army and insulated them from the revolutionary chaos that was threatening to engulf the Reich. Some of the British

---

21. The delays and problems besetting the advance are described in the Quarter-master-General's Diary, 'The Problems of the Advance', pp. 4–6, WO 95/40.
22. Lt. Goodman to parents, 4.12.18, IWM 71/59/1.
23. Haking to CGS, GHQ, 4.12.18, p. 2 (D 18), WO 144/4 fos 65–70.
24. Diary of Pte D.H. Doe, 15.12.18, IWM P.326/T.

commanders were positively embarrassed by the friendliness of the German officials. General Sir Aylmer Haldane found it 'rather a strain to force oneself not to give way to one's natural inclinations to be somewhat friendly to individuals' but resisted the temptation by reminding himself of the German occupation of Belgium.[25]

On 3 December there were urgent requests from both the German General Staff at Cologne and the Oberbürgermeister, Konrad Adenauer, for a quick occupation of the city to prevent a dangerous hiatus developing between the withdrawal of the German army and the arrival of the British.[26] Plumer and Foch readily agreed and a force composed of cavalry and armoured cars under the command of General Lawson arrived at Cologne at midday on 6 December. Lawson immediately met Adenauer to discuss the city's security and the more unwelcome question of billeting. He insisted on the dissolution of the city's home guard and vetoed any participation of the newly created Soldiers' and Workers' Councils in their discussions. Adenauer unsuccessfully pressed for an immediate parade of troops through the city centre. Also worried by the possible consequences of a clash between British troops and gangs of local youths, he warned Lawson not to confuse their mischievous but essentially innocent trick of putting detonators on the tram lines with the first stages of a general uprising. Lawson, amused, assured him that 'his troops and the Cologne children would soon become the best of friends', but the interview ended on a more ambiguous note when Adenauer, who naturally wished to know the approximate number of troops to be stationed in Cologne, was cryptically told that he should regard Lawson's men as the '*hors d'oeuvre* to an unknown number of dishes'.[27]

During the next three days the Guards and the Second and Third Divisions marched into Cologne. The crowds watched them in sullen silence or with indifference, although one guardsman was pleased to note that 'the younger female population, however, greeted us with calls, handkerchiefs waving, etc'.[28] By 14 December the advance had reached the outer perimeter of the bridgehead, where the troops were ordered to dig trenches and lay wire en-

25. Diary of General Sir Aylmer Haldane, 16.12.18, NLOS MS.20250.
26. Edmunds, *The Occupation*, p. 90; Recker, 'Adenauer und die englische Besatzungsmacht', p. 101.
27. 'Verhandlung mit General Lawson', 6.12.18, HA d SK 902/241/1; T. Prittie, *Konrad Adenauer*, London, 1972, p. 42; Williamson, 'Cologne and the British', pp. 695–6; Recker, 'Adenauer und die englische Besatzungsmacht', pp. 100–1.
28. J.W. Drury, Diary of a Guardsman, 14.12.18, IWM P.191.

tanglements in case of a renewal of hostilities.[29] The Military Governor and his staff arrived on 11 December and set up their headquarters in the Hotel Monopol, 'visitors being turned out, bedroom furniture removed and office furniture installed'.[30]

The following day Fergusson saw Adenauer and told him that while the civil population would be disturbed as little as possible, it might be necessary 'to impose certain rules and regulations which may be very annoying, but which will have to be obeyed'. Adenauer's efforts to soften the impact of martial law met with no success, even though he cleverly tried to play on British Prussophobia by pleading eloquently that 'the population of Cologne is somewhat different from other German tribes. For many hundreds of years there has been a mixture of blood in the population of Cologne resulting in lightheartedness in the city.' Unmoved, Fergusson merely commented that the British regulations were identical with those enforced by the Germans in Belgium. Fergusson was assured that the Soldiers' and Workers' Councils were no threat, but he was ominously told that the city had only five or six weeks' food supply left and Adenauer gloomily predicted that 'there may be fear for the worst in a short time owing to difficulties of transport'.[31]

By mid-December the full rigour of martial law had been established in the Cologne Zone. Frontier control posts were set up between occupied and unoccupied Germany. The Zone was divided into areas and sub-areas under divisional and brigade commanders, which as far as possible corresponded to the Prussian units of Kreis and Gemeinde.[32] On all matters requiring policy decisions the area commandants consulted the Military Governor through their corps commanders. In principle the Military Government interfered with local administration as little as possible. Following precedents set by the Germans themselves in their occupation of French territory in 1871–4, the main point of contact between the military and civil authorities was at the top.[33] The Military Governor issued instructions to the mayors, district presidents and the chief of police, who then passed them down the

29. Edmonds, *The Occupation*, pp. 99–104.
30. 'Short Record of the Work of the Military Governor . . .', WO 95/277.
31. 'Minutes of a Conference between the Military Governor and the Oberbürgermeister, Cologne at the Monopol Hotel, 12.12.18', HA d SK 902/241/1
32. See Fergusson's synopsis for General Robertson, 16.4.19, LHCMA, Robertson I/28/2a.
33. J.H. Morgan, 'The British occupation of the Rhineland', 4.5.19 (no. 477/1/8–9325), FO 608/142 fos 147–50.

administrative hierarchy. The local police were placed under the supervision of the Provost Marshall's office. The German courts continued to exercise jurisdiction over German citizens who broke the Reich penal code, but offences against the occupation authorities were tried under martial law. Minor offences, such as failing to salute a British officer, were heard before a summary court, which could impose a maximum fine of 7,000 marks or imprisonment for six months. More serious offences went before a military court, which could award the death sentence, subject to confirmation from the Commander-in-Chief. In the first months of the occupation some thirty to forty cases were heard daily in the Cologne summary courts and many a respected and worthy Kölner, 'who had never thought that they would be involved in criminal proceedings, learnt in this way what the inside of Klingelputz Jail looked like . . . .'[34] Seeking to describe the occupation of Cologne, *The Times* correspondent quoted Abdhur Rahmen of Afghanistan who is supposed to have remarked 'that British rule settles on a district as softly as snow, but freezes as hard as ice'.[35]

In the chaotic circumstances of December 1918 such a 'freeze' was not entirely unwelcome to those desiring the status quo in the Rhineland. As the Cologne Zone was a part of the German Federal State of Prussia, the British insistence on dealing with the legally constituted Prussian authorities not only blocked attempts by soldiers' and workers' councils to take over local government, but also pre-empted plans of local separatists to set up an independent Rhineland. The British were paradoxically both conquerors and defenders of the constitutional status quo in the Rhineland.

---

34. J. Becker, 'Sieben Jahre britischer Herrschaft in Köln', p. 45, HA d Sk Chron.u. Darst. Nr.501, HA d SK.
35. *The Times*, 14.12.18. See also Recker, 'Adenauer und die englische Besatzungsmacht', pp. 99–100.

—2—

The Reluctant Assumption of Commitments, January–June 1919

When the Peace Conference began at Paris on 18 January, the essential British war aims had already been achieved: Britain had maintained her position as a great power, the majority of the German navy was anchored ignominiously in Scapa Flow, German commercial rivalry had, at least temporarily, been eliminated and her overseas empire was dissolved. Despite the anti-German hysteria of much of the electorate and many politicians in the general election of December 1918, the re-elected coalition government led by Lloyd George still envisaged the maintenance of a chastened, democratic Germany as a European great power, which would both be able to pay the reparations Lloyd George had pledged his government to demand, and act as a bulwark against bolshevik Russia. Above all Lloyd George wanted to avoid long-term European commitments and the perpetration of any new 'Alsace-Lorraines' in the Rhineland, Danzig or Upper Silesia, which would sow the seeds of a fresh war. Inevitably then, British objectives were fundamentally opposed to French policy, which was intent on securing material guarantees against a German military revival either by negotiating a long-term Anglo-American military guarantee of France's frontiers or by partial dismemberment of the German Empire. It was ironic that in his desperate attempts to modify French policy, Lloyd George ended by accepting commitments in Germany that were to keep British troops and administrators tied up for a decade after the signature of the peace.

The Genesis of the Control Commissions

At the end of December 1918, the British Cabinet decided to make disarmament an immediate priority on the grounds that this would enable it both to end conscription in Britain, which was deeply unpopular, and by weakening Germany's offensive capacity, to moderate French aims in the Rhineland. The extensive demobilization riots amongst British troops in France and England in January only served to emphasize the need to accelerate German disarmament. Consequently on 24 January[1] Lloyd George proposed to the Supreme War Council that a reduction in the size of the German army, the surrender of weapons and munitions and the destruction of key war factories should be made a precondition for the renewal of the Armistice. The subsequent discussions foreshadowed one of the more contentious Anglo–French arguments that were later to complicate the work of inter-Allied control in Germany. Foch sceptically observed that the controlling parties which would have to verify the destruction of the plants would only be allowed to see 'what the Germans wished them to see' and urged the Allied statesmen to keep the Rhineland occupation up to strength, while Lloyd George optimistically argued that 'in every country two or three factories alone were absolutely essential and when these went, the others would prove inadequate'. On his suggestion a committee was set up to draft a plan for controlling the German manufacture of armaments. Its proposals marked the genesis of the Inter-Allied Military Control Commission (IAMCC) that was to remain in Germany up to 1927.

The report was given a mixed reception on 7 February by the Supreme War Council,[2] where Lloyd George candidly conceded that 'all he wanted was to get the guns away from the Germans so that it might not be necessary to maintain huge armies'. A week later in Lloyd George's absence the Americans persuaded the British delegation to secure German disarmament as part of the peace treaty, rather than as a precondition for the renewal of the Armistice. On 12 February[3] the Supreme War Council renewed the Armistice indefinitely and appointed a fresh committee chaired by Foch to draw up the necessary military terms, the recommendations of which were reviewed on 3 March. The duration of the

1. 'Process-verbal of a meeting of the S.W.C. held in M. Pichon's Room', 24.1.19 (IC 118/BC A9), USFR, PPC vol. 3, pp. 704–14. For a background to the Peace Conference see A.J. Mayer, *Politics and Diplomacy of Peacemaking. Containment and Counter-revolution at Versailles, 1918–1919*, London, 1968, ch. 22; M.L. Dockrill and J.D. Goold, *Peace without Promise. Britain and the Peace Conferences, 1919–23*, London, 1981, ch. 2; M. Trachtenberg, 'Versailles after Sixty Years', *Journal of Contemporary History*, vol. 17, no. 3, 1982, pp. 487–506.
2. Minutes of the 1st Meeting of the 13th Session of the SWC, 7.2.19 (IC 135/BC 25) (Appendix B contains the report), USFR, PPC vol. 3, pp. 895–914.
3. Minutes of the 5th Meeting of the 13th Session of the SWC, 12.2.19 (IC 140/BC 29), USFR, PPC vol. 3, pp. 971–9.

Military Control Commission's activities in Germany and whether Germany should have a conscript or professional army emerged as key issues dividing Britain and France. France's determination not to compromise on German armaments was emphasized when Clemenceau angrily remarked that 'other countries might perhaps be content with transitory naval terms, but he himself was not prepared to sign an invitation to Germany to prepare for another attack by land after an interval of 3, 10, or even 40 years. He was not prepared to sign a peace on those conditions.'[4] Lloyd George wished to destroy conscription in Germany which the political Left in Britain, in Smuts' graphic phrase, believed was 'the taproot of militarism',[5] since he was convinced that if only Germany could be completely disarmed for five years, its people would never again tolerate rearmament and the reintroduction of conscription. Unlike the French, who pragmatically viewed German disarmament 'as merely another means of weakening Germany',[6] he also regarded German disarmament as the first step towards general European disarmament, which would have the added bonus of checking nascent French bonapartism. He did not share Foch's fear of the potential of German manpower, as in his eyes 'without cannon men alone constituted a small danger'.[7] With the support of Colonel House on 7 March,[8] he forced Clemenceau to drop Foch's plan for a German short service conscript army of 200,000 and to accept the principle of a regular army, although reluctantly he had to agree to a force of 100,000 rather than 200,000 men. It was left to Balfour to point out on 10 March[9] that if the German army became a mere police force, the Allies would have to guarantee the Reich against attack from Poland and Bohemia. Further proposals for the creation of Allied military, naval and aeronautical control commissions, the abolition of the German General Staff, a dramatic reduction in arms, munitions and war material, the demolition of all fortifications in the west, the complete dissolution of the airforce and the reduction of the navy to a handful of ships were accepted by the Supreme Council without serious debate.[10] On 17 March

4. Meeting of the 16th Session of the SWC, 3.3.19 (IC 153/BC 43), USFR, PPC vol. 4, pp. 182–90.
5. Jaffe, *The Decision to Disarm Germany*, p. 189.
6. Ibid., p. 188.
7. USFR, PPC vol. 3 (IC 118/BC A9), p. 710.
8. 'Notes of an Interview between M. Clemenceau, Col. House and Myself. . . 10.30 a.m. 7.3.19', HLRO, LG F/147/1.
9. Minutes of the 4th Meeting of the 17th Session of the SWC, 10.3.19 (IC 158/BC 48), USFR, PPC vol. 4, pp. 294–304.
10. Salewski, *Entwaffnung*, pp. 30–6; Jaffe, *The Decision*, pp. 192 and 257.

Wilson attempted to set a time limit to the activities of the Control Commissions but succeeded merely in having a clause inserted, which boldly stated that a 'time limit' was set, without defining precisely what this limit was.[11] This would prevent the French maintaining a permanent commission in Germany, but the moment of its withdrawal would be open to interminable debate.

Further modifications designed to reconcile Germany to the treaty merely introduced more ambiguities.[12] On 26 April Anglo-American pressure secured the statement that German disarmament was a preliminary to general disarmament. By ignoring the more robust French interpretation of disarmament as solely a means for destroying German power, the Allies gave the Germans a moral hostage for the future. In May, in response to German observations on the draft treaty, two more concessions were granted. The promise of Germany's entry into the League of Nations was held out as a reward once she had demonstrated her good faith by fulfilling the disarmament clauses. She was also given a transitional period until 31 March 1920 to effect a reduction in the size of her army.

The disarmament clauses of the treaty were a compromise, which on balance were more favourable to Britain than to France, but their ambiguity ensured that argument over their interpretation continued and enabled the French to insist on the IAMCC remaining in Germany until January 1927, when initially President Wilson had envisaged only a three-month period![13]

The Fifteen-Year Occupation of the Rhineland

In the first months of the occupation the Rhineland was a power vacuum, and the population, reeling under the impact of military defeat and fearful of bolshevism, was open to considerable political manipulation by the Allies. Beyond keeping the Rhineland as 'a liquid asset'[14] to ensure the surrender of the German fleet and agreement on reparations, the British government had no ambi-

11. Minutes of the 3rd Meeting of the 18th Session of the SWC, 17.3.19 (IC 162/BC 52), USFR, PPC vol. 4, pp. 355–78.
12. Jaffe, *The Decision*, pp. 195–213.
13. Salewski, *Entwaffnung*, p. 33.
14. 'Report by the Civil Commissioner . . .', 11.3.19, p. 5, FO 382/2316 fos 2461–2489.
15. See J.C. King, *Foch versus Clemenceau*, Cambridge MA, 1960, ch. 1; McDougall, *Rhineland Diplomacy*, ch. 1; R. McCrum, 'French Rhineland Policy at the Peace Conference, 1919', *Historical Journal*, vol. 21, no. 3, 1978, pp. 623–48.

tions on the Rhine, but to the French the occupation was a unique opportunity to weaken Germany permanently by detaching, through one means or another, the whole area from the Reich.[15]

In November 1918 Foch gave French plans in the Rhineland 'a momentum which no one else could supply',[16] when he drew up for Clemenceau a memorandum[17] in which he argued strongly that the Allies should create a series of client states on the Rhine and draw them into a military alliance with France, Belgium and Luxemburg. Clemenceau broadly accepted Foch's proposals, although in deference to anticipated American objections he deleted the plans for Rhenish conscription. Clemenceau did not officially raise the Rhenish question at the Peace Conference until the end of February as he hoped to soften potential Anglo-American hostility to the proposals by first securing Allied agreement on less contentious issues. On a visit to London in early December 1918 Clemenceau was careful to absent himself when Foch discussed the future of the Rhineland with Lloyd George and Bonar Law, the leader of the Conservative Party.[18] Both British politicians were unimpressed by Foch's assurances that he would avoid creating 'a new Alsace-Lorraine' by taking 'precautions to conciliate the feelings and interests [of the Rhinelanders]'. Bonar Law pessimistically observed 'that Germany had said exactly the same thing. We ourselves had tried for years to conciliate the Irish.' After attempting in vain for three months privately to drive a bargain with the Allies, Clemenceau first officially raised the Rhineland question at the Paris Conference on 25 February in a memorandum drafted by Tardieu, one of his closest advisers and a member of the French negotiating team. It was proposed that Germany's western frontier should be fixed at the Rhine, that the bridgeheads should be occupied by an inter-Allied force and that no permanent territorial annexation should be forced upon the Rhinelanders. The British and American delegations were initially impressed by the apparent moderation of the French proposals. After further talks with Tardieu, Balfour gained the impression that the French were thinking merely of setting up a temporary Rhineland state, which would after an interim period have the right to opt for reunion with Germany.

The War Cabinet discussed the French proposals for occupying

16. King, *Foch versus Clemenceau*, p. 14.
17. 'Note', 28.11.19, Vincennes 4N92-1.
18. 'Notes of a Conversation at 10 Downing St., 1.12.18' (IC 97), CAB 28/5 fo. 107.

the bridgeheads on 28 February.[19] While it was fundamentally hostile to them, the knowledge that Britain needed French support in the Middle East prevented any outright veto. Churchill caught the mood of the meeting when he advised his colleagues 'that in handling this question, we should show ourselves as sympathetic as possible to the French, for two reasons: first in order that she might show herself accommodating in regard to our eastern policy and second, to enable us to acquire great influence over France and the Peace Conference generally'. He was therefore ready to contemplate an occupation of the bridgeheads, 'subject to America bearing her share', and, to meet French security fears, he advocated the construction of a channel tunnel to facilitate the transport of an expeditionary force. On 4 March, however, the Cabinet was more outspoken against committing British troops to an occupation of the bridgeheads.[20] The Prime Minister expressed doubts whether Clemenceau really supported the occupation of the Rhineland and hoped that France could be appeased by assurances of German disarmament and support from the League of Nations. Lord Curzon, who was then the Lord President, dismissed the prospect of a permanent British occupation of the Rhine as 'intolerable', while the Chancellor of the Exchequer, Austen Chamberlain, observed that 'no British government . . . could propose garrisoning the Rhine with our troops beyond the period required to extract reparations and indemnity'. Churchill cynically remarked that 'if the French proposals were to be turned down . . . he should prefer that the veto should be imposed by the United States and not by ourselves'. The General Staff were also opposed to a permanent occupation; they argued that a military alliance with France would deter Germany more effectively and suggested that the British army should initially form part of the general reserve in any plans for another war against Germany, and that a channel tunnel capable of taking two or even four lines of rail traffic should be constructed to ensure its rapid deployment behind the Meuse.[21]

The whole issue of the Rhineland was discussed in Paris on 11–12 March in a special committee set up by Lloyd George, Clemenceau

---

19. War Cabinet, 28.2.19 (538A), CAB 23/15 fos 25–9; H. Nelson, *Land and Power*, pp. 206–9. For a general background see also D. Lloyd George, *Memoirs of the Peace Conference*, Yale, 1939, vol. 2, ch. 8.
20. War Cabinet, 4.3.19 (541A), CAB 23/15 fos 31–43.
21. See Note of 1.3.19 by the General Staff (no. 0.2/9/30), on War Cabinet paper: WCP 135, WO 158/109.

and Colonel House to draw up Germany's post-war boundaries.[22] The French delegate, André Tardieu, argued forcefully that 'the drawing of the German frontier on the Rhine, the constitution of an independent Rhenish state and the Allied command of the bridges were three legs of one plan and stood or fell together', and brushed aside objections by Phillip Kerr, the British delegate, that strong opposition to separation would be inevitable.[23] Although Kerr regarded Tardieu's proposals as 'a shell shock proposition', which he would 'resist . . . to the end', he nevertheless conceded that Allied forces would probably have to occupy the Rhine bridges 'for a year or so', both to ensure the execution of key articles of the Peace Treaty and to prevent Germany 'being overwhelmed by Bolshevism'.[24]

Lloyd George effectively broke the impasse by persuading Wilson on 14 March to agree to offer France a joint Anglo-American military guarantee. This, together with German disarmament, would most likely have enabled Britain to have achieved her dual aim of containing Germany, whilst stabilizing Europe. The chances of Germany daring to challenge such a combination in the future were virtually nil. Although Clemenceau welcomed the military guarantee, he still insisted on a permanent post-war Allied occupation of the Rhineland, but his cogently argued memorandum merely elicited from Balfour the pessimistic observation that unless there was a radical change in the international system 'no manipulation of the Rhine frontier is going to make France anything more than a second rate power trembling at the nod of its great neighbours on the East, and depending from day to day on the changes and chances of a shifting diplomacy and uncertain alliances'.[25] It was only after another month of protracted and often heated negotiations that compromise was at last reached. Despite intense opposition from Foch, the President of the Republic, Poincaré, and the War Aims bloc in the Chamber, Clemenceau finally accepted the Anglo-American guarantee, provided the Allies agreed on a fifteen-year occupation of the Rhineland. This was to be divided into three sections: the northern one, which included the British Cologne zone, would be evacuated after five years, the central one after ten years and the southern one after fifteen. Wilson agreed on

22. For further details of the Rhineland Question see H. Nelson, *Land and Power*, pp. 209–48, and F.S. Northedge, *The Troubled Giant*, London, 1966, pp. 104–10.
23. Kerr's 'Notes of a Conversation with M. Tardieu, and Dr Mazes, 11–12 March, 1919', p. 14, FO 608/142 fos 119–41.
24. Ibid. Minute for Balfour, 13.3.19, fos 116–18.
25. Minutes by Balfour, 18.3.19 (5455), FO 608/141 fos 9–12.

15 April and Lloyd George reluctantly followed suit a week later.

The compromise was bitterly attacked by Foch, Poincaré and many of the officials at the Quai d'Orsay. Although Clemenceau allowed Foch to air his criticisms both at a session of the Council of Ministers on 25 April, and at a plenary session of the Peace Conference on 6 May, a day before the terms were handed to the Germans, he did not allow the question to be re-opened. Consequently the only hope of averting what seemed to Foch and the French army a disastrous peace, which underpinned German unity, lay in encouraging a separatist *fait accompli* in the Rhineland. Between April and June there began, in the words of one historian, 'a blind race in which Clemenceau and the generals competed to finish their work before the other'.[26] The French generals in the Rhineland realized that a peace treaty recognizing German unity would pre-empt Rhenish separatism, while Clemenceau feared that a Rhineland *putsch* backed by the French army would lead Britain and America to re-open the whole question of the fifteen-year occupation. In fact the separatist uprisings in Wiesbaden and Speyer on 1 June coincided with a series of meetings of the British Empire Delegation and the Cabinet to discuss the German proposals for modifying the Peace Treaty, and strengthened their desire to revise the draft treaty and above all to modify the Rhineland occupation clauses.[27] The following day, at a meeting of the Council of Four, Lloyd George fought hard to reduce the occupation to two years, but he failed to win American backing, and consequently was unable to secure more from Clemenceau than a pledge to keep the costs of the occupation as low as possible.[28] However, two weeks later he did secure the vague assurance, which in essence became Article 431 of the Treaty, that once Germany had given concrete evidence of her willingness to fulfil her obligations, 'the Allied and Associated Powers . . . will be ready to come to an agreement between themselves for the earlier termination of the period of occupation'.[29]

An uneasy compromise was thus again created, which neither side considered final and which both attempted to revise almost up to the final departure of the last French troops on 30 June 1930.

26. McDougall, *Rhineland Diplomacy*, p. 66.
27. CAB nos. 32, 33 and 34; CAB 29/28 fos 266–93.
28. K. Nelson, *Victors Divided*, p. 117.
29. 'Notes of a Meeting held at Mr. Lloyd George's Residence', 16.6.19 (CF-73A), USFR, PPC vol. 4, pp. 521–2.

Schleswig, Danzig and the Eastern Borders

Paradoxically it was a measure of Lloyd George's very success in moderating the terms of the Peace Treaty that British troops and officials became involved in policing and administering Danzig, the great industrial triangle of Upper Silesia and the rural backwaters of Allenstein, Marienwerder and Schleswig. The French sought to complement their attempts to create an independent Rhineland by building a strong Poland in the east, which would include Poznania, Upper Silesia, most of West Prussia and the southern regions of East Prussia, and by encouraging Denmark in the north to claim the greater part of Schleswig. Like the Rhenish problem, the Polish question was to provoke a major clash between the contradictory French and British concepts of the future role of Germany in Europe.

During the inter-Allied discussions preceding the Armistice, Balfour and Lloyd George managed to veto French attempts to define the future frontiers of Poland and to occupy Danzig.[30] Consequently, although an independent Polish government was set up by Pilsudski as a result of a coup in former Russian Poland, throughout the Peace Conference Germany continued to enjoy the advantage of controlling a large part of the territory, to which the new regime in Warsaw laid claim. The Commission on Polish Affairs, set up by the Supreme Council, recommended on 12 March that Danzig, Marienwerder and Upper Silesia should all be included in the new Polish state, and, on the insistence of the British members, that the future of Allenstein should be decided by plebiscite. This 'happy harmony of views between the experts'[31] was not echoed when the Supreme Council discussed the report. Lloyd George vigorously opposed the inclusion of Danzig and Marienwerder. Not only did he once again make comparisons with the history of Alsace-Lorraine under German rule, but he also argued that outright annexation would drive Germany into the arms of the bolsheviks. By threatening to withdraw the British offer of a military guarantee he forced the reluctant Clemenceau to agree on 3 April to the establishment of a free and autonomous city of Danzig, to be linked with Poland by a customs union and presided over by a High Commissioner appointed by the League of Nations, and to determine Marienwerder's future by plebiscite.

Lloyd George renewed his attacks on the Polish clauses of the

30. H. Nelson, *Land and Power*, pp. 82–3.
31. P.S. Wandycz, *France and Her Eastern Allies*, Minneapolis, 1962, p. 37.

Treaty, when the German Peace Delegation in their reply of 29 May to the peace terms vehemently criticized the Upper Silesian settlement. The British Empire Delegation agreed with him 'that the Germans had made out a strong *prima facie* case on the eastern boundaries',[32] and, after a combined meeting with the Cabinet, authorized him 'to use the full weight of the entire British Empire to secure modifications', even to the point of refusing military and naval assistance should Germany not sign the Treaty.[33] On 2 June Lloyd George proposed to the Council of Four that a plebiscite should also be held in Upper Silesia. After twenty-four hours of intense argument he won grudging support from Wilson and again forced Clemenceau to make concessions.[34] The details were worked out in a new commission set up to re-examine the eastern frontiers of Germany. Despite initial attempts by Le Rond, the French chairman, to prove that a plebiscite was unnecessary, the Commission reported unanimously on 10 June on all points except the length of time to be allowed before the voting. The British representatives were anxious to hold the plebiscite as soon as possible to avoid a prolonged and unsettling period which 'would be marked by an aggravation of the antagonism between Poles and Germans', but their French, American and Italian colleagues argued that a 'cooling off period of one or two years was necessary to enable popular passions to subside and public order to be restored'.[35] On 11 June the Council of Four approved these recommendations and ambiguously decided that the vote should take place at any time between six and eighteen months after the ratification of peace. Lloyd George had won an important battle in his struggle to avoid the creation of new 'Alsace-Lorraines' in eastern Europe and to recreate a European balance of power, but at this stage he could not realize quite how onerous the task of administering Upper Silesia and Danzig would be in the transitional period until the new and sometimes unworkable arrangements outlined in the Treaty could be brought into force.

The British advocated plebiscites on Germany's eastern borders as a means of preventing the transfer of large German minorities to Poland. In Northern Schleswig, where the majority of the popula-

32. Minutes of Meeting of the British Empire Delegation, 30.5.19 (no. 32), pp. 3–4, CAB 29/28 fos 266–70; H. Nelson, *Land and Power*, pp. 333–4.
33. Minutes of Meeting of the British Empire Delegation, 1.6.19 (no. 34) p. 11, fos 283–93.
34. H. Nelson *Land and Power*, p. 347.
35. 'Commission on the Eastern Frontiers of Germany', 8.6.19, 1st Session, pp. 3–6, FO 608/126 fos 366–77.

tion was Danish, the French welcomed the chance to hold the plebiscite which Bismarck had promised in 1866, and encouraged the Danes to demand the extension of the plebiscite virtually to the Dannevirke, a mere twenty miles from Kiel.[36] On 15 April the Council of Four agreed to a plebiscite to be held in three zones comprising virtually the whole of Schleswig. Unlike the Poles, the Danes were intent on demanding the absolute minimum of German territory. According to one British official at Paris, 'the main thing in their mind was to avoid trouble with Germany [which would be caused] by annexing anyone who might be found a crypto-German'.[37] On 7 May the Danish government protested sharply at the inclusion of the third zone, which was consequently omitted by the Council of Four as part of the overall revision of the Treaty on 14 June. Given this eminently reasonable attitude on the part of the Danes, it is hardly surprising that the Schleswig Plebiscite was the easiest of the tasks confronting the British when enforcing the Peace Treaty in 1920.

---

36. Wambaugh, *Plebiscites since the World War*, vol. I, pp. 46–63; Sir James W. Headlam-Morley, *A Memoir of the Paris Peace Conference, 1919*, ed. A. Headlam-Morley *et al.*, London, 1972, p. 165.
37. Headlam-Morley, *A Memoir of the Paris Peace Conference*, p. 51.

—3—

The British in the Rhineland, 1919

While Lloyd George was attempting in vain to extricate Britain as soon as possible from Continental military involvements, the British Military Government in Cologne was wrestling with the potentially explosive social, political and economic problems of post-war Germany. The problems of unemployment, hunger and the threat of bolshevism were experienced more acutely in the British Zone than in the predominantly rural zones of her allies. Cologne itself was an industrial conurbation with a population of 600,000 with extensive suburbs that were commercial centres in their own right, while up in the north-east corner of the zone there were a number of small industrial towns such as Benrath and Solingen, which bordered the bolshevik 'cholera area' of the Ruhr. The problems of the Military Government were compounded by the fact that it had to rely upon a conscript army, whose enthusiasm and loyalty were visibly flagging, for its ultimate coercive power. For much of the next year there lurked in the minds of the politicians and generals the fear that the British army would mutiny like the Germans and that the whole Armistice Agreement and subsequent peace treaty would come crashing down like a pack of cards.

The Crisis in Morale

The weakness and unreliability of the British forces on the Rhine in 1919 was a powerful incentive for British politicians to oppose an occupation of the Rhineland and to work, at France's expense, for a quick and acceptable peace with Germany. Doubts about the morale of the Second Army and of its successor, the Rhine Army, were a constant source of anxiety both to its commanding officers and to the Military Government at Cologne, which feared the vulnerability of the soldiers to bolshevik propaganda and their consequent ineffectiveness as an occupying force; these doubts strengthened the War Office's reluctance to commit British troops to peace-keeping duties in eastern Germany and impressed upon senior British officers in Germany the paramount importance of restoring some semblance of order and economic prosperity in both the occupied and unoccupied territories.

In 1917 Haig had warned the War Office that once demobilization began 'a feeling of jealousy will arise, men will keenly watch the dates of departure of others', and had particularly emphasized that 'the temper of the troops during this period will be a factor not to be lightly disregarded'.[1] His initial suggestion that demobilization should proceed on the principle of releasing whole units at a time was rejected in favour of 'pivotalism', which was a scheme designed to give priority to the release of key groups of industrial workers; but when demobilization became an election issue in December 1918, Lloyd George bowed to the pressure of public opinion and did all he could to accelerate its pace regardless of the carefully laid plans of the War Office. Regulations were changed rapidly and were interpreted so liberally that they appeared to the impatient men left behind to lack both justice and logic.[2] For instance a subaltern in Cologne, waiting to return home to medical school, observed ironically that 'the Olympians have issued an order that anyone going on leave if he received an offer of a job can stay and take it, which means, of course, that no temporary officers or men will ever come back off leave and all the War Office's fine schemes of demobilization are washed out'.[3] By 14 January 1919 it was clear to Haig that if the tempo of demobilization continued at its current rate, the Second Army would be reduced to 'a medley of all arms and not a properly balanced force'.[4]

The mood of the troops in France and Britain became increasingly ugly. There were strikes and demobilization riots on both sides of the Channel.[5] Winston Churchill, who took over the post of War Minister on 10 January, rapidly grasped that 'a few more weeks on present lines and there will be nothing left but [a]

1. Haig to the Secretary, 2.10.17 (no. A.G./E/8/5), WO 32/5241.
2. Quartermaster-General's Diary, Dec. 1918–Jan. 1919, 'Demobilization', pp. 8–9, WO 95/41. See also C.E. Carrington, *Soldier from the War Returning*, London, 1965, pp. 254–6, and for a more detailed survey of the demobilization crisis, A. Rothstein, *The Soldiers' Strikes of 1919*, London, 1980.
3. Lt Goodman to parents, 25.12.18 IWM 71/59/1.
4. Paper drawn up by GHQ France headed 'Demobilisation' and handed to CIGS, 14.1.19, WO 32/52422.
5. There are interesting accounts of these incidents in the reports of General Corvisart, Chief of the French Military Mission in London, to M. le Président du Conseil, Ministre de la Guerre, in Vincennes, 7N 1255.

demoralized and angry mob, made up of men left behind on no principle that they consider fair and without the slightest regard to military formation'.[6] He drew up a plan for stabilizing the situation and meeting the continuing military commitments on the Rhine, in northern Russia, the Middle East and the Empire. The majority of fighting troops would be demobilized but some 900,000 men, picked predominantly from the younger age groups, who had been conscripted at the end of the war, would be retained on increased pay for a further year. The Cologne Zone was to be garrisoned by what was in effect a new army composed of 69 battalions of 'young soldiers', who had finished their basic training too late to fight, strengthened by a number of specialist units and NCOs retained from the old Second Army. The Cabinet, persuaded by Churchill that any British evacuation of the Cologne Zone would 'fatally weaken our position at the Peace Conference', readily approved the plan.[7]

Although German officers serving with the Armistice Commission at Spa eagerly reported back to Berlin in mid-January rumours of imminent mutiny,[8] there were no disturbances in the Zone on the scale of those in France or Britain. Indeed, the weekly postal censorship reports in January emphasized the relatively contented mood of the men on the Rhine, but in February and March there was a marked increase in drunkeness, and strikes occurred in several units.[9] The very success of the new demobilization plans rapidly depleted the number of troops available for picket and guard duties and consequently threw an extra burden on those left behind. At Malmedy a private in the Black Watch complained in his diary that 'owing to the two platoons being below strength [he] was continually on guard duty every alternate day'. In contrast it seemed that the officers, secure in comfortable billets, were having a 'whale of a time'.[10]

The situation was exacerbated by the initial appalling delays that occurred in moving goods and personnel by rail from the base camps in northern France, so ensuring that the supply of rations and luxuries to the Second Army had to be restricted to the

6. Churchill to Lloyd George, 20.1.19, LG, HLRO, F/8/3/5.
7. Churchill to Lloyd George, 29.1.18, LG, HLRO, F/8/3/9; see also M.Gilbert, *Winston Churchill*, vol. 4, London, 1975, pp. 181–96.
8. Bevollmächtigter des Kriegsministeriums bei der Wako, an das Kriegsministerium, 14.1.19 (no. 6503), FCO Lib 4080D921815-816.
9. Postal Censorship Reports on Demobilization, Haig papers, NLOS Acc. 3155/220(d). See also Haldane's Diary, 13.2.19, NLOS MS.20250.
10. Diary of Pte J.A. Douglas, vol. 7, 14.3.19, IWM 81/20/20.

absolute minimum. Leave journeys home became an endurance test in cattle trucks, or, at best, unheated carriages where in the exceptionally cold weather of early February it was not unusual to contract frost-bite.[11] Neither was morale improved by a shortage of cooks and the impossibility of eking out rations by purchasing local food, every bit of which was needed for the German population. Consequently, even as late as March, it was only possible to provide the 8th Battalion of the Black Watch, after a long march, with a meal consisting of soups and rice pudding.[12]

The process of replacing the Second Army with young soldier battalions caused considerable dislocation, which was not effectively overcome until mid-summer. The majority of the 'young soldier' battalions were moved intact to the Rhine, but some twenty-two were broken up and distributed amongst existing battalions.[13] Their arrival intensified the desire of the veterans for demobilization. One corporal in the South Wales Borderers wrote in a letter home complaining that the 'young soldiers' battalion to which he had been transferred 'does seem a mob after being in the 1st Battalion', and then warned that unless demobilization came quickly, he was afraid that 'there will be a rumpus with us boys out here. They are not playing the game with us at all.'[14]

The formation of the new Army of the Rhine was supposed to be completed by 2 April, but when Robertson took over from Plumer on 20 April, it was clear that this was an optimistic target. At a time when Foch had emphasized that the occupation armies should be ready to advance at short notice into Germany, the Rhine Army was suffering from a crippling shortage of NCOs, commanding officers and gunners. Robertson was also critical of the 'easy going spirit prevailing', and concerned by the mood in the Heavy Artillery, which was 'largely composed not of young soldiers but of middle aged men who are anxious to return to their wives and families; some of them doubt the fidelity of their wives; others have sick wives or sick children, while others are forfeiting their means of livelihood'.[15]

He informed his senior officers that 'high morale, a contented spirit and good discipline were in present circumstances more important than any standard military training', and he was emphatic that 'officers must do the same parades as the men . . . .'.[16]

11. Ibid., 11–13.2.19.
12. Ibid., 2.3.19.
13. Edmonds, *The Occupation*, p. 145.
14. Cpl J.L. Morgan to Annie and Arthur, 20.3.19, IWM, P. 265.
15. Robertson to the Secretary, WO, 28.4.19, LHCMA Robertson 1/28/20a.

Where possible he alleviated what he accepted was the object of justifiable complaints. He improved messing arrangements and also attempted to accelerate the demobilization of the older men. Nevertheless he was faced with several strikes, particularly in the Artillery,[17] and he was so unsure of his men's mood that he was uncertain whether they would obey the order to cheer on the King's birthday parade.[18]

The reorganization of the British occupying forces inevitably affected their operational efficiency. In 1919 the Rhine Army had two major responsibilities: it had both to police the Cologne Zone and to be ready at a moment's notice to advance into Germany. The possible rejection of the Allied peace terms by the Germans posed the Rhine Army with a challenge potentially far beyond its strength. On 25 April Foch outlined his plans for a full-scale advance into Germany: the British, with a force of six divisions, were to advance north-east through the Ruhr and then on to the Weser.[19] Foch wanted the Allied armies to be ready to move at short notice, but an operation on that scale would have been virtually impossible for Robertson to mount, as there were serious manpower shortages in both the cavalry and specialized units, while the Royal Artillery was urgently awaiting the arrival of 50 per cent of its officers.[20]

The peace terms were handed to the Germans on 7 May, and in anticipation of a possible rejection, Foch was instructed by the Allied leaders to be ready for an advance into Germany any time after 27 May.[21] Although Foch, who had been briefed on the Rhine Army's manpower shortages, secured assurances from the British government that reinforcements would be sent,[22] both Churchill and Robertson were acutely aware of the dangers of an advance into the interior of Germany. In May, Churchill urged Lloyd George to press for a quick peace with Berlin, as otherwise 'we may easily be caught, as Napoleon was in Spain, and gripped in a position from which there is no retreat and where our strength will steadily be consumed',[23] while Robertson pointed out to the CIGS

16. 'Notes of a Conference held at the C.in.C's House . . . 17.5.19', ibid., I/28/8a.
17. Haldane Diary, 30.5.19, NLOS, MS.20250.
18. Ibid., 31.5.19.
19. Grant to DMO, 22.4.19 (no. 237) WO 158/84, Pt. 6.
20. Robertson to Secretary, WO, 28.4.19. See also Sir W. Robertson, *From Private to Field Marshal*, London, 1921, p. 365.
21. Foch to Robertson (no. 2559), 19.5.19, Vincennes, 14N49–2.
22. Ibid.
23. Gilbert, *Winston Churchill*, vol. 4, p. 896.

that after detaching troops to guard his lines of communication, he would have only two or three divisions left by the time he reached the Weser.[24] Nevertheless, in the first two weeks of June, while the Council of Four were deliberating on their reply to the German observations on the peace terms, intensive and ostentatious preparations for advance were made; but on 23 June the Germans agreed to sign and five days later the troops were brought back from the frontier,[25] although plans were kept updated for the 'remote contingency' that the Reichstag would refuse to ratify the Treaty.[26]

The British Army had survived the traumatic period from the Armistice to the signature of the peace, by undergoing a disorientating metamorphosis, which ultimately reduced its size from 3.5 million to 370,000 in November 1920. Ironically, as a result of the unprecedented expansion of British commitments, the army was 'plunged without a break into world wide garrison, occupation and policing duties'.[27] The General Staff[28] relegated the Army's German responsibilities to the lowest order of importance and consequently the Rhine, and later in January 1920, Danzig and Allenstein became training garrisons for young inexperienced troops[29] or else potentially unreliable units like the Southern Irish regiments, which could not be used against Sinn Fein in Ireland. The British army was thus in 1919 and 1920 a patently unreliable instrument for exerting pressure on Germany and it is arguable that Britain's position on the Rhine by the summer of 1919 depended largely on bluff. That this was not called was the true measure of Germany's defeat and demoralization.

The Inter-Allied Dimension, December 1918–May 1919

Although French attempts to create an independent Rhineland were defeated in the Council of Four in April 1919, had determined

24. Wilson Diary, 20.6.19, IWM 73/1/26.
25. War Diary, May, June 1919, British Army of the Rhine, General Staff, WO 95/24.
26. Secretary, WO to Robertson, 25.7.19, LHCMA, Robertson I/28/25.
27. B. Bond, *British Military Policy between the Two World Wars*, Oxford, 1980. p. 38.
28. Ibid., p. 29.
29. See letter from R.B. Gooden to 'Ad. and Maud' about the Royal Fusiliers in Danzig, 10/6/20, IWM 73/137/6. See also entry in Henry Wilson's Diary, 13.3.20, on inspection of units of the West Kents in the Rhineland: 'Again weak, young and untrained with 200–300 men who have never been on the range, and none of the Lewis gunners have ever fired the gun off'; IWM 73/1/26.

action in March and April by British and American officials not resulted in the creation of the inter-Allied Rhineland Commission, it would have been almost impossible for Britain and America to have coordinated Allied economic policy in occupied Germany. Consequently, it would have been much easier for the French to have persisted unchecked with a programme of economic separatism.[30]

At the end of December 1918, Foch and the French generals on the Rhine embarked upon an economic and political programme for engineering a *de facto* separation of the Rhineland from Germany. As Supreme Commander of the Allied forces, Foch was in a powerful position to influence French policy on the Rhine. In mid-December, when it was obvious that the diplomats would not be able to come to a quick decision on the future status of the Rhineland, Foch set up Le Contrôle Générale de l'Administration des Territoires Rhénans at his advanced headquarter in Luxemburg, to supervise and coordinate the Allied military authorities in the Rhineland. In charge of it he placed Paul Tirard, a brilliant and politically motivated civil servant, who in pre-war Morocco had already observed at first hand how a well-planned paternalistic programme could appease a potentially hostile population. Although the Contrôle Générale was theoretically an inter-Allied body, it was dominated by French civil and military officials and was the *de facto* civil arm of the French army of occupation.[31] Foch also created the Luxemburg Economic Committee to regulate the economic relations of the occupied territories with unoccupied Germany, the neutral states and the Allied powers. The Luxemburg Committee was, in fact, in all but name a department of the Contrôle Générale,[32] and as such subordinate to Foch, who did not hesitate to influence its decisions, even though it was nominally responsible to another newly constituted inter-Allied body, the Paris Left Bank Committee, which was theoretically supposed to settle the general lines of the economic policy to be pursued in the occupied territories.

British and American suspicions of French Rhineland policy were inevitably fanned by Foch's attempts to re-orientate the Rhineland economy towards France. Haig was particularly worried by Foch's directive of 8 January ordering the Luxemburg Committee to set up inter-Allied sub-committees or economic sections

---

30. K. Nelson, *Victors Divided*, pp. 99–101.
31. R. McCrum, 'French Rhineland Policy', p. 629.
32. Webster, 'The Administration of the German Armistice and the Politico-Economic Direction of the Rhineland Occupation, 1918–19' (U.4110/25/70), 20.8.43, p. 17, CAB 45/82 fo. 145. K. Nelson, *Victors Divided*, p. 99.

in each zone to deal with economic questions, as he quickly perceived that they would 'trench upon the authority of the Field Marshal, C. in C. of the British Armies'.[33] His concern was shared both by Waterlow, the British representative on the Left Bank Committee, and Travers Clarke, the Quartermaster General of the British forces in France and Germany, who warned that the army could not 'tolerate interference by an inter-Allied body with all the openings which it gives for intrigue in the actual administration of the occupied zone for which they are responsible'.[34] Such opposition compelled Foch virtually to eliminate the inter-Allied element on the economic sections. In the British Zone he was able to appoint only one French technical officer, who in practice was excluded from any real participation and reduced to the status of a mere liaison officer.[35] Initially both Britain and America were at a considerable disadvantage because their armies lacked the necessary experts to sit on the key inter-Allied economic committees. Haking warned Haig that 'unless we insist on the representation of all the Allies on every commission which sits, we are likely to jeopardize British interests'.[36] On 12 January, when the first meeting of the Luxemburg Committee took place, Haig was only able to second a staff officer to attend on a temporary basis.[37]

Both the British and the Americans were anxious to strengthen the influence of the civilian experts and to create an effective body, which would be independent of Marshal Foch, to formulate and to coordinate inter-Allied economic policy in the Rhineland. At first Waterlow was optimistic that the Left Bank Committee would be able to fulfil its supervisory role effectively. Its first meeting on 8 February[38] was surprisingly constructive despite a speech by Tirard arguing strongly for the use of economic inducements to win over the Rhinelanders 'to the side of the *Entente*'. Waterlow in his turn pressed British demands for turning the Luxemburg Committee into a purely civil body, and then put forward proposals, which were accepted, for streamlining the decision-making process of the Left Bank Committee. At the end of the day he was sufficiently confident to report to Curzon that he saw 'no reason why the Paris

33. Haig to Sec. WO, 11.1.19 (no. 14129/3QD2), Appendix XIII, File/72, QMG, WO 95/41.
34. Waterlow's Memorandum on Economic District sub-commissions, 28.1.19, FO 608/222 fos 246–7.
35. Webster (U.4110/25/70), p. 18.
36. Haking to CGS, 11.1.19 (D.55), p. 3, WO 144/7, fos 125–7.
37. Haig to Sec. WO, 11.1.19 (no. 14129/3QD2).
38. Minutes of La Commission interalliée de la Rive Gauche du Rhin, 8.2.19. FO 382/2306 fos 512–19.

Commission should not eventually become a useful instrument for advising the associated governments and for coordinating their action in matters of economic policy relating to the Left Bank of the Rhine'.[39] However, his optimism was not well founded. Neither the Left Bank nor the Luxemburg Committees were able to control the individual economic sections in the occupied territories, nor check French commercial initiatives in the Rhineland. On discovering in early March that British officials in Cologne had no knowledge of the very existence of the Left Bank Committee, Waterlow urgently cabled Curzon 'that unless present entire lack of coordination between various authorities is remedied there is no prospect of getting systematic procedure for trade between U.K. and Left Bank of the Rhine into working order. Consequence must be that British interests will suffer.'[40]

In March Anglo–American dissatisfaction with the complete lack of coordination between the Allies and distrust of French machinations in the Rhineland came to a head. To provide effective 'leverage'[41] against the Supreme Command and to impose some order on the economic administration of the occupied territories, British and American officials increasingly urged that the Supreme Economic Council, which had been set up in February on President Wilson's initiative to deal with the financial and economic questions affecting unoccupied Germany, should also be given similar responsibilities for the Rhineland. Thus E.F. Wise, one of the British representatives on the Supreme Economic Council, came to the conclusion that 'the Luxemburg Committee should act as a clearing house of information and should secure co-ordination of policy throughout the occupied area' and refer 'points of principle' to the Supreme Economic Council at Paris.[42]

The case for such a move was strengthened by the decision at the Brussels Conference on 14 March to treat both occupied and unoccupied Germany as one unit for revictualment purposes. Wise elaborated his ideas more precisely in his report to the Supreme Economic Council on 15 April in which he cogently argued that whilst:

> there can be no question that in matters of military importance the authority of the Army Command acting under direction of the High

39. Waterlow to Curzon, 9.2.19 (no. 2W), FO 382/2306 fos 450–1.
40. Waterlow to Curzon, 3.3.19 (no. C902), FO 608/279 fos 79–80.
41. Webster (U.4110/25/70), p. 19.
42. 'Notes on the Food supply for the Left Bank of the Rhine, 1.3.19', LG, HLRO, F/8/3/26, fo. 271.

Command, must be supreme . . . many of the problems to be dealt with are of civil, economic or industrial rather than of a military nature, and they must be considered in their bearing on the general problem of economic relations with Germany as a whole.[43]

He consequently recommended the replacement of the Luxemburg Committee by an inter-Allied Rhineland Commission under the chairmanship of Tirard, 'to co-ordinate the administration of the four Army Commands on all economic, industrial and food questions in accordance with the policy laid down by the Supreme Economic Council'. To ensure the uniform treatment of both occupied and unoccupied Germany he went on further to suggest that the Supreme Economic Council should set up a special sub-committee, to which the Rhineland Commission should report, that would coordinate all the Council's work on both occupied and unoccupied Germany. Despite a rival French plan,[44] Wise's proposals were in essence accepted by the Supreme Economic Council on 14 April, subject only to two American amendments, both aimed at diminishing French influence still further: these proposed that the Rhineland Commission should sit in Cologne rather than Luxemburg and that Tirard should give up his post as director of the Contrôle Générale, and were approved by the Council of Foreign Ministers on 21 April.[45]

In practice it took another month before the responsibilities of the inter-Allied Rhineland Commission were defined. Pierrepoint Noyes and Sir Harold Stuart, the new American and British Commissioners, both reported to Luxemburg to start work on 30 April, but Tirard remained absent until compelled to appear on 10 May after Noyes and Stuart threatened to begin without him. He managed to avert the eventual move of the Rhineland Commission to Cologne only by agreeing to its transfer to Coblenz.[46] Sir Harold Stuart, who had been in the Indian Civil Service before the war and then worked in the Ministry of Food from 1916 to 1918, was a forceful character, who was to make a considerable reputation for himself in the Rhineland and Upper Silesia as the man who

43. Memorandum by the Supreme Economic Council for the Council of Ten, Enclosures 1 and 2, 15.4.19, pp. 117–120, FO 374/21. K. Nelson, *Victors Divided*, p. 101.
44. Tirard to Foch, 9.4.19, Vincennes 4N92-1.
45. K. Nelson, *Victors Divided*, pp. 101–2.
46. Ibid., pp. 103–4.

could stand up to and outwit the French. He played a key part in the decisive clash with Tirard on 13 May[47] when he vigorously questioned the doctrine that France, by virtue of the predominance of her interests in the Rhineland, could automatically claim a preponderant role in the Commission, and argued strongly that 'nothing prevents us from examining political questions which bear upon economic, industrial and food problems'. He thus insisted that the inter-Allied Military Food Committee was responsible to the Rhineland Commission rather than to the Supreme Command and rejected Foch's claims that all directives from the Rhineland Commission 'should be submitted to the Marshal, Commander of the Allied Armies, who will ensure their execution'.[48] He also emphasized the Supreme Economic Council's own recommendation that it should be the final instance for clarifying the powers of the Rhineland Commission. On 19 May at a special session of the Council[49] a compromise was reached, whereby Foch agreed to Tirard's resignation as Director of the Contrôle Générale and recognized the Commission's responsibility for civil and economic affairs in the Rhineland, while Tirard in his new role as president of the Commission would be given the right by the Supreme Command to 'transmit to [the] commanders of [the Rhine] armies instructions discussed and approved by the Commission'.

The establishment of the inter-Allied Rhineland Commission was a significant check to French power in the Rhineland. By coordinating Allied economic policy in the Rhineland along lines laid down by the Supreme Economic Council, it created a new institutional framework in which Britain together with America could effectively block French attempts to create an independent Rhineland by manipulating the Rhineland economy.

The British Military Government in the Cologne Zone

The organization of the Military Governor's office was initially modest, reflecting the total lack of preparation by Haig for an

47. Minutes of 3rd Session, Inter-Allied Rhineland Commission, 13.5.19, CAB 29/15 fos 138–41.
48. 'Memorandum by the Sub-Committee on Germany for the Supreme Economic Council', no. 38, CAB 29/15 fo. 136.
49. For a summary of compromise see Minutes of 20th Session of Supreme Economic Council, 26.5.19 (WCP 879), CAB 29/15 fos 474–82. K. Nelson, *Victors Divided*, p. 105.

occupation. At first policy decisions were made on a hit or miss basis after conferences with Plumer and the Corps Commanders,[50] but this quickly changed. As early as 27 December 1918 Fergusson asked for an increase in the number of staff.[51] In January 1919 he was considerably assisted by the appointment of Frank Tiarks, a partner of J. Henry Schroders in the City, as Civil Commissioner to act as adviser on financial and commercial matters. Tiarks, who was married to a German and was himself of German extraction, was able to exploit his pre-war contacts to gain useful information for the Military Government.[52] By the spring the Military Government had become a sophisticated organization with sections on policy, personnel, circulation, censorship and on all aspects of the economy, involving labour, food, coal and industries.

British policy within the Zone was described in April 1919 as 'conservative' in that its 'sole aim . . . has been to ensure . . . the continuance in office of members of local bodies, who have not only had administrative experience but have grown accustomed to cooperating with us in our occupation'.[53] Nevertheless in the early days of the occupation British officers were aware of the political vacuum that had opened up in the Rhineland and of the unique opportunities afforded to the Allies for influencing its future. One of the first reports from the Second Army in Cologne stressed that 'the German popular mind is at present apprehensive and receptive; all its old ideals have been swept away; it has no rallying point at home; it is vague as to the future. The people particularly of the industrial Rhine provinces would welcome almost any scheme which would ensure order and enable business to proceed.'[54]

The Military Government was uncertain how to deal with the Rhenish separatist movement, which was anxious to win Allied support before challenging Prussian control of the Rhineland. Initially Colonel Ryan, the director of Fergusson's Political Department, encouraged Adenauer to flirt with separatism, in the hope that the movement would become pro-British.[55] When an inter-

50. See entry in Clive's diary, 14.12.18, LHCMA, Clive II/4.
51. 'Short Record of the Work of the Civil Government under the Military Governor, British Occupied Territories', p. 2, WO 95/277. This gives a good overall survey. See also Recker, 'Adenauer und die englische Besatzungsmacht', pp. 102–8.
52. Tiarks to his wife, 16.1.19, Tiarks papers.
53. 'The British Occupation of the Rhineland', 4.5.19 (no. 477/1/8-9325), p. 3, FO 608/142 fos 147–50.
54. Report from the Second Army (1), 17.12.18, FO 608/268 fos 18–19.
55. J.C. King, *Foch versus Clemenceau*, p. 32. For Adenauer's role see K.D. Erdmann,

Allied propaganda mission visited Cologne on 1 February, Ryan told it that a Rhenish Westphalian Republic, albeit 'loosely federated with the rest of Germany', was a real possibility and could 'be influenced by propaganda to drift into sympathy rather with the Western powers than with the Central European system'.[56] However, when clarification was sought from the Foreign Office, Fergusson's Chief of Staff General Clive was told unambiguously that, despite the Foreign Secretary's personal inclination for a Rhenish–Westphalian republic, either as an independent entity or as a state federated with the rest of Germany, it was British policy not to interfere in internal German politics and that it was therefore 'of the utmost importance that no step should be taken which would in the slightest degree tend to expose us to the risk of being considered to have officially favoured either proposal'.[57] Consequently the British army remained politically neutral, despite the initial sympathy of some of the Military Governor's staff for the separatists. When, at the end of May, Clive was approached by Colonel Hellé, the Chief of Staff to General Mangin, Commander of the French Tenth Army at Mainz, and asked how the British would react to a separatist coup backed by the French, he was curtly informed that 'we are here to keep order [and] that is what we shall do'.[58] Clive was sufficiently worried to go to Paris to seek more precise guidance from Lloyd George, who unambiguously informed him that Germany was too important a barrier against bolshevik Russia to be further weakened by a Rhineland secession.[59] When, shortly after his return from Paris, the separatists launched an abortive and farcical series of coups in Speyer, Wiesbaden and Mainz, he wisely avoided any provocative show of force in Cologne and allowed the reports in the local newspapers of the events in the French Zone to speak for themselves.[60] Separatism remained a latent threat to the stability of the British Zone; in August the Military Government was sufficiently concerned that the separatists would try to pre-empt the ratification of the Peace Treaty, which guaranteed a united Germany, by declaring an independent republic, to post up

Adenauer in der Rheinlandpolitik nach dem Ersten Weltkrieg, Stuttgart, 1966, pp. 21–70.
56. 'Inter-Allied Propaganda Mission to the Occupied Districts of Germany', report by Capt. Kelly, 14.2.19 (no. 2293), p. 16, FO 608/135 fos 170–91.
57. S.G. Guest to Clive (no. 2094), 13.2.19 FO 608/136 fo. 305.
58. Clive to Edmonds, 'III. Independence of Rhineland', Oct/Nov. 1943, CAB 45/81 (iii).
59. Clive, ibid.
60. Clive, ibid.

notices emphasizing that 'no change in the German administration . . . will be permitted, and no new authority will be
recognised, without the previous sanction of the British Military
Authorities'.[61]

A greater threat to the stability of the Zone was posed by the
volatile situation in unoccupied Germany and by the chronic shortages of food and raw materials in the Cologne area, which consequently exacerbated unemployment and encouraged the spread of
bolshevism. In Cologne itself the bolshevik threat was not great. In
November 1918 the Independent Socialists had set up Soldiers' and
Workers' Councils in the Rathaus, but shortly before the British
came the local officials had reasserted their independence,[62] and the
Councils themselves were dissolved on 20 December.[63] In the
north-eastern section of the Bridgehead, particularly in the industrial areas of Solingen, Benrath and Reisholz, which bordered the
Ruhr, the Spartacists and Independent Socialists were much
stronger, and their activities were constantly monitored by agents
who were recruited locally by British intelligence officers.[64]

Although there was some suspicion in the Foreign Office that the
Germans were exaggerating the threat of revolution as 'an elaborate
trick to cheat the Allies into moderation',[65] British military intelligence was convinced of the reality of the threat of communism in
unoccupied Germany.[66] Throughout February and March there
were frequent alerts in the British Zone which reminded General
Haldane of the endless 'cries of wolf' in the trenches.[67] On 25
March, for instance, rumours reached Fergusson's office that '7,000
ruffians led by Spartacists were to assemble in the Cologne Stadt-
wald and march on the Rathaus and jail . . .'.[68] A convoy of
motorcyclists was immediately dispatched, but closer inspection

61. Proclamation dated 21.8.19 (S/3001), FO 608/136 fo. 365.
62. Monograph by Sir Charles Fergusson: 'Military Governor's Office', Second
Army GS War Diary, WO 95/277.
63. 'Minutes of a Conference between the Military Governor and the Oberbürgermeister, Cologne, 21.12.18', HA d SK 902/241/1.
64. For an example see the confessions of one Albert Schuster, who had originally
been imprisoned in Germany for his part in the naval mutinies of October 1918. He
had escaped and together with his wife was subsequently recruited by British
Intelligence. After a spell of working for the French they defected back to the
Germans. *Freiwillig erklärt Albert Schuster, 1.6.20*, Nr. 214/L20/SP Bundesarchiv,
Koblenz (hereafter BA.KO) R.43I/177 fos 149–51.
65. Minute by M. Sadler, 27.2.19, no. 3125, FO 608/129/fo. 184.
66. See for example 'Conditions in Germany', report compiled by fourteen officers
who visited Germany, 18 Jan.–12 Feb. 1919, FO 608/129 fos 271–376.
67. Haldane Diary, 25.3.19 NLOS MS. 20250.
68. Ibid.

revealed that the meeting was peaceful and law-abiding.[69] A more serious threat was presented by Communist attempts to exploit the unrest in the army. In January 'a serious conspiracy'[70] aimed at disseminating bolshevik literature amongst American and British soldiers was uncovered and its members arrested.

In practice the Military Government had more to fear from strikes on the railways, and in the power stations. The labour force in the Zone was affected by the same strike fever that gripped unoccupied Germany. Four years of war and malnutrition had sapped industrial discipline, and the creation of the new Republic with the subsequent introduction of the eight-hour day, worker representation committees and plans for nationalizing the coal mines had naturally raised the workers' expectations at the very point when inflation was eroding their wages.[71] As far as possible, British policy was to intervene in industrial and labour questions only when the security of the Zone seemed threatened. Thus the coal magnate Carl Silverberg was prevented from attending a meeting of the Socialization Commission in Berlin in January 1919 on the grounds that it was desirable 'to keep subversive tendencies and ideas of this nature out of occupied territory and to demonstrate clearly that no such measures would be tolerated under Allied Administration'.[72] The extension of the German 'Socialization' Coal Law of 23 March to the occupied territories was vetoed by Foch until February 1920,[73] but the British authorities after some initial hesitation permitted the formation of workers' committees in the coal mines and even forced the textile employers to follow suit.[74] They similarly tolerated the introduction of the eight-hour day, despite opposition from local employers, although as a result of directives from Foch and the Inter-Allied Railway Commission, the miners and railway personnel continued to work a full ten-hour day.[75]

On the whole the officers in the Labour Section of the Military Governor's staff displayed a considerable aptitude for the complex subject of industrial relations, but inevitably there were times when their inexperience complicated the situation. For instance, at the end of January when some of Silverberg's workers were pressing

69. VI Corps G.S. War Diary, 25.3.19, vol. XLVI, WO 95/775.
70. Monograph, p. 2, WO 95/277. See also Williamson, 'Cologne and the British', p. 697.
71. 'Work of the Labour Section of the Military Governor's Branch, British Army of the Rhine', WO 95/277.
72. Clive to Silverberg, 18.1.19, BA.KO *Nachlaß* Silverberg/142.
73. Eighth Sitting of the IARHC, 4.2.20, §IX Min. 128, FO 894/1 fo 232.
74. 'The British Occupation of the Rhineland', p. 5, FO 608/142 fos 147–50.
75. Ibid., p. 5.

for the immediate introduction of the eight-hour day, 'four or five British officers' prematurely promised their support only to find that both Silverberg and the local trade union leaders believed that the changes should only be gradually phased in so as to avoid disruption to production. Consequently both the Military Government and Silverberg had to devise a formula which maintained the prestige of the British army, while informing the workers that they had 'misunderstood the officers'.[76]

In March accelerating inflation and growing food shortages led to a marked increase in strikes and labour unrest. A particularly alarming development was that, while the workers were pressing for higher wages and improved conditions, it was often 'quite immaterial to [the] employers whether their men [went] on strike or not',[77] as factories, particularly in north-western areas of the Zone, were operating at a dead loss since their running costs were far higher than their profits. Consequently on 16 April General Plumer issued a proclamation, which, while promising increased supplies of food and the protection of 'the rights of the workers to the fullest degree',[78] nevertheless introduced a compulsory arbitration system. If the existing German arbitration courts failed to solve a labour dispute, it would be heard before a final British court of appeal, which was constituted by the end of April and consisted of two officers and one civilian adviser, seconded from the Ministry of Munitions, together with a German advisory committee composed of two employers nominated by the Regierungspräsident and four trade union officials.

These new labour laws were first challenged by the metal workers in Benrath,[79] who went on strike for increased pay, the award of a lump sum bonus and longer holidays. As the German arbitration court failed to find a solution, the dispute was referred to the new appeal court, which rejected the bonus claim but recommended a wage increase for the lowest paid. The compromise was turned down by the workers' leader, Carl Husch, who then called a general strike in the Benrath area, which threatened to close down a key power station that supplied some 75 per cent of the local factories with their energy. The Military Government reacted swiftly by either imprisoning or deporting the ringleaders, and the

76. 'Rücksprache mit Herrn Major Piggott am 22.1.1919,' BA.KO/Nachlaß Silverberg/142 fo.11.
77. 'The Labour Situation in the Territory occupied by the British', 7.4.19, FO 608/281 fos 497–500.
78. 'The Work of the Labour Section', p. 4, WO 95/277.
79. Ibid., p. 7.

strike quickly collapsed. The Labour Section had no doubt that this action 'had a salutary effect on the whole of the occupied territory, as all the industrial areas and trade unions were watching this as a test case in which the British authority in trade disputes either established itself or went by the Board [*sic*]'.[80]

As a result of their daily experiences in both occupied and unoccupied Germany, British military officials quickly came to the conclusion that only a rapid increase in the supply of food and raw materials could avert famine, mass unemployment and eventual revolution. When the Second Army occupied Cologne, the shops and cafés seemed to be well stocked with food, but appearances were deceptive. The troops rapidly discovered that the cakes were 'abominable flourless, sugarless concoctions' and began to notice 'the little child skeletons' hanging round 'the officers' messes for crusts and refuse'.[81] By February reports were unanimous that Germany faced imminent famine. An intelligence report from the II Corps warned, for instance, that 'the situation . . . appears to be getting more acute daily. Most people predict that by the end of February or March there will be a state of famine unless foodstuffs are imported at once.'[82] This view was shared by E.F. Wise, one of the British delegates on the newly created Supreme Economic Council, who visited the Rhineland later in February. In a strongly worded and cogently argued memorandum,[83] which was circulated to the War Cabinet on 6 March, he pointed out:

> Public opinion in this country and America shed no tears over the vigorous enforcement of the blockade with the view of starving Germany so long as the war lasted, but since the war has ceased the contact between the British and American soldiers and the German civil population has profoundly modified the point of view of the soldiers. It is open to doubt whether public opinion in this country or in America would be prepared to acquit the Government of criminal negligence if the civil population of the territories administered by the Allied Armies is allowed to starve.

He also warned that in the event of large-scale bread riots, the occupying troops might refuse to undertake 'the task of policing

80. Ibid., p. 10.
81. Gedye in the *Bystander*, 13.8.19, IWM Gedye/12. See also Tiarks to wife, 20.1.19, Tiarks papers.
82. Intelligence Report, 8.2.19 (no. L. 239) II Corps War Diary (Appendix to February 1919), WO 95/645.
83. 'Notes on Food Supplies for the Left Bank of the Rhine', 1.3.19, HLRO, LG, F/8/3/26 fo.271.

and repressing a starving population', and stressed that a quiescent and well-fed population in the Rhineland would 'enormously simplify the task of a further advance into Germany if such an advance is to be made'.

At the end of February the practical consequences of the near-famine conditions in the British Zone were brought home to General Clive and his staff when they noticed that 'the school children whom we passed in walking to our office had entirely stopped running about and playing on their way to school'.[84] The Military Government's immediate reaction was to dispatch Tiarks to persuade Lloyd George to sanction the immediate dispatch of food to Cologne.[85] However, the whole question of revictualling both occupied and unoccupied Germany raised important political questions, which could only be solved on an inter-Allied level. In January a provisional agreement had been negotiated with the Germans at Trier allowing Germany to purchase cereals and fats in exchange for the surrender of her merchant fleet, but the German government delayed its implementation in the hope that the threats of famine and bolshevism would stampede the Allies into further concessions. The Americans, and the British after an initial period of apathy,[86] were anxious to relax the blockade and treat Germany economically as one unit, whereas the French, worried that Germany's scant gold reserves would be used for purchasing American grain and fats rather than for paying reparations, and intent on encouraging Rhineland separatism by an exclusive policy of generosity to the occupied territories, were determined on obstruction. Consequently little progress had been made in implementing the agreement.

The reports from British officers in Germany had already convinced Lloyd George that the only effective *cordon sanitaire* against bolshevism 'was to feed Germany'.[87] Thus Tiarks, who arrived at an opportune moment with much relevant information, had little difficulty in persuading him 'to consider at once the steps that must be taken for bringing auxiliary emergency food supplies to the occupied area for the use of the civil population'.[88] The following day decisive progress was made in the revictualment question. At a

84. Clive to Edmonds ('II. Note on p. 26') Oct./Nov. 1943, CAB 45/81 (III).
85. Ibid. See also Tiarks to wife, 7,9, and 11 March 1919, Tiarks papers; and 'Report by the Civil Commissioner to the Military Governor of Cologne', pp. 1–28, FO 382/2316 fos 2463–2489.
86. McDougall, *Rhineland Diplomacy*, p. 55.
87. 'Notes of a Conversation at the Prime Minister's Flat, 6.3.19', HLRO, LG, F/121/3.
88. 'Report by the Civil Commissioner', p. 13.

meeting of the Council of Ten, the body initially directing the work of the Peace Conference, Lloyd George sharply attacked French obstructionism, and countered the argument that the Germans were merely blackmailing the Allies into making concessions by quoting copiously from a telegram which he had received from General Plumer the preceding afternoon describing conditions in the British Zone. He then insisted that any further negotiations with the Germans on food supplies should be presided over by a British chairman. Subsequently on 13–14 March at Brussels an agreement was secured with the Germans, which effectively treated Germany as one unit as far as food supplies were concerned.[89] Tiarks also learnt from Austen Chamberlain, the Chancellor of the Exchequer, that the Treasury had agreed to fund an immediate delivery of some 200,000 tons of potatoes and surplus army rations for the British and American Zones, subject, of course, to eventual repayment from Washington and Berlin.[90]

Before returning to Cologne Tiarks scribbled a triumphant note to his wife claiming that the work he had done 'in getting things moving in every sort of branch of the peace conference is simply huge and the affects [*sic*] of it on the whole organisation here will be lasting'.[91] This is an understandable exaggeration, although the first-hand knowledge he brought from Cologne did reinforce Wise's arguments for the creation of the Rhineland Commission. The immediate effect of his intervention on the revictualment of Cologne was, however, disappointing. It was not until April that any food was ready for distribution to the occupied territories. Then, when the boats arrived with the first consignment of Norfolk potatoes at Cologne, the municipal food organization was unable to pay for them owing to a sudden fall in the value of the mark, and they were not unloaded until the bargees complained that 'they were rotting the sides out of their barges'.[92] Some twenty years later General Clive vividly recalled 'a crowd of German women pushing the potatoes in a state of almost liquid putrescence into sacks and carrying them off'.[93] Distribution and the fixing of maximum prices was left to the German authorities, who devised a scheme, which was theoretically effective but in practice frequently evaded, and consequently large quantities of

89. S.P. Tillman, *Anglo-American Relations at the Paris Peace Conference of 1919*, Princeton, 1961, pp. 265–6.
90. 'Report by the Civil Commissioner', pp. 16–18.
91. Tiarks to wife, 11.3.19, Tiarks papers.
92. Clive to Edmonds ('II. Note on p. 26').
93. Ibid.

food continued to be sold on the black market. As the poor rate of exchange ensured that every four-pennyworth of imported British food cost the German a shilling,[94] the price of even the emergency rations remained too high for the poorer sections of society, or those on a fixed income, such as the army of middle-class administrators employed in the 'vast administrative machine of modern Germany'.[95] At the end of May the urban population was still 'listless, depressed and anaemic',[96] yet even so, it was better fed than the proletariat in unoccupied Germany, whose rations were some 30 per cent less than those in the occupied territories.[97]

In July and August there was a temporary but dramatic improvement in the situation as a consequence of the signature of the Peace Treaty, the increase in dairy imports from France and Holland and an abundant fresh fruit harvest. The steady increase in the number of men finding employment also ensured that more families could afford to supplement their rations. Colonel Strange, the Food Commissioner at Cologne, reported that 'the shops are full of provisions . . . The people are more cheerful, and at the time of closing the wineshops and cafés, even uproarious'.[98] The *Bystander* confidently foresaw the restoration of the 'the Hun [to] his national magnificence of bulk'.[99] Nevertheless food supplies were far from assured. Throughout the war years the soil had been starved of vital fertilizers; there was a persistent shortage of cattle feeding stuffs, which in turn affected milk production, and the municipal authorities were unable to stockpile food for the coming winter. By December the population was again caught in the vicious circle of inflation and food scarcity. Little crossed the Rhine and neither the Belgian nor the French Zone had reserves to spare. By January 1920 the average daily ration in the Cologne Zone had sunk to a mere 1,090 calories per day.[100]

Whilst food was an absolutely fundamental requirement for the civil population, coal was hardly less important as it was the key to

94. 'Food Conditions in the British Zone', report by Lt Col. Strange, 2.7.19, FO 608/279 fos 263–83. See also Fergusson, 'Army of the Rhine, Military Governor's Branch', 16.4.19, p. 2, LHCMA Robertson I/28/2a.
95. 'Report on the Food Conditions in the British and American Occupied Areas' by Professor E. H. Starling and J. H. Garvin, 25 May 1919, p. 5, FO 608/222 fos 143–9.
96. Ibid., p. 4.
97. Ibid., p. 2.
98. Strange, 'Food Conditions in the British Zone', p. 12.
99. Gedye, the *Bystander*, 13.8.19.
100. 'Report on Food Conditions in Occupied Territory', by E. M. Troughton, Feb. 1920 (no. 179118), FO 371/4344.

the revival of industry and full employment. Although the British Zone contained large deposits of lignite, which met domestic needs,[101] a constant supply of black coal from unoccupied Germany was essential to keep the majority of power stations and factories running. Thus even when the frontier between the occupied and unoccupied territories was closed on 14 December 1918, coal continued to cross the Rhine, although not in sufficient quantities to guarantee normal production. In March, when even this inadequate supply was threatened by the precipitous decline in production in the Ruhr coal fields, Tiarks was so concerned for the future of the economy of the British Zone that he urged on Lloyd George the occupation of Westphalia by Allied troops.[102] Understandably Lloyd George remained unconvinced, and consequently the Zone's vital coal supplies remained at the mercy of factors outside British control. On 28 March British officials arranged a meeting through 'banking channels' with the great Westphalian mine owner, Hugo Stinnes, and agreed that production would not appreciably rise until the colliers were better fed.[103] During the summer coal production rose in the Ruhr, but a steady supply was still by no means assured. In August the 'only reserves held at all [were] kept by the railways; . . . other undertakings had often literally to shovel coal from the track to the furnace'.[104] By mid-November coal shortages were again acute and General Robertson was alarmed that many factories in the Zone would have to close down.[105]

In the struggle to prevent a total breakdown of the economy in the British Zone, coal supplies were an essential prerequisite, but ultimately the only real guarantee of success was the restoration of economic links with unoccupied Germany, which had been almost completely cut by decrees issued on Foch's orders by the Military Government on 14 December 1918 and on 1 January 1919.[106] Haig was privately critical of these orders as he was convinced that they would lead to large-scale unemployment, and he openly questioned whether the army should be involved.[107] Their impact was, however, mitigated by a concession granted by the Allies on 18 January

101. Robertson to Churchill, 16.11.19, LHCMA Robertson I/28/27a.
102. 'Report by the Civil Commissioner', pp. 10–11.
103. 'Meeting at 11.15 a.m. Held in Room 16 (Hotel Monopol)', 28.3.19, FO 608/281 fos 344–9. Ryan and Tiarks were both there.
104. 'Report on the Present Situation and Outlook of the Coal Supply in Occupied Territory', by Major G.J. Saunders, 30.8.19. FO 371/4341 fos 253–4.
105. Robertson to Churchill, 16.11.19, LHCMA Robertson I/28/27a.
106. Becker, 'Sieben Jahre', vol. 1, pp. 114.
107. Haig to Sec. WO (14129/3. Q.D.2) 11.1.19, WO 95/41.

1919 whereby not only was the import from unoccupied Germany of vital raw materials permitted but also, under certain circumstances, permission would be granted for all products which could be recognized as essential for the economic life of the Rhineland. A month later Fergusson allowed industrialists to cut red tape by applying for import permits on a regular monthly basis.[108] This significantly helped the economy of the British Zone survive until the ban on trade with unoccupied Germany was lifted on 12 July. In February trade was permitted between the occupied territories, neutrals and the Allies. The British Military Government, like its French, Belgian and American counterparts, urged its countrymen to exploit the unique opportunities provided by the occupation to capture markets. In February and March the Commercial Department of the Military Governor's office was strengthened by an additional number of civilians recruited from the Ministry of Munitions, and a technical commission was sent out to Cologne to advise on trade between the occupied territories and Britain and to report on the state of manufacturing in the Rhineland.[109] The Commission was so impressed by the modern design of the factories, the high standard of the mechanized equipment in them and good welfare arrangements for the workers that it advised British industrialists to 'exploit this unique opportunity for studying German methods in detail'.[110] In May a high-powered delegation of industrialists methodically inspected all branches of the engineering industry in the Rhineland.[111] The British textile industry was particularly interested in the dye stocks at the Bayer Chemical works at Leverkusen, near Cologne, and at the Badischer Aniline factories at Ludwigshafen in the French Zone.[112]

Although the Technical Commission reported in March that there were excellent market opportunities for boots, clothing and raw materials of all kinds,[113] there was a considerable delay before British goods reached the Rhineland in bulk both because the trade routes through Rotterdam and Antwerp had not yet been reopened and because the Board of Trade, in its anxiety not to pre-empt the conditions of a later more comprehensive Anglo–German trade agreement, felt that 'until peace terms had been agreed, merchants

---

108. Becker, 'Sieben Jahre', vol. 1, pp. 115–16.
109. 'Report by the Civil Commissioner', pp. 1–2.
110. 'Report of the Commission Appointed by Lord Moulton to advise General Plummer on Technical and Trade Matters in the British Occupied Territory of Germany', 1.4.19, p. 86. FO 382/2316 fos 2269–2459.
111. Details on FO 608/280 (Section 2, 'Inspection of Factories').
112. Minute by Cooper, 15.9.19, FO 371/4341 fo. 6.
113. 'Report by the Civil Commissioner', p. 4.

should be allowed to find their own channels for carrying on trade'.[114] The Military Government in Cologne, convinced of the need to revive local industry, was much more helpful. It collected statistics, found billets for visiting businessmen, arranged for industrial delegations to visit German factories,[115] and from October onwards the *Cologne Post*, the British Army newspaper, regularly published a column for British businessmen in the Rhineland in which it fully reported any relevant commercial information.[116] Initially the soldiers were critical of the apparent lethargy of British traders. General Fergusson observed in April that whilst the 'French, Belgian and Americans are active and have either sent in quantities of second hand rubbish or have booked orders for millions of marks of goods, the British probably owing to sentiment and partly from apathy, are doing nothing'.[117] In May the British Reception Office at Cologne provided some 2,190 billets for visiting businessmen out of which only 98 were taken up by British traders.[118] However, once the Peace Treaty was signed and more normal commercial conditions restored to the occupied territories, there was a surge of interest. In July there was an increase of 600 per cent in visiting British businessmen, and T. H. Urwick, a British official on the inter-Allied Rhineland Commission, was pleased 'to note that though the British traders started very late, they are now beginning to realise the importance of trade that can be done in these areas'.[119]

There was considerable resentment amongst both British officials and businessmen at the French commercial offensive in the Rhineland, although there were similar complaints made by French officers and journalists about the efforts of the Military Government to assist British traders and to impede their French rivals.[120] The French were accused frequently of not 'playing the game' by either ignoring or bending the complex commercial regulations in their favour.[121] The American and British authorities were con-

114. Ibid., p. 28.
115. See FO 608/279 Section 7, 'Inspection of Factories', and 608 280 Section 2, 'Inspection of Factories'.
116. Beginning 31.10.19.
117. 'Army of the Rhine, Military Governor's Branch', 16.4.19, LHCMA Robertson I/28/2a.
118. Urwick to Waterlow, 11.6.19 (Lux. no. 158), FO 608/280 fo. 133.
119. Urwick to Waterlow, 25.7.19 (no. 218), FO 608/280 fo. 125.
120. See Memorandum by the Commercial Counsellor at the British Embassy, Paris, 24.6.19, FO 608/280 fos 414–16, and also the Complaints in the 'Travail du Commandant Berger', Vincennes, 7N2664–1.
121. See the letter from one Harry Lomax, 1.8.19: 'Whilst England has been playing

cerned by the large-scale smuggling of French goods over the frontier into unoccupied Germany. Major A.F. Vernon, the head of the Commercial Department of the Military Government, complained that contrary to the regulations which forbade the re-export of goods from the occupied to the unoccupied territories, 'an enormous trade had been developed between France and the interior of Germany'. He gloomily prophesied in May that 'if the French continued . . . the blockade will cease to exist . . . and merely become an ingenious device for opening the doors to French trade while keeping them locked in the face of Britain'.[122] Despite attempts by both the British and Americans to close it, 'the hole in the West' remained open until Germany ratified the Treaty of Versailles on 10 January 1920 and regained the freedom to extend her tariff system to cover the occupied territories.[123]

The British Military Government showed a considerable – even ruthless – awareness of the commercial opportunities in the Rhineland, but as it represented a power which had no political ambitions there, it could afford to conduct a reasonably just caretaker regime, which as the middle classes appreciated, protected Cologne against the tide of bolshevism.[124] Visitors were impressed by the lack of 'cheap and petty jingo hatred'[125] for the Germans amongst many of the troops, but there were, of course, the inevitable petty tyrannies, and incorrigible 'hun haters' like the Area Commandant of the western suburbs of Cologne, who hoped in early January that 'there would be . . . someone shot so that [the Germans] could see that there was an iron hand under a kid glove'.[126] Another officer recalled later how he became suspicious that some of the local villagers were trying to beat the curfew by pretending that their wives were in labour, and that under the pretext of fetching the midwife, they were in fact playing cards with friends. One night he burst into a cottage with an armed escort and saw 'to my horror the woman lying on the bed with no clothes on and a baby half born. Needless to say I beat a hasty retreat and remarked inwardly 'better luck next time'.'[127] However, despite such incidents as these, the

the game, French traders set at nought the terms of the Armistice and sent in hundreds of lorry loads of stuff. . .'; FO 382/2322 fo. 3397.
122. Vernon to Urwick, 31.5.19, FO 608/280 fos 435–7.
123. McDougall, *Rhineland Diplomacy*, p. 130.
124. W. Bergmann to K. Bartel in Weekly Report on Censorship of German Press in Cologne, Bonn, etc., ending 29.3.19, Section 7, p. 4, WO 95/775.
125. Tiarks to wife, 24.1.19, Tiarks papers.
126. Lt Goodman to parents, 14.1.19, IWM 71/59/1.
127. Memoirs of Lt Col. Fleetwood-Wilson, IWM 75/52/1.

record of the British Military Government in 1919 was on balance both humane and just.

A Clash between Two Worlds:
Anglo–German Relations in the Cologne Zone in 1919

Inevitably the army of occupation placed a considerable strain on the civil population, particularly in Cologne, where according to one visitor from England in 1919 'khaki–clad soldiers swarm in every direction. Soldiers, soldiers: they overflow the railway station, the square, the Hohenzollern bridge.'[128] Two different worlds clashed: a large military presence with its own organizations and way of life was superimposed upon the civilian population. Consequently there was friction at almost every level between soldier and civilian, and the bureau which Adenauer set up to deal with occupation questions was inundated with complaints ranging from the harmful effects of army lorries reversing on pavements to the RAF exercising over cemeteries.[129] There were also fatal accidents caused by careless driving and several incidents where civilians were shot because unwittingly they did not respond to a sentry's challenge. In May 1919 an incident occurred which illustrates only too clearly that a 'military occupation, however honestly the "occupiers" may strive to be just to the "occupied", remains always an unpleasant business'.[130] Three schoolboys on bikes raced passed a column of British troops. When one of the boys yelled out to his friends, 'Don't go so fast, you rabble', the lieutenant leading the column instantly suspected an insult and fired some warning shots which fatally wounded the boy. The army offered the boy's family a derisory amount of compensation, which hardly covered the medical fees, but cashiered the lieutenant, despite his plea that he had often employed similar methods in the colonies.[131]

The army's billeting and requisitioning policy also complicated the life of the civilian population. Not only were all the large hotels and three hundred houses taken over for offices and messes, but

---

128. Markham, *A Woman's Watch on the Rhine*, p. 9.
129. See also Williamson, 'Cologne and the British', pp. 695–702.
130. G.E.R. Gedye, *The Revolver Republic*, London, 1930, p. 248.
131. Williamson, 'Cologne and the British', p. 700. See also Haldane's Diary, 12.5.19, NLOS MS. 20250. Details of this and other incidents are in 'Gewalt und Fahrlässige Handlungen von Besatzungszugehörigen', HA d SK, Best. 83/1/17, 2, pp. 1–18.

ninety-six schools in the Cologne area were requisitioned for use as temporary barracks. The educational authorities tried in vain to find alternative accommodation and a large number of children were left to run wild in the streets, with the predictable result that, in the words of Dr Becker, the Director of the Occupation Department at the Town Hall, 'their demoralization and barbarization made frightening progress'.[132]

It is difficult to generalize on the behaviour and attitudes of the British troops. There were so many cases of looting that Dr Becker had to set up a special office to deal with complaints.[133] Amongst the subalterns there was an understandable but irritating upsurge of boisterous 'undergraduate' behaviour. On the evening of 4 January 1919, for instance, two drunken officers placed chamber-pots on the heads of the statues of Kaiser Wilhelm and Kaiserin Augusta, and a further group assaulted a night-watchman when he was unable to conjure up women for them.[134] In the pages of the Rhine Army's newspaper, the *Cologne Post*, and in a fortnightly diary in the *Bystander*, which was written by Captain Eric Gedye, an intelligence officer on Fergusson's staff, the Rhinelander was usually seen as a figure of amusement rather than of hatred. Gedye was making a conventional judgement when he observed that 'removed from the influence of the Prussian officials and placed under the healthier and certainly not more severe rule of the Briton, the Rhinelander appears an amiable person enough – possibly due to the drop of French blood in his veins, possibly to his sunny lazy climate'.[135] There was virtually universal agreement amongst the officers, in whose own education organized games had played such a key part,[136] that the Germans suffered from a surfeit of book-learning and needed to learn quite literally how 'to play the game'. Thus the *Cologne Post* could tell its readers in all seriousness that 'after a clean and sane peace, Germany must try to get by means of sport a sane mind in a sane body'.[137] Nevertheless, German efficiency was widely admired. Many of the troops were impressed by the good quality of working-class housing in Cologne,[138] and official inspections of factories revealed the advanced state of her technology. After visiting a sugar beet factory General Haldane

132. Quoted in Williamson, 'Cologne and the British', p. 699.
133. Ibid., pp. 699–700.
134. Ibid., p. 700.
135. *Bystander*, 20.8.20.
136. See Bond, *British Military Policy*, ch. 2.
137. *Cologne Post*, 22.4.19.
138. Ibid., 1.7.19.

was convinced that 'unless we radically change our methods, drop some of our conservativism, and above all really work, the Germans must inevitably get ahead of us'.[139]

Until the Peace Treaty was signed fraternization with German women was banned, but inevitably it took place despite all attempts by the military authorities to stop it. Soldiers picked up girls in cinema or cafés and most officers had their pet *fräulein*.[140] In July 1919 fraternization was at last officially permitted, but it was still not encouraged by either the British or German authorities. The more strait-laced members of the Cologne bourgeoisie were horrified at the philandering that took place between the British soldiery and the local *Mädel*,[141] while the English girls, employed as secretaries, nurses or canteen assistants, were frankly jealous. At the Cologne races in July Gedye noted that 'one or two rather self-conscious parties of English and Germans put in an appearance, but the glances of the English girls at any officer who talked to a golden haired Rhinemaiden must have kept him from feeling the somewhat oppressive heat of the day'.[142] The *Cologne Post* thundered against the dangers of intermarriage. In one leader readers were warned that 'for five years or more the German nation has been nourished on hatred for Britain and it would be an unpleasant event for an English father if the first words his offspring spoke were "Gott Strafe England".'[143]

The attention of gossips and the press naturally focused on sexual relationships, but there were numerous examples on both sides of individual acts of kindness and generosity. At Christmas in 1918 men billeted with German families were surprised to receive gifts of food and wine.[144] One subaltern, after braving the rigours of the Cologne–Boulogne leave train, arrived back at his billets in Zülpich with a bad cold, where, as he recorded in his diary, 'my landlady ordered me "a hot bath and off to bed"! There she plied me with hot milk and honey, cough mixture and so forth and was delighted to find next morning that the cold had gone.'[145]

In the summer of 1919 civilians visiting the Cologne Zone were astonished by the apparently amicable relations between the occupiers and the occupied. In England the predominant mood was still

139. Haldane's Diary, 10.2.19, NLOS MS. 20250.
140. See, for example, *Bystander*, 6.8.19.
141. Williamson, 'Cologne and the British', p. 699.
142. *Bystander*, 13.8.19.
143. *Cologne Post*, 25.7.19.
144. See 'The Reminiscences of Pte. G.W. Sullivan', p. 109, IWM P. 253.
145. Diary of Lt C. Carter, 2.2.19, IWM PP/MCR/141.

one of fierce hatred for Germany, but on the Rhine British troops had learnt to appreciate the Germans as individuals rather than as a collective 'blood terror called the Boche'.[146] To Violet Carruthers, a Liberal, journalist and wife of a Rhine Army colonel, this growing understanding between British troops and Germans was a welcome by-product of the occupation, and she was moved to comment:

> Better relations between nations will, I believe, be built up ultimately on working class laws. The diplomacy of the politicians in power is too bitter and too tortuous to further the cause of European reconstruction. From this point of view the occupation has been wholly to the good inasmuch as tens of thousands of Englishmen who have passed through the country have gone home with a saner appreciation of the situation.[147]

There is little doubt that the soldiers returning home to Britain and the Dominions did take back with them a 'saner appreciation of the situation' in Germany. They had witnessed at first hand the effects of the blockade on German women and children, and as the many surviving collections of letters and diaries show, had also been treated for the most part with warmth by the local population. To what extent these impressions contributed to the changes in attitude in Britain towards Germany and the growth of support for revising the Treaty of Versailles over the next three years is hard to assess, but at the very least they could hardly have hindered the process. They contributed to the growing perception of the Germans as the underdog.

---

146. *Bystander*, 20.8.19.
147. Markham, *A Woman's Watch on the Rhine*, p. 233. Mrs Carruthers preferred to be known by her maiden name, Markham.

—4—

Preparing for Ratification, June–December 1919

It was only after the signature of the Peace Treaty that the extent of Britain's responsibilities in Germany emerged. At a time when industrial troubles at home and unrest in Ireland, India and Egypt were claiming both attention and military manpower, Britain had to find troops and skilled administrators to preside over the execution of the Peace in Germany. Not only was it difficult to find sufficient personnel with a knowledge of German, but in order to survive the machiavellian intrigues within the inter-Allied commissions, where French generals and bureaucrats sought every opportunity to effect a *de facto* revision of the Treaty, senior British officials in Germany needed to be experienced and forceful administrators and well versed in the problems of contemporary Europe. The lack of officials of the necessary calibre was to cause serious difficulties in Danzig, Upper Silesia and on the Military Control Commission in Berlin.

To coordinate after ratification the innumerable inter-Allied bodies set up by the peace treaties of 1919, of which the Inter-Allied Rhineland High Commission (IARHC), the plebiscite commissions and disarmament control commissions were only a fraction, the Allied and Associated Powers agreed in July to set up a standing committee in Paris, later known as the Ambassadors' Conference. Initially the Ambassadors' Conference was envisaged as a compromise between the Anglo-American concept of a 'clearing house' for collecting information and exchanging opinions and the Franco-Italian wish to set up a committee with far-reaching powers to interpret and execute the Treaty of Versailles. In practice, with the consent of the Foreign Office the Franco-Italian model was adhered to more closely. Staffed by professional diplomats and headed by the formidable Jules Cambon, the former French Ambassador in Berlin, it developed an impressive *esprit de corps* of its own. In January 1920 its membership was composed of the British, Italian and Japanese Ambassadors. The Belgian Ambassador attended when topics affecting his country were discussed, while the American Ambassador was present only as an observer, as Congress had not yet ratified the Treaty. On military matters it was to be advised by the inter-Allied Military Committee of Versailles. The Ambassadors' Conference was the visible expression of Allied unity and was later described by Gustav Stresemann, the German Foreign Secretary, as 'a sort of penal committee' against Germany,[1] but increasingly over the years 1920–23, it became the arena in which Anglo-French differences on the interpretation of the peace were fought out. When, as frequently happened, deadlock ensued, only the Supreme Council, which was the peacetime reincarnation of the old Supreme War Council, could decide Allied policy. The Supreme War Council was not officially dissolved during the Peace Conference and temporarily functioned in the interregnum between the signature of the Versailles Treaty and its ratification by the signatory powers under the name of the Council of the Heads of Delegation. In January 1920 the Allied leaders agreed on the continuing need for a supreme international body to meet periodically to discuss questions of principle. Thus the Supreme War Council evolved into the Supreme Council and incongruously combined elements of the old Congress and diplomacy from the period 1814–22 with the 'Summitry' of the twentieth century.[2]

The Triumph of the Civilians in the Rhineland

Once the principle of the fifteen-year occupation had been conceded, it became necessary to determine its organization, and there began, in the words of one British Foreign Office official, 'the development of two inter-woven dramas, namely the struggle between the civil and military powers for supremacy and also the struggle of the French to be supreme amongst the Allies'.[3] By late

1. W.M. Jordan, *Great Britain, France and the German Problem, 1918–1939,* London, 1943 (new impression, 1971), p. 60.
2. For a brief description of these bodies see A.J. Toynbee, *Survey of International Affairs, 1920–23,* London, 1925, pp. 1–5; Jordan, *Great Britain, France and the German Problem,* pp. 57–60. The most detailed study is in J. Heideking, 'Oberster Rat – Botschafterkonferenz – Völkerbund', *Historische Zeitschrift,* vol. 231, 1980, pp. 589–630. See also P. Cambon, *Correspondance, 1870–1924,* 3 vols, Paris, 1940–6, vol.3, pp. 273–438.
3. FO Minute on Waterlow's letter of 16.6.19 (no. 156, Commercial W) (90999) to Curzon, FO 382/2319 fos 3058–3063.

March 1919 British military and legal experts in Paris had unofficially assumed that some sort of *post bellum* occupation of the Rhineland was inevitable. Brigadier-General J. H. Morgan, the personal representative of the Adjutant-General at the Peace Conference, had already drawn up a set of draft clauses for inclusion in the Peace Treaty to safeguard the rights of the occupying powers.[4] Although he conceded six weeks later that the growing importance of the Rhineland Commission necessitated 'the infiltration into the administration of a very considerable civil element of an expert character', he nevertheless still deemed it essential that the occupation should be 'nothing less than a military dictatorship with unlimited powers' as the Germans 'both by temperament and training [were] indisposed to take orders from anyone not in uniform'.[5]

The soldiers' assumption that the Rhineland should be governed by a military regime was sharply challenged by Britain's representative on the Paris Left Bank Committee, Sydney Waterlow, who argued that only the new Rhineland Commission could effectively guarantee 'the smooth working of the machinery of commerce and the distribution of food and raw materials imported into the area'. He warned that in an emergency it would have

> to be developed into a body of the greatest importance. Germany may collapse into Bolshevism, and, cut off from imported food and raw materials, remain economically prostrate. In that event the very interests of the occupying armies will . . . require a separate economic regime for the occupied territory, and the Commission will necessarily become the organ through which the Associated Governments will control the relations of the occupied territory with the rest of the world.[6]

The Council of Four on 8 May instructed their military advisers to draw up a draft convention providing for a military occupation of the Rhineland.[7] Within three days a draft was produced which would have perpetuated the same system of military control which had been in force since November 1918 with the added provision of powers to veto German industrial regulations and agreements. It was, however, subjected to such searching criticism from Stuart,

---

4. 'The Allied Occupation of Germany' (Article 47 of the 'Preliminaries of the Peace'), 24.3.19 (5091), FO 608/141 fos 376–80.
5. J.H. Morgan, 'The British Occupation of the Rhineland,' p. 2, FO 608/142.
6. S.P. Waterlow, 'Future Economic Control of the Occupied Part of Germany', 4.5.19 (no. 10190), FO 608/222 fos 303–7.
7. A draft had been ready since 23 April. See Thwaites to Hankey, 23.4.19, IWM Wilson 73/1/26, file 45.

Noyes and Waterlow, who all feared that the overwhelming numerical superiority of the French army would enable the French to control the Rhineland, that Lord Robert Cecil, the chief British representative on the Supreme Economic Council, and General Thwaites, the Director of Military Intelligence, drafted a compromise proposal which was submitted, together with the original draft, to the Council of Four on 29 May. Two days earlier Noyes, incensed by the recent attempt by General Mangin, the Commander of the French 10th Army at Mainz, to encourage a separatist revolt at Coblenz, had written directly to President Wilson outlining a plan for subordinating the armies in the Rhineland to a civilian inter-Allied commission, which would have the power to make regulations whenever German law or actions threatened the execution of the Treaty or the safety of the troops. Wilson was convinced by Noyes' arguements, while Lloyd George opportunely seized on the chance to reopen the whole question of the fifteen-year occupation. Clemenceau cleverly divided his critics. He agreed to the appointment of a committee under the chairmanship of Louis Loucheur to rewrite the draft convention on the basis of the Noyes proposals, but he adamantly refused to make any concession on the principle of the fifteen-year occupation.[8]

The Loucheur Committee accepted two basic proposals from the Noyes plan when it recommended the termination of martial law and the creation of a civilian commission to represent the occupying powers in the Rhineland. It refused, however, to endorse the scheme for endowing the Commission with the potentially limitless power of making new regulations or of amending old ones when German actions or laws threatened the execution of the Treaty. Also in deference to the persuasive arguments from Foch that the Noyes Plan would invest a civilian High Commission with such sweeping powers that it would in fact lead to a far greater Allied involvement in civilian affairs than a simple military regime based on martial law,[9] the British, Italian and American delegates on the Committee suggested that the convention should be limited to an initial period of two years, after which a further convention could be negotiated.[10] Lloyd George, of course, welcomed the

8. 'The Working of the Rhineland Agreement', 18.2.44 (U.1344/104/70), p. 5, paras 14–16; Copy in LSE, Webster Papers, 11/2. See also E. Fraenkel, *Military Occupation and the Rule of Law*, London and New York, 1944, pp. 71–80; K. Nelson, *Victors Divided*, pp. 109–12.
9. Commission interallieé de la Rive Gauche du Rhine, procès-verbaux, 29.5.19–9.6.19, Séance du 31.5.19 (Matin), pp. 5–10, FO 608/142 fos 306–83. Fraenkel, *Military Occupation*, pp. 75–6.
10. 'Report presented to the Council of the Principal Allied and Associated Powers

two-year limit,[11] but Clemenceau, opposed to renewed British attempts to reduce the overall period of occupation, rejected the compromise, although he did mollify Lloyd George by agreeing that an earlier termination of the occupation was theoretically possible provided Germany had already fulfilled the demands of the Treaty.[12] The Council of Four therefore accepted the modified Noyes Plan as the basis of the Rhineland Agreement[13] and incorporated Clemenceau's condition for an earlier evacuation into Article 431 of the Treaty.

Upon ratification a civilian High Commission consisting of one representative each from Belgium, France, America and Britain would preside over the Allied occupation of the Rhineland. The French Commissioner was to be chairman or president, and, although decisions were to be taken by a majority vote, in the event of a deadlock the president would be entitled to give the casting vote. Each High Commissioner was responsible to his own government, to whom he could appeal if outvoted, although he could not delay the implementation of decisions taken. The High Commission was not an administrative body. It existed solely to protect the occupying forces and, in a clause which invested the Commissioners with considerable potential powers, it was authorized to issue any ordinance necessary for their safety and maintenance and to declare martial law whenever necessary. All Allied personnel and any Germans employed by them were subject exclusively to military law and could only be tried in Allied military courts. Rather ambiguously, the Rhineland Agreement also stated in Article III that 'any person who commits any offense against the persons or property of the armed forces of the Allied and Associated Powers may be made amenable to the military jurisdiction of the said forces'. The German civil authorities were to be required to provide all necessary billets and barracks, and if these were insufficient, Allied commanders could requisition more. German railway, postal and telephone personnel would come under the authority of the Allied Commander-in-Chief, whenever military interests required it. The High Commission was bound to consult the military

by the Inter-Allied Commission on the Left Bank of the Rhine' (WCP 978), FO 608/142 fos 173–6.

11. K. Nelson, *Victors Divided*, pp. 116–20.

12. 'Notes of a Meeting held at Mr. Lloyd George's Residence', 16.6.19 (CF 73A), HLRO, LG, F/124.

13. See 'Convention Regarding the Military Occupation of the Territories of the Rhine' (WCP 993), FO 608/142 fos 177–82. The text is also published in Fraenkel, *Military Occupation*, pp. 233–6 and Edmonds, *The Occupation*, pp. 402–6.

authorities before issuing any ordinances affecting them, but in the event of a declaration of martial law, the army commanders could intervene in the German civil administration only after obtaining specific approval from the High Commission.

On 16 June the Rhineland Agreement was initialled. Together with the agreement to allow a plebiscite in Upper Silesia, it composed the major Allied concession to the German note of 29 May rejecting the draft peace terms of 6 May, and arguably played a part in persuading the Berlin government to accept the Treaty of Versailles, which was signed with the Rhineland Agreement on 28 June. The Allies agreed informally to discuss with German officials the details of the application of the Rhineland Agreement. 'Explanatory discussions'[14] started on 11 July at Versailles where the Germans pressed hard for a supplementary agreement guaranteeing the civil rights of the population and the restoration of political, judicial, administrative and economic links with Berlin, and also for official recognition of the appointment of a civil commissioner as their representative in the Rhineland. Although the Allies rejected a formal agreement, they nevertheless tried to be conciliatory. They agreed to accept, on an unofficial basis only, a German civil commissioner, but stressed that the High Commission still reserved the right 'to enter into relations with any local authority whatsoever'.[15]

The Rhineland Agreement, like the Versailles Treaty itself, was a compromise. To the Anglo-Saxon powers it was an attempt to make the occupation more palatable to the German government, whilst placing the French armies in the Rhineland firmly under the control of a civilian inter-Allied Commission. To the French it was a necessary cosmetic concession to their allies, which still preserved much of their influence intact in the Rhineland.

British military and civil officials gave the Rhineland Agreement a mixed reception. Waterlow was convinced that it would end French attempts 'to preserve the position of permanent influence in the whole of the occupied territory',[16] but not everybody was so optimistic. General Robertson predicted 'a most complicated and difficult time'.[17] Stuart's assistant on the Rhineland Commission, T.H. Urwick, pointed out that France and Belgium, strengthened

14. K. Nelson, *Victors Divided*, pp. 157–8.
15. 'Draft Reply to the German Note regarding the occupation of the Left Bank of the Rhine', FO 608/142 fos 264–72 (eventually dispatched as no. 15702/511/1/9).
16. Waterlow to Curzon, 16.6.19 (no. 156, Commercial W), FO 382/2319 fos 3059–3063.
17. Robertson to CIGS, 3.7.19, LHCMA Robertson I/28/15a.

by Tirard's casting vote, would be able to force through any policy they wished; drawing on his experiences over the past year he warned Waterlow that the French 'are persistently and exclusively working for their own particular interest, and further that their methods and the action that they take, unless under constant check, are liable to cause the very greatest irritation and friction; they seem incapable of taking a fair and common-sense view'.[18] He recommended urgently that an Italian Commissioner should be appointed and the casting vote abolished. Waterlow agreed on the desirability of Italian membership, but believed that 'in the long run French cleverness is no match for British persistency' provided that 'our representative on the spot is a strong man thoroughly up to his work and that he is properly supported at home'.[19] This was indeed to be a crucial proviso!

After the signature of the Rhineland Agreement the Rhineland Commission became the 'Committee of Organization'[20] for the future High Commission. Wise successfully urged the Foreign Office to nominate Sir Harold Stuart as the British High Commissioner, and also advised them strongly to fend off any attempts by the Treasury to enforce cheese-paring economies on personnel and salaries as 'it would be a fatal mistake, especially in view of the activity of the French in covering the occupied territory with a large and expert staff to attempt . . . to make shift with a second rate personnel'.[21] On 31 July Waterlow was moved back to London to head a specially created Rhineland Department in the Foreign Office.[22]

Detailed work on the organization of both the High Commission in Coblenz and of the administration of the Cologne Zone began in June.[23] At Cologne a sub-committee was set up under Colonel Ryan, General Clive's former chief of staff, and divided into sections covering such crucial subjects as food supplies, labour, political affairs, legal matters and billeting. The existing area and sub-area commandants were to be replaced by Kreis officers, whose task was essentially to act as 'an umpire between Allied Military and German civil interests'.[24] Stuart was adamant that the

18. Urwick to Waterlow, 24.6.19, FO 608/279 fos 215–17.
19. Waterlow to Urwick, 27.6.19, FO 608/279 fos 218–19.
20. Memorandum 'On Measures to be taken by the IARHC as soon as it comes into existence', 28.6.19, FO 608/279 fos 110–16.
21. Wise to FO, 24.6.19, FO 608/279 fos 239–41.
22. See Minutes, 31.7.19, FO 371/4336 fos 88–91.
23. Stuart to Waterlow, 30.6.19 (Lux. no. 180 no. 02), FO 608/279 fos 194–6.
24. 'Administration of the British Zone of Occupation after the Ratification of the Peace Treaty', 17.9.19, FO 371/4345 fos 306–20.

key to the effective organization of the High Commission in Coblenz was to create a system of sub-committees to which problems could be submitted, before proceeding to the High Commission. 'Any other procedure would overwhelm the Commission with detail.'[25] With a few exceptions like the professional diplomat Arnold Robertson, who was his deputy, most of his personal staff in Coblenz were also drawn from the army. Later this was to draw accusations of a 'bastard military system',[26] but Stuart deliberately gave preference to soldiers on the grounds that they would be more respected by the Germans and that they were, above all, available.[27] He recruited a gifted staff, which was more than able to hold its own with the French. Some were former expatriates, like Quarry, who before the war had been a concert pianist in Germany, or the 'fiery' Georgi, who had grown up in the French Colonies.[28] Others, like Gedye or Ryan himself, who had already been offered the post of manager of the Cologne branch of Lloyds Bank,[29] preffered life in occupied Germany to the uncertainties of post-war Britain.

Stuart also had to ensure that his staff had adequate secretarial back-up. By July there were over thirty girls working for the British section of the Rhineland Commission in Coblenz, who were naturally of considerable interest to the local American garrison. In early August the redoubtable Violet Carruthers was sent down there to make recommendations for their future welfare. She rapidly came to the conclusion that the girls lacked proper discipline and supervision and that as their office hours were light, it was 'not surprising that pleasure [had] assumed outstanding proportions in their eyes'.[30] She consequently recommended a more careful selection process in London and the provision of proper hostels in Coblenz where the girls would be supervised and only given late passes twice a week.

25. Minute no. 441 of the 32nd Meeting of the IARHC, 24.10.19, FO 371/4347.
26. E.C. Lawrence to Huddleston, 16.12.23, FO 371/8691 fo. 128.
27. Stuart to Waterlow, 30.6.19 (Lux. no. 180 no. 02), FO 608/279 fos 194–6.
28. C. Repington, *After the War*, London, 1922, pp. 225–6. See also G. Mutius to Rosenberg, 9.12.22, p. 4, FCO Lib. 3058 D603035-58. Francis Quarry's son informed me that his father 'went to Germany initially from school, but tiring of the rigours of student life after two years, joined the British Army and served in several campaigns in Africa at the turn of the century, returning to Germany in 1905 and resuming his piano studies under Paderewski in Heidelberg'. Patrick Quarry to author, 14.4.82.
29. Lloyds Bank Archives, Lloyds Bank (France) and National Provincial Bank (France) Ltd, Minute Book no. 4, 14.8.18, no. 2336.
30. E.F. Wise to Violet Carruthers (Mrs Markham), 15.7.19, 'Report on Women Clerical Staff at Coblenz', LSE Archives, Markham 2/7.

On the whole the preparatory work progressed satisfactorily, but it was sometimes interrupted by inter-Allied disagreements. For instance a potentially serious dispute arose in August when the French argued that, as the Rhineland Agreement laid down that Allied troops should be quartered in barracks, their soldiers should occupy Cologne since the small British garrison there would hardly fill up the local barracks. Stuart lived up to his reputation as the hammer of the French by pointing out forcefully to both the War Office and the Foreign office that

> a British Commissioner with no independent source of information at his disposal would be like a blind and deaf man. With Cologne held by the French he loses his eyes and ears, and consequently if his Government wish him to oppose, or even to temper and control the trend of French policy . . . he cannot carry out his instructions effectively.[31]

His arguments had considerable effect, and shortly afterwards the War Office decided to keep the Rhine Army in Cologne.[32]

By the end of November the Rhineland Commission was ready for its official transformation into the High Commission. The basic ordinances had been drafted, its organization agreed upon and the necessary personnel appointed. Sir Harold Stuart hoped that its role in the Rhineland would be merely one of 'judicious watchfulness',[33] but the London *Spectator* was more realistic when it observed that its future 'seems to lie in a sealed book that few care to open'.[34]

Setting up the Control Commissions

On the assumption that ratification would quickly follow the signature of the peace, the military representatives of the *Entente* powers and America were instructed on 28 June to organize inter-Allied Military (IAMCC), Naval (IANCC) and Aeronautical (IAACC) Control Commissions.[35] Their draft report, which was approved without discussion by the Heads of Delegation,[36] recommended that all three commissions should have their headquarters in Berlin

31. Memorandum on the Retention of Cologne, 21.8.19 (no. 120099), FO 371/4336 fos 181–6.
32. FO to Derby, 27.8.19 (no. 120099), FO 371/4336 fo. 188.
33. Stuart to Waterlow, 23.6.19 (Lux. no. 167, no. 02), FO 608/279 fo. 23.
34. *Spectator*, 16.8.19, p. 204.
35. Admiralty (Paris) to Admiralty (London), 27.6.19 (no. 35), ADM 116 1933.
36. DBFP Ser. 1, vol. 1 (no. 70), pp. 52–7; Salewski, *Entwaffnung*, pp. 48–52.

and then be divided into sub-commissions, each dealing with different aspects of disarmament. Within the IAMCC, which was by far the largest, three subdivisions were created covering Munitions and Armaments, Effectives (or military personnel) and Fortifications. The first two sub-commissions were to be based at Munich, Dresden, Stuttgart and 'at other such places as may be necessary',[37] while the Fortifications sub-Commission, the scope of which was given a more precise geographical definition by the Treaty, was to set up provincial headquarters in Königsberg, Kiel, Stettin, Mainz, Strassburg and Cologne.

French influence in the key Military Commission was safeguarded by the appointment of a French president. Responding to the advice of the Military Representatives of the Supreme War Council that he 'should be a general officer chosen with special reference to his military standing and reputation, as well as his energy and activity',[38] Foch selected General Claude Nollet, a formidable staff officer with an incisive mind that was rapidly able to penetrate the arcane details of the German military-industrial complex. Foch made the importance of his mission abundantly clear when he informed him that ' La Guerre n'est pas finie.'[39] The two other French generals on the commission were men of similar stature and, like Nollet, both had taught at the prestigious Ecole de Guerre.[40] General Walch was an artillery expert, who had commanded the artillery corps at St Quentin and Verdun, while Barthélemy, the head of the Effectives sub-Commission, had been in charge of the Deuxième Bureau of the French War Office.

The senior British appointments are likewise a guide to the degree of importance London attached to their activities. Admiral Charlton, who, as president of the Allied Naval Armistice Commission, already had experience of a *de facto* system of control of the German naval bases,[41] was transferred to the presidency of the IANCC, while Air Commodore Masterman, a former Director of the Admiralty's Air Department before transferring to the RAF in 1918, became the president of IAACC. The appointment of General Sir Francis Bingham to command the British section of the IAMCC emphasized the British conviction that German disarmament was

---

37. Inserted on Bingham's advice. 'Process verbal of a Joint Meeting of Military Naval and Air Representatives, held at Versailles on 7 July 1919', ADM 116 1933.
38. DBFP Ser. 1, vol. 1 (no. 7), pp. 52–3.
39. C. Nollet, *Une Expérience De Désarmament. Cinque Ans de Contrôle militaire en Allemagne*, Paris, 1932, p. II.
40. J.H. Morgan, *Assize of Arms*, vol. 2, 'Galley Slip VI', ch. XVII. See also below, ch. 7 footnote 1.
41. See ADM 116 1939 for details of periodic inspections during the Armistice.

primarily a matter of destruction of guns and munitions. Bingham was a man of great charm, but lacked the stature of a successful field officer and had no knowledge of German or of Germany.[42] He had served as Director General of Design in the Ministry of Munitions. The only senior officer who could match the intellectual calibre of the French generals was Brigadier-General Morgan, who in civilian life was Professor of Law at University College, London. He was appointed on the strength of his successful role as legal adviser to the Adjutant-General, whom he had represented at the Paris Peace Conference. He was to be brilliantly successful in unravelling the Reichswehr's attempts to evade the Treaty, but his pronounced francophil tendencies, contempt for Bingham and lack of sympathy for his own government's foreign policy led to bitter disputes within the British section of the IAMCC. His appointment was also resented by many regular officers. General Sackville-West, the British Military Representative on the Supreme War Council, for instance, complained to Henry Wilson that 'there are 4,000 unemployed regular officers. I should think one of them might be as good as Morgan.'[43]

On 8 August Nollet's request for a staff of 350 Allied, American and Japanese officers, 150 interpreters and 800 other ranks for the IAMCC, was readily approved by the Heads of Delegation.[44] Originally, only 20 per cent of the IAMCC was to be British, but, as the United States did not ratify the Treaty, the British share had to be increased to 32 per cent, while the French increased theirs to 45 per cent, thereby decisively strengthening their grip on the Commission.[45] Bingham had built up a nucleus of his staff in April, when it was known that control commissions would be sent to Germany.[46] He recruited the bulk of his staff from the Rhine Army,[47] but advertisements were also placed in British papers inviting 'anyone interested in German affairs . . . to visit the nearest recruiting office'.[48] Charlton had to supplement his technical

42. Morgan, *Assize of Arms*, vol. 2, Galley Slip VI. Bingham's son aptly remarked: 'Having such experience of the industrial side of creating war material, my father was in an ideal position to tackle the job of breaking it up in Germany' (H. Bingham to author, 28.11.75).
43. Sackville-West to Wilson, 3.11.19, IWM Wilson papers, 73/1/26, file 12E.
44. DBFP Ser. 1, vol. 1 (no. 31), pp. 379–80.
45. Salewski, *Entwaffnung*, pp. 48–52.
46. S. Roddie, *Peace Patrol*, London, 1932, pp. 31–3.
47. Diary of Major-General Sir Francis Bingham, September 1919–May 1920, p. 12 (28 or 29 September), IWM, Ball Papers, 72/116/4.
48. W.G. Cook's Memoirs, P. 25, IWM 77/183/1.

personnel by recruiting experts from such firms as Armstrong Whitworth and Vickers.[49]

Intent on both completing the whole process of control as quickly as possible and hoping also to modify some of the procedures before they could be applied, the German government invited the Allies to send 'une Commission qualifiée' to enter into negotiations on some of the practical details of control. On Foch's advice the Heads of Delegation consented to send 'une sorte d'avant-garde des Commissions de Contrôle' on the strict understanding that it would merely discuss methods of carrying out the treaty and in no way embark on negotiations.[50] After some prevarication by the Germans, the preliminary commission travelled via Cologne on 12 September into 'the dark hinterland'[51] of Germany. Bingham and his staff were given rooms in the Esplanade Hotel, which according to Bingham was 'frequented by the most villainous-looking war profiteers – fat and greasy with hideous female belongings'.[52]

Like his colleagues on the other commissions, Nollet had to weld a disparate, international personnel into a harmonious and effective unity by developing 'des liens de confiance réciproque, des habitudes de travail en commun, qui créent une pensée et une doctrine uniques et faisant de la Commission de Contrôle une organisme cohérent'.[53] He therefore held daily meetings of the Council of the Commission attended by all senior officers and heads of subcommissions in an effort to iron out 'les petits divergences' within his multinational team.[54] Bingham supported Nollet fully in this. In October he loyally declined an invitation to dinner from Noske, the German Defence Minister, for fear that this would give rise to rumours of Anglo–French differences.[55] Potential friction between the IANCC and the IAMCC was also avoided when the Admiralty agreed that Charlton should recognize Nollet as the Senior Allied Officer when joint meetings took place in Berlin.[56] Nollet at this stage was so touched by Bingham's behaviour that he praised his

49. Memorandum and Minute from Director of Naval Ordinance, 25.11.19 (no. G.O. 1155/19), ADM 116/1936 (Pack no. 8A/11).
50. DBFP Ser. 1, vol. 1 (no. 40), pp. 488–9.
51. Morgan, *Assize of Arms*, vol. 1, p. 16.
52. Bingham, Diary, 21.10.19, IWM 72/116/4.
53. Nollet to Foch, 21.10.19, p. 1, Vincennes 4N99-1.
54. Ibid.
55. Bingham, Diary, 11.10.19, IWM 72/116/4.
56. Admiralty (Military Branch) to Naval Section, Paris, 15.10.19, ADM 116 1934 (Pack no. 23).

'loyauté et l'élevation de pensée' to Foch.[57] In reality, however, Bingham lacked the essential 'passion'[58] for his job, which Nollet was trying to inculcate. He more realistically saw the work of the Commission as a medium-term task 'for putting Germany out of business as a military nation for sometime to come. Needless to say they can begin building up when we have gone, but if we are successful, they will find themselves faced with the same problem that we had in 1914.'[59] Essentially, like Lloyd George, he felt that the effectiveness of Allied disarmament measures rested ultimately on the attitude of the German population, and he was convinced that in the autumn of 1919 'if Germany wanted to go to war against the Entente powers not fifty per cent of the nation would have anything to do with it'.[60]

In September 1919 the Reichswehrministerium set up the Army, Navy and Air Peace Commissions, which developed into a system of virtual counter-control. The Army Peace Commission was directed by the formidable Generalleutnant von Cramon, whose views were the mirror image of Nollet's. He too, felt that the war was not over and 'sought to execute the task given him in such a way that a maximum of demands made by the IAMCC were balanced by the absolute minimum of concessions made by the Army Peace Commission'.[61] As the Germans were ready to dispute the intricacies of the disarmament clauses in Section V of the Treaty of Versailles with a skilful tenacity, Nollet was anxious not to be lured prematurely into conference with von Crammon, accompanied by colleagues, who had not yet had time to prepare their briefs. He thus refused an initial invitation on 17 September to discuss 'a number of questions' [62] until he had been informed in writing what they were, and had set up a coordinating committee consisting of the senior officers of the Commission. Nollet's determination to avoid procedural traps led to his first disagreement with Bingham. A seemingly innocuous invitation by the Germans to meet at the Auswärtiges Amt to discuss the allocation of billets was suspected by Nollet of being a trap, and he promptly insisted that the Acting Quartermaster-General of the Commission should himself both convene and chair the meeting, despite Bingham's plea that 'as Peace has been signed . . ., the Foreign Office is the

57. Nollet to Foch, 21.10.19, p. 2, Vincennes 4N99-1.
58. Ibid., p. 9.
59. Bingham, Diary, 3.10.19, IWM 72/116/4.
60. Ibid.
61. Salewski, *Entwaffnung*, p. 60.
62. Bingham, Diary, 17.9.19, IWM 72/116/4.

proper person [*sic*] to convene the meeting, and that it is right for us to go into it especially as we are at present here by invitation and not by right as we shall be after ratification'.[63] The question was eventually solved by a Gilbertian compromise, whereby, until ratification, all meetings would be chaired by an Allied and a German officer, who would enter the conference room simultaneously.[64]

On 5 November the senior officers of the IAMCC formerly handed over to their German opposite numbers a series of questionnaires on the German armed forces, and on the 14th a further meeting took place to discuss them. Nollet, by acting as sole spokesman on the Allied side, hid any potential Allied disagreements from the Germans. The German generals first tried to argue 'with the verbal ingenuity of a medieval schoolman'[65] that the wording of Article 205, which allowed the Allies to 'proceed to any point whatever in German territory', in fact provided no legal justification for stationing sub-committees in the provinces, but merely permitted Allied officers, based in Berlin, to make flying visits. They also contended that while the Treaty permitted the Commission to monitor the demobilization of the old Imperial army, it did not authorize it to check on the creation of the new Reichswehr. They made one further well-argued point, which Bingham called 'a real porer',[66] when they insisted that, as the Treaty afforded the German government three months to reduce its army to 200,000 men, there was no cause for Allied control during this period. Nollet rejected all these points outright, but Bingham privately thought that, as far as the last argument went, the Allies did not have 'a good case'.[67] After this failure to outwit Nollet, there were no more conferences until 29 January 1920.

Although the Germans failed to gain any concessions from the Control Commission, in a wider context they made significant progress in winning a degree of sympathy and understanding for Germany's post-war predicament amongst some of the British members of the IAMCC. Bingham was in close contact with General Malcolm, the Head of the British Military Mission in Berlin since April 1919, whose regular and comprehensive reports back to London never ceased to urge that as it was in Britain's own

63. Ibid., 18.9.19.
64. Ibid., 21–27.9.19.
65. Morgan, *Assize of Arms*, vol. 1, p. 27. See also Bingham, Diary, 5.11.19, IWM 72/116/4.
66. Bingham, Diary, 15.11.19, IWM 72/116/4.
67. Ibid.

interests to maintain 'an orderly and stable government in Germany . . . it [was] not wise to press our claims . . . in what might appear an unreasonable spirit'.[68] Bingham rapidly came to share these views. He agreed that a 'Germany with an army whittled down to practically nothing will be in a state of chaos'[69] and he appreciated that the IAMCC was 'not going to ease matters as we shall have to order factories to close and the tract we shall leave behind us will be unemployment and trouble'.[70]

In December 1919, the German government skilfully exploited the growing understanding of Bingham's Adjutant, Colonel Roddie, for the intractable problems facing the new Republican regime. Roddie was invited to dinner by Prince Münster to meet the Reich President, Ebert, and Noske, who then most effectively pressed upon him the disastrous consequences for the future of democracy in Germany if the Allies really insisted on the surrender of Hindenburg and Ludendorff for trial as War Criminals under Articles 228 and 229 of the Versailles Treaty. Immediately afterwards, with Bingham's blessing, Roddie went straight back to London and saw not only the CIGS and Winston Churchill, but also managed through Sir Almeric Fitzroy, the Clerk of the Privy Council, to have a somewhat melodramatic letter circulated to the Cabinet, which was 'much impressed' by it. The Cabinet decided to urge the French government to include in the War Criminal list only those whose offences were so flagrant that they could not be disputed by the German government.[71]

It was thus clear that even before control had begun the basic attitudes towards post-war Germany of the leaders of the French and British sections of the IAMCC were so different that they would increasingly find difficulty in working in tandem.

Danzig and the Plebiscite Commissions

In Eastern Europe, thanks to the concessions extracted from the French during the peace negotiations, Britain was faced with demands for contributing troops and administrative personnel to the

68. 'Memorandum on Relations with Germany', 7.1.20, Malcolm Papers, 'Demi-official correspondence', St Antony's College, Oxford.
69. Bingham, Diary, 23.10.19, IWM 72/116/4.
70. Ibid., 11.10.19.
71. 'Conclusions of a Meeting held in Mr. Bonar Law's Room . . .', 23.12.19 (18(19)), CAB 23/18 fos 260–3. See also Roddie, *Peace Patrol*, pp. 127–35; Carsten, *Britain and the Weimar Republic*, p. 56.

plebiscite commissions and the transitional Allied administration in Danzig. The planning and the execution of the plebiscites in rural Schleswig, Marienwerder and Allenstein were relatively simple, but in Danzig and Upper Silesia the problems facing the Allies were of a completely different nature. In Danzig the ambiguous wording of Articles 101–104[72] of the Peace Treaty committed the Allies to appointing a temporary High Commissioner with virtually sovereign power, to preside over negotiations between the Poles and the Danzig Germans of a complex treaty defining their mutual commercial, economic and diplomatic relations, before placing the city under the protection of the League of Nations. The High Commissioner, whom much to the dismay of French public opinion[73] the Heads of Delegation decided was to be a British appointment, would have to govern a city where hunger, unemployment and an implacable hatred of the Poles were volcanic forces, which threatened to explode at any moment. Similarly in Upper Silesia where the Plebiscite Commission was entrusted with administering the territory for a minimum of six months before organizing the plebiscite, the Allied administration would inherit a province with the largest concentration of industry in Germany outside the Ruhr, which was not only beset by the social and economic problems prevailing throughout post-war Germany, but where in addition the German and Polish populations were bitterly divided. In Danzig and Upper Silesia it was, therefore, vital that the Foreign Office should appoint tenacious and experienced diplomats, who both understood the post-war German situation and were able to block French attempts subtly to revise the Treaty whilst it was in the process of execution. It was equally important that they should be backed up by an adequate military force.

The War Office recommended the appointment of General Spears, the Head of the British Military Mission in Paris,[74] but this was squashed by the Foreign Office on the grounds that somebody was required ' who has had the experience of foreign or colonial administration or at any rate has had the management of men or conducted negotiations in distant places'. It favoured, rather inappropriately, 'a leading light from either the Levant or Far Eastern Service',[75] but eventually settled for Sir Reginald Tower,[76] who had rightly gained the reputation of being an energetic defender of

72. DBFP Ser. 1, vol. 1 (no. 12), p. 116.
73. Derby to FO, 13.7.19 (C102675), FO 371/3899.
74. Balfour to Curzon, 18.8.19 (C117922), FO 371/3925.
75. Gregory to Drummond, 29.8.19 (117922), FO 371/3925.
76. FO to Crowe, 20.10.19 (134661), FO 371/3925.

British interests in Argentina during the war.[77] Sir William Marling, the British Ambassador at Copenhagen, was appointed the British representative on the Schleswig Commission, while two other career diplomats who had served in South America, Ernest Rennie and Henry Beaumont, were later seconded to the Allenstein and Marienwerder Commissions. For the key post on the Upper Silesian Commission the Foreign Office, despite its reservations about employing soldiers in diplomatic posts, agreed to the appointment in July of Colonel Percival as no one else could apparently be found 'at such short notice with similar qualifications'.[78] As AQMG of the British Military Mission in Berlin, Percival had already been on a fact-finding mission to Danzig[79] and had some knowledge of Polish–German relations, but he was to be no match for his immensely hardworking and unscrupulous French colleague, General Le Rond, who had been Foch's Adjutant-General and the French expert on the Polish Commission in the Peace Negotiations at Paris. Conscious of Percival's relatively low rank, the Foreign Office attempted in vain to persuade the CIGS to promote him to the rank of temporary general.[80]

The Council of the Heads of Delegation followed the guidelines laid down by Foch that in each of the plebiscite areas 'the presidency of the commission and the command of the occupying forces [should] be exercised by personalities belonging to the same nation'.[81] Thus, as British forces were to play a dominant role in peace-keeping operations in Schleswig and Allenstein, Marling and Rennie both presided over their respective commissions, while the French were allotted the presidency of the Upper Silesian Commission, and the Italians the Marienwerder Commission. The British, influenced by their tradition of indirect rule within the Empire, were anxious to reduce interference by the Commissions in the local administration to the absolute minimum. Rennie's desire to 'utilize existing organisations as far as possible' was echoed in almost identical words by both Tower and Marling.[82] As

77. Tower's career in Argentina and Danzig is well covered in the ten volumes of press cuttings and souvenirs in the FCO Library, DA 566.9 T.65.
78. Minute by J.C. Heath (?), 27 (?) July 1919, FO 371/4301 fo. 3.
79. See 'Extracts from Notes taken by Col. Percival during visit to Danzig, 8–9 July, 1919', Steward's Papers, Christ Church, Oxford, S XVIII/68.
80. Hardinge to Thwaites, 13.11.19 and Thwaites to Hardinge, 24.11.19, FO 371/4301 fos 22–4.
81. DBFP Ser. 1 vol. 2 (no. 2), p. 22.
82. Report of a Meeting with Jean Couget, 29.10.19 (148272), FO 371/4294 fos 198–201; Marling to Curzon, 3.9.19 (no. 247), FO 608/127 fo. 136; Tower to Conference of Ambassadors, 20.2.20 (181201), FO 371/3925.

the task of the Schleswig Commission was the least complicated of all the plebiscite commissions, it was the first to be formed and to begin its preparations for the occupation. Responsibility for supervising the local administration was divided between the British, French, Norwegian and Swedish Commissioners. The American Commissioner elect, General Sladen, was forbidden to attend by his government until the Treaty had been ratified by Congress. Marling took over responsibility for the departments of food supplies and the local economy.[83] The deliberations of the commission were, however, accompanied by frequent clashes between Claudel, the French Commissioner, and Marling, who was scathingly critical of his colleague for attending meetings unprepared and for making irrelevant comments, which apparently indicated that he had 'not found time to read the agenda before arriving'.[84]

The organization of the Allenstein and Marienwerder Commissions began more harmoniously in November. Following the pattern of the Silesian and Schleswig Commissions administrative responsibilities were divided between departments, each headed by an Allied official, while, as in Upper Silesia, supervisory control was exercised locally through Kreis officers. The number of posts to be filled by British appointments was relatively small. The army provided the Kreis officers and most of the technical personnel, but the Post Office seconded one official from its pensions department to supervise the postal and telegraph systems in Marienwerder.[85]

As the scale of the problems in Upper Silesia was so much greater, the scope of its plebiscite commission had been defined more carefully in the Treaty, which had authorized it in Article 88 to assume 'all the powers exercised by the German and Prussian Governments, except those of legislation or taxation'. Le Rond and Percival agreed quickly on a draft plan, which followed the Schleswig model of setting up a general secretariat and dividing the administration of the province into seven departments under the direction of the British, French, Italian and American Commissioners. Food supplies and communications were to be the specific responsibility of Percival. An important innovation was the creation of twenty Kreis or district officers, of which six were to be British, to exercise control over the administration at local level. Overall, thirty-five British officials were needed for Upper

83. 'Memorandum on the Slesvig [*sic*] Plebiscite', 26.11.19 (11456), FO 608/139 fos 98–9. Wambaugh, *Plebiscites*, vol. 1, pp. 67–8.
84. Marling to Curzon, 3.9.19 (no. 247), FO 608/127 fo. 136.
85. The files FO 371/4294 and 4295 contain details of the appointment of personnel to the Allenstein and Marienwerder Commissions.

Silesia,[86] many of whom needed to be fluent in German and to possess technical expertise. Crowe managed to overcome Foreign Office objections to this number by reminding Curzon of the Commission's vital role in administering 'for a period of from 6 to 18 months, an important industrial area where national and political tension is high'.[87] He also secured the grudging consent of the Treasury to Le Rond's 'extravagant' proposals for generous salaries for the personnel on all the plebiscite Commissions in Germany.[88]

Tower appointed in November a small staff consisting of an administrative assistant, a railway expert and naval, military and commercial advisers.[89] He was supposed to receive instructions from the Supreme Council, but Crowe, alarmed at the hostility his appointment had aroused in France, advised against seeking precise instructions, as this 'might lead to an attempt to place inconvenient limitations on his powers'.[90]

Although the Treaty explicitly committed the Allies to a military occupation of Silesia, it was left to the discretion of the Supreme Council as to whether troops should be sent to the other plebiscite areas and to Danzig. The military representatives of the Supreme War Council quickly agreed that a force of 13,000 men was needed in Silesia,[91] but the British and Americans were deeply reluctant to commit any troops to Danzig. Sir Henry Wilson was adamant that 'not one British soldier'[92] could be spared and General Thwaites warned Crowe, then sitting as British representative on the Heads of Delegation, that 'they must not be taken from the Rhine now as it is doubtful how they would behave'.[93] Nevertheless it was clear from the reports of British officials who had visited Danzig that, as 'the general feeling . . . is that one is rather sitting on a safety valve and does not quite know when it will go off',[94] a military occupation was unavoidable. It was agreed on 8 August[95] that the Allies and the USA should each supply an equal number of troops to Upper Silesia, but the French met with strong opposition when

86. 'Personnel for Upper Silesian Commission', 25.10.19, FO 608/127 fos 271–4.
87. Crowe to Curzon, 27.10.19 (19891), FO 608/127 fos 277–8.
88. FO to Crowe, 21.11.19, FO 371/4294 fos 358–60.
89. FO to Crowe, 4.11.19 (no. 1326R), FO 371/3925.
90. Crowe to Curzon, 19.12.19 (no. 1716), FO 371/3925.
91. DBFP Ser. 1, vol. 1 (no. 11), p. 101.
92. 'Notes made by CIGS after telephone conversation with Thwaites', 9.7.19, IWM 73/1/26 file 45.
93. Thwaites to Crowe, 21.7.19, IWM 73/1/26 file 45.
94. Report by Capt. Crewdson, 26.6.19 (C99123), FO 371/3899.
95. DBFP Ser. 1, vol. 1 (no. 31), p. 377.

they proposed that the troops in both Danzig and Upper Silesia should be formed into a multinational force, as a demonstration of Allied unity. The British Army immediately suspected the French of political manoeuvering to subordinate the Allied contingents to their own command,[96] and Crowe tenaciously supported the soldiers' arguments for independent national commands, despite furious objections from the French.[97] Arrangements for the occupation of Allenstein, Marienwerder, Danzig and Upper Silesia were drawn up by the Military Representatives on 18 October. Sackville-West, instructed by Henry Wilson not 'to budge a decimal of an inch', achieved virtually all that the War Office wanted: the British were given sole command of Danzig, Allenstein and Schleswig, while in Upper Silesia and Marienwerder British forces would operate under their own officers, even though accepting orders from inter-Allied high commands.[98]

The long delay before ratification exacerbated racial tension in Danzig and the plebiscite zones, and created an administrative and economic hiatus, in which virtually no decision could be taken.[99] In Silesia a full-scale Polish uprising in Kattowitz and Pless had erupted in August and been ruthlessly crushed by the Reichswehr.[100] Worried by the impact of this on the province's coal production, the representatives of the Heads of Delegation had considered asking Berlin to permit an Allied occupation of Upper Silesia before the ratification of peace, but decided instead to send a mission composed of the Chiefs of the Allied Military Missions in Berlin in early September.[101] Their attempts to mediate between the Poles and Germans 'had a soothing effect on local conditions',[102] and a small inter-Allied sub-commission remained in Silesia until ratification. Privately, General Malcolm showed the same deep distaste for the Poles that his compatriots were to display elsewhere in eastern Germany and was appalled at the prospect of Upper Silesia becoming Polish, as the Polish Jews would 'swarm into and devour the

96. Sackville-West to Wilson, 19.9.19, IWM 73/1/26 file 12D.
97. DBFP Ser. 1, vol. 1 (no. 62), pp. 756–61.
98. Ibid., vol. 2 (no. 2), pp. 22–3; Wilson to Sackville-West, 14.10.19 and British Delegation, Paris, to Sec. WO, 18.10.19, IWM 73/1/26 file 12D.
99. Commander E.L. Wharton, 'Report on the Situation in Danzig', 13.10.19 (no. PM5/23), FO 371/3925; Marling to Curzon, 31.12.19, no. 363, FO 852/3; Wambaugh, *Plebiscites*, vol. 1, p. 109.
100. Wambaugh, *Plebiscites*, vol. 1, pp. 219–20; A. Cienciela and T. Komarnicki, *From Versailles to Locarno*, pp. 49–50.
101. DBFP Ser. 1, vol. 1 (no. 36 and no. 40), pp. 421–4 and 483–4.
102. E.H. Carr's Minute of 12.9.19 on 'Premier Rapport De la Commission de Haute Silesia, 5.9.19', FO 608/127 fo. 215.

present prosperous community and we shall have the Jewish question added to all others'.[103] Nevertheless, the delay did enable the Allies to complete their logistical and administrative arrangements and to re-allocate their troop contingents and officials to fill the gaps left by the Americans' refusal to participate until the Senate had ratified the Treaty.

On the very eve of the departure of the various plebiscite parties, a serious blow was delivered to Allied plans when, on 20 January, the British government reneged suddenly and unexpectedly on its military commitments.[104] Tower valiantly but unrealistically insisted that he was prepared to go 'when and where the Supreme Council sent him with or without troops'.[105] Foch was left with the virtually impossible task of having to conjure up six battalions out of France's own already over-stretched resources. He was reported to have observed acidly that Britain was no longer a 'puissance alliée, but, like the Americans, rather a puissance associée'.[106] The situation was only eased when Lloyd George in a reluctant change of heart conceded that 'it might be possible . . . by a special effort' to send one battalion supported by naval units to Danzig and a further one to Allenstein, both to be under the command of General Haking. Foch then found two more French battalions and Italy promised to 'make every effort' to do the same for Silesia.[107]

Thus, although the British government was in the end just about able to provide minimum forces for Danzig, Schleswig and Allenstein, their inability to support Percival at Oppeln with even a battalion of British troops at a time when French influence would clearly be strengthened by America's inability to participate in the Upper Silesian Administrative Commission, was to make his task of asserting Britain's influence over the proceedings of the Commission almost impossible. The wisdom of Sackville-West's observation that 'diplomacy without the support of the military is a frail reed to rely upon'[108] was to be proved many times over in the next year in Upper Silesia.

103. Malcolm's Diary, 7.9.19, Malcolm Papers.
104. DBFP Ser. 1, vol. 2 (no. 78), p. 938.
105. Diary of Francis Bourdillon, 20.1.20, Bourdillon Papers.
106. Ibid.
107. DBFP Ser. 1, vol. 2 (no. 79), p. 949.
108. Sackville-West to Wilson, 5.8.19, IWM 73/1/26, file 12D.

PART II

1920: Enforcing the Treaty

Introduction: 1920 – A Sombre Prospect

When the Treaty was ratified on 10 January 1920, British officials were committed to work on a whole range of inter-Allied Commissions, which all represented entirely novel attempts to solve international problems. In Schleswig, Marienwerder and Allenstein their tasks were relatively simple as the ethnic composition of the local population ensured an unambiguous response to the plebiscites, but in Danzig and Upper Silesia, Sir Reginald Tower and Colonel Percival wrestled with problems which were at the flashpoint of Anglo–French differences. Within Germany the control commissions began to operate but, despite Nollet's painstaking efforts to create a team, by the end of 1920 the IAMCC was seriously split by both Anglo–French disagreements on the state of German disarmament and by the increasingly bitter dispute within the British element between Morgan and Bingham. Only in Coblenz did a fragile and temporary inter-Allied harmony exist where Sir Harold Stuart, the most experienced of all the British civil officials in German affairs, was able to establish a workable *modus vivendi* with Tirard.

In 1920 both the internal state of Germany and the international situation could scarcely have been less propitious for the execution of the peace. The prospects for a pacification of Europe were irreparably damaged by the refusal of the American Senate to ratify the Treaty of Versailles. Britain, whose own guarantee to assist France against any future act of German aggression was conditional upon American participation, seized the chance to regain her diplomatic freedom, and thus refused to honour the promise made to Clemenceau in April 1919 of a defensive treaty,[1] while France appreciated that without the restraining hand of Washington, she would be able to exert pressure more effectively on Germany. However, without the ultimate force of America underwriting the Treaty, neither power, alone or in combination with the other, had the strength to uphold its provisions for Eastern Europe. This was made painfully clear by the course of the Russo–Polish War in 1920. In the summer the whole structure of post-war Europe was threatened when the Bolsheviks, provoked by the Polish invasion

1. Northedge, *The Troubled Giant*, p. 160.

of the Ukraine, advanced almost up to Warsaw, and the formation of a Russo-German revisionist pact seemed a real possibility. In anticipation of Poland's defeat 'all Germany began to boil up',[2] and it was only the victory by Pilsudski, the Commander of the Polish forces, over the Bolsheviks in August that saved the Treaty.

Until the autumn of 1920 the French economy was dependent on British coal supplies. The British ruthlessly exploited their monopoly and charged extortionate rates until September when their hold over the French economy was broken by the recession. The coal crisis not only exacerbated Anglo–French relations, but also encouraged the French to look upon the Ruhr as a 'black Eldorado'.[3] As early as January 1920 Millerand consulted the French army about the possibility of an occupation,[4] and at each confrontation with the Germans, it was the ultimate threat made to force their compliance to Allied demands. By December 1920 a Ruhr occupation was a Damocles' sword hanging over Europe. It was avidly desired by France and dreaded by Britain.

For all Germans the overriding aim of their country's foreign policy was to bring about a revision of the Treaty of Versailles, which through its financial and military clauses, as well as by the occupation of the Rhineland and plebiscite areas, affected large numbers of the population. After an initial success in April 1920 in extracting concessions from the Allies, which permitted the Germans to try war criminals in their own courts, the weak Weimar coalition governments drew the conclusion that further treaty revisions could only be achieved both by standing firm against Allied demands and by appealing to Britain to moderate French policy. The success of this policy was constantly threatened by the 'chaos of conflicting forces'[5] that threatened to plunge Germany into civil war. Besides the embattled moderates of the democratic parties, there were the extreme nationalists like Ludendorff, who pursued fantastic plans for German expansion in eastern Europe, particularist conservatives like Escherich, who built up a strong anti-Communist Bavarian defence force, and at the opposite end of the political spectrum, the Independent Socialists and Spartacists with their bastions of working-class support in the Ruhr, Hamburg, Berlin and Saxony. On 12 March Germany was plunged into a serious crisis, which could have ended in civil war when the

2. Lenin, quoted in Wandycz, *France*, p. 161.
3. Maier, *Recasting Bourgeois Europe*, p. 195.
4. McDougall, *Rhineland Diplomacy*, p. 108.
5. Northedge, *The Troubled Giant*, p. 171.

Nationalists, led by Kapp and Lüttwitz, backed by the Freikorps and units of the Reichswehr, seized Berlin. The government fled to Stuttgart but the Kapp regime, paralysed by a general strike, collapsed within days. In the Ruhr the workers rose up and seized control of the whole area east of Düsseldorf and Mülheim.[6] To regain control necessitated the advance into the demilitarized zone by German troops and Freikorps units. This violated the Versailles Treaty and played straight into the hands of the French by giving them an opportunity to occupy, as a penalty, the towns of Frankfurt, Darmstadt, Hanau and Homburg.

The Ruhr revolt and the subsequent action of the French strengthened the determination of the Reichswehr and the self-defence forces to oppose the disarmament clauses of the Treaty, and made a conciliatory policy by the German government even more difficult to follow. In the elections of 6 June 1920 there was a marked swing to the right. The mood in Germany was thus far from conducive to the orderly execution of the Treaty. Allied demands were met at every level by a mixture of outright defiance and a more subtle policy of procrastination. Although the Reparation Commission was not scheduled to announce the exact figure for German reparation debts until 1 May 1921, according to the Treaty Germany in the meantime was to pay 20 billion (American billions or milliards) gold marks to meet the costs of the armies of occupation and to supply some 40 million tons of coal to France, Belgium, Italy and Luxemburg; but the German government, deeply resentful that the justification for reparations rested on the war guilt clause of the Treaty, refused to cooperate in any effective assessment of reparations.[7] There was a similar deadlock over disarmament where the Reichswehr waged what one German historian has called 'ein zäher Kleinkrieg' ('a tenacious guerrilla war')[8] against the inter-Allied Control Commissions.

During 1920 diverging policies in Britain and France began to crystallize. As the Allies confronted one German crisis after another, it became clear that London cared little about the strict execution of the Treaty, and was ready to make considerable concessions to preserve a united Germany under a moderate government as a bulwark against bolshevism in the east and what increasingly became to be regarded as French bonapartism on the Rhine. It was axiomatic in London that only a united and quiescent

6. J. Erger, *Der Kapp-Lüttwitz Putsch. Ein Beitrag zur deutschen Innenpolitik, 1919–20*, Düsseldorf, 1967; G. Eliasberg, *Der Ruhrkrieg von 1920*, Bonn, 1974.
7. Maier, *Recasting Bourgeois Europe*, p.233.
8. Salewski, *Entwaffnung*, p. 57.

Germany could pay reparations and assist in the revival of world trade. France, on the other hand, was far from being a saturated power and sought to use the Treaty of Versailles as a means decisively to weaken Germany both economically and militarily. French aims were therefore frequently diametrically opposed to British policy on Germany, but as a consequence of America's refusal to ratify the Treaty or to accept a League of Nations mandate over any of the former Turkish territories in the Middle East, Britain had no option but to keep the *Entente* as the sheet anchor of her foreign policy. The British still needed French support in negotiating the Treaty of Sèvres with Turkey and in executing the Versailles settlement. Ultimately the British government could not afford to turn its back on Europe. Lord Curzon, the new British Foreign Minister, realized only too well that Britain's 'position renders it impossible for us to sever ourselves from European politics. If we did so, whatever happened to others, we should sink in a few years to the insignificance of Spain or the impotence of Portugal.'[9] Neither the British concept of a balance of power with Germany playing its part in a new European concert, nor the French concept of establishing a decisive hegemony over Germany was strong enough to prevail. Both competed uneasily with each other.[10]

9. Quoted in Kaiser, *Lord D'Abernon*, p. 9.
10. Lowe and Dockrill, *The Mirage of Power*, pp. 338–74; Niedhart, 'Multipolares Gleichgewicht', p. 113; Porter, *Britain, Europe and the World*, ch. 4; Krüger, *Die Außenpolitik der Republik von Weimar*, pp. 1–6. For a general survey of French policy in the inter-war period, see A. François-Poncet, *De Versailles à Potsdam*, Paris, 1948, chs 1–11; A. Cobban, *A History of Modern France*, vol. 3, section II; and J. Néré, *The Foreign Policy of France from 1914 to 1945*, London and Boston, 1975, ch. 3.

-5-

The Plebiscites

Although the Schleswig, Marienwerder and Allenstein plebiscites were relatively successful operations, nevertheless in embryo they contained many of the problems that were to paralyse the Upper Silesian Plebiscite Commission. In the absence of American representation their deliberations became polarized between the British and French with the Italians and Japanese, in Marienwerder and Allenstein, caught in the middle. In all three plebiscites the French disagreed with the majority reports and attempted to revise the Commission's recommendations. In Marienwerder and Allenstein the Poles threatened to disrupt the plebiscites and to terrorize the voters, while even in Schleswig the Danish nationalists attempted to overturn a German majority in the second zone by arguing for its internationalization under British protection. The problems facing British officials in these rural backwaters paled into insignificance beside the task awaiting Percival in Upper Silesia where in its mining and industrial areas all the post-war problems of Germany were compounded by bitter racial tension between the mixed German and Polish population.

Schleswig, January–June 1920

Sarah Wambaugh, the historian of the post-war plebiscites, described in almost lyrical terms the successful execution of the Schleswig plebiscite and concluded that 'there can be no question that the Plebiscite reflects the greatest credit not only on the International Commission but on the two opposed nationalities'.[1] The Schleswig plebiscite was certainly a relatively simple and civilized operation, largely because the majority of Danes, frightened of creating a German irredentia within their frontiers, were

1. Wambaugh, *Plebiscites*, vol. 1, p. 95.

unique in asking for 'less rather than more than belonged' to them.[2]

Owing to delays in ratification, it was not until 25 January that the Schleswig Commission was able to install itself at Flensburg. The occupying forces consisted of a battalion each of the Chasseurs Alpins and of the Sherwood Foresters, which for some of the time were stationed in small detachments throughout the province, and of a squadron of warships, anchored off Flensburg, Murwick, Apenrade and Sonderburg, under the command of Admiral Sheppard.[3] The attitude of the personnel of the two occupying powers towards the inhabitants of Schleswig contrasted sharply. The French were inclined indiscriminantly 'to treat Slesvig as a conquered enemy country'.[4] The captain of the French cruiser the *Marseillaise*, for instance, caused considerable resentment at Murwick when he ordered the wooden figure of Marshal Blücher in the local Torpedo School to be removed from its pedestal and put in the cellar on the grounds that it 'hurt the feelings of the French troops to see this statue every day'.[5] The British battalion, on the other hand, was correct but aloof in its attitude to the Germans. Its colonel was determined that 'there should be as little intercourse as possible' between his men and the Germans, and relied on the services of the personnel of the Church Army sent from Cologne to run canteens, a reading room and a roller skating centre to cocoon his troops from the German population. Towards the Danes in the northern zone a more relaxed attitude prevailed. The correspondent of the *Cologne Post* was able to indulge himself safely in a romantic predilection for Britain's Scandinavian kith and kin when he described how the Sherwood Foresters were 'getting the heartiest reception wherever they appear. Many of the people speak English and the similarity in national characteristics and racial kinship facilitate intimacy.'[6] As in the Rhineland, British personnel were preferred to the French by the German population. When the Commander of the Allied forces in Schleswig toured the plebiscite zones before the arrival of the troops, he was asked in 'nearly all towns' to send British rather than French troops.[7] Some Germans were even tempted to see the British as a *deus ex machina* which

2. Headlam-Morley, *A Memoir of the Paris Peace Conference*, p. 51.
3. Sheppard to Sec. of Admiralty, 30.1.20 (no. 10/21), ADM 116 2077. For a useful account of the Sherwood Foresters see *The Sherwood Foresters Regimental Annual*, 1920, pp. 5–10.
4. DBFP Ser. 1, vol. 10 (no. 420), p. 574.
5. Report of Proceedings, 9.2.20 (no. 20/21), ADM 116 2077.
6. *Cologne Post*, 12.2.20.
7. Report of Proceedings, 30.1.20 (no. 10/21), ADM 116 2077.

could save them from their painful dilemmas by annexing Schleswig outright to the Empire.[8]

The commission's arrangements for the plebiscite in the first zone worked smoothly and encountered little opposition. The actual voting took place 'in perfect order'[9] and the Danes, as expected, won an overwhelming majority. The plebiscite campaign in the second or southern zone, where the population was predominantly German, also proceeded peacefully, although there were isolated reports of Danish meetings being interrupted. One of Admiral Sheppard's staff officers discovered a party of four German officers and thirty five ratings on the island of Sylt, which, under the pretext of mine clearing, was attempting to influence the vote of the local population. All but one officer and ten men were subsequently expelled.[10] The greatest potential threat to public order occurred when the German outvoters, nearly 8,000 in number, descended by train on Flensburg during the three days before the voting in the second zone took place.[11] All available troops were moved into the city and each train was met by a small detachment of soldiers. The local German plebiscite committees arranged accommodation for their compatriots, while the 1,300 Danes who arrived by sea remained on board their ships in the harbour. All alcohol was prohibited during the three days before the plebiscite.[12] The actual vote on 14 March gave the Germans a 75 per cent majority in Flensburg and 80 per cent in the outlying districts.[13]

The news of the Kapp *Putsch* on the preceding day arrived too late to influence the voting, but over the next week its repercussions were felt in the plebiscite zones. Just across the border there was rioting in the town of Schleswig and Sheppard decided to set up outposts on the southern frontier of the zone 'to watch traffic and report any unusual movements'.[14] There were also wild but inaccurate reports of an imminent Spartacist *coup* in Flensburg. The

---

8. See the letter in Marling's scrapbook on 'Slesvig' from 'ein älterer Flensburger', who wrote: 'Als gebürtiger Flensburger habe ich die Verpflichtung Ihnen mitteilen zu können, daß die allgemeine Gesinnung hier in Flensburg mehr für einen Anschluß an England als für Dänemark gestimmt ist.' Marling commented that this was an example of 'scores of similar letters' sent to the Plebiscite Commission.
9. DBFP Ser. 1, vol. 10 (no. 420), pp. 573–6.
10. Sheppard to Sec. of Admiralty, 22.2.20 (no. 27/21) and 29.2.20 (no. 33/21), ADM 116 2077.
11. Ibid., 7.3.20 (no. 44/21) and 16.3.20 (no. 50/21).
12. DBFP Ser. 1, vol. 10 (nos 422 and 426), pp. 577–9, 583–5.
13. Sheppard to Sec. of Admiralty, 16.3.20 (no. 50/21), ADM 116 2077.
14. Ibid., 21.3.20 (no. 57/21).

main impact of the *Putsch* was to revive the movement in the second zone for setting up an autonomous Schleswig-Holstein in order to cut free from 'the political storm centre of Berlin'.[15] Marling, like his colleagues in Cologne a year earlier, was inclined to view this northern separatism sympathetically on the grounds that it would not only give the Danish minority protection against petty discrimination by Prussian officials, but also offer 'the promise of considerable advantage to our own Allied interest without necessarily involving us in fresh obligations and responsibilities'.[16] The Foreign Office treated Marling's dispatch with understandable scepticism and, as with the parallel case of Rhineland separatism, argued that 'unless such a scheme is put forward and accepted as a purely internal problem dependent only upon the decision of Germany herself we ought to have nothing to do with it'. French support for the idea was dismissed as 'typically "French" and absurd right through'.[17]

Although the return of the formidable Dr Todsen, the former Bürgermeister of Flensburg, led to a marked decline in popular support for the Schleswig-Holstein separatist movement,[18] the French, supported by the Norwegians, fought a determined rearguard action to modify the majority decision in the second zone. When the Commission met on 26 March to draw up recommendations for the new frontier, the Norwegian and French Commissioners attempted ingeniously to exploit the provision in Article 110 of the Peace Treaty for 'taking into account the particular geographical and economic conditions of the localities in question' to argue that Denmark would be justified in claiming a fifth of the total area of the second zone. Despite Marling's efforts to preserve the unanimity of the commission, Claudel insisted on incorporating these arguments in a minority report, the drafting of which he delayed until after Easter, as he hoped to exploit the political crisis which had suddenly erupted in Copenhagen, where the mildly pro-German Social Democratic government had been dismissed by the King who, pending an election, had appointed a more nationalist Conservative administration.[19]

The new Danish Cabinet did not disappoint Claudel. It proceeded to embark upon a propaganda campaign to influence the

15. DBFP Ser. 1, vol. 10 (no. 427), pp. 585–90.
16. Ibid., p. 589.
17. Minute by Crowe of 14.4.20 on Marling's Dispatch (DBFP Ser. 1, vol. 10, no. 427) (191454), 23.3.20, FO 371/4065.
18. DBFP Ser. 1, vol. 10 (no. 427), p. 590.
19. Ibid. (nos 428–430), pp. 590–602; Wambaugh, *Plebiscites*, vol. 1, pp. 86–8.

Entente powers to agree to an internationalization of the second zone. Particular efforts were made by the nationalist press in Copenhagen to tempt Britain by proposing that the zone should be placed under British sovereignty, thereby enabling the Royal Navy to control the Baltic. Professor Vinding Cruse was sent to London to win over the Foreign Office, but Curzon, anxious that Britain should disengage from the area, rejected the proposal outright.[20] When the majority and minority reports were discussed at the Conference of Ambassadors on 5 May, Cambon tried to win support for Claudel's proposals by arguing that while it was 'impossible to contest in a general manner the results of the plebiscite', nevertheless the Conference would be 'justified in not taking them too much as gospel truth'.[21] However, the British representative, Lord Derby, impatiently brushed aside these obviously untenable arguments, and the Anglo–Swedish proposals were accepted, although the Conference detailed Marling and Laroche, the Director of the European section of the Quai d'Orsay, to draft a clause protecting minorities in both zones. The text of the convention transferring northern Schleswig to Denmark was approved on 22 May and notified to Berlin and Copenhagen on 15 June.[22]

The transfer of sovereignty of the first zone from the German government to the Danish government was a complex process. The Commission was prepared to concede to the Danes the right to occupy the first zone before the final frontier had been fixed, and while it was still theoretically German territory. It had therefore to reconcile Denmark's desire to assume the administration of the zone with the residual German rights there. The Danes were authorized to begin occupation on 5 May. The Assistant Commissioner, Bruce, overcame German objections to the immediate appointment of Danish judges by proposing that the outgoing German judiciary should be permitted to continue to preside over all cases currently before the courts, while all new trials would be conducted by the incoming Danes.[23] A more serious problem emerged when the Commission decided to introduce the Kroner currency into the first zone on 20 May.[24] The German population in the second zone, which was still under the administration of the Commission, and shut off from the Reich, feared that the Kroner

20. DBFP Ser. 1, vol. 10 (no. 445), p. 623.
21. Ibid. (no. 433), p. 606.
22. Ibid. (no. 454), pp. 633–4.
23. Ibid. (no. 431), p. 602; Note by Brudenell Bruce, 3.5.20 (no. 4b/1920), FO 852/4.
24. DBFP Ser. 1, vol. 10 (no. 441), pp. 618–21.

currency in the north would have a disastrous impact on the cost of living in the southern zone. Workers' committees in Hadersleben and Apenrade threatened a general strike.[25] This was enthusiastically encouraged by the German representative to the Commission, Dr Mezger, who brought in agitators to whip up public opinion against the Danes 'in order to stifle any tendency in the population towards entertaining the internationalization idea'.[26] The threats evaporated when the Commission reassured a workers' delegation that there would be an effective economic barrier between the two zones and that all trade restrictions between Germany and the southern zone would be removed.[27] Bruce also insisted on the removal of Mezger, and for the remaining few weeks of its existence, dealt directly with the Auswärtiges Amt through the British chargé d'affaires at Berlin.[28] In early June strikes broke out in the four main towns in the first zone against the rise in the cost of living caused by the introduction of the Kroner. Bruce, shocked by 'the almost incredible weakness of the Danish administration'[29] in consenting to negotiate with the local Spartacists, intervened, like a colonial governor, and ordered the ringleaders to be arrested and brought to Flensburg. Far from resenting Bruce's intervention, the Danish administrator, 'who was very confused and apologetic',[30] apparently appreciated the Commission's show of strength.

The Commission was dissolved on 15 June[31] after handing back the second zone to Germany. The unique nature of this plebiscite was emphasized by the reception given to the Allies by the Danish government. On their way home the Sherwood Foresters were fêted in Copenhagen, like the Chausseurs before them, and thanked by the Danish Parliament for carrying through 'the exalted principle of the self-determination of peoples'.[32] The senior officers were invited to dine with the King, while the soldiers themselves were treated to lavish meals in the Tivoli Gardens and the Town Hall. It is thus not surprising that the *Cologne Post* should report that the Sherwood Foresters felt that 'in saying farewell . . . we all felt that we are not saying good bye to foreigners, but to our kith

25. Mezger to AA, 16.5.20 (no. 167), FCO Lib. 4718, E229149–152.
26. Ibid., 19.5.20 (no. 3963), 3139 D651461–64.
27. DBFP Ser. 1, vol. 10 (no. 452), p. 630.
28. Brudenell Bruce to Köster, 17.5.20 (no. 28), FO 852/14.
29. DBFP Ser. 1, vol. 10 (no. 462), p. 645.
30. Ibid., p. 646.
31. Ibid. (no. 464), pp. 648–9.
32. Speech by Harold Scavenius at 'the luncheon in the Danish Houses of Parliament in honour of the British soldiers in occupation', 17.6.20. Marling papers, Album on 'Slesvig'; *Sherwood Foresters Annual*, p. 10.

and kin'.[33] It was noticed, however, by the German Embassy that the Danish nationalists were markedly cool towards the celebrations.[34]

Curzon privately thanked Marling for presiding over so successful an operation and stressed that 'had the arrangements for the plebiscite miscarried, or even been delayed, a bad precedent would have been created, which might have had far reaching effects'.[35] It is, of course, true that the plebiscite was conducted peacefully, partly because the Danes had only modest territorial claims, but also because many Germans conceded that the plebiscite, which Bismarck had promised in 1866, cleared up 'a really dark chapter in our history'.[36] Nevertheless the attempts by the French and the Danish nationalists to manipulate the results and modify the relevant Treaty clauses retrospectively indicated the potential problems that could arise on the east German frontier with Poland where two strong nationalisms clashed and both Britain and France were at cross-purposes.

Allenstein and Marienwerder, January–August 1920

The decision to hold plebiscites in Marienwerder and Allenstein essentially favoured the status quo. In Marienwerder, the Poles could only realistically hope to win a majority in Stuhm, while in Allenstein, despite the fact that the majority of the population spoke a Polish dialect, it was predicted that 'the utmost limits of their success' would be a few inconsequential gains along the southern borders as the inhabitants were Lutheran and indifferent to Polish nationalism.[37] The Polish government, encouraged by the French, was reluctant to accept this, as it hoped to broaden the Danzig Corridor to protect the Vistula and the vital rail links between Warsaw and Danzig.[38] Unlike the Danes, the Poles had no qualms about absorbing a large cohesive German-speaking minority and were ready to exploit ruthlessly, if incompetently, every

33. *Cologne Post*, 3.7.20.
34. Deutsche Gesandtschaft (Kopenhagen) to AA, 22.6.20 (P.A. no. 572), FCO Lib. 3139 D651484–91.
35. Curzon to Marling, 21.7.20, Marling Papers, 'Slesvig Album'.
36. Hans Delbrück to 'Herr Minister (Müller)', 18.2.20, FCO Lib. 3137D.651086.
37. DBFP Ser. 1, vol. 10 (no. 581), pp. 771–3. Wambaugh, *Plebiscites*, vol. 1, pp. 99–100.
38. Beaumont, 'Diplomatic Butterfly', p. 527, Beaumont papers. See also IWM PPMCR 113.

opportunity to achieve their aims. In both areas British policy was to complete the plebiscites quickly and wind up the Commissions without delay before either the Poles or the French could devise reasons for prolonging their existence. The Foreign Office was under considerable pressure from the Treasury and the War Office[39] to restrict British involvement in east Germany to the absolute minimum, and their parsimony at times threatened the operational efficiency of the British element on the two Commissions. Sir Timothy Eden, the British secretary to the Marienwerder Commission, complained, for instance, that 'the motor cars issued to His Britannic Majesty's Commissioner . . . are such as can only be regarded with respect from the point of view of a souvenir hunter or antiquarian'.[40]

The Allied officials and occupying troops arrived in mid-February.[41] In both areas the Commissions exercised supervision over all the public services by setting up departments to whom the relevant German officials could report.[42] In Allenstein Rennie secured the appointment of British officials to head the departments of the Interior and Communications, as he realized that these would have 'the most frequent dealings with the German officials',[43] while in Marienwerder Beaumont was given responsibility for the key post of the director of the department of Traffic and Communications, which was to involve him in bitter conflict with the Poles.

British officials on both Commissions rapidly established good working relations with their German counterparts and the population at large. In Allenstein one British visitor from Cologne was naively surprised by how 'one can wander through the streets and woods of this stronghold of Prussianism with as little concern as one can walk down the Hohe Strasse' (in Cologne) and noted how 'the natives' would come to British officials when their own officials would give them no satisfaction.[44] In Marienwerder Beaumont, and sometimes his staff, were invited to the houses of the local magnates, such as Count Dohna-Finckenstein; Pavia, the Italian Commissioner, and Beaumont also entertained regularly.[45]

39. See FO to Treasury, 3.6.20 (no. 199603/39), FO 371/4299 fos 231–3.
40. Report by Sir Timothy Eden, 19.3.23 (188912), FO 371/4297, fos 152–5.
41. Details in DBFP Ser. 1, vol. 9 (no. 56), pp. 89–92 and ibid., vol. 10 (no. 532), pp. 721–2.
42. Wambaugh, *Plebiscites*, vol. 1, p. 144.
43. DBFP Ser. 1, vol. 10 (no. 532), p. 721.
44. *Cologne Post*, 9.7.20. DBFP Ser. 1, vol. 10 (no. 538), pp. 730–3.
45. Beaumont, 'Diplomatic Butterfly', pp. 547–9.

Beaumont had wisely taken the precaution of picking up through a friend a Polish chef, who 'more perhaps than anything else . . . reconciled [him] to the disagreeable side of living for six months in an atmosphere of acute racial antagonism accentuated rather than softened by the arrival of our mission'.[46] British prestige in Allenstein was reinforced by the pipe band of the 1st battalion of the Royal Irish Regiment, which played regularly outside the Commission's headquarters on Sundays. The population was understandably fascinated by 'the weird strains of the bagpipes'.[47]

At the outset relations between the Commissioners were cordial in both Allenstein and Marienwerder,[48] but nothing could disguise for long the fundamental tension between British and French policy. Beaumont later observed that the French officials acted on the principle 'that we are in occupation of conquered territory and are only here to protect and help Poland. The plebiscite was for them quite a secondary consideration and only a very bad means of trying to make up the shortcomings of the Peace Treaty.'[49] Unlike their colleagues in Schleswig, the Commissioners were given a free hand to arrange the dates for the plebiscites, as the Peace Treaty did not commit them to a definite timetable. Their immediate task was to ensure for both the local Poles and the Germans the necessary freedom and security in which to conduct the plebiscite campaign. Although the Foreign Office viewed the Commissions' rather leisurely progress towards a plebiscite with impatience, privately attributing it to the 'intention of the French and Italian members, who are drawing . . . huge salaries, to protract the proceedings to the utmost',[50] it was made very clear by Rennie that if the plebiscite was held prematurely, the Poles would be prevented by German intimidation from campaigning freely.[51]

Initially neither Commission created a plebiscite police force. In Marienwerder the paramilitary Sipo and the voluntary Einwohnerwehr, which outnumbered the Italian army of occupation, were disarmed but not disbanded, while, despite opposition from the French Commissioner, the Allenstein Commission placed the Sipo (the Security Police) and the Grenzschütz (the Frontier Police) under the control of two British officers, and only gradually

---

46. Ibid., p. 531.
47. *Cologne Post*, 11.3.20.
48. Beaumont, 'Diplomatic Butterfly', p. 527; DBFP Ser. 1, vol. 10 (no. 532), p. 721.
49. Beaumont to Phipps, 5.8.20 (C3523), FO 371/4764 fos 43–4.
50. Minute by Waterlow, 24.3.20, FO 371/4296 fo. 614.
51. DBFP Ser. 1, vol. 10 (no. 538), p. 733.

disarmed them, a process which was delayed by the Kapp *Putsch* in March.[52] Under pressure from the Poles, who were understandably suspicious of what were basically still German paramilitary forces, the Marienwerder Commission in April set up a special plebiscite gendarmerie, under Italian command, to which a proportion of Polish volunteers were recruited. Rennie was reluctant to follow suit, unless significant military reinforcements were sent, as the initial performance of the Marienwerder force had, in E.H. Carr's words, been 'more dangerous than useful';[53] but eventually in May he set up a similar force, which was supervised locally by Kreis officers and controlled centrally by a British Inspector-General, Colonel Hawker, whose secondment as an expert in police matters was the most Rennie could extract from the War Office.[54]

Although the potential for public disorder was always present, the Commissions were able to consolidate their authority and draw up the plebiscite regulations in relative calm. The Germans, assured of victory, could tolerate the Commissions with equanimity provided they proceeded quickly with the plebiscite.[55] The Poles oscillated uneasily between a defiant assertion of their rights, a boycott of the plebiscite procedures and attempts by the Warsaw government to intimidate the Germans by disrupting rail traffic in the Corridor. Beaumont rapidly developed an almost pathological hatred of what he called the 'Frankenstein' Polish state.[56] Much to the irritation of the Foreign Office he openly criticized the Polish peace settlement, which he suggested was either based on an 'over-estimate of Polish capacities and superficial knowledge of local conditions', or had been 'deliberately designed for the purpose of leaving an open sore between Poland and Germany, which time is more likely to envenom than to heal'.[57] Not surprisingly he earned a magisterial 'semi-official' rebuke from Crowe,[58] the permanent Under-Secretary at the Foreign Office, who increasingly began to doubt Beaumont's judgement.[59] Beaumont, however, remained unrepentant and defended himself in a dispatch, which

52. Ibid., vol. 10 (nos 532, 535, 538), pp. 722, 728, 731–2.
53. E.H. Carr, DBFP Ser. 1, vol. 10 (no. 581), p. 771.
54. Rennie to FO, 27.5.20 (no. 200559) and FO to Rennie, 2.6.20 (200559/39), FO 371/4299 fos 412 and 414.
55. *Allensteiner Zeitung*, 15.2.20.
56. DBFP Ser. 1, vol. 10 (no. 574), p. 764.
57. Ibid. (no. 542), p. 737.
58. Minute by Crowe, 1.4.20 (189176), FO 371/4297 fo. 175.
59. Ibid., Minute by Crowe, 15.4.20 (191754), fo. 475.

can be regarded as a classic statement of the views of British officials serving in eastern Germany:

> We all came here sympathising with Poland, but since we have seen things at close quarters, we have without exception changed our views. Even Prussian militarism was gentle compared with what is going on all round our frontiers. Our impression is that aggression is more likely from the side of Poland than Germany. Germany is bound hand and foot and can hardly be aggressive for a long time to come.[60]

The publication of the plebiscite regulations in mid–April marked the beginning of the plebiscite campaigns and a corresponding heightening of tension. Polish propaganda campaigns, which sometimes took the form of mounted parades of horsemen dressed in eighteenth–century costume or of concerts of Polish folk music, inevitably drew sharp responses from the Germans.[61] Despite serious misgivings about dispersing troops in small numbers, Rennie was persuaded by the French Commissioner to agree to a series of military 'promenades' through Allenstein in order to show the flag.[62] There was considerable truth in the Polish complaints that in Allenstein the Commission could not realistically guarantee to hold the plebiscite in the necessary 'freedom, fairness and secrecy' demanded by Article 95 of the Treaty,[63] but the Foreign Office, only too aware, in the incisive words of Crowe, 'that an insufficient number of troops were sent for the reason that no more could be found',[64] could only wring its hands and advise that it should be held at 'the earliest possible moment'.[65] The Poles, on the other hand, argued strongly for a delay on the grounds that German officials still predominated in the police forces and local government, and that there was consequently little chance of conducting the plebiscite peacefully.[66] These arguments failed, however, to swing the Conference of Ambassadors where Lord Derby and the Italian Ambassador blocked Cambon's attempt to delay the plebiscite until the occupying forces had been reinforced.[67]

The plebiscite campaigns gathered momentum once polling day

60. DBFP Ser. 1, vol. 10 (no. 574), p. 764.
61. Beaumont, 'Diplomatic Butterfly', p. 545.
62. Rennie to Curzon, 13.4.20 (no. 194141), FO 371/4298 fo. 178.
63. Rennie to Curzon, 22.4.20, FO 371/4298 fo. 429.
64. Minutes on Rumbold to Curzon, 24.4.20 (195727), FO 371/4298 fo. 447.
65. Minutes by Wigram, 20.4.20 (192924), FO 371/4297 fos 567–8.
66. Wambaugh, *Plebiscites*, vol. 1, p. 126.
67. DBFP Ser. 1, vol. 10 (no. 579), pp. 767–8. Bülow to AA, 5.5.20 (no. 53), FCO Lib. 2286 K644398.

was fixed for 11 July. In June the centre of controversy shifted to the preparations for bringing in the outvoters, the overwhelming majority of whom were German. As both Rennie and Beaumont feared that the Poles would attempt to disrupt rail traffic in the Corridor, Derby raised the question at the Conference of Ambassadors, where, despite vigorous French opposition, it was agreed that Allied officers should escort the outvoters across the Corridor.[68] In Allenstein Rennie complained that his work was hindered by the propensity of the newly appointed French Commissioner, M. Chevally, 'to raise objections to questions [rather] than to solve them'.[69] Chevally confidentially told him that he was being criticized in Paris 'for not doing what was expected of him in the Polish question'.[70] In the final week before the voting the mood in the two zones was tense, but there were no large-scale outbreaks of violence. An attempt by Polish irregulars to infiltrate across the border into Marienwerder shortly before polling day was checked by Italian troops,[71] while intensive patrolling by the Royal Irish and the Plebiscite Police ensured relative peace in Allenstein.[72]

Once the results were declared, which showed in both areas an overwhelming majority for remaining within the Reich,[73] the War Office pressed for the immediate withdrawal of the Royal Irish. Wilson, alarmed by Haking's reports that some of the men were overt Sinn Fein sympathizers,[74] desperately wanted to avoid any possibility of their close contact with the Russian bolshevik forces, which had already pushed the Poles back to the borders of East Prussia. The Royal Irish in Allenstein and the Italian troops in Marienwerder had already disarmed detachments of the Red Army which had strayed over the frontier.[75] As there had been disturbances amongst Irish troops in India and in the Irish Guards at Caterham,[76] Haking's fears were understandable, but exaggerated. He based his advice on the behaviour of a small detachment of the Royal Irish, who had caused 'a lot of trouble'[77] when they visited

68. DBFP Ser. 1, vol. 10 (no. 595), pp. 787–8.
69. Rennie to Curzon, 4.7.20 (C577), FO 371/4762 fo. 37.
70. Ibid., 6.7.20 (C1293) fos 117–19.
71. Beaumont, 'Diplomatic Butterfly', pp. 546–7.
72. DBFP Ser. 1, vol. 10 (no. 615), pp. 803–5.
73. Ibid. and no. 617, pp. 806–8.
74. Haking to Wilson, 16.7.20, IWM 73/1/26, file 48A.
75. Wigram to Curzon, 27.7.20 (C2293), FO 371/4763 fo. 117. Beaumont, 'Diplomatic Butterfly', p. 552.
76. *Cologne Post*, 5.2.20 and letter to the author from Mrs E. Smith, Lord Chancellor's Dept., 19.3.85, Ref. MS39/1/33.
77. Haking to Wilson, 16.7.20, IWM 73/1/26, file 48A.

Danzig for dental treatment. The Foreign Office, however, gave the battalion a glowing recommendation when the Commission left Allenstein in August.[78] Crowe suspected that the War Office was making use of the Sinn Fein scare 'as a pretext . . . to withdraw their troops in accordance with the general policy of scuttle',[79] but he underestimated the ever-present fear of mutiny, which still haunted the higher echelons of the British Army in 1920.

Both Commissions presented their recommendations for the new frontier lines to the Ambassadors' Conference on 24 July. Rennie had little trouble in securing agreement for the proposal to cede the three villages on the frontier which had opted for Poland, while denying the right of cession to six others which formed isolated enclaves in German-speaking territory;[80] but the Marienwerder Commission, faced with the more intractable problem of having to reconcile the result of the plebiscite with Article 97 of the Treaty, which expressly stipulated that Poland was to be 'in any case' guaranteed 'full and complete control' of the Vistula, was unable to draft a unanimous report.[81]

Anticipating this problem Beaumont had, back in April, urged the setting up of an international commission to control the Vistula,[82] and Pavia had also sounded out in May the German representative attached to the Commission, with proposals for scrapping the plebiscite and, 'either by means of a court of Arbitration or some other commission', for engineering the award of Kreis Stuhm to Poland.[83] Bülow reported that there was no doubt that 'the inter-Allied Commission had come to the conclusion that the pre-conditions [*Voraussetzungen*] for an annexation by Poland of this area could in no way be achieved by a plebiscite'.[84] Neither initiative received any backing from London or Paris and it was thus left to the Commission to recommend the line of the new frontier in the light of the plebiscite.

Pavia had a difficult task to mediate between the conflicting proposals of the French and British Commissioners. The French were pressing to award Poland sufficient territory to enable her

78. See S. Geoghegan, *The Campaigns and History of the Royal Irish Regiment*, vol. 2, Edinburgh, 1927, pp. 132–4.
79. Minute 26.7.20, on telegram from Derby to Curzon (C2165), FO 371/4762 fos 186–90.
80. DBFP Ser. 1, vol. 10 (no. 634), pp. 821–6.
81. Ibid. (no. 617), pp. 806–10.
82. Beaumont to Curzon, 24.4.20, FO 371/4298 (195560) fos 413–15.
83. Note by Meyer, 13.5.20 (no. 3071), FCO Lib. 2286 K644405–08.
84. Ibid.

strategically to dominate the Vistula, while Beaumont proposed that a small Polish bridgehead should be formed on the right bank of the Vistula out of the two villages that had voted for Poland.[85] Pavia drew up a rushed and, in places, nebulous report that recommended that the harbour of Kurzebrack and some five villages should be ceded to Poland.[86]

When the Ambassadors met on 24 July, Derby capitalized on the War Office's threat to recall the Royal Irish battalion from Allenstein, and attempted to bulldoze his colleagues into taking a 'final and immediate decision', but Cambon insisted on deferring a decision in order to give Chérisey time to present his case.[87] Millerand also prevailed upon Lloyd George to delay evacuation until mid-August so that the vital rail and river communications with Danzig would have some protection at the very moment when the Russians were threatening Warsaw,[88] but French attempts to modify the details of the Allenstein and Marienwerder settlements in favour of the Poles proved unsuccessful.[89] On 16 August the small number of villages ceded to Poland were handed over with almost indecent haste. In Allenstein, as the arrival of Polish officials was blocked by the Russian advance, the villages were temporarily returned to the local German authorities, even though they had now officially become part of Poland.[90]

The Commissions left the same day without any of the festivities that marked the departure of the Schleswig Commission. Both the French and Poles were surprised by the size of the pro-German vote and feared its possible repercussions on the more important plebiscite in Upper Silesia.[91] For the British government the plebiscite results were a vindication of the correctness of their policy of moderating Polish claims on German territory. Many British officials in the attractive town of Allenstein were loath to end what one junior member of the Commission called 'the best six months of my life'.[92] In Marienwerder, however, Beaumont was so horrified by the brutal treatment meted out to the Germans in the

85. Meyer, 'Für Staatssekretär von Haniel' (no. 85), 15.7.20, FCO Lib. 2286 K644426–32; Beaumont, 'Diplomatic Butterfly', pp. 553–4.
86. DBFP Ser. 1, vol. 10 (no. 617), pp. 808–9. Wambaugh, *Plebiscites*, vol. 1, pp. 136–9.
87. Derby to Curzon, 24.7.20 (C2164), FO 371/4762 fo. 184.
88. FO to Rumbold, 28.7.20 (no. 347), FO 371/4763 fo. 123.
89. DBFP Ser. 1, vol. 10 (nos 629 and 631), pp. 817–19. Beaumont to Curzon, 11.8.20 (C3953), FO 371/4764 fos 126–7.
90. DBFP Ser. 1, vol. 10 (no. 638), p. 828.
91. Wandycz, *France*, p. 42.
92. *Cologne Post*, 26.8.20.

Corridor that he bitterly opposed the transfer to Poland of any more German minorities, which had for long enjoyed 'the benefits of perhaps the most efficient administration in the world',[93] as little less than a betrayal of civilization to barbarism. This view, shared by British officials in Danzig and Upper Silesia, contributed powerfully to the growing sympathy in Britain with the German 'underdog'.

The Upper Silesian Commission: The Attempt to Pacify Upper Silesia

The Upper Silesian question did much to crystallize the differences between the British and French approaches to post-war Germany. For the British the plebiscite was essentially an exercise in damage limitation, to ensure that too much German territory was not swallowed up by an unstable Poland. Already by the end of 1920 with the onset of the post-war depression it was beginning to be appreciated in Britain that a revived German economy was the only engine that could pull Europe out of recession. It was thus hardly in Britain's interests to weaken Germany still further by detaching the vital industrial province of Upper Silesia from her. The British government therefore hoped that in a plebiscite fairly organized, the majority of the population would decide to stay with Germany. The French, on the other hand, desperate to strengthen Poland and weaken Germany, did all they could to bring about the opposite result.[94]

Even without this fundamental clash between British and French aims the task facing the Upper Silesian Plebiscite Commission in February 1920 was as complex as any that confronted the *Entente* powers in Germany. The Commission assumed responsibility for a large Prussian province, containing a concentration of coal mines and iron and steel industries second in size only to the Ruhr, and with a population of some 2,280,000 inhabitants, who were racially deeply divided. The Commission had not only to ensure law and order during what was to be a long and bitter plebiscite campaign, but also to guarantee the production of the coal mines, on which the economic life of much of Central Europe depended.

93. Beaumont, 'Diplomatic Butterfly', p. 532.
94. Bertram–Libal, 'Die britische Politik in der Oberschlesienfrage, 1919–22', pp. 105–8; P. Gajda, *Postscript to Victory, British Policy and the German–Polish Borderland, 1919–1925*, Washington, 1982, p. 212; Cienciala and Komarnicki, *From Versailles to Locarno*, pp. 59–62; Kaiser, *Lord D'Abernon*, pp. 189–221.

If the British government's arbitrary cancellations of the decision to contribute three battalions to the army of occupation in early January was not to lead to a weakening of British influence on the Commission, Colonel Percival would have to demonstrate exceptional strength of character and a diplomatic finesse with which his previous career as a military administrator scarcely fitted him. His task was to be made more difficult by the formidable character of General Le Rond, who by virtue of his position as president of the Commission and of the French military and administrative preponderance in Upper Silesia, enjoyed considerable advantages over his British and Italian colleagues. Le Rond was a fluent and persuasive speaker and an immensely hard worker. As president he drew up the agenda for each day's meeting and had the advantage of actually living in the Commission's headquarters. The commander of the occupying forces, General Gratier, was his military subordinate while French officials filled the majority of the senior posts of the Commission and directed key departments of the Interior, Finance and the economy.[95] Out in the districts the six British Kreis officers had a simpler task because they were supported by a small but useful staff composed of British nationals and were consequently spared the daily inter-Allied bickering that became the norm in Oppeln; but they were, of course, dependent on French or Italian troops in any emergency.

The Commission had a minimum of six months in which to stabilize the situation in Upper Silesia before proceeding to hold the plebiscite. Apart from the ever-present danger of racial strife, the greatest threat to the provinces lay in the chronic lack of food and the adverse impact of this on production and labour relations. As elsewhere in Germany, the surest way to combat bolshevism was to provide adequate food supplies. J.I. Craig, the British Director of the Food Department, was able to mitigate the worst shortages with supplementary supplies of flour, rye, lard and condensed milk from Poland, Czechoslovakia and Hungary.[96] The Commission initially treated the Silesian proletariat with considerable circumspection. When the railway workers at Ratibor demonstrated against the newly introduced piece-rates, an official was hastily sent

95. Material on Percival's earlier career can be found in the Steward's Papers, Christ Church, Oxford, S.XVIII.b.1–5. There is a good assessment of Le Rond in F. Bourdillon, 'Report on the Upper Silesian Plebiscite Commission', pp. 20–1 (C9145), FO 371/8810.
96. 'Report on the Administration of Food Control of the inter-Allied Administrative and Plebiscite Comission, Upper Silesia', FO 890/16 fos 146–85.

down to withdraw them and to assure the workers that the Commission had 'the sincere desire to help the people and not least of all the working classes'.[97] The British Kreis officers, in particular, appeared to win the confidence of the workers by their readiness to listen to their complaints. When, for instance, the Sipo attempted to break a strike at the Bismarckhütte in the Beuthen rural district by occupying the foundries on 1 April, Lieutenant Fenton ordered them to withdraw 'amidst tremendous cheering of the workmen', and the local Kreis officer, Major Ottley, was able to negotiate a compromise which made a return to work possible.[98] Percival was instrumental in overcoming Le Rond's opposition to the introduction of the new Works Council Law into Silesia.[99]

During the first month of the occupation both the Germans and the Poles adopted 'a waiting attitude',[100] and the province remained peaceful, but the hostile reaction of the German government to the Commission's introduction of its own courts, and the subsequent judges' strike, which was only broken by the expulsion of the Chief Justice,[101] led to a hardening in the attitude of the Germans against the Commission. On 13 March the Commission feared that when the Kappist troops occupied Breslau, a German invasion was imminent and that sympathetic uprisings would take place in Oppeln, Gleiwitz and Kattowitz.[102] The Poles responded by massing troops on the frontier and mobilizing their own paramilitary organizations within Silesia, and consequently discouraged the Germans from any precipitate action.[103]

The unfortunate conjunction of Labour Day on 1 May with Poland's National Day on 3 May confronted the Plebiscite Commission with its first major test. The labour demonstrations passed off relatively peacefully, but when the predominantly German centres of Ratibor, Lublinitz and Oppeln were invaded on 2 and 3 May by large crowds of Polish demonstrators, the Germans staged counter-demonstrations.[104] To avoid a dangerous escalation local Allied officials concentrated on keeping the rival demonstrations apart. At Oppeln Percival himself intervened and separated the

---

97. 'Diary of Colonel Sir H.F.P. Percival . . ., 9.2.20–16.9.20' (22.3.20), FO 890/16 fos 241–543.
98. Ibid., 1.4.20.
99. Ibid., 19.4.20.
100. DBFP Ser. 1, vol. 11 (no. 11), p. 11.
101. Percival, Diary, 14.3.20, FO 890/16.
102. Ibid., 15.3.20.
103. DBFP Ser. 1, vol. 11 (no. 11), pp. 11–14.
104. Percival to Curzon, 4.5.20 (19700), FO 371/4303 fos 262–3.

demonstrators.[105] After two days of 'intense' public excitement[106] peace was restored, but on 7 May Korfanty, the Polish government's representative in Upper Silesia, announced a two-day strike of Polish coal miners as a demonstration against the Germans.[107] As a result of an initiative by Percival, who feared that the strike might trigger a civil war, the three Commissioners met Korfanty in the woods between Bierdzan and Rosenberg[108] and managed to persuade him to keep the strikers on a tight leash, even though it was too late to call off the strike, by promising him that plans were under way to disband the German paramilitary police force (the Sipo) and raise a new mixed gendarmerie under an Allied officer.[109]

Throughout the early summer of 1920, isolated but frequent incidents of communal violence continued to erupt. Amongst the Germans a hatred and distrust of the French fuelled an exaggerated pro–British sentiment. For instance at Beuthen after a series of severe disturbances, which culminated in the sacking of Korfanty's Headquarters, a crowd besieged Major Ottley's office and begged him to take over from his French colleague the responsibility for the Beuthen town Kreis.[110] The French troops naturally reciprocated the hatred shown them by the Germans. Le Rond confided in Percival that 'even the troops were inclined to go against him because . . . he is not sufficiently firm against the Germans'.[111] Ironically, at that very point he was interrupted by General Hammond, the British Head of the Transport and Communications Department, who insisted that a group of French soldiers should be ordered to stop throwing stones at German workmen in the Malapanerstraße.[112] Although at first Percival and Le Rond tried hard to work as a team,[113] by early summer their relations were becoming increasingly strained. On Sunday 9 May the two clashed bitterly before lunch on the subject of Korfanty's role in the demonstrations of 3 May.[114] Throughout the summer internal disagreements continued to multiply. At a meeting of the

105. Percival, Diary, 2.5.20, FO 890/16.
106. DBFP Ser. 1, vol. 11 (no. 12), p. 16.
107. Ibid. (no. 12), p. 15.
108. Percival, Diary, 7.5.20, FO 890/16.
109. DBFP Ser. 1, vol. 11 (no. 12), pp. 15–18. Percival in fact uses the original name of the force, Sicherheitswehr.
110. Percival to Curzon, 29.5.20 (201200), FO 371/4303 fos 524–7.
111. Percival, Diary, 11.6.20, FO 890/16.
112. Ibid.
113. Percival, for instance, supported Le Rond's attempt to merge the Allied Officials on the Commission into an effective international team. See Percival to Oliphant, 22.2.20 (181586), FO 371/4301 fos 625–9.
114. Percival, Diary, 9.5.20, FO 890/16.

Commission on 1 July the Italian Commissioner, General de Marinis, was so irritated by Le Rond 'that he felt very much inclined . . . to leave the room, as, whenever any Polish delinquencies were dealt with, they are always glossed over by the president'.[115] In his determination to pursue a purely French policy in Upper Silesia, Le Rond attempted to reduce his colleagues to cyphers. He resented any attempt by Percival to emphasize the British element of the Commission and even complained about the Royal Coat of Arms on Percival's notepaper.[116] Le Rond skilfully resisted any attempts by Percival or de Marinis to tie him down by having the Commission's meetings minuted, but eventually he did concede that immediately after a meeting had ended, the Secretary should be called in to record the decisions taken.[117]

The Bolshevik advance on Warsaw and Berlin's provocative declaration of neutrality on 25 July, banning the transit of munitions across Germany to Poland, heightened the tension in Upper Silesia.[118] On 17 August von Moltke invited the Commission to adhere to this declaration.[119] When it understandably refused, the German workers held a twelve-hour protest strike which in Kattowitz led to an attack on the headquarters of the local French Kreis officer and the subsequent declaration of martial law.[120] German action merely played into the hands of Korfanty, who on 19 August issued a proclamation calling on the Poles to defend their lives and property against the Germans. There was an immediate response, which brought the province to the brink of civil war. The Polish miners struck and armed reinforcements poured in over the frontier. Within forty-eight hours the Poles controlled Tarnowitz, Hindenburg and Rybnik and sizeable areas of five other Kreise, where they immediately disarmed and expelled all German officials and the predominantly German Sipo.[121] Some semblance of peace was restored when the Poles and Germans negotiated a provisional agreement on 31 August, which was confirmed two days later, whereby they both agreed to petition the Commission to accelerate its plans for creating a new police force composed of equal numbers of Germans and Poles and to expel all political agitators who had

115. Ibid., 1.7.20.
116. Ibid., 24.6.20.
117. Ibid., 5.8.20. An example of Le Rond's 'eel-like' qualities can be seen in ibid., 3.8.20.
118. Wambaugh, *Plebiscites*, vol. 1, p. 235; Cienciala and Komarnicki, *From Versailles to Locarno*, pp. 52–3.
119. DBFP Ser. 1, vol. 11 (no. 26), p. 36, footnote 3.
120. Ibid., pp. 36–7.
121. Percival to Curzon, 21.8.20 (C4487), FO 371/4815 fo. 61.

entered the province illegally after 1 August 1919.[122]

The crisis shattered what remained of Allied unity in Upper Silesia. British officials were appalled by the overtly pro-Polish bias of the French occupying forces. Ottley complained that the French Controller of Beuthen Town overruled his request for more troops to defend the German population, while Perry, the Kreis officer for Gross Strehlitz, informed Percival bluntly that he had 'no confidence in the impartiality of the Commission, who . . . were pursuing a policy which it was discreditable for any British officer to have anything to do with'.[123] Both Ottley and Perry, together with Captain Macpherson, an assistant to the Commissioner of Lublinitz, decided to resign in protest against the partisan action of their French colleagues. Confronted by determined French support for the Poles, they were powerless without British troops to uphold the impartiality of the Commission. They resorted to noble but impotent bluster. Macpherson, for instance, observed in his letter of resignation that: 'During the War I served in France and always lived on terms of closest friendship with our French allies . . . But I will not further take part in the policy they are now pursuing – a British standard of justice, impartiality and integrity does not permit me . . .'[124] These British officials were decent men who could afford to 'play the game' as it lay in their country's interests to hold a fair plebiscite. They had little sympathy for the dilemma of the French, who on so vital an issue could not afford to allow the Poles to lose 'the game'.

In Oppeln Percival and de Marinis launched a strong attack on Le Rond at the meeting of the Commission on 21 August when they complained 'that he was attempting to do everything himself, that in all his publications he talked about himself instead of the Commission . . . in other words that at every opportunity we were being eliminated . . .'[125] Le Rond lost his temper and according to Percival 'fairly wiped the floor' with his critics. Later de Marinis observed privately to Percival that 'sooner or later' they would both have to resign.[126] Curzon's reaction to Percival's initial reports on these differences with Le Rond was to instruct the Embassy in Paris to urge the Quai d'Orsay 'to take all possible steps'[127] to ensure the impartiality of French troops in Upper

122. Percival to Curzon, 31.8.20 (C5661), FO 371/4816 fos 9–20.
123. Percival, Diary, 22 and 26.8.20, FO 890/16.
124. Macpherson to Percival, 1.9.20, p. 4, FO 371/4816 fos 227–30.
125. Percival, Diary, 21.8.20, FO 890/16.
126. Ibid.
127. Curzon to Buchanan, 31.8.20 (C5136), FO 371/4815 fo. 160.

Silesia, but as further details emerged of the gravity of the crisis, it rapidly became clear that the whole question of the Commission's future would have to be considered by the Conference of Ambassadors.[128] Derby was thus instructed to press for the recall of Le Rond and Gratier, even if it meant the resignation of Percival. Curzon was adamant that if French consent was not forthcoming, Britain would withdraw in protest from the Commission.[129] The Conference of Ambassadors met on 16 September, but deferred discussion of Upper Silesia for a further four days until Millerand and Le Rond could attend.[130] This gave the Foreign Office time to supply Derby with detailed evidence of Le Rond's machinations and to brief him on the changes in the Commission recommended by Percival, who urged the reallocation of the responsibility for the industrial areas of Beuthen and Gleiwitz to British and Italian controllers, the creation of a new police department under a British official and the setting up of an effective inter-Allied secretariat through which all the official correspondence of the Commission would be channelled.[131]

On 21 September Le Rond defended his position at the Conference of Ambassadors with a skilful and conciliatory speech, which made his position virtually unassailable.[132] Derby was forced to agree to a compromise, which in essence made 'aucune concession importante'.[133] Minutes of the Commission's meetings were to be kept and its papers and details of all financial transactions were to be open to inspection by all Allied officials. An independent police department was to be set up, but it was to remain under the control of a French Commandant with British and Italian assistants. There was to be no re-allocation of the industrial districts amongst the Allies.[134] Opinion in the Foreign Office differed as to whether or not it represented a diplomatic defeat for Britain,[135] but at least Le

128. Curzon's Minute on Percival's Telegram (no. 192), 31.8.20, FO 371/4816 fo. 8.
129. DBFP Ser. 1, vol. 11 (no. 42), pp. 54–5.
130. Ibid. (no. 47), p. 66.
131. Ibid. (nos 46 and 49), pp. 58–65 and 67–9.
132. Ibid. (no. 56), p. 76.
133. 'Haute-Silesie', MAE Allemagne 216 fo. 1.
134. DBFP Ser. 1, vol. 11 (no. 62), pp. 81–2. These changes necessitated the further recruitment of some thirty-nine officials, the majority of whom were ex-officers or men with experience of other inter-Allied missions (ibid. nos 59 and 68, pp. 79 and 88).
135. Waterlow regarded it as 'a defeat for us', while Crowe and Hardinge disagreed: Minutes, 12.10.21, FO 371/4818 fos 159–61. The Germans also realized that in all essentials the French had preserved their position intact: see note dated 20.10.20 (no.

Rond was forced on to the defensive and for the time being compelled to adopt a more conciliatory attitude towards the Germans. As Percival was ill for much of the autumn, the difficult task of ensuring that Le Rond interpreted the directives of the Ambassadors' Conference fell to his assistant Bourdillon. Le Rond initially attempted 'to slip out of the obligation to keep "procès verbaux" by maintaining that practically all the business dealt with by the Commission [was] of a secret nature'.[136] Nevertheless, under pressure from Bourdillon and de Marinis, he conceded in principle the formation of an inter-Allied secretariat at Oppeln and also agreed that each Kreis officer should have an inter-Allied staff representing all three Allied powers.[137] The limits to British influence were, however, sharply illustrated when the Foreign Office, anxious for 'some concrete step'[138] which would dramatically demonstrate the new balance of power on the Commission, overreached itself by urging Percival in November to insist on the expulsion of Korfanty. Using evidence from an intercepted German wireless message and quoting from a particularly inflammatory speech by Korfanty made at Rosenberg on 23 November, Percival pressed strongly, but unsuccessfully, for his expulsion.[139] Predictably it rapidly threatened to become yet another trial of strength between London and Paris, but when the issue was referred to the Ambassadors' Conference, it soon became clear that the French would rather face a British withdrawal from Upper Silesia than concede.[140] Consequently, despite the ringing declaration of Waterlow that 'to yield will be to make ourselves parties to a plebiscite held under auspices, which no one can pretend are impartial',[141] Curzon quietly allowed the demand to drop in mid-January.[142]

The winter months of 1920–1 passed without another insurrection. Extra rations, authorized at the Spa Conference and further supplemented by irregular deliveries of sugar, flour and tobacco from Czechoslovakia, which the Reparation Commission had per-

IV PO16242) (signed Meyer), FCO Lib. K1809 K456471–72, and also letter from the Staatskommissar für öffentliche Ordnung to AA, 18.11.20 (no. 14363/20G), FCO Lib. K1809 K456525–26.
136. Bourdillon to Carr, 20.10.20 (9660), FO 371/4819 fos 161–3.
137. Percival to Curzon, 27.10.20 (C10205), FO 371/4820 fos 2–3.
138. DBFP Ser. 1, vol. 11 (no. 69), p. 90.
139. Ibid. (no. 94), pp. 116–18.
140. Ibid. (no. 119), pp. 141–2.
141. Minute of 15.12.20 on no. 1390 from Hardinge to FO (C13862), FO 371/4822 fos 180–1.
142. DBFP Ser. 1, vol. 11 (no. 128), p. 150 (footnote 1).

mitted to be paid for by coal produced in overtime shifts by the Upper Silesian miners, went some way towards blunting the hunger of the miners and avoiding unrest.[143] Nevertheless violence and assassination were virtually daily events in the mining districts. In early January 1921 Percival reported that 'bands of brigands infest the country and murder and robberies by violence are caused almost daily not only in the open country, but even in the larger towns'.[144]

Faced with the intractable problems of inter-communal strife in Upper Silesia and the growing evidence that the October reforms were merely cosmetic, the morale of many British officials declined and the British element on the Commission viewed the future pessimistically. One officer lamented that 'trying to get a move on with anything [was] like trying to push a steam roller',[145] while Percival, who had regularly to contend with Le Rond, feared 'a return of the unsatisfactory state of affairs prevailing in Upper Silesia in August 1920'.[146] There was also some evidence of indiscipline amongst the British officials. In January several officials were sacked for 'unseemly behaviour' involving 'being seen in public places in uniform with women of doubtful character, having rows with, and failing generally to get on with other members of the Commission [and] remaining in bed until 11 or 12 in the morning instead of attending their respective offices and doing their work'.[147] The prospects for an orderly plebiscite campaign and the calm appraisal of its results seemed remote by the end of 1920.

143. Dept. of Food Control, pp. 16–17, FO 890/16 fos 163–6.
144. Percival to Curzon, 11.1.21 (C1286), FO 371/5887 fos 119–20.
145. Tidbury to Wigram, 12.1.21 (C1380), FO 371/5887 fos 146–7.
146. Percival to Curzon, 16.2.21 (C3758), FO 371/5889 fo. 196.
147. Tidbury to Wigram, 12.1.21 (C1380), FO 371/5887 fos 146–7.

–6–

Cologne and Danzig: The Gibraltars of the North

In 1920 Cologne and Danzig appeared to be the new bastions of British influence on the Continent. Even a year later General Degoutte, the French Commander-in-Chief of the Allied armies on the Rhine, still regarded Danzig as a link in a chain of British bases around the periphery of Europe stretching from Constantinople through Malta and Gibraltar, which 'grâce à sa politique de réalisation égoïste, assuré son hégémonie sur l'Europe au lieu et place de l'Allemagne'.[1] In both cities the British occupation was initially greeted by the local German population as providing a bulwark against anarchy and the protégés of the French, the separatists in Cologne and the Poles in Danzig. However, while Cologne did indeed become a stable island of British influence in the Rhineland, Danzig remained a turbulent and violent city from which British troops and officials were only too happy to extricate themselves in December 1920.

Sir Reginald Tower at Danzig

While it was the French in Schleswig, Marienwerder and Allenstein who stretched the interpretation of the Treaty to the utmost, in attempts to justify their policy, in Danzig it was the British who were anxious to reinterpret, in a sense favourable to their own interests, the key Articles 103 to 108. In their desire to strengthen Germany, British officials in London, Paris and Danzig fought tenaciously to give Danzig a greater degree of independence from Poland than a literal interpretation of the Treaty warranted.

---

1. Rapport Mensuel, Mois de Novembre et Decembre 1921, p. 92, Vincennes 7N2656.

Tower was invested with formidable powers.[2] Responsible only to the Conference of Ambassadors, he was to prepare Danzig for its metamorphosis into a free city under the League of Nations. He thus had not only to negotiate a convention between Danzig and Warsaw, but also to divide up the former property of the Reich between the two successor powers and to 'tender to the authorities of Danzig such assistance and advice as [he might] think proper in framing the constitution of the Free City'.[3] Tower reached Danzig on 10 February where he was greeted in a manner 'reminiscent of the arrival of a colonial governor in some isolated colony'.[4] Both in his introductory speech to the reception committee at the station and subsequently at every other opportunity Tower attempted to enthuse the Danzigers with the prospect of their new role as members of an international free city, and to paint a glowing picture of their future economic prosperity.[5] In Danzig, where there was a widespread assumption that the city was about to become a British protectorate,[6] the imposing figure of Tower appeared to symbolize the might of the British Empire, but in reality he was in an exposed and dangerous situation. Not only had he to negotiate a treaty between two irreconcilable enemies, but he presided over a volatile population facing unemployment and near starvation. His only military support, apart from visiting British and French warships, was a battalion of French Chausseurs, which was stationed outside the city, and the 3rd Battalion of the Royal Fusiliers. In February 1920 it was still composed of raw and untrained troops, and lacked experienced NCOs.[7] He was further handicapped by the attitude of General Haking, the military

2. Gregory at the FO minuted that Tower 'will virtually be Governor of Danzig', 6.11.19 (no. 1-3201), FO 371/3925.
3. DBFP Ser. 1 vol. 11 (no. 181), pp. 208–9. His instructions from the League were sent on 16.2.20 (no. 179327), FO 371/3925.
4. *Vossische Zeitung*, 11.2.20. Most of the newspaper references in this chapter come from Tower's collection of cuttings, FCO Library, DA 566.9. T.65.
5. 'To the People of Danzig' (no. 179471), FO 371/3925; *Manchester Guardian*, 13.2.20. His niece, Miss Winifred Tower, who went to Danzig with him, told me that he was determined to be accessible to the inhabitants and initially insisted on walking around the city alone. When her brother, who was the adjutant of the Fusiliers, remonstrated with him, he replied: 'If they think we are afraid of them, we ought to go home immediately.' Interview with the author with Miss Tower, 29.1.83.
6. See also *Neuste Nachrichten*, Stettin, 17.2.20: 'so war es gedacht: Danzig – englische kolonie auf dem Kontinent'. In April Haking reported that one of his staff had a conversation with 'two or three labourers', who were alarmed about rumours of a British military withdrawal; they 'said that they wished that the British would take over the permanent control of Danzig': Haking, 'The Situation in Europe', 18.4.20, IWM 73/1/26 file 48A.
7. R.B. Gooden to Ad. and Maud, 10.6.20, IWM Gooden papers, 73/137/6.

commander of the Allied forces in Danzig and Allenstein, who had gained a considerable insight into German affairs as British representative on the Armistice Commission. He had himself hoped to be commissioner[8] and was contemptuous of Tower's apparent lack of relevant experience of contemporary Germany.[9]

Tower's first task was to create a council of state to administer the city until a constituent assembly could be elected and be entrusted with the task of drawing up a democratic constitution. As his intention was to disturb 'as little as possible the existing machinery of government',[10] he nominated a small executive council, led by the Lord Mayor of Danzig, Heinrich Sahm, with whom he soon established a considerable rapport. Under Sahm's able leadership the council rapidly drew up plans for an elective town council of 120 and a new High Court of Justice.[11] Tower had little understanding of labour politics. Haking was critical that he had not appointed a labour representative to the council of state and had prophetically warned him that it would be 'from labour that you will have chief trouble';[12] indeed, within days of his arrival Tower was faced with a series of crippling strikes by gas, water and power station workers. On 25 February Tower issued a proclamation banning all strikes in essential services. Haking feared that this would merely intensify labour hostility in Danzig and cause 'a howl from the labour unions' in Britain.[13] The socialist *Danziger Volksstimme* was quick to observe that 'one would certainly have expected a little more independence for the masses from representatives of the League of Nations, which was to bring all the blessings of democracy to Germany too',[14] but the trade unions in Danzig decided against a confrontation with Tower and, instead, attempted in vain to persuade him to set up an industrial court of arbitration which would have brought the Danzig labour laws into line with those in the occupied Rhineland.[15]

8. Drummond to Balfour, 17.7.19 (copy enclosed in no. 124552, Drummond to Gregory, 1.9.19), FO 371/3925. Haking was eventually appointed the League of Nations Commissioner in 1921.
9. 'Of course they ought to have sent someone here who thoroughly understands the Germans, and not a man who has been in South America since the war began', Haking to Wilson, 6.3.20, IWM 73/1/26 file 48A.
10. Tower to Conference of Ambassadors, 20.2.20 (no. 181201), FO 371/3925.
11. Ibid., 6.3.20 (no. 184230) and 16.3.20 (no. 187558), FO 371/3932. C.M. Kimmich, *The Free City*, pp. 24–8.
12. To the CIGS, March 1920, IWM 73/1/26 file 48A.
13. Ibid., Haking to Wilson, 6.3.20.
14. Quoted in Intelligence Report, 4.3.20, which Haking sent to Wilson. IWM 73/1/26 file 48A
15. Ibid.

The defeat of the Kapp *Putsch* and the subsequent Spartacist uprising in the Ruhr led to a more militant atmosphere in Danzig. There were threats to kidnap Tower, to lock up the Fusiliers in their barracks and call a general strike. At one stage the Fusiliers were sent out in the middle of the night to occupy Tower's residence in the Oberpräsidium.[16] Tower was so alarmed by plans of the Independent Socialists for holding a mass rally to demand the repeal of the strike ban, that he seriously considered declaring a state of siege, but under pressure from Haking who argued that this would 'alienate not only the working men, but also the ten thousand unemployed . . . and produce a situation exactly opposite to what we desire, and one which we may have the greatest difficulty in dealing with', he relented and allowed the demonstration to go ahead.[17]

Both Haking and Tower were anxious to encourage any projects which could provide work for the unemployed. Tower had attempted in November 1919 to encourage Allied investment in the city,[18] and Haking conceived of a bold scheme for creating work for virtually all the unemployed by demolishing the old medieval fortifications, and paying for the men's wages out of a loan raised on the security of the building land subsequently released.[19] After some hesitation Tower backed the plan,[20] but it was never put into practice, and in mid-summer there was still a hard core of 8,000 unemployed.[21]

Potentially Danzig, with Poland as its economic hinterland, was an inviting target for British commerce and investment. Headlam Morley, the historical adviser to the Foreign Office, while dismissing rumours that it was about to become a British colony, conceded:

> that we ought to do everything in our power to encourage British trade with Poland through Danzig: it is a part of the world in which we ought to maintain and establish our interests and influence . . . It is contrary to all the sound traditions of our policy to get mixed up in the affairs of Poland, but Danzig is within the sphere of our interests and influence.[22]

16. Haking to Wilson, 27.3.20 (no. 189855), FO 371/3934. Also information from an interview by the author with Miss Winifred Tower, 29.1.83.
17. Ibid. (Haking to Wilson, 27.3.20).
18. 'Notes on a Journey to Danzig', 17–29 Nov. (no. 169160), FO 371/3925.
19. Haking to Wilson, 21.3.20, IWM 73/1/26 file 48A.
20. Tower to Conf. of Amb., 27.3.20 (no. 189189), FO 371/3934.
21. Haking to CIGS, 9.7.20: 'The Military Occupation of Danzig', IWM 73/1/26 file 48A.
22. Minute by Headlam Morley, 16.2.20 (C173632), FO 371/3925.

The British Trade Corporation opened up banking premises there in the autumn of 1919 and Tower attempted to attract investment from Vickers, Armstrong, Whitworth and Co. and Pearson and Sons,[23] but apart from the allegedly extensive black market dealings on behalf of the Royal Fusiliers by a local African entrepreneur, Marengo Dyck,[24] the anarchic conditions in Danzig in 1920 seemed to have deterred most foreign businessmen. In 1920 Danzig was not an attractive prospect for investment. Its main industries had been the Imperial shipyards and munitions factories, which had closed down in December 1918. The Free City was faced with the painful and slow task of re-orientating its economy towards Poland, a process which Tower compared to 'an attempt to graft the head of a bee on the body of a wasp'.[25]

For coal and food supplies Danzig was dependent on Poland, which was itself desperately short of them. In January and April Tower negotiated agreements with Warsaw whereby the Poles supplied potatoes, flour and rye in exchange for deliveries of marmalade and sugar, but deliveries were tardy and usually inadequate,[26] especially as, for some of the time, Poland was

23. 'Notes on a Journey to Danzig, 17.11.19–29.11.19' (no. 169160), FO 371/3925. For the work of the British Trade Corporation see R.P.T. Davenport-Hines, *Dudley Docker. The Life and 'i nes of a Trade Warrior*, London, 1984, pp. 133–49.

24. *Danziger Volksstimme*, 20.3.20, FCO Lib. DA 566.9. T.65. He had lived for several years in Danzig. His career would be worthy of the pen of a social historian of the eminence of Professor Cobb! With the signature of the Polish-Danzig Convention in November 1920, there was some evidence of British initiatives. In February 1921 the Lloyds (France) and National Provincial (France) Bank branch at Cologne sanctioned a loan to the British Trading Corporation of ten to fifteen million marks for use in Danzig, and by October a client advised the bank that there was sufficient business to make it profitable to open up a branch there. In late 1921 an international consortium in which the Sheffield firm Cravens and Co. was represented began to negotiate for the purchase of the Danzig shipyards and railway shops, but by the autumn of 1922 the rapid deterioration of the Reichsmark, which still circulated in Danzig, caused the consortium to delay a decision. It was not until a new central Bank was set up and an independent currency introduced with the help of the Bank of England in 1923/24 that Danzig became a more attractive place for foreign investments, although according to a Midland Bank report in 1925, 'the continuous difficulties' with Poland were still a potential deterrent to British investment. See Lloyds Bank (France) and National Provincial Bank (France) Ltd, Minute Book no. 6, 17.2.21, no. 4003 and Minute Book no. 7, 31.10.21, no. 4638; British Overseas Bank, Intelligence Dept, Sept. 1922, Report on Danzig, Appendix: Danzig Shipyards and Railway Shops, pp. 16–17, Bank of England OV 120/6 fo. 3; Montague Norman to Havenstein, 3.10.23, Bank of England OV 34/72 fo. 3; Midland Bank Ltd, Overseas Branch, Report on Poland (prepared by C.A. Wurth), p. 22, Midland Bank Archives, 192/4 (I am grateful to Mr Edwin Green, the Archivist, who sent me a copy of this).

25. 'Economic Conditions in Danzig', (no. 214861), FO 371/3935.

26. Ibid.; Tower to Conf. of Amb., 31.3.20 (no. 19058), FO 371/3934.

fighting for its life against Soviet Russia. Tower's niece was so moved by a visit to a children's ward in a Danzig hospital where she saw babies suffering from malnutrition that she was instrumental in obtaining from the Save the Children Fund in London two thousand boxes of condensed milk and sixteen bales of clothing, but even this remarkable effort, as the *Volksstimme* pointed out, was 'less than a drop in the ocean'.[27] Deliveries of coal from both Poland and Germany totalled a mere 22,000 tons a month, which was less than 50 per cent of its requirements. In September Tower despairingly observed that 'it was simply not possible to follow any definite economic policy in Danzig owing to the uncertainty of supplies'.[28]

These deprivations, for which the Danzigers held the Poles responsible, made the negotiation of the convention between the Free City and Warsaw even more difficult. Neither side was ready to compromise on their interpretations of Article 104. The Danzigers were intent on keeping Polish influence in their city to an absolute minimum, while the Poles argued that their treaty rights involving the use of the docks, the control of the Vistula, the railway, posts and telegraphic system gave them a *de facto* sovereignty over the city. Tower rapidly came to the conclusion that the creation of a genuine Free City was incompatible with the concessions which Poland claimed under Article 104. Tower conceived his duty to be the creation of an independent city under the League of Nations and made clear to the Poles that 'he could not contemplate a solution by which Danzig would be made immediately a Polish city, with all her resources controlled by Poland and at the same time encourage the citizens of Danzig to believe that the Allies had granted to them the privileges of a free city'.[29] He tried unsuccessfully to convince the Conference of Ambassadors to sanction an indefinite prolongation of the Allied administration of the city.[30]

At the end of April Tower went to Paris to explain the intricacies of the negotiations and to plead for a revision of Article 104.[31] Predictably he met strong French opposition. One British Foreign Office official minuted: 'The pity of it is that the line of cleavage in Paris seems to be the same as that on the spot: "the French and the

27. Interview with Miss W. Tower, 29.1.83; *Danziger Volksstimme*, 10.8.20.
28. 'Economic Conditions', FO 371/3935.
29. Tower to Conf. of Amb., 8.4.20 (no. 191749), p. 3, FO 371/3931.
30. Tower to Conf. of Amb., 17.3.20 (no. 187854), FO 371/3932; Rumbold to Curzon, 29.3.20 (no. 190052), FO 371/3932.
31. DBFP Ser. 1, vol. 11 (no. 262), pp. 306–7.

Poles, His Majesty's Government and Sir Reginald Tower and the Danzigers".'[32] Derby was quite convinced by Tower that a too literal interpretation of Article 104 would jeopardize Danzig's very existence, and suspected that the French were attempting 'to produce a situation in which the "freedom of Danzig" becomes nothing but a name'.[33] It was thus agreed[34] that only the Allied Prime Ministers could settle the question in the forthcoming Spa conference, and in the meantime Tower was instructed to draw up a memorandum on the conflicting proposals of the Danzigers and the Poles and append his own recommendations for a compromise.[35]

On 26 and 28 May Tower chaired meetings between Sahm and the Poles, but, as both sides submitted drafts which were 'on every point of importance . . . completely and irreconcilably at variance',[36] they ended in deadlock. Tower therefore drafted for the Allied heads of state his own recommendations, which were based on the assumption that the Allies, 'while according the utmost economic benefits to Poland', also wanted to 'maintain the reality of a free city'.[37] He repeated the proposal that had originally been made by Lord Derby for setting up harbour and railway boards on which would sit an equal number of Poles and Danzigers with a neutral chairman appointed by the League, to administer Danzig's port facilities and railways. He also recommended that Danzig should be permitted to appoint its own 'commercial commissioners' in foreign countries, even though Article 104 made Poland responsible for the city's foreign relations.[38]

In Danzig itself the months of May and June were relatively peaceful. The Royal Fusiliers were able to set up camp just outside Danzig at Brosen and begin to concentrate on basic military training.[39] No disorders accompanied the elections to the Constituent Assembly, which was opened by Tower, wearing in the words of one journalist 'a ceremonial suit which was so laden with gold and decorations that one involuntarily had to ask oneself how he could carry the burden'.[40] There was also such a marked

32. Minute by Cruikshank, 12.5.20 (no. 196943), FO 371/3934.
33. DBFP Ser. 1, vol. 11 (no. 265), p. 310.
34. Ibid. (no. 269), p. 316.
35. Ibid. (no. 265), pp. 309–11.
36. Ibid. (no. 281), p. 336. The Minutes of the meeting are printed in *Danziger Zeitung*, 10.7.20.
37. DBFP Ser. 1, vol. 11 (no. 281), p. 336.
38. Ibid., pp. 336–7. See also Cienciala and Komarnicki, *From Versailles to Locarno*, p. 101.
39. *Royal Fusiliers Chronicle*, March 1921, p. 39.
40. *Das Freie Volk*, 16.6.20.

improvement in labour relations that Tower was able to lift the strike ban in return for assurances from the union leaders that they would first exhaust every possibility of negotiation before embarking on a strike.[41] However, Tower was uncomfortably aware that beneath the surface there were still acute tensions. In early June he informed Curzon that the unemployed were showing 'signs of desperation', and that taxation was being raised to the 'highest possible figure' by the municipal authorities in a desperate attempt to remain solvent.[42] He was particularly anxious that Danzig should be permitted to defer meeting the costs of the temporary Allied administration until its economy had recovered, and he even threatened to close down the High Commission if the British Treasury did not agree to defray its costs for a further period of three months.[43] His persistence paid off when the Conference of Ambassadors decided in September that, since Danzig had served as a base for the plebiscite garrisons in Allenstein and Marienwerder, Germany and Poland would defray the costs of the British garrison up to August.[44]

Labour unrest and the hatred of Poland on the part of the Danzig Germans were fused together into a formidable revolutionary force by the apparent imminent defeat of the Polish army by the Bolsheviks in July.[45] As the Polish forces fell back towards Warsaw, Danzig's position as the one port through which munitions and reinforcements could reach Warsaw became crucially important. The city's dockers were quick to exploit their potential stranglehold, when they refused to unload the *Triton*, a Greek merchantman carrying munitions, which berthed at Danzig on 21 July. When Tower and Haking met the dockers' leaders in an attempt to break the deadlock, Haking successfully persuaded them to agree to British troops unloading the *Triton*,[46] but Tower, uncomfortably aware, as indeed Haking himself was, that one battalion could not both work in the docks and at the same time be prepared to maintain order in the city, asked Haking to seek specific instructions from the newly installed Anglo-French diplomatic mission in Warsaw, the British member of which was Lord D'Abernon, the Ambassador in Berlin.[47] Haking, however, presented D'Abernon

41. *Danziger Neuste Nachrichten*, 5.6.20.
42. Tower to Curzon, 8.6.20 (no. 203818), FO 371/3926.
43. Ibid.
44. Derby to FO, 29.9.20 (no. 215498), FO 371/3926.
45. Cienciala and Komarnicki, *From Versailles to Locarno*, pp. 102–3.
46. Haking to CIGS, 25.7.20 (no. 209641), FO 371/3916; J.B. Mason, *The Danzig Dilemma: A Study in Peacemaking by Compromise*, London, 1946, pp. 116–17.
47. Tower to Conf. of Amb., 28.7.20 (no. 210289), FO 371/3916 fos 45–8.

with such a damning report on Tower's alleged vacillations in Danzig that D'Abernon, much to Crowe's fury in London,[48] advised Curzon to recall him and replace him by Haking himself.[49] D'Abernon approved Haking's plan for using troops to unload the *Triton* and called upon Tower to give him 'all possible assistance'.[50] Tower reluctantly agreed, and work began on 27 July,[51] although a day later a telegram arrived informing Tower of the decision taken by Lloyd George and Millerand at Boulogne to the effect that 'it was most desirable to get the cargo unloaded by other than military labour' and that 'no effort' should be spared 'to obtain this'.[52]

In the short term, Tower had no option but to continue to use troops on the *Triton*, but he may, entirely unofficially, just possibly have tried to square the circle by employing remnants of the White Russian army of General Avalov-Bermondt. The Commander of the French Baltic Squadron, Captain Brisson, informed the French Admiralty that he had been visited by 'un Colonel russe, déguisé en officier anglais', the day after 'la manifestation' (of 29 July), who had apparently informed him that his troops, 'habillés en soldats anglais', had been working in the docks. Brisson sarcastically observed that they 'servent en ce moment de paravent à Sir Reginald Tower qui peut dire que l'Angleterre n'aide pas les Polonais, et qui peut d'un autre côté affirmer qu'il a fait tout ce que qu'il a pu pour le faire'.[53] The *Triton*'s cargo was unloaded and sent up to Dirschau under police escort without incident, but the use of British troops, or at least troops in British uniforms, undoubtedly raised the political temperature in Danzig. On the afternoon of 29 July several thousand workers demonstrated in the Hay Market against high taxation. After storming the town hall and forcing Sahm to promise immediate cuts, they attacked the local prison (where it was rumoured that twenty British soldiers were confined for refusing to unload the *Triton*) but were dispersed by the police.[54] That evening there were attacks on Polish travellers and officials in

48. Minute by Crowe, 28.7.20 (on no. 210129), FO 371/3916.
49. DBFP Ser. 1, vol. 11 (no. 356), pp. 405–6.
50. Ibid.
51. Ibid. (no. 359), p. 407.
52. Ibid. (no. 358), pp. 406–7.
53. 'Extrait d'une lettre du Capitaine de Vaisseau Brisson, Commandant de la Division Navale de la Baltique à M. le Ministre de la Marine', 9.8.20 (no. 125), MAE Dantzig, 5, fos 40–51. There is no confirmation by Haking of this; indeed he refers specifically to the Fusiliers unloading the *Triton*: Haking to Wilson, 26.8.20, IWM 73/1/26 file 48A.
54. 'Rioting at Danzig', *The Times*, 31.7.20.

Danzig station, and mobs forced their way into the city's main hotels in search of further victims.[55] Tower handed over the responsibility for maintaining law and order to Haking, who later boasted to the CIGS that 'the only thing that has kept this town quiet when the victorious Soviet army was approaching was my constant touch with the local leaders, which has always been looked upon with the deepest suspicion by the High Commissioner and only permitted grudgingly because he saw I was going to do it whether he liked it or not'.[56] To the French both Tower's and Haking's attitude appeared to be one of craven appeasement. Colonel Lorillard, the military liaison officer at Danzig, complained bitterly to Weygand that even 'les événements du 29 juin [*sic*] . . . ne lui ont pas encore ouvert les yeux. . . . Dans la Proclamation à l'eau de rose qu'il publie à la suite de ces incidents, il fait surtout part au Danzigois de "son plus sérieux désir d'être leur *ami*"!!!'[57]

For the first two weeks of August the Russian advance into Poland continued and the strategic value of Danzig remained of crucial importance. Lloyd George and Millerand attempted to coordinate a joint Anglo–French policy on Poland at the Supreme Council meeting at Lympne on 8 and 9 August. While Lloyd George had promised British assistance to Poland in the event of a Soviet threat to its independence, he was also interested in securing an Anglo–Russian trade agreement. Consequently at Lympne he made no secret of his opinion that 'the Russians were entitled to punish the Poles' for invading the Ukraine.[58] Eventually a compromise was agreed upon whereby if the Soviet government refused an armistice on the basis of granting recognition to an independent Poland within her ethnographic frontiers, Britain and France would blockade Russia, supply military equipment to Poland and keep open her lines of communication with Danzig. However, this was shattered when the British government, under intense pressure from the Labour movement at home, which had set up on 9 August a Council of Action pledged to harness the 'whole industrial power of the organised workers'[59] in opposition to intervention, ap-

55. Le Chef de Bataillon Lorillard, 30.7.20, 'Manifestations Du 29 juillet', Mission Militaire français, Delegation De Dantzig, no. 67/R.T., Vincennes 7N2988.
56. Haking to Wilson, 26.8.20, IWM 73/1/26 file 48A.
57. Lorillard's 'Note (redigée sur l'ordre de Monsieur le Général Weygand)', 1.8.20, Vincennes 7N2988.
58. Wandycz, *France*, p. 170.
59. S. White, 'Labour's Council of Action, 1920', *Journal of Contemporary History*, vol. 9, no. 4, 1974, p. 99.

proved on 10 August[60] a draft peace drawn up by the Russian government, which would have reduced the Polish army to a force of 50,000 men. The Poles were implacably opposed to peace on these terms, while to the French they were a betrayal of the Lympne Agreement. Anglo–French relations were further exacerbated by French recognition on 13 August of General Wrangel's White Russian government in the Crimea, an action which Curzon described as 'tantamount to a declaration of war against Soviet Russia'.[61]

It was thus not surprising that in early August the British government neither reinforced Danzig nor vigorously ordered Tower to keep the port and the railways open. Curzon conceded the vital importance of Danzig, but the Foreign Office did not seriously challenge the War Office's pleas that it could not raise the necessary four battalions to protect Danzig and the lines of communication with Poland,[62] although it was more sceptical about the alleged Sinn Fein sympathies of the Royal Irish battalion in Allenstein, which was whisked away in August to the Rhineland to avoid possible contamination by bolshevism[63] in Danzig. Haking's and Tower's arguments that the use of British military labour to unload any more ships would merely precipitate fresh rioting were accepted in London, and the War Office specifically forbade Haking to use his troops for dock labour.[64] Consequently in early August the Danzigers were able to tighten their embargo on Polish war material with impunity. The French Vice-Consul observed bitterly that 'le sentiment dominant est la joie devant l'écrasement de la Pologne', and pleaded for the despatch of a French warship.[65]

The French used every channel available to them to persuade the British government to issue positive instructions to Tower and to reinforce the city. Foch approached Wilson through the French military attaché in London[66] and on 20 August de Fleuriau, the French chargé d'affaires, called at the Foreign Office and argued strongly that Tower's action was contrary to the Treaty of Versailles,[67] but ultimately the issue could only be resolved by the

60. Wandycz, *France*, pp. 170–1.
61. DBFP Ser. 1, vol. 11 (no. 431), p. 480.
62. Ibid. (no. 393), p. 442. Curzon Minuted on 18.8.20 (211996); 'who is to supply the Labour battalions?' FO 371/3918.
63. See above, ch. 5, pp. 98–9.
64. DBFP Ser. 1, vol. 11 (no. 404), p. 449.
65. Vice-Consul at Danzig (Gueritte) to M. le Ministre (no. 40), 7.8.20, MAE Dantzig 4, fos 231–2.
66. De La Panouse to Wilson, 16.8.20 (no. 212236), FO 371/3918.
67. DBFP Ser. 1 vol. 11 (no. 468), pp. 512–13.

Supreme Council or by the Conference of Ambassadors, which could not be convened until 24 August.[68] In the meantime Foch and Weygand attempted to force Tower's hand by sending 400 tons of rifles and ammunition on board the French cruiser *Gueydon*, which docked on 22 August.[69] If necessary Foch threatened to use French troops to supervise the unloading of the cruiser.[70] Alarmed at the possible consequences for public order, Haking managed to persuade the captain to delay unloading until Tower received an answer to his telegram requesting precise instructions from the Conference of Ambassadors.[71] On 24 August Tower was at last sent unambiguous instructions, when the Conference of Ambassadors ordered him 'to employ any available labour under protection of [the] Allied powers'.[72] This somewhat tardy display of Allied unity had its effect and within days the dockers and railwaymen were handling Polish military cargoes without opposition.[73] Gueritte, the French Vice-Consul in Danzig, claimed that the collapse of the embargo on Polish war material merely demonstrated Tower's 'faiblesse ou sa mauvaise volonté systématique à l'égard des Polonais' that had allowed the crisis at Danzig to become so menacing.[74] Tower's dislike of the Poles and reluctance to risk large-scale rioting probably did encourage the defiance of the Danzig dockers and railwaymen,[75] but the most decisive factor in creating a new mood of compliance in Danzig was Pilsudski's rout of the bolshevik forces outside Warsaw on 17 August, which deprived the Danzigers of the prospect of the imminent defeat of the despised and hated Poles, rather than the firm commands issued belatedly to Tower and Haking by the Conference of Ambassadors.

The new chastened mood of the Danzig Germans did not facilitate negotiation of the Danzig–Polish convention. At Spa in July the British proposal for setting up a joint harbour board under a chairman appointed by the League of Nations had been accepted[76] but by September, when Tower went to Paris, it was becoming

68. Ibid.
69. Ibid. (no. 471), p. 516.
70. Ibid.
71. 'Compte Rendue sur la situation à Dantzig, le 24.8.20' (no. 92/R), Vincennes 7N2988.
72. DBFP Ser. 1, vol. 11 (no. 480), p. 521.
73. Ibid. (no. 502), p. 538.
74. Gueritte to M. le Ministre (no. 48), 27.8.20, MAE Dantzig 5, fos 32–3.
75. Ibid. (no. 12), 24.8.20, MAE Dantzig 4, fos 276–8.
76. Cienciala and Komarnicki, *From Versailles to Locarno*, pp. 103–4.

clear that the Allies would have to impose a treaty on both sides. A sub-committee of the Conference of Ambassadors was set up to draft a convention and reported back to the Conference in mid-October. Despite amendments insisted upon by the French, it was broadly acceptable to the British and favourable to Danzig.[77] The joint harbour board remained an integral part of the agreement, and in order to deprive Poland of an excuse to garrison troops in the city, Derby successfully persuaded the Ambassadors to recommend that the League should have the freedom in a time of crisis to call upon whichever power seemed appropriate to defend the city.[78] Despite last minute attempts by the Poles to raise further matters of principle,[79] the Free City was formally recognized on 15 November and the convention was signed by the Poles three days later. Tower himself was *persona non grata* at the Quai d'Orsay. Worn out by his time at Danzig he returned home to retirement. Although Britain had achieved its aim in Danzig, Tower, unfairly, but probably unavoidably, had become an embarrassment to the British Embassy in Paris.[80] For the remaining weeks of British custodianship in Danzig Colonel Strutt acted as temporary High Commissioner.

Meanwhile, strike threats and demonstrations continued in Danzig. In August Haking had warned the CIGS that 'without a promise of coal'[81] he would be able to do little to stabilize the situation, which by November was so desperate that, in words reminiscent of Sir William Robertson in Cologne in April 1919, he cabled to the War Office: 'I do not think that the Army Council would approve of their soldiers being called upon to risk their lives in suppressing a disturbance, which has been brought about by the failure of the Administration to look after the poorest and most helpless members of the community . . .'[82] It was not until the end of November that officials from the Upper Silesian Coal Commission visited Danzig and recommended diverting some 35,000 tons of coal monthly to the city.[83] By that time, however, Britain had extricated herself from the daunting prospect of presiding over the impoverished city in winter. Strutt ceased to have any official

77. Kimmich, *The Free City*, p. 29.
78. DBFP Ser. 1, vol. 11 (no. 634), pp. 655–6; Fisher to FO, 18.11.20 (N2739), FO 371/5409 fo. 6.
79. 'Memorandum by Mr. Cruikshank', 29.10.20 (N1626), FO 371/5408.
80. E.H. Carr to J.D. Gregory, 18.9.20 (no. 215378), FO 371/3926.
81. Haking to Wilson, 19.8.20, IWM 73/1/26 file 48A.
82. Haking to CIGS, 4.11.20 (N2378), FO 371/5413 fos 108–9.
83. 'Report by Lt. Col. Ditmas of the Permanent Coal Delegation of the Reparation Commission', 30.11.20 (N4083), FO 371/5413.

responsibility once the convention was signed,[84] and the Royal Fusiliers were withdrawn by the end of December.[85]

Although large crowds saw them off at the station, Danzig had been an uncomfortable and sometimes dangerous place for the British. At first the Fusiliers were welcomed as protectors against the Poles, but the attitude of the local Socialists and Spartacists was ambivalent towards them. In the early spring, when food supplies were at their scarcest, the soldiers' ability to use the strength of sterling to buy up food supplies was understandably resented by much of the population.[86] During the troubles of July women who had consorted with British troops reportedly had their hair shorn off.[87]

The British, whose European and global position rested on their ability to hold the balance of power, an aspect of which, from time to time, was playing 'the honest broker', were convinced that their role in Danzig was to mediate between the Danzigers and the Poles to produce a viable Free City.[88] As the stakes were so high, neither side was prepared 'to play the game'. The *Manchester Guardian* compared Tower to 'an umpire at a cricket match where both teams are infuriated, where there is no book of the rules and no M.C.C. to whom the matter can be referred'.[89] Viewed, however, from Paris or Warsaw, Sir Reginald appeared far from being an impartial umpire. He was, on the contrary, like so many of his countrymen in 1920, alienated by the strident aggression of the Poles and instinctively sympathetic to the pro-consular bureaucratic efficiency of men like Sahm. On every issue of importance he came down on the side of the Danzigers. He successfully pleaded for the modification of Article 104, which, as it stood, could have justified the Polish administration of the port. Although he was later prematurely recalled from Danzig by the Foreign Office in an attempt to improve Anglo–French relations, he in fact interpreted the policy of his government accurately, and played an important part in ensuring the independence of the Free City.

84. Derby to Strutt, 12.11.20 (N2444), FO 371/5409 fo. 216.
85. *Royal Fusiliers Chronicle*, p. 40.
86. *Deutsche Volksstimme*, 20.3.20.
87. Hankey to Balfour, December 1920, IWM 73/1/26 file 6.
88. The Royal Fusiliers were instructed by the *Cologne Post* (11.3.20), for instance, in answer to the question why they were there: 'Well, I suppose the answer to that should be something like this: the Allies must see to it that the Free State is properly constituted and that she is not overawed by Prussia or Poland and peace and order is secured during the time of transition.'
89. *Manchester Guardian*, 25.8.20.

Sir Harold Stuart and Arnold Robertson at Coblenz

The Rhineland High Commission officially came into existence with the German ratification of the Peace Treaty on 10 January. Its basic powers were defined in the six ordinances, which replaced the proclamations issued by the Allied and American armies during the Armistice. The High Commission was a compromise between Wilsonian idealism and military realism; 'It represented the exercise of power politics against a conquered enemy, and at the same time . . . it reflected an almost unlimited belief in the rule of law'.[90] It was therefore an ambiguous instrument, which paradoxically increased the powers of the occupying forces in the Rhineland. By giving the High Commission power to issue ordinances to protect the occupying armies wherever necessary, it proved, in Professor Webster's words, 'a flexible instrument of power more far reaching, as Marshall Foch himself pointed out, than the Commander-in-Chief's traditional regulatory authority'.[91] In effect, far from abolishing martial law, the Commission, arguably up to the autumn of 1924, maintained a partial state of siege. British policy in 1920, and indeed for the subsequent four years, consisted in cooperating with the French whilst attempting to persuade them strictly to adhere to the Rhineland Agreement and the Treaty of Versailles.

Within the British Zone the transfer of power went smoothly. Orders issued by the outgoing military government to strikers in the brown coal mines and the railway repair shop at Nippes to return to work were confirmed 'provisionally' by the High Commission.[92] The potentially more difficult problem caused by Washington's refusal to accept the jurisdiction of the High Commission over the American Zone until the ratification of the Treaty by the Senate was solved by a compromise put forward by General Allen. He agreed to tolerate within the American Zone the ordinances of the High Commission, provided they did not contradict the terms of the Armistice agreement. Stuart realized that this 'bristle[d] with points on which conflict of authority'[93] could at any time arise, but was grateful for any arrangement that left American troops in the Rhineland and Noyes with a seat on the High Com-

90. Fraenkel, *Military Occupation and the Rule of Law*, p. 4.
91. Webster, 'The Working of the Rhineland Agreement', 18.2.44 (u.1344/104/70), p. 16, LSE, Webster papers, 11/2. See also Kaiser, *Lord D'Abernon*, ch. 6; Recker, 'Adenauer und die englische Besatzungsmacht', pp. 108–13.
92. Minutes of IARHC, 11.1.20, 1st Session, §VI, Min. 7, FO 894/1 fo. 7.
93. DBFP Ser. 1, vol. 9 (no. 1), pp. 1–2.

mission, albeit only as liaison officer with Allen's military government, since it acted as some check on French influence at Coblenz. Initially the Commission's efficient dispatch of work was hindered by language differences and Tirard's frequent visits to Paris to confer with the Quai d'Orsay. Stuart's attempt to delegate to sub-committees much of the routine work of vetting German legislation, before it could be applied to the Rhineland, was blocked by Tirard 'with the result that the wheels of the High Commission became most infernally clogged'.[94] Reflecting on his first impressions of the workings of the High Commission at Coblenz, Arnold Robertson informed Waterlow that its meetings were 'becoming rarer and we practically never have the four High Commissioners here together at the same time . . . Our procedure is thus intolerably delayed and we are becoming the laughing stock of the army as well as . . . of the German officials'.[95]

General Degoutte, the French Commander-in-Chief of the Allied armies in the Rhineland, may have regarded the IARHC as an ineffectual talking shop, where all decisions were taken by a majority,[96] but its ultimate supremacy over the army in all civil matters was rigorously defended by Stuart. For instance, Generals Sir William Robertson and Degoutte failed to obtain *carte blanche* to introduce an effective censorship of mails in their respective zones.[97] In June Stuart decisively routed an attempt by the Army Council to claim that the British army of the Rhine could ultimately 'take any step necessary either through military courts or by executive action for the maintenance of public security or order within occupied territory', by threatening to resign.[98]

To the German government the High Commission was a body not to be lightly dismissed: rather it was projected, not entirely inaccurately, as an insidious, French-dominated tyranny. On the publication of the Six Ordinances, Koch, the Reich Minister of the Interior, immediately sent a note to the Supreme Council in Paris complaining that they damaged German sovereignty.[99] The

---

94. A. Robertson to Waterlow, 26.1.20, Robertson Papers, File I, Germany (The Rhine).
95. Ibid., 19.2.20.
96. Armée Du Rhin, Rapport Mensuel, juin 1920, IV, p. 1, Vincennes 7N2655.
97. DBFP Ser. 1, vol. 9 (no. 35), pp. 53–5; Minutes of IARHC, 11.2.20, §XIII, Min. 152, FO 894/1 fo. 269.
98. Army Council to Undersec., FO, 4.6.20 (20180), and Stuart to Waterlow, 26.6.20, FO 371/4351 fos 269, 273–4.
99. 'A Short History of the General Administration and Activity of the Rhineland High Commission and of the Conditions in the Rhineland during the year 1920' (C9474), p. 2, FO 371/9844 fos 131–7.

German government also initially conducted a policy of non-cooperation with the Commission. There were long delays in furnishing the Kreis officers with information, and the local Bürgermeister were advised to ignore questions which were not authorized by the Ordinances.[100] This made the Commission's task of monitoring food supplies in the Rhineland virtually impossible. In December 1919, the average daily ration was down to a little over one thousand calories a day,[101] and in mid–February Stuart reported that 'the people in the towns are already showing signs of deficient nourishment'.[102] Tirard accused Berlin of deliberately neglecting the occupied territory and proposed that the law giving the German government the monopoly of importing food-stuffs into the occupied territory should be suspended and that the Allied governments should draw up contingency plans for feeding the Rhineland. Stuart, convinced that Tirard was trying to use the food crisis as a lever to create an independent Rhineland, was far more cautious, and while he did not rule out Allied intervention 'if it becomes clear that the food shortage . . . will be so great as to create a state of starvation', he believed that in fact the Berlin government was giving the Rhineland preferential treatment.[103] At the end of March the new Müller administration encouraged German officials to cultivate unofficial contacts with the staff of the High Commission in order to 'find out more about the manifestly considerable differences of opinion between the Allies'.[104] Thus the German Ministry for Food and Agriculture evinced a greater readiness to cooperate with the High Commission, and on 7 May Dr Hermes, its new Minister, actually met Stuart in Cologne[105] and promised in the future to send him all the relevant statistics on food supplies so that the Commission would have the necessary facts at its disposal.

Inevitably, in early 1920 the food and fuel shortages, combined with a rapid deterioration in the value of the mark, exacerbated an already tense labour situation in the British Zone. Unrest came to a head when negotiations for the renewal of wage contracts began in the New Year. There were strikes on the railways in Cologne, in the power station at Knapsack, amongst the municipal and trans-

100. DBFP Ser. 1, vol. 9 (nos 59, 61, 185), pp. 95–9, 213–4. Hatzfeldt to AA, 1.4.20 (A.Nr.16), p. 4, FCO Lib. L1766 L515571–75.
101. 'Report on Food Conditions in the Occupied Territory', Feb. 1920 (179118), FO 371/4344 fos 415–420B.
102. DBFP Ser. 1, vol. 9 (no. 43), pp. 69–71.
103. Ibid.
104. Hatzfeldt to AA (A.Nr.16), p. 5, FCO Lib. L1766 L515571-75.
105. DBFP Ser. 1, vol. 9 (no. 465), pp. 475–8.

port workers at Solingen and Opladen and in the brown coal mines.[106] On the day before the High Commission came into being, the British military authorities had issued an ultimatum threatening to arrest, virtually as hostages, a hundred miners at Knapsack, twenty at Brühl and thirty railwaymen at Opladen if work was not resumed. In fact the arrest of only twenty-nine men and the visible deployment of troops was sufficient to persuade the strikers to return to work on 14 January.[107]

Labour unrest continued spasmodically in the British Zone for the next month. Colonel Ryan attributed the blame for this to the Independent Socialists, and warned the Commission that they were 'practically indistinguishable from bolshevism. . . . In every difficulty between employer and employed the USP [Independent Social Democratic Party] press is on the watch to turn events to the party's political profit. Scarcity of food, high prices, profiteering, the fall of the mark, strikes and general discontent, are all used as means to swell the party vote.'[108] On 9 February the High Commission was faced with one of the largest strikes that had occurred in the British Zone since the Armistice, when the metal workers in Solingen struck for higher wages as a result of rising inflation. The employers' tactics of locking out the workers escalated the conflict and led to sympathetic strikes. The strike became a decisive test of strength between the Commission and the Independent Socialists, who had chosen in Solingen 'a favourable field of battle'.[109] They controlled the town councils of Solingen, Wald and Ohligs and were therefore able to finance communal kitchens for feeding the strikers. In its early stages the strike spread rapidly. The Prussian authorities were sufficiently alarmed to cooperate with the High Commission. While the Prussian government declared a state of emergency in Düsseldorf, Elberfeld and Barmen, British officials in Cologne were able to avert the threat of sympathetic strike action by warning that secondary action would be in breach of Ordinance No. 5 and by the prominent deployment of troops. The strike was thus confined to the metal workers in Solingen, where it dragged on until 21 March.[110]

In January 1920 Germany seemed to be teetering on the verge of

---

106. 'Report of the Labour Situation in German Occupied Territory . . . for the period 1.1.20–15.2.20' (no. 18668), FO 371/4349 fos 10–26.
107. War Diary of the General Staff, British Army on the Rhine, 1 Jan. to 31 Jan. 1920, WO 95/24.
108. Ryan, 'Political Report, 31.1.20' (177635), FO 371/3779 fos 495–9.
109. 'A Short History', p. 8.
110. Ibid., pp. 7–8.

revolution or civil war. Stuart was so alarmed by the implications of this for the Rhineland and by the opportunities it opened up for French separatist policies that he sent Curzon a review of the options open to the Allies should either a successful Spartacist or monarchist revolution break out in unoccupied Germany. His own view, which Curzon endorsed, was that they 'should in principle . . . support the existing form of government so long as it continues, and any other . . . which establishes itself as a *de facto* government in unoccupied Germany unless the majority of the inhabitants. . . . [were] clearly opposed to it'.[111]

The Kapp *Putsch* on 13 March and the subsequent uprising in the Ruhr appeared at first to bear out Stuart's sombre assessments, especially when a delegation of the Ruhr workers told the High Commission that the workers would prefer occupation by French troops rather than by the Reichswehr.[112] Under the protective umbrella of the Allied troops the Rhineland remained relatively tranquil. Cologne was so quiet throughout the weekend of 13 and 14 March that 'the cabarets, restaurants and other resorts of the *schieber* were as full as ever, and no one could have dreamt that anything unusual was afloat'.[113] In Wiesdorf, Langenfeld and Opladen a more threatening situation developed when Workers' Councils took over the town halls and the railway workshops, but they were evacuated when convinced by British officials that Kapp's writ did not run in the Rhineland.[114]

Stuart was convinced that the key to British security in the industrial areas of Cologne and Solingen depended upon an 'attitude of complete neutrality'[115] towards the uprising in the Ruhr, while General Morland, the new Commander of the Rhine Army, was confident 'that our safety here lies in the fact of the balance of power between the militarists on the one hand and the workmen on the other'.[116] Consequently when 1,500 Reichswehr troops retreated across the frontier from the Ruhr into the British Zone on 19 March, they were disarmed and interned for over three weeks, despite requests for their immediate release by the legitimate German government, as British officials feared that a premature move would give rise to 'very strong feelings against the Allies among the industrial population' both in the Ruhr and the Cologne Zone,

---

111. DBFP Ser. 1, vol. 9 (no. 34), pp. 51–2.
112. Ibid., pp. 339–40 (no. 317); see also p. 272 (no. 239).
113. Gedye, *Bystander*, 14 April 1920.
114. 'A Short History', p. 10.
115. DBFP Ser. 1, vol. 9 (no. 193), p. 220.
116. Morland to Wilson, 22.4.20, IWM 73/1/26 file 57.

and lead to further rioting 'and even armed attacks on our own troops'.[117] By the end of March an increasing number of Ruhr insurgents were fleeing over the frontier to escape from the Reichswehr and to surrender to the British authorities. As by 7 April there were 5,000 of them in the British Zone, the Reichswehr soldiers were moved out to camps in the French Zone and from there released in batches back into the unoccupied territory.[118] The dispersal of the insurgent forces was a slower and more complex operation. Simply to drive them back over the border would have invited embarrassing incidents that might have led to awkward questions being asked by Labour MPs in the Commons.[119] The Allied chargés d'affaires in Berlin therefore extracted an offer of a general amnesty from the German government,[120] but as this excluded the leaders of the uprising and escaped criminals, a hard core of some 1,600 insurgents decided to remain in the British Zone.[121] The Allied chargés d'affaires were instructed to seek further clarification in Berlin, but the matter was allowed to drop as the remaining insurgents had all apparently returned by 4 May.[122]

Throughout this period of acute crisis in Germany, the facade of Anglo–French cooperation on the Commission was maintained despite the rupture in relations between London and Paris when the French occupied Frankfurt, Darmstadt, Hanau and Homburg in retaliation against the entry of the Reichswehr into the Neutral Zone. It was Noyes who emerged as the most vociferous critic of the French, and who opposed Degoutte's request for discretionary powers to declare a state of siege in the Mainz bridgehead on the eve of the operation.[123] When Tirard, after Rolin-Jaequemyns, the Belgian Commissioner, had been instructed by Brussels to support the French unconditionally, publicly announced that the High Commission's support for the occupation was now unanimous, Noyes published in the press a notice dissociating himself from the action.[124] Robertson was appalled at this public breach of Allied unity, even though the British government was later to play a key role in forcing French withdrawal.

117. Stuart to Curzon (no. 188125), 22.3.20, FO 371/3781 fos 394–6.
118. 'A Short History', p. 12.
119. DBFP Ser. 1, vol. 9 (no. 430), p. 448.
120. Ibid. (no. 435), pp. 451–2.
121. 'Aufzeichnung', 26.4.20 (RK4233II), FCO Lib. K2131 K585953.
122. DBFP Ser. 1, vol. 9 (no. 435), p. 452.
123. K. Nelson, *Victors Divided*, pp. 164–8.
124. Ibid., p. 167.

The Kapp *Putsch* and the Ruhr uprising gave considerable impetus to French attempts to encourage Rhineland and Bavarian separatism. Degoutte in his monthly report for March emphasized that in the aftermath of the *Putsch* it should be relatively easy 'd'ouvrir à l'influence français les milieux disposés a s'orienter vers nous'.[125] Millerand was influenced by what appeared to be growing support for the anti-Prussian federalist movement in his decision to occupy Frankfurt, which was a key junction for north–south rail traffic. Paléologue, the new Secretary-General at the Quai d'Orsay, even pledged one and a half million francs to finance the setting up of a Catholic press organization and drew up a detailed plan for engineering a Bavarian secession from the Reich.[126] The British government's attitude towards the separatist movements continued to be one of strict neutrality although British officials in Cologne tolerated the setting up of a counter-separatist department by the local Polizeipräsident.[127] This note of ambiguity in the British attitude puzzled German officials in Cologne and Coblenz, who believed that the British wanted to leave their options open in order, later perhaps, to be able to strike some political bargain with the French.[128]

With the collapse of the Kapp *Putsch* and the Ruhr revolt, and Millerand's reluctant agreement at the meeting of the Supreme Council at San Remo in April to evacuate the Maingau, the prospects for unravelling Germany for the time being receded, although the French continued to remain 'in constant and very close contact with all circles . . . which desire to bring about a change in the present structure of the *Reich*'.[129] In September the personnel of the French Press and Information Bureau, which supplied information to the French propaganda newspaper, *Echo du Rhin*, was actually increased.[130] French machinations were primarily opposed in the Rhineland by the Nationalist Society, the Heimatdienst, which was run from Frankfurt and had offices and propaganda departments in Cologne and the other main Rhineland towns.[131] The intense

125. Armée Du Rhin, Rapport Mensuel, Mars 1920, III, p. 5, Vincennes 7N2655.
126. McDougall, *Rhineland Diplomacy*, p. 120.
127. Report by [?] von Prittwitz to Ministerium des Innerns, 4.5.20, FCO Lib. L1766 L515580–83.
128. Ibid.
129. Bernstorff to AA, 23.7.20 (no. 910), Bericht 278, FCO Lib. L1766 L515603–607.
130. Ibid., 24.9.20 (no. 1130), Bericht 351 L515611–13.
131. DBFP Ser. 1, vol. 10 (no. 224), pp. 317–20. See also reports on activities of the Heimatdienst in the British Zone 23.8.20 (C4706) and 9.8.20 (C6976) FO 371/4835 fos 16–23.

unpopularity of the French naturally facilitated the campaign against separatism. Local agents were more suspicious of the British for the very reason that they did not 'follow the foolish French policy of pinpricks, but instead treated the population with understanding without once losing sight of their aims'.[132] What these 'aims' were was not spelt out, but the British were credited with an immense fund of machiavellian cunning!

British prestige in the Rhineland in 1920 was a result of a combination of a small but adequate garrison in Cologne, which was able to block sporadic French efforts to take over the occupation of the city,[133] and of a strong High Commissioner in Coblenz. Frequently with the backing of Noyes, Stuart worked as a good-humoured but effective 'brake' on Tirard in the Commission.[134] In March, no doubt aware that the Reich Factory Council Law had in reality turned the Workers' Councils in unoccupied Germany into mere 'grievance committees',[135] he overcame Tirard's more rigid authoritarianism and persuaded the Commission to agree to their introduction into the Rhineland in June.[136] Later in July, at a sitting of the High Commission 'during which feelings had run high'[137] about the kidnapping of the separatist leader, Dorten, by German agents in occupied territory, Stuart, with the help of General Allen, managed to dissuade Tirard from pressing for draconian punishments against a large number of petty officials indirectly involved, and instead to work through the Conference of Ambassadors to demand the return of Dorten and the punishment of only the most culpable officials. Thanks to Stuart's good working relationship with Tirard, the distrust and bitterness that bedevilled Anglo–French cooperation in Danzig, Upper Silesia and on the IAMCC in Berlin were largely absent in Coblenz. As Robertson observed in his first speech as High Commissioner to the Commission, 'It is hardly a secret that this is almost the only inter-Allied Commission which has progressed without any serious disagreement.'[138]

132. 'Situationsbericht der Rheinischen Volkspflege', 15.8.20. ʒA.KO R43 I/177 fo. 198.
133. Rumours of French attempts to move into Cologne were frequently mentioned by Morland and Wilson. See letters of 12.4.20 (Wilson to Morland) and 4.11.20 (Morland to Wilson), IWM 73/1/26, file 57.
134. Bernstorff called him 'Hemmschuh gegenüber den Franzosen', Bernstorff to AA, 24.9.20 (no. 1130), Bericht 351, FCO Lib. L1766 L1515611-13.
135. Maier, *Recasting Bourgeois Europe*, p. 146.
136. Stuart to Curzon, 10.3.20 (C185107), FO 371/4349 fos 53–7.
137. 'A Short History', p. 19.
138. Minutes of the High Commission, 28 and 29.10.20, 59th Sitting, §I, Min. 1203, FO 894/7 fos 234–5.

Sir Harold Stuart's retirement and replacement by Arnold Robertson was viewed with misgiving both in some quarters of the Foreign Office and by the Germans.[139] One official in London feared that 'his kindly nature will make [him] suffer when there is need for truculence against the wishes of the good Tirard'.[140] He was certainly more francophil than Stuart and was as suspicious of Germany's intentions as General Degoutte. He wrote to the Editor of *The Times*, for instance, that 'as far as we British are concerned there is one essential fact we must never lose sight of, and that is that it is us the Germans still hate and still envy more than any other nation in the world'.[141] Nevertheless he was determined to check French attempts to revise the Treaty unilaterally and to 'prevent [them] from making fools of themselves and from making themselves more hated by the Germans than must necessarily be the case'. He was convinced that Germany wanted to separate France and Britain so that it 'may fall upon the former and then deal with the latter at his [*sic*] leisure'.[142]

Robertson made a vigorous start as High Commissioner. He forcefully dismissed (arguably justified) German complaints, to which the Foreign Office was inclined to give credence, that the High Commission had systematically extended its powers since January.[143] He also reacted sharply to a critical speech on the occupation made by the German Minister of the Interior in the Reichstag, and insisted that it be referred to the Conference of Ambassadors.[144] He was fortunate that there was a lull in strikes and that the Independent Socialist movement had split in October. In November British officials noted as 'a healthy sign' how poorly attended the Communist meetings in the zone were.[145] The food problem was also eased by the activities of the Quakers, who in the absence of any official assistance from London were asked by 'the British military (sic) authorities' to feed the schoolchildren through-

139. Bernstorff to AA, 24.9.20 (Bericht 351); K. Nelson, *Victors Divided*, p. 350.
140. Cooper to Robertson, 7.10.20, Robertson Papers, File I, Germany (The Rhine).
141. Ibid., Robertson to Wickham Steed, 26.4.20.
142. Ibid., Robertson to Cooper, 8.10.20.
143. Robertson to Curzon, 25.10.20 (C9751), and Oliphant to Robertson, 10.11.20 (C10209), FO 371/4805 fos 182–8 and 206–7; 'A Short History', pp. 27–8.
144. Bernstorff to AA, 18.12.20 (no. 1402), Bericht 434, FCO Lib. L1766 L515627-29. Robertson's arguments are contained in 'Memorandum on the speech of Herr Koch . . .', 13.11.20, BA.KO *Nachlass* Kochweser 83 fos 1–4. See also 'A Short History', pp. 28–9.
145. Herbertson, Political Report, no. 16, for period ending 5.11.20 (C10667), FO 371/4805 fos 24–30.

out the British Zone.[146] By tapping local businessmen in Cologne for funds the Quakers were able to feed five thousand children by November and nearly eighteen thousand in February 1921.[147]

To the Germans and many British officials in the Rhineland, however, this calm seemed to be a lull before the storm. On all sides there were rumours that a French occupation of the Ruhr was inevitable and that France would use the issue of the Bavarian Einwohnerwehr as a pretext for action.

146. Library of the Society of Friends, London, Friends Emergency and War Victims Relief Committee, General Committee minutes: Secretary's reports, 31.8.20.
147. Ibid., 2.11.20 and 1.2.21.

−7−

Control Commences

Of the three inter-Allied Control Commissions which began work in January 1920, the IAMCC has rightly claimed most attention from historians, as on it devolved the major part of the task of disarming Germany both economically and militarily. Its work was frequently controversial and potentially impinged on vital political and economic questions affecting the future of the German economy. Inevitably its activities became a focus for the Anglo–French debate on the future of Germany and the execution of the Treaty. The novelty of its duties attracted a number of able and independent-minded officers to the British element of the IAMCC, who as Anglo–French differences intensified, did not hesitate to make their own contributions to the inter-Allied debate. The evaluation of the unpublished second volume of Morgan's *Assize of Arms* and the Ball Papers enable the internal divisions of the British element of the IAMCC to be more fully explored than was possible when Salewski wrote his classic study.[1]

In contrast to the IAMCC, the Naval and Aeronautical Commissions had a much more closely defined and limited task, which the French viewed as basically of secondary importance. In both Commissions there appeared to be an essential identity of interests between the British and French and an absence of ambitious officers dashing off unofficial memoranda to politicians or civil servants in

1. The Ball Papers, which include a fragment of Bingham's Diary, are in the Imperial War Museum. The sole remaining copy of the second volume of the *Assize of Arms*, which is partly still in proofs, and is not complete, is with Mr Barry O'Brien, who most kindly lent it to me. John Fox briefly consulted a copy still in the possession of Methuen and Co. for his seminal article 'Britain and the inter-Allied Military Commission of Control, 1925–26', but in 1976 I was informed that this had disappeared in the firm's amalgamation with Eyre and Spottiswoode and move to New Fetter Lane (G. Strachan to author, 4.5.76). Quite why this volume was never published in 1945 is a mystery. Was Methuen afraid of possible libel cases, or was it that Morgan in fact never completed the text? These sources enable a few more officers in the IAMCC, besides Nollet, 'aus der Anonymität herauszutreten'. (Salewski, *Entwaffnung*, p. 44.)

London. In his own way Admiral Charlton was as rigorous an advocate of the total execution of the naval clauses of the Treaty as Nollet was of the military clauses.

As soon as the Treaty was ratified, the three Control Commissions were able to summon their full complement of personnel into Germany. They were initially faced with an almost impossible task to be executed within an absurdly short time scale. To enforce the Treaty, not only did the IAMCC have to ensure the dissolution of the various paramilitary groups set up since the Armistice, such as the Freikorps, and the Einwohnerwehren, but within three months it had to monitor the metamorphosis of the Imperial Army into the new Reichswehr of 100,000 men, ensure the closure of superfluous armament factories and monitor the destruction of all surplus arms, munitions and war material. The Naval Commission was similarly bound to oversee the demobilization of personnel, take the surrender of all warships in excess of the number permitted by the Treaty and destroy any surplus war material, all within three months.

Inevitably the impossibility, and indeed desirability, of meeting this time scale in the chaotic conditions of early 1920 led to fresh demands in early February by British officials, which were tantamount to a *de facto* Treaty revision. The British General Staff, advised by Malcolm, Haking and Bingham, argued strongly for propping up the existing German government by conceding, 'at all events for 1920', Berlin's demands for a 200,000-man army.[2] Even when the Supreme Council agreed to extend the deadline for creating the 100,000-man army until 10 July, the Army Council still found the reductions premature.[3]

The ambiguity of some of the disarmament clauses exacerbated Anglo–French differences within the IAMCC. It was, for instance, difficult to define what was meant by war material: in an age of total war it could embrace virtually everything. Thus in dealing with the plants used for war production, the Control Commissions could quite literally follow the letter of the Treaty and cripple German industry, or they could use their discretion and destroy only the machinery specifically engaged in manufacturing munitions.[4] Several British members of the Armaments sub-Commission, which Bingham personally commanded, strongly advocated the revival of Anglo–German trade links. Dr Watts, its civilian technical adviser, informed Lord Kilmarnock, then chargé

2. 'Present State of Germany', Memo. by Gen. Staff, 5.2.20 (18C), WO 155/2.
3. H.J. Creedy to Undersecretary of State, FO, 26.2.20 (no. 01545033) and B. Cubitt to the same, 20.4.20, WO 155/2.
4. Morgan, *Assize of Arms*, vol. 2, pp. 316–17. Salewski, *Entwaffnung*, p. 100.

d'affaires in Berlin, that the German chemical industry was anxious to resume commercial relations with British firms, and urged that an arrangement should be reached whereby British manufacturers should supply German industry with raw materials, which could then be worked up into products that could be re-imported into Britain.[5] Another member, based at Cologne, Major C.J.P. Ball, who was later to become an industrialist of international standing and the pioneer of the UK magnesium industry, used his position to establish commercial links between the factories he inspected and the London company of F.A. Hughes and Co. Ltd, general merchants, importers and exporters, for which he seems to have been working in his free time as a 'freelance'. Later in 1923 he joined the company and became its managing director.[6] Given this practical commitment to re-establishing trade links with Germany within his own sub-Commission, it is not surprising that Bingham played a key part in pressing for clarification from the Conference of Ambassadors of the interpretation of Article 168, which prescribed the suppression of all establishments used for the manufacture of war materials within three months. The Conference on 10 February accepted the substance of Bingham's advice and defined the scope of Article 168 to mean that only plant designed solely for war manufacture should be destroyed; semi-specialized plant would have to be converted for commercial purposes, while all 'non-specialized' plant could be left intact.[7] In coming to this decision 'la Conférence répondait aux nécessités du moment',[8] by recognizing that mass unemployment would aggravate the internal situation and that the destruction of German industry and payment of reparations were mutually incompatible opposites. In retrospect Morgan commented that 'the result of these concessions was that Germany was left by us in possession of more than 90 per cent of all machines, which had been employed in manufacture during the war'.[9]

Although the factory owners, particularly in the British Zone,

5. DBFP Ser. 1, vol. 10 (no. 122), pp. 199–200.

6. Ball Papers, IWM 72/116/3. See for example Ball to Hethey, 8 and 29.1.20. Ball eventually built up a factory for the production of rockite synthetic resins and moulding powders at Feltham (Anon., *F.A. Hughes Centenary Year*, Epsom, 1968: Centenary brochure). When Bingham retired from the Lieutenant-Generalship of Jersey in 1929 he did some part-time personnel work there for Ball. (Information given to the author by Humphrey Bingham and Mr Jim Ball.) See also below ch. 11, pp. 213–14.

7. DBFP Ser. 1, vol. 10 (no. 8), p. 18.

8. Nollet, quoted in Salewski, *Entwaffnung*, p. 104.

9. Morgan, *Assize of Arms*, vol. 2, p. 319.

were anxious to have their plants cleared for peacetime production, the Control Commissions initially encountered a stubborn passive resistance from the German military and naval authorities. A conference between the senior members of the IAMCC and the Germany Army Peace Commission on 29 January, for instance, foundered acrimoniously on von Cramon's determination to chair the meeting;[10] while the German Naval Peace Commission, despite Charlton's stern injunction 'to work and not to talk', pleaded that a lack of coal would delay the punctual delivery of the warships to the Allies, and fought a skilful rearguard action against handing over the relevant technical documents demanded in Article 209 of the Treaty.[11] What little progress that was being achieved was abruptly halted by the publication on 3 February of the War Criminals list, which included the names of the German Crown Prince, Hindenburg, Tirpitz and Ludendorff. Bingham was convinced that the demands were 'idiotic' and had done more to unite Germany than any other incident since the Armistice. However, the acceptance by the Allies on 13 February of the German proposal that the War Criminals should be tried before a German rather than an Allied Court, opened up the way for the resumption of control.[12]

On the eve of the Kapp *Putsch* it is not surprising that the Allied inspection committees should have run into considerable hostility from both the Reichswehr and civilians. At Bremen officers of the Naval Control Commission were assaulted by a hostile crowd. Major Geary, the president of a 'travelling committee' inspecting arsenals and fortifications in central Germany, met with less overtly aggressive behaviour, but he was nevertheless treated to a noisy demonstration in the Dresden barracks on the day before the Kapp *Putsch*, which he described later in his report: 'When we arrived in the barracks, from all the windows the soldiers put their heads out and started blowing trumpets, shouting and making cat calls and then started singing "Deutschland ober [*sic*] Alles" . . .'[13] Only by exploiting the Germans' desire to get rid of the Allied Committee did Geary manage to complete his inspection.

10. Bingham, Diary, 3.2.20, IWM 72/116/4; Roddie, *Peace Patrol*, p. 78; Morgan, *Assize of Arms*, vol. 1, p. 48.
11. 'Minutes of First Meeting between IAMCC and German Naval Peace Commission on board HMS "Malaya"', 17.1.20, pp. 11–12, ADM 116 1932, Pack no. 46/A; Salewski, *Entwaffnung*, pp. 94–5.
12. Bingham, Diary, 13.2.20, IWM 72/116/4; Toynbee, *Survey of International Affairs, 1920–23*, London, 1925, p. 98.
13. DBFP Ser. 1, vol. 10 (no. 22), p. 32; Bingham, Diary, 'Experiences of Major Geary from March 1st to March 22nd', IWM 72/116/4.

The Kapp *Putsch* and the subsequent uprising in the Ruhr again brought the work of the Control Commissions to a complete halt. Kapp, backed by units of the Reichswehr and several Freikorp brigades, seized Berlin, Breslau and Königsberg, forcing the legitimate Bauer government to flee to Stuttgart. Berlin and most other cities were paralysed by a general strike, called in protest against Kapp by the trade unions. Allied diplomats and Control Commission personnel in Berlin were cut off for nearly a week from any contact with the outside world. Bingham had to rely on the British garrison in Danzig to send up provisions by destroyer to Stettin, where they could be collected by an army lorry from Berlin. For a week life in Berlin was both intensely uncomfortable and potentially dangerous. There was 'no heating, very little food . . . no electric light . . . and no railways. A wretched existence'.[14] Outside Berlin there was the risk that the small isolated Allied Committees would be caught up in the cross-fire between the Kapp forces and workers. General Morland at Cologne reported that there were 'screams for help from various detached officers', who wanted lorries to bring them safely back to the Rhineland.[15] In fact, British officers returning to Berlin had little trouble negotiating the numerous road blocks set up by the rival forces; for instance, one officer arriving from Breslau by car was warmly greeted by a local Einwohnerwehr unit, and its commander insisted on accompanying him to the next barrier, so that he would be able to negotiate it safely. However, at Dresden Major Geary blundered twice into heavy street fighting whilst sight-seeing and narrowly escaped being hit by a couple of stick grenades.[16]

Kapp, of course, had no desire to harm Allied personnel, as it was vital to gain Allied recognition. Both Nollet and Bingham were informed through von Cramon that Kapp would honour the Peace Treaty 'as far as the honour and capacity of the German people allowed'.[17] Although a joint meeting of the Allied representatives on 13 March in Berlin decided to ignore the Kapp regime, Kapp and his press officer, the notorious Trebitsch-Lincoln, the former Liberal MP, who had been imprisoned in Britain during the war for espionage, spread rumours which oscillated between claiming that either the whole British Cabinet or

14. Bingham, Diary, 17 and 22.3.20, IWM 72/116/4. For fuller details of the *Putsch* see Erger, *Der Kapp–Lüttwitz Putsch*; also F.L. Carsten, *The Reichswehr and Politics*, Oxford, 1966, pp. 78–88.
15. Morland to Wilson, 22.3.20, IWM 73/1/26, file 57.
16. Bingham, Diary, 18.3.20 and 'Experiences of Major Geary', IWM 72/116/4.
17. Kapp to General von Crammon, 17.3.21 (3u FM.4228), FCO Lib. L321 L098398.

individual British officers supported the *Putsch*, which despite energetic denials by both Kilmarnock and Bingham continued to be published in foreign newspapers.[18] On 17 March, isolated and defeated by the general strike, Kapp fled Berlin, to be followed on the next day by the Naval Division, which was then replaced by units of the Reichswehr, 'believed to be faithful to the Ebert (sic) Government'.[19]

When Bauer returned to Berlin, he was anxious to send in troops to pacify the Ruhr, which lay in the demilitarized zone. Nollet, who had been instructed to withhold permission unless he received a contrary order from Foch, was adamant that Reichswehr intervention would be both useless and dangerous. Bingham was inclined to agree and observed in his dairy: 'in the Ruhr District, wherever there are troops, there are troubles: where there are no troops, there are no troubles. It is the old French conundrum: Does the egg come from the chicken or the chicken from the egg?'[20] Ultimately, however, this was an issue that could only be decided by the Supreme Council itself. When on 3 April the German government finally sent in the Reichswehr, the French precipitated a major crisis in the *Entente* by occupying Darmstadt, Frankfurt, Hanau and Homburg without consulting their Allies. The British government protested vigorously against this unilateral French action, and Derby was instructed consequently to boycott all further discussions on the execution of the Treaty until the French agreed in the future to confer first with their allies before taking any similar action again. It was not until 11 April that Millerand agreed and a serious Anglo–French rift was closed.[21]

When the Supreme Council met at San Remo on 19 April the slow progress of the Control Commissions was reviewed. Millerand pressed strongly for an immediate occupation of the Ruhr as a '*gage*' or pledge to guarantee the prompt execution of the reparation and disarmament clauses of the Treaty, but in the face of British opposition conceded, instead, to Lloyd George's proposal to summon the German leaders to a conference at Spa in order to 'see what explanation they could give and what they could do',[22] provided the Allies agreed first to threaten sanctions should their demands

18. DBFP Ser. 1, vol. 9 (nos 95 and 142), pp. 136 and 166; J.T. Trebitsch-Lincoln, *The Autobiography of an Adventurer*, London, 1931, pp. 168–81; Roddie, *Peace Patrol*, pp. 147–51.
19. DBFP Ser. 1, vol. 9, (no. 202), p. 236.
20. Ibid. (no. 130), pp. 158–60; Bingham, Diary, 22.3.20, IWM 72/116/4.
21. Carsten, *Britain and The Weimar Republic*, pp. 38–43.
22. DBFP Ser. 1, vol. 8 (no. 2), p. 7; G. Riddell, *Lord Riddell's Intimate Diary of the Peace Conference and After, 1918–23*, London, 1933, pp. 185–90.

not then be carried out. In preparation for the Spa Conference, Bingham was instructed to compile a detailed progress report of the IAMCC's work.

Morgan meanwhile redoubled his efforts to unmask von Seeckt's subterfuges. Of all the British officers in the Effectives Sub-Commission, Morgan was the only one with sufficient German and intellectual training to master the subject. He wrote his reports 'like a Counsel's opinion for clients, with the utmost economy of language and no frills, they ran into tens of thousands of words and involved . . . a most intensive study of the vast and intricate organisation of the German Army from top to bottom'.[23] The key to his work lay in the discovery that the pension offices throughout Germany were really camouflaged mobilization offices corresponding to the old *Bezirk* departments of the pre-war army.[24]

The monitoring of the destruction of German artillery and the inspection of factories in unoccupied Germany did not recommence until late April. Bingham himself visited the depots in Schweinemünde and admired the 'beautiful new heavy guns and carriages' and confided in his diary that 'it seem[ed] wicked to break them up, but from the point of view of our job it must be done.'[25] He was optimistic that the bulk of the 20,000 guns, the existence of which the Germans had reported to his sub-Commission, would be destroyed within three months. The inspection of the enormous number of factories which had been producing war material was only in 'its infancy'.[26] At Krupp a Control Committee was set up in May. The reactions of Bingham and Nollet to the discovery that the company was completing an order of some sixty 77 mm guns to replace existing models for the Reichswehr illustrates the different approaches these two generals had to German disarmament: Bingham initially approved the manufacture on the grounds that Krupp was legitimately replacing older guns, which the Reichswehr were permitted to keep; Nollet on the other hand was adamant that construction could not start until the IAMCC had decided which factories would be allowed to continue to produce war material.[27] Bingham shared his own government's more relaxed attitude to the interpretation of the Versailles clauses. In his memorandum to the War Office in prep-

23. Morgan, *Assize of Arms*, vol. 2, Galley slip VI (01-929).
24. Ibid., pp. 196–201 (ch. XIV, 'Von Seeckt's First Move').
25. Bingham, Diary, 11.5.20, IWM 72/116/4.
26. DBFP Ser. 1, vol. 10 (no. 110), p. 162.
27. For the setting up of the Committee see Vincennes, Jacobsen, IK 3, Box 3; Krupp to von Haniel, 20.5.20 (A.A. FM 6300), FCO Lib. L320 L097966-70.

aration for the Spa Conference, Bingham gave a moderately optimistic report on the progress made by the IAMCC and reported that 'generally speaking' the disarmament clauses were being executed. Essentially he was convinced of the good will of both the German government and people and that 'the very sight of a soldier is a red rag to 90 per cent of the inhabitants of the country'.[28] It is arguable that Bingham was over-optimistic and therefore rather careless of detail and red tape, but in 1920 his attitude was closer to the mainstream of British thinking on Germany than was Morgan's insistence on absolute disarmament.

In the course of the summer Morgan became increasingly critical of Bingham's apparent naivety and accused him of accepting dangerously inaccurate statistics from the Germans on the numbers of field guns, rifles and machine guns destroyed. He also dispatched his reports on the structure of the German army independently of Bingham to the War Office, and in an attempt to dissuade Lloyd George's 'feline mind'[29] from conceding to German demands for an army of 200,000, in May briefed Lloyd George's private Secretary, Phillip Kerr, with the full details of von Seeckt's policies. This had little effect as Lloyd George remained 'much more alarmed about the failure to destroy the guns than about the reduction of the German Army'.[30] In August Bingham attempted to impose a 'muzzling order' on Morgan, which was later rescinded at the direct request of the Director of Military Intelligence at the War Office, to stop his independent dispatch of reports to London. It is likely that Bingham wished to ensure that as head of the British element on the Commission, his own views were not consistently contradicted by one of his colleagues. To counter this attempt to isolate Morgan, Nollet appointed him to the newly constituted 'inner cabinet' of the Commission, which Bingham significantly was not invited to join. Morgan was instructed 'directly to report for the information of Marshal Foch, on all kinds of vital questions at issue with the German Government'.[31] The whole incident inflamed relations between Bingham and Morgan and damaged the effectiveness of the British element on the Commission, which increasingly became polarized between these two men. The leading supporters of Bingham were Roddie in Berlin and Colonel Weber and Major Ball of the Cologne District Armaments

28. DBFP Ser. 1, vol. 10 (no. 110), p. 154; Bingham, Diary, 4.5.20, IWM 72/116/4.
29. Morgan, *Assize of Arms*, vol. 2, p. 243.
30. DBFP Ser. 1, vol. 8 (no. 32), p. 342.
31. For details of this incident see Morgan, *Assize of Arms*, vol. 2, Galley slips VI (01-929) and VII (02-907).

sub-Commission, all of whom did not hesitate to speak their minds freely to their German contacts.[32] Ball was intent on building up a business based on Anglo–German trade and therefore had a vested interest in opposing French policy which could only result in French economic domination of the Ruhr and Rhineland. The Bingham–Roddie–Weber–Ball axis was significantly strengthened by the appointment of Lord D'Abernon as British Ambassador in Berlin in June 1920.[33] He had been appointed by Lloyd George primarily as an economic expert, to encourage the restoration of the German economy so that Germany could pay reparations. He had therefore little understanding of the intricacies of disarmament and was more alarmed by the threat of communism than by a revival of German militarism. In 1944 Morgan castigated him as being 'of all Englishmen . . . more responsible than any other for the present catastrophe' and blamed him for deliberately misleading the British government about the true state of German disarmament. According to Morgan he completely overshadowed Bingham: 'a melancholy story . . . of a well meaning but weak man dominated by a strong man'.[34]

When the Spa Conference opened on 6 July, it was clear that German disarmament was far from completed. The reduction of the Army to 100,000 men had not been carried out, many of the paramilitary formations like the Einwohnerwehr were still intact, the General Staff survived in the guise of the Abwickelungsamt and thousands of factories awaited inspection. Neither had the Reichstag yet passed the necessary legislation to ban the import and export of war material or to abolish conscription. The Germans were thus presented with what appeared to be an ultimatum, although in reality it contained important concessions: Lloyd George proposed that the final reduction of the Reichswehr should be delayed until 1 January 1921, provided that the Sipo and the Einwohnerwehr were immediately disarmed, all surplus armaments and equipment surrendered, legislation passed abolishing conscription and the remaining aerial and naval clauses of the Treaty fulfilled. This was accepted by Millerand on condition that if the Reichstag had not

32. See for instance the report from Nonn, Deutsche Verbindungsstelle, Köln, to Hauptverbindungsstelle, Berlin, 22.1.21 (no. 4170), FCO Lib. 9285 H255030-34.
33. D.A. Holt, 'The British Embassy of Lord D'Abernon, 1920–26', May, 1971, pp. 103 ff. (thesis submitted for the degree of PhD to University of London, but author died before the award was made), FCO Library. See D'Abernon, *An Ambassador of Peace, 1920–26*, vol. 1 (25.6.20), London, 1929/30, p. 53.
34. Morgan, *Assize of Arms*, vol. 2, Galley slips IV (62V CR 167) and V (62V CR 168).

passed the necessary legislation by 1 September or if the German army was not reduced to 150,000 by 1 October, the Allies would 'proceed to occupy a further part of German territory, whether it be the Ruhr basin or some other district, and [would] only evacuate it on the date when all the conditions of this arrangement have been fulfilled'.[35]

Strengthened by the threat of sanctions in Spa, the tempo of the IAMCC's activities accelerated over the next five months. By November a seemingly impressive record of progress was reported by Bingham: conscription was legally abolished, the army cut to 150,000 men and large quantities of artillery surrendered for destruction. Over 2,000 factories had been finally cleared for peacetime production.[36] Yet opportunities for procrastination and subterfuge by the German authorities abounded. Admiral Charlton, for instance, reported in December that the IAMCC was 'experiencing great and increasing opposition to their work' and that 'naval war material [was] being secretly distributed and concealed throughout Germany, palpably with the consent and active participation of the naval representatives of the German Government'.[37] The Bavarians also stubbornly refused to dissolve the Einwohnerwehr. By the end of the year this became the key issue between the IAMCC and the Reich government and threatened to trigger off a French occupation of the Ruhr. Allied pressure for the simultaneous disarmament of both the Sipo and the Einwohnerwehr placed the German government in a genuine predicament. Disarming the police and attempts to call in weapons held by the civil population paradoxically enhanced the role of the Einwohnerwehr as a bulwark against revolution.[38] The Bavarians also appeared to accept the prospect of a Ruhr occupation with equanimity, believing rumours spread by French agents to the effect that they would be given preferential terms for the delivery of coal, and in the event of their declaration of independence, even allowed to maintain an armed Einwohnerwehr. The chill warning of the Prussian envoy in Munich that the Bavarians could become 'the grave diggers of the Reich'[39] may have made little impact in Munich, but it was certainly heeded in London where both the

35. DBFP Ser. 1, vol. 8 (nos 42 and 50), pp. 418–20, 479; Salewski, *Entwaffnung*, p. 136.
36. DBFP Ser. 1, vol. 10 (no. 312), pp. 413–27.
37. Charlton to Conf. of Amb., 18.12.20 (69/38/A/1), ADM 116 1932, Pack no. 38/A/1.
38. Mayer to AA, 9.9.20 (no. 419), FCO Lib. 9861 H319372-73.
39. Preussische Gesandschaft, München to AA, 22.9.20 (no. 374), p. 3, FCO Lib. L722 L222651-56.

government and industry and the banks dreaded the consequences for European recovery of a French occupation of the Ruhr. The attitude of key British officials in Berlin was ambivalent towards the Einwohnerwehr. D'Abernon, Malcolm and Bingham all agreed that the Einwohnerwehr and the Orgesch in the event of a communist uprising 'would powerfully serve the cause of order'.[40] D'Abernon advised that the IAMCC should in the short term concentrate on the destruction of war material and allow the Reich government time to negotiate with the Bavarians a gradual disarmament of the Einwohnerwehr. This line was endorsed by both the Foreign Office and the Army Council, which laconically observed that 'there is no doubt that Bolshevism and not Germany, is at present the danger to the peace of Europe'.[41]

These views were, of course, not shared by Nollet. On 9 November, when the German Foreign Minister, Simons, asked Nollet to give the Bavarians more time to disarm the Einwohnerwehr, he grudgingly agreed to send the request on to Paris, but stressed that 'the matter must go forward'.[42] A month later the Council of the IAMCC dispatched a 'very stiff and uncompromising'[43] letter to the German government demanding the immediate disarmament and dissolution of the Einwohnerwehr. Bingham, isolated on the Council, 'made no remark, although he showed an inclination to admit to the carrying out of the disarmament of the *Selbstschutzorganisationen* the possibility of a delay, though he said nothing of its duration'.[44] Bingham's ineffectual attempts to delay the dispatch were destroyed by his old enemy Morgan, who 'made certain observations intended to strengthen the arguments contained in the letter'.[45] Inevitably Nollet's note risked precipitating an issue, which the British felt was no longer acute, into a major crisis. At the Foreign Office one official observed that '[t]aking into consideration the view of our own War Office, of Lord D'Abernon and presumably General Bingham, . . . it is difficult to understand how [the note] . . . can be said to represent the views of an inter-Allied Commission on which HMG are represented . . .', and suggested that the War

40. DBFP Ser. 1, vol. 10 (no. 325), p. 449. Crowe minuted on this: 'Lord D'Abernon gives very sound advice'; FO 371/4758 (28.11.20), fo. 44. See also D'Abernon, *Ambassador of Peace*, vol. 1 (23.11.20), p. 92.
41. Cubitt to Undersecretary of State, FO 24.12.20 (C14711), FO 371/4758 fo. 172.
42. Report of Meeting between Simons and Nollet (no. F12736), 9.11.20, FCO Lib. 9285 H254624.
43. DBFP Ser. 1, vol. 10 (no. 334), p. 458.
44. Nollet to Foch, 18.12.20 (no. 1252), FO 371/4758 fo. 189.
45. Ibid.

Office should 'enquire how General Bingham came to consent to the despatch of a note like this, which raises grave political issues'.[46] Despite some reservations by Crowe, who pointed out that Nollet was only enforcing the Treaty, Curzon secured Cabinet support for requesting the French government to instruct Nollet to refer back in the future all such contentious issues to the Conference of Ambassadors.[47] His action won the backing of the Italians, whose Ambassador in Berlin felt that the whole question of disarmament 'had grown beyond the competence of the Control Commission'.[48]

By the end of 1920 the potential for disagreement between London and Paris over the progress made by Germany was great. Both the War Office and the Foreign Office agreed that Germany was no longer a military threat to Britain. The War Office consistently urged a 'policy of conciliation'[49] towards Germany. By November Bingham was sure that 'Germany at the present moment, both in men, materials and factories . . . [was] in an infinitely worse state of preparedness [*sic*] for a great war than England in 1914'.[50] The British government felt sufficiently optimistic to consider, in the autumn of 1920, plans for the eventual replacement of the Control Commissions by a permanent League of Nations committee in Geneva.[51] British officials were becoming increasingly impatient with French insistence on the absolute fulfilment of the Treaty under threat of further occupation of German territory. In January 1921 Waterlow argued that it was 'vital to the peace and recovery of Europe that the penal method should be, if not replaced, at least modified, by some system of good conduct prizes', and suggested that in return for completing disarmament, Germany should be rewarded with a cut in the size of the armies of occupation.[52]

46. Wigram's Minute of 17.12.20 on Nollet's Note to German Government of 11.12.20, FO 371/4758 fo. 101.
47. Ibid., fo. 102; Cabinet Conclusions of 30.12.20 (80/20), CAB 23/23 fos 348–9.
48. AA Presseabteilung der Reichsregierung to von Haniel (no. F59) 30.12.20, FCO Lib. L319 L097794.
49. General Staff Memorandum, 6.8.20 (C7032), FO 371/4741 fos 71–2; D'Abernon, *Ambassador of Peace*, vol. 1 (28.12.20), p. 106.
50. 'Report on Germany's Military Strength on 1.11.20', 2.11.20, FO 371/4757 fos 206–10.
51. D'Abernon to Curzon, 13.11.20 (C11471), FO 371/4758 fos 6–8; FO reply to D'Abernon (signed L. Oliphant), 22.11.20 (no. 1068), FO 371/4758 fo. 9.
52. DBFP Ser. 1, vol. 16 (no. 577), p. 621.

PART III

The Disintegrating Entente,
January 1921–December 1922

Introduction: The Diplomatic Background

The problems facing British officials in Germany during the crisis-ridden years of 1921–2 cannot be fully understood without an initial summary of the continuing and intensifying Anglo–French divergences over the execution of the Treaty of Versailles, which determined both the context and the diplomatic climate in which they had to discharge their duties. Britain and France were not strong enough to enforce their own interpretations of the Treaty upon each other; consequently neither the French plan for establishing an absolute hegemony over Germany nor the British desire to recreate a workable balance of power triumphed, and Europe continued to stagger from crisis to crisis.

When the Briand administration was formed in January 1921, ominously for Lloyd George, France's international position was stronger than it had been a year earlier. The Franco–Polish alliance, which was on the verge of being signed, buttressed French influence in eastern Europe, while the collapse in coal prices and the devastating impact of the post-war slump on Britain temporarily liberated France from British restraint.[1] The most pressing problem confronting the Allies in early 1921 was the question of German reparation payments.[2] At the Paris Conference in January, Britain and France agreed upon a provisional schedule for reparation payments, totalling 226 billion (milliards, or American billions) gold marks over a 42-year period, but this was rejected by the German government, which, bowing to opposition from the industrialists and public opinion, produced its own figures a month later at the first London Conference. These amounted to a modest overall payment of 30 billion gold marks, and were also conditional upon the retention of Upper Silesia. The offer was so obviously inadequate that Lloyd George had little option but to agree to the immediate occupation of Düsseldorf, Duisburg and Ruhrort, the

1. McDougall, *Rhineland Diplomacy*, pp. 139 ff.
2. For a succinct account of the reparation issue see H. Ronde, *Von Versailles bis Lausanne*, Stuttgart and Cologne, 1950, pp. 42 ff.; Northedge, *The Troubled Giant*, pp. 173 ff., and Maier, *Recasting Bourgeois Europe*, pp. 233 ff.

setting up of a Rhenish customs regime under Allied control and a payment of a 50 per cent export levy by the German government. This failure to agree on a global sum for reparation at the London Conference was to have significant consequences for the future of Anglo–French relations. Lloyd George's policy of pursuing a step-by-step normalization of relations with Germany through a series of international conferences received a severe check, while it put Briand under immense pressure from French public opinion to resort to draconian sanctions against the Germans and to concede nothing in Upper Silesia or over the disarmament question. It accentuated the differences between London and Paris and in the summer of 1921 put the *Entente* under great strain.

At the end of April the Reparation Commission completed its study of Germany's financial liabilities under the Treaty of Versailles and finally fixed the German debt at 132 billion gold marks. The report was first discussed at Lympne where Briand was able to manoeuvre a reluctant and hesitant Lloyd George into agreeing to a Ruhr occupation should Germany not accept its findings. Given American isolation, it was still axiomatic in London that only by cooperating with France could Britain mitigate the worst consequences of a Ruhr occupation.[3]

On 5 May at the second London Conference the Allied leaders dispatched an ultimatum to Berlin giving the Germans a week to accept the new schedule of reparation payments and the disarmament measures stipulated first in their note of 29 January.[4] As the Fehrenbach government had fallen, Lloyd George successfully encouraged Joseph Wirth to form a government willing to accept the ultimatum by hinting that he would support an interpretation of the ambiguous plebiscite result in Upper Silesia, which would ensure the retention of the key industrial region by Germany.[5]

In May Upper Silesia was plunged into chaos by an armed revolt led by Korfanty, who was intent on demonstrating the region's essentially Polish character. His forces quickly established themselves at the so-called Korfantry line some 80 kilometres to the west of Kattowitz. The Plebiscite Commission, bowing to *force majeure*, signed a preliminary agreement with the insurgents recognizing their position. In a speech that reverberated through the capitals of Europe Lloyd George rejected the agreement on 14 May and pointedly argued that if the Allies could not restore order, the

3. DBFP Ser. 1, vol. 16 (no. 446), p. 473.
4. Salewski, *Entwaffnung*, p. 173.
5. Cienciala and Komarnicki, *From Versailles to Locarno*, p. 66.

Germans should be permitted to do so. Briand threatened an occupation of the Ruhr should the Reichswehr intervene, while in Silesia German Selbstschutz forces began their counter-attack. The dispatch of British troops to Silesia eased the tension between London and Paris, but at the Supreme Council in August complete deadlock was reached, and was only broken by referring the whole problem of the future of Upper Silesia to the League of Nations, which ultimately gave a judgement more in accord with French rather than British interests.[6]

By the early autumn of 1921 France had temporarily regained the initiative in Europe. Not only did her will prevail in Upper Silesia, but Loucheur, Briand's Minister for the Liberated Regions, negotiated the Wiesbaden Accords with Rathenau, the German Minister for Reconstruction, which aimed to increase the amount of reparations delivered in kind and envisaged 'direct Franco–German cooperation as the core of western European reconstruction'.[7] For Britain the Accords raised the spectre of a potentially powerful challenge of a Franco–German economic combine; but by December Lloyd George, no longer distracted by the Irish problem, which had been partly solved by the conclusion of the Free State Treaty, was rapidly re-establishing his leadership within the *Entente*. Opposition from both French and German industrialists had effectively vetoed the implementation of the Accords and consequently the way was open for his 'grand design'[8] for rebuilding Russia with German assistance. He was persuaded both by British bankers[9] and by the persuasive arguments of Walter Rathenau himself, who visited London in December 1921,[10] that in the short term Germany needed to be granted a temporary moratorium, but in the longer term he was convinced that the key to the payment of reparations and European economic revival lay in the prosperity which an international scheme for the reconstruction of Russia would generate. It appeared to square the circle. It would bring

6. Wandycz, *France*, pp. 226–37; F.G. Campbell, 'The Struggle for Upper Silesia, 1919–22', *Journal of Modern History*, vol. 42, no. 3, 1970, pp. 361–85; Cienciala and Komarnicki, *From Versailles to Locarno*, pp. 65–82.
7. C. Fink, *The Genoa Conference*, Chapel Hill and London, 1984, p. 18. See also D. Felix, *Walther Rathenau and the Weimar Republic*, Baltimore, 1971, pp. 75–8.
8. McDougall, *Rhineland Diplomacy*, p. 175.
9. 'Copy of Memorandum dated 24.11.21 handed by the Governor to the Chancellor of the Exchequer, 30.11.21'; Memorandum (by M. Norman) for Cabinet, 27.11.21; Memorandum by Sir Robert Kindersley 28.11.21, Back of England OV 34/100 fos 6–8, 12, 13.
10. Felix, *Walther Rathenau*, pp. 112–14; see also H. Kessler, *Walther Rathenau, Sein Leben und sein Werk*, 2nd edn, Wiesbaden, 1962, ch. 10.

back Russia and Germany to the concert of powers under conditions laid down by a British-dominated *Entente*. It would also have the added bonus that it would direct German exports into eastern Europe rather than towards the Empire.

Escalating German inflation in November and the subsequent announcement by Wirth on 15 December that Germany could not meet the next instalment of reparation payments made an Anglo–French agreement on reparations a matter of urgency. Briand came to London on 18 December where he made the one demand, which if granted would have given the French government sufficient confidence to introduce an element of flexibility into their reparation policy. He proposed an Anglo–French pact or 'broad alliance in which the two powers would guarantee each other's interests in all parts of the world, act closely together in all things, and go to each other's assistance wherever these . . . were threatened'.[11]

Both Lloyd George's reconstruction plans for Russia and Briand's alliance proposal were discussed at Cannes on 6 January 1922, where Briand agreed, in principle, to calling an economic conference on Russia to be held at Genoa, but rejected a British offer of a ten-year defence pact to protect France against unprovoked aggression, as it failed to guarantee the permanent demilitarization of the Rhineland. Briand's apparent subordination to Lloyd George led to his downfall. He was summoned by the Senate's Foreign Affairs Commission to Paris and ordered to cancel any engagements he had already entered into. To avoid possible defeat in the Chamber Briand resigned on 12 January and was replaced by Raymond Poincaré three days later.[12]

Poincaré was determined to strengthen the *Entente*, but the essential prerequisite for this remained a British guarantee both of the Rhineland's long-term demilitarization and of the status quo in eastern Europe. The Cabinet's fear that this was tantamount to conceding French hegemony in Europe, denied France the necessary security which would have enabled her to grant concessions to Germany. Poincaré's dilemma was further intensified by the insolubility of the reparation problem. The financial pressure on France could have been eased if America had negotiated a generous debt settlement with Britain, but American fiscal and economic policy blocked this. American tariffs prevented the building up of favourable trade balances by the European powers, and the creation of the World Debt Funding Commission by Congress ensured that

11. Fink, *Genoa Conference*, p. 35.
12. McDougall, *Rhineland Diplomacy*, pp. 178–80.

Washington could cut neither British nor French debts. This in turn ensured that Britain could make no financial concessions to France, who consequently redoubled the pressure on Germany.[13]

The Conference opened on 10 April 1922 and was a disaster. In the absence of concessions from either London or Washington, Poincaré stubbornly vetoed the raising of any topics that might have resulted in the revision of the Peace Treaty; Britain's hopes of finding the key to reparation payments and economic revival were thus blocked, and Lloyd George was unable to prevent Germany and Russia from negotiating the Rapallo Agreement in which both powers mutually renounced claims for war damages. It was assumed immediately in Paris that the Agreement contained secret military clauses and thus intensified French fears and suspicions of Germany. Throughout the summer Poincaré remained adamantly opposed to any concessions to Germany. In June the French delegate on the Reparation Commission rejected proposals by the Banker's Committee for reducing Germany's total debt and stabilizing the German economy in preparation for the issue of an international loan. Within Germany the assassination of Rathenau, who had become Foreign Minister in January 1922, in June marked the virtual collapse of Wirth's policy of fulfilment and on 12 July the German government headed for a confrontation with Poincaré, when it requested a two-year moratorium. Any remaining chances of concessions from Poincaré were destroyed on 1 August when Britain announced in the Balfour note that in the absence of a general scheme for the cancellation of inter-Allied debts, she would insist on the repayment from her debtors of the sum she owed America.[14] Superficially this appeared a generous offer, but in reality Britain's demand for punctual payment from her allies contrasted painfully with the concessions Lloyd George was advocating for Germany in order to facilitate the payment of reparations and economic recovery. The Balfour note decisively hardened opinion in France and arguably more than anything else made the Ruhr occupation inevitable. At the London Conference in August Poincaré insisted that the price of a moratorium would have to be the expropriation by the Reparation Commission of the state-owned mines of the Ruhr, the supervision both of the state-owned forests and of the dyestuff industry on the left bank by the Rhineland High Commission, the reintroduction of customs barriers surrounding the Rhineland and the Ruhr ports and a 26 per cent

13. Ibid., p. 200.
14. Ibid., p. 222.

general duty on German exports. Despite reservations by Curzon on the awkward consequences for British interests of French hostility 'in every part of the world', the Cabinet rejected Poincaré's proposals and concluded that 'in the event of final disagreement with France the Prime Minister and his colleagues should offer to refer the question at issue for settlement to the Reparation Commission or the League of Nations'.[15] Lloyd George was ready to call France's bluff and if necessary force an open breach.

Some of the strain was taken out of Anglo–French relations by Lloyd George's fall in October. The new Conservative administration under Bonar Law was more sympathetic to Curzon's desire to achieve an overall settlement with France, not least in the hope of buttressing British interests in the Near and Middle East, but Bonar Law was unwilling to revise the guidelines of the Balfour note of 1 August. Consequently on 27 November the Poincaré cabinet decided finally on the occupation of the Ruhr. The Allied meetings in London in December and in Paris in January, called to consider a fresh German request for a moratorium and an international loan to stabilize the mark, 'were strictly pro forma'.[16] The London Conference was adjourned on 11 December, but before the Allied leaders could reconvene in Paris on 2 January Poincaré had already engineered a legal justification for a Ruhr occupation by establishing through a majority decision an 'almost microscopic'[17] German default in the delivery of wood and telegraph poles. The Paris meeting which broke up on 5 January thus had served little purpose except as a forum for demonstrating the unbridgeable divide between the British and French approaches to reparations. Poincaré summed up the situation in the final session of the conference when, as reported by Lord Crewe, he said:

> there was a ditch between us; that not only the views of the French government and of the French delegation, but the views of the French people made it impossible they could cross it . . . The ground of principle constituting that ditch was this simple question: Is there to be a moratorium with pledges [*gages*] or without pledges?[18]

---

15. Cabinet Conclusions 10.8.22 (44/22), pp. 11 and 15, CAB 23/30 fos 396–411.
16. McDougall, *Rhineland Diplomacy*, p. 239.
17. Sir John Bradbury quoted in Toynbee, *Survey of International Affairs, 1920–23*, p. 191.
18. DBFP Ser. 1 vol. 21 (no. 4), pp. 5–6.

8

The Double Crisis:
Sanctions and Upper Silesia

In the early spring of 1921, to both the Foreign Office and much of British public opinion, the sanctions crisis in the Rhineland and the stubborn and ultimately successful French attempts to secure the industrial regions of Upper Silesia for Poland appeared to be part of a two-pronged attack on Germany aimed at irreparably weakening her, regardless of her Treaty commitment to pay reparations. In December 1920 Lord Hardinge had warned that a Polish victory would, by depriving Germany of the Upper Silesian coal mines, render the French threat to occupy the Ruhr basin 'the more potent'.[1]

The two crises put the local British officials under an almost unbearable strain, by brutally illustrating how weak the basis of British power was on the Continent in the spring of 1921. Both Robertson and Percival were put in the unenviable position of having to maintain British influence without adequate military support. In June the British position in Upper Silesia was powerfully reinforced by persuading Stuart to come out of retirement to replace Percival and by backing his authority with 5,000 troops, but this in turn denuded the Cologne garrison and intensified the pressures on Robertson. It was thus not surprising that Percival broke under the strain in May and that Robertson's increasingly outspoken criticism of the Foreign Office caused him to be transferred to the Consulate of Tangier by the end of the year.

The Rhineland and the Sanctions Crisis, 1921

For British officials in the Rhineland, 1921 was almost as difficult a year as it was for their colleagues in Upper Silesia. The collapse of

1. DBFP Ser. 1, vol. II (no. 119), p. 142.

the British economy,[2] the subsequent emancipation of Paris from British domination of the *Entente*, and the weakness of the British army, ensured that the British element on the Rhineland Commission was essentially on the defensive against French initiatives throughout the year. Relentlessly at all levels French officials continued to encourage the growth of French influence on the Rhine. Tirard explained his tactics in his annual report[3] for 1920: 'Notre action n'y est conçue que sous la forme d'appuis discrets fournis à certains partis, et sous l'aspect d'un effort de rapprochement intellectuel et économique ayant pour objet d'inciter les populations à nous mieux connaître et à se lier à nos intérêts.' He ominously added: 'Mais le champ reste ouvert à une action diplomatique qui pourrait nous fournir, pour la solution du problème, les moyens d'action que le Traité de Versailles a refusé'.

The influence of the French army remained strong within the French element of the High Commission, which in 1919, like the British, had been staffed with a large number of ex-officers.[4] The generals viewed Tirard's propaganda campaign with growing impatience and, as General de Metz, the French Sub-Commissioner in the Palatinate ironically remarked, their overwhelming desire was 'to present France with a province, as Salome . . . produced the head of John the Baptist on a silver bowl . . .'[5] Even in the Cologne Zone British influence seemed to be under siege. General Morland feared that the French would seize the chance to reinforce the bridgehead with their own troops, when the dispatch of four battalions in March to supervise the plebiscite in Upper Silesia virtually halved the British garrison.[6] Robertson felt that the British Zone in the eyes of Whitehall was a remote outpost, worthy of little direct attention.[7] To add insult to injury the Treasury provoked his clerical staff into near revolt by proposing to cut their foreign allowance.[8]

The coincidence of the sanctions crisis with the Upper Silesian plebiscite stretched the Rhine Army to its limit. The actual occupation of the three Ruhr ports on 7 March was swift and without any incidents, except for Belgian troops accidentally firing at the British Rhine Flotilla.[9] The British contribution to the operation

2. A.J.P. Taylor, *English History 1914–45*, Oxford, 1965, p. 145.
3. Tirard to MAE, 12.1.21 (no. 697), MAE Rive Gauche 3 fos 45–63.
4. Lerehenfeld to AA, 16.2.21 (no. 60), p. 2, FCO Lib. 3058 D602894–909.
5. Ibid., p. 4.
6. Morland to Wilson, 26.2.21, IWM 73/1/26 file 57.
7. Robertson to Waterlow, 10.2.21, Robertson Papers, Germany (The Rhine), 2.
8. Petition dispatched by Robertson to FO, 25.2.21 (C4263), FO 371/5882 fos 86–8.
9. Morland to Wilson, 10.3.21, IWM 73/1/26 file 57.

consisted of two squadrons of cavalry, a few tanks, five boats of the Rhineland Flotilla and a squadron of planes, which made demonstration sorties over Düsseldorf.[10] Degoutte had intended the British to occupy the high ground north-east of Oberhausen, but Morland, on discovering that it faced 'a mass of mines and factories' and would be virtually impossible to reinforce in an emergency, moved the line marginally further west.[11] The High Commission, anticipating the establishment of a customs barrier in the west, had already asked its Financial, Economic and Intelligence Committees to prepare a plan which could be put into operation immediately, and was therefore ready on 7 March to apply the customs sanctions on the western frontier. The establishment of an eastern customs frontier was more complex.[12] Robertson was at first not clear whether it was intended as a short-term punitive measure or as a more permanent means for raising revenue, although he was reassured by Curzon that it was primarily a scheme for temporarily exerting pressure on Germany.[13] On the other hand, Tirard was determined to exploit the plan 'to separate the Rhineland, at any rate commercially, from the rest of Germany'.[14] Nevertheless the Commission was able to agree on a rough and ready scheme for levying initially 25 per cent of the existing German tariff, subsequently 50 per cent and then ultimately the full tariff along the border between occupied and unoccupied Germany. Robertson forwarded a copy of these proposals to London, where on 23 March they were endorsed by an inter-departmental committee composed of officials from the Foreign Office, the War Office, the Treasury and the Board of Trade, which also warned of 'the probability that a severance of the Rhineland from Germany by a high customs barrier would lead to the merger of Rhineland and French interests'.[15] After further consideration by the Conference of Ambassadors, the High Commission was empowered to announce that the customs cordon would come into force on 20 April along the borders with unoccupied Germany.[16] It was to be operated by a Customs Managing Board, consisting of British, French and Belgian representatives. General Allen accepted the extension

10. War Diary of General Staff, British Army on the Rhine, 7.3.21, WO 95/24.
11. Morland to Wilson, 10.3.21, IWM 73/1/26 file 57.
12. 'Report for 1921 on the Occupied Territory' (C5036) pp. 31–4, FO 371/10756 fo. 89.
13. DBFP Ser. 1, vol. 16 (no. 453), p. 480.
14. Ibid., (no. 467), p. 496.
15. Inter-Departmental Conference on the Report of the Inter-Allied Rhineland High Commission, 23.3.21 (C6448), FO 371/6021 fos 41–8.
16. 'Report', 1921, p. 32.

of the customs line to the American Zone, provided it could be supervised by personnel of all three Allied powers on the Commission. Despite considerable reservations from the Quai d'Orsay,[17] the Italians were permitted to appoint an official to the Commission with the right to participate in all matters dealing with sanctions.[18] The considerable delay in implementing this scheme caused uncertainty and disruption to trade in the Rhineland. Adenauer and the Cologne Chamber of Commerce ceaselessly bombarded both British officials and the Berlin government with graphic visions of economic ruin.[19]

British officials in Cologne above all feared the impact that sanctions would have on the economy within their own zone. Piggott believed that the Ruhr coal magnates and industrialists would retaliate by creating an artificial coal shortage, which would immediately cause acute unemployment, and that the workers would subsequently direct their anger against the Allies rather than their employers, especially as their union leaders were Prussians or at least firm supporters of the central government in Berlin.[20] Several members of his staff pessimistically conceded to the French that the separation of the Rhineland was now almost inevitable and that Germany could only win it back by another war.[21] Although Robertson was fully aware of the dangers of the customs barrier to British trade and to the Rhineland's economy[22] he saw no option but to support the French fully. He was convinced that 'the only way of bringing the present intolerable situation to an end is to hit the Germans as hard as we can with the customs frontier weapon so . . . that it will frighten the Government at Berlin and make them fear that they may lose the Rhineland'.[23] His most immediate problem was to find the manpower to supervise the customs cordon within the British Zone. This inevitably strained British resources to the utmost. Morland could only provide sufficient troops if a further draft of a minimum of 800 men were sent over to Cologne,[24] but reinforcements were an impossibility because of

17. Note for M. Berthelot, 8.3.21, MAE Rive Gauche 200 fos 32–3.
18. 'Report', 1921, p. 32.
19. Adenauer to Reichskanzler, 4.3.21, and Handelskammer, Köln to same, 5.3.21, FCO. Lib. L1711 L502478-82, 92-93.
20. Le Délégué dans la Zone Britannique to Tirard, 16.3.21 (no. 69 ZW/3), AN AJ 9 4289.
21. Ibid., 8.3.21 (no. 59 ZW/3).
22. DBFP, Ser. 1, vol. 16 (no. 461), pp. 486–8.
23. Ibid. (no. 475), p. 511.
24. Morland to Wilson, 15.3.21, IWM 73/1/26 file 27; Edmonds, *The Occupation*, p. 222.

both the Irish troubles and the imminent threat of strikes by the 'Triple Alliance' of miners, railwaymen and transport workers at home. Indeed in early April four battalions were ordered back from Cologne to England.[25] Wilson was quite frank that in his opinion it was 'more important to knock out a (sic) Sinn Fein than it [was] to catch a battleship coming in through an outpost in front of Cologne',[26] but Robertson was not to be deterred. A few days later he again wrote to Wilson pleading for reinforcements on the grounds that 'the customs barrier along the Rhine and Bridgeheads will effect little or nothing unless we "go all out"', the consequences of which would produce unemployment 'on a large scale', thereby making military reinforcements even more urgent.[27] Wilson, however, remained adamant and insisted that 'owing to the Frocks [the politicians] having flung the British Army out of the window the day after the Armistice, the British Empire at the present moment has no Army worth the name.'[28] The Cabinet tardily granted permission for the recruitment of 150 temporary frontier officials on 9 April,[29] but by the end of the month recruitment had still not begun as a result of protracted negotiations with the Treasury.[30] Robertson was in a situation which had already become familiar to many British officials in Germany: he lacked sufficient manpower to carry out the duties laid upon him. With the help of twenty British customs officials, who arrived in Cologne on 6 April, and fifty-five NCOs and men spared by Morland,[31] Robertson managed to create a skeleton force, of which only seventeen men would be on duty at any one time. In an ironic and critical letter to Curzon,[32] Robertson observed that until such a time as reinforcements came from Britain 'it has been suggested to me that placards with collecting boxes might be erected at the crossroads. On the placards would run the legend: England expects every German to pay his Duty.'

On 20 April the customs barrier between occupied and unoccupied Germany came into force. Initially control was only carried out on the railways and waterways: road traffic was not subject to any control until 10 May.[33] Tirard, however, viewed the progress

25. Edmonds, *The Occupation*, pp. 218–19.
26. Wilson to Robertson, 19.3.21, IWM 73/1/26 file 23.
27. Ibid., Robertson to Wilson 22.3.21.
28. Ibid., Wilson to Robertson, 30.3.21.
29. Cab. conclusions of 9.4.21 (C7742), FO 371/6023 fos 11–12.
30. FO to Ryan, 30.4.21 (C8051), FO 371/6024 fo. 32.
31. DBFP Ser. 1, vol. 16 (no. 512), pp. 548–9.
32. Ibid., p. 549.
33. 'Report', 1921, pp. 32–3.

made with great satisfaction. He rejoiced that within a month the Allies had regained all the economic powers they had possessed in the Rhineland during the Armistice, and warned Briand that there must be no return to the impotence imposed by the Versailles Treaty.[34] The French generals were, of course, more interested in seizing the Ruhr itself. Buoyed up by the ease with which the Ruhr ports were occupied, they were convinced that French troops would meet no resistance and consequently pressed their government to act quickly.[35] Planning for the occupation of the Ruhr began in mid-March.[36] On the assumption that British troops would take part, Degoutte allocated to the Rhine Army the task of occupying Remscheid and Elberfeld. Neither Morland nor Robertson relished the prospect of a Ruhr occupation. Robertson particularly feared that 'our little friends will bite off more than they can chew',[37] but the prevailing feeling amongst the British in the Rhineland was that a Ruhr occupation was 'almost inevitable'.[38] At Lympne Lloyd George reluctantly came to the conclusion that 'at the present moment there was no government in Germany strong enough to carry out the Treaty of Versailles, without a threat of force'.[39] By the time the London ultimatum was dispatched on 5 May the French had over a quarter of a million men mobilized in the Rhineland;[40] a considerable number were billeted in the British Zone, which caused mounting friction with the local German authorities.[41] The British contingent, which consisted of two squadrons of cavalry, an 18-pounder battery and four tanks, was placed under the command of the 77th French division at Solingen.[42]

When the new Wirth government accepted the ultimatum on 12 May, nobody was more surprised than Robertson. He had suspected that the German government would deliberately court occupation in order to set American and British public opinion against France.[43] British officials in Coblenz and Cologne had braced themselves for the occupation, only at the last moment to

34. Tirard to Briand, 28.4.21, MAE Rive Gauche 111 fos 34–5.
35. See for example General Denvignes to Degoutte, 23.4.21, pp. 6–8, Vincennes 7N2644-2.
36. Morland to Wilson, 20.4.21, IWM 73/1/26 file 57.
37. Ibid., Robertson to Wilson, 26.4.21, file 23.
38. Ibid., Morland to Wilson, 20.4.21, file 57.
39. DBFP Ser. 1, vol. 15 (no. 71), p. 464.
40. McDougall, *Rhineland Diplomacy*, p. 155.
41. Regierung Düsseldorf to Staatskommissar für öffentliche Ordnung, 11.5.21 (no. 3025/21), FCO Lib. L1711 L502507; Morland to Wilson, 18.5.21, IWM 73/1/26 file 57.
42. Edmonds, *The Occupation*, p. 224.
43. Robertson to Wilson, 28.5.21, IWM 73/1/26 file 23.

find it cancelled. Not surprisingly the French representative at Cologne reported that most of them 'ne cachent pas leur joie de voir contremander l'occupation de la Ruhr'.[44] To rub salt into the wound 'certaines personnes dans les mêmes milieux' suggested that France had lost a unique chance of occupying the Ruhr.[45] One Senior British official chided the French for accusing the British of bad will when they themselves lacked 'd'estomac' for the operation.[46] In the opinion of French officials there was little doubt that the cancellation of the Ruhr occupation had damaged their prestige and caused 'une immense sensation de découragement dans les milieux séparistes et francophiles de Cologne', as the occupation of the Ruhr was considered to be the main aim of French policy.[47]

Following the acceptance of the London ultimatum, the German customs officials began to cooperate in operating the new eastern customs frontier, and soon, paradoxically, more duties were being collected in the British Zone than in the French Zone.[48] The German officials were supervised by a handful of British troops and customs officers. Reflecting on this some twenty years later Robertson wrote: 'Give me a British subaltern and a posse of British troops, without any interference of any kind, and I guarantee that they will keep order almost anywhere.'[49] Nevertheless, although the French had suffered a setback to their Ruhr policy, the Korfanty uprising in Upper Silesia and the subsequent fear of intervention there by the Reichswehr gave them the opportunity to maintain the pressure on Germany. A large number of French troops still remained in the British Zone under orders to move into the Ruhr within twenty-four hours' notice.[50] Their removal was further delayed by the transfer of virtually the whole of the British Rhine Army to Silesia at the end of May. According to the *Bystander* Cologne became so full of French *képis* that it could be called 'Paris-sur-Rhine'.[51] Temporarily the French army occupied almost the whole stretch of the Rhineland from the Dutch border to Alsace-Lorraine.[52] Like

---

44. Le Délégue dans la Zone Britannique to Tirard, 12.5.21 (no. 108 ZW/3), AN AJ⁹ 4289.
45. Ibid.
46. Ibid.
47. Ibid.
48. 'Report', 1921, p. 33. Robertson's unpublished memoirs, chapter on 'Germany', p. 6, Robertson Papers.
49. Robertson, ibid.
50. Morland to CIGS, 17.5.21 (no. GO. 165), FO 371/6029 fo. 116; see also Morland to CIGS, 18.5.21, IWM 73/1/26 file 57.
51. 'Paris-Sur-Rhine', *Bystander*, 13.7.21.
52. DBFP Ser. 1, vol. 16 (no. 800), p. 897.

Percival in Upper Silesia Robertson had to defend his country's interests from a position of humiliating weakness. He wrote bitterly to Wilson in June: 'I went down to Cologne the other day to look for our army, but could not find it. I have subsequently learnt that it passed me on the road and it was playing polo at Coblenz.'[53] Everywhere the French appeared to be seizing the initiative. Tirard was strongly lobbying the Quai d'Orsay to maintain sanctions despite the German acceptance of the London ultimatum, as they were an indispensable weapon in the hands of the High Commission.[54] Neither had the French forsaken their ultimate desire to occupy the Ruhr; General de Metz quite openly boasted in the Palatinate that 'We are going straight for the Ruhr.'[55] The French cultural department at Coblenz organized an impressive Fine Arts exhibition at Wiesbaden which was patronized by leading French artists from Paris; it was 'the high watermark reached by the waves of French propaganda, which had been beating at the Rhineland since the beginning of the occupation'.[56]

Throughout the summer of 1921 Robertson ceaselessly advocated the dismantling of the customs barriers[57] and some symbolic gesture from London, such as a visit by either Curzon or Lloyd George, that would indicate that the government took the Rhineland seriously.[58] He pressed hard for the return to Cologne of the six battalions in Silesia, which had been transferred there as a result of the Korfanty revolt,[59] and warned Curzon that unless the British and Americans were prepared to take 'a more active and open interest in the Rhineland', the German population would be goaded by French policy into an explosion of popular anger, which 'would bring the next war immeasurably nearer'.[60] In a memorable phrase he accused the French of 'playing ducks and drakes with the peace of the world'.[61] He was painfully aware that the Germans had practically written off the British in the Rhineland, and informed the Foreign Office that 'if we cannot adequately fulfil our obligations, we had better get out altogether'.[62] Robertson's opinions were ill-received by the Foreign Office, and were to play a part

53. Robertson to Wilson, 15.6.21, IWM 73/1/26 file 23.
54. Tirard to MAE, 19.5.21, MAE Rive Gauche 111 fos 64–5.
55. Niederschrift (Dr Knoch), 19.5.21 (no. 982), p. 4, FCO Lib. L1766 L515664–74.
56. 'Report', 1921, p. 11; Tirard, *La France Sur le Rhin*, Paris, 1930, ch. 4.
57. See, for example, DBFP Ser. 1, vol. 16 (no. 633), p. 684.
58. Robertson to Leith Ross, 23.7.21, Robertson Papers, Germany (The Rhine), 2.
59. Robertson to Tufton, 15.6.21 (C12643), FO 371/5972 fos 15–17.
60. Robertson to Curzon, 15.7.21 (C14614), FO 371/5973 fos 5–9.
61. Robertson to Wigram, 16.6.21, Robertson Papers, Germany (The Rhine), 2.
62. Robertson to Tufton, 15.6.21 (C12643).

in his transfer to the Consulate in Tangier in November.[63] Understandably, Robertson, who was having to bear the brunt of the consequences of British impotence in the Rhineland, tended to forget that viewed from London it was just one problem amongst many. Morland, on the other hand, exaggerated when he observed that 'the Rhine to us is nothing, whereas it is everything to France'.[64]

The British government wanted the Rhineland to remain an integral economic and territorial part of Germany. Both the Foreign Office[65] and British banking and business interests pressed for the abolition of sanctions together with the retention of the industrial triangle of Upper Silesia on the grounds that it would assist Wirth's government of fulfilment and so stabilize Europe and make reparations possible. British businessmen, for instance, anxious to negotiate economic agreements with Germany in the summer of 1921 and to use German know-how to exploit markets in Russia and in the British Empire, found sanctions an active barrier to cooperation.[66] Initially the French were unreceptive to the British arguments for the abolition of sanctions. Tirard indeed, when approached by Robertson at a private reception, mischievously suggested that Britain 'recherche dans la restitution des Colonies allemande les moyens de fournir à l'Allemagne un élément de prosperité économique autrement plus puissant que la suppression de quelques taxes qui subsistent sur le Rhin'. When Robertson replied that it was Britain's duty to protect 'les indigènes contre les horreurs de l'administration allemandes', Tirard ironically observed that it was a pity that the same 'bienveillance humanitaire' was not available for the Poles in Upper Silesia.[67] Nevertheless, privately Briand realized that the sanctions policy would have to be modified,[68] and in August at the Supreme Council he proposed the replacement of the customs barriers by a new inter-Allied licensing organization which would ensure that the Germans would not discriminate against Allied imports, but he refused to agree to the evacuation of the Ruhr ports.[69] The customs sanctions were lifted

---

63. See Crowe's Minutes on Robertson's letter of 15 July (C12643): 'He apparently expects us to send an army and drive the French out', FO 371/5973 fos 2–3.
64. Morland to Wilson, 5.9.21, IWM 73/1/26 file 57. A year earlier he had himself stressed the political and commercial importance of the occupation. See below ch. 11.
65. DBFP Ser. 1, vol. 16 (no. 626), Memorandum by Lord Curzon, pp. 678–80.
66. See 'Aufzeichnung', 16.7.21, FCO Lib. K131 K013941-42.
67. Tirard to Briand, 27.7.21 (no. 2008), MAE Rive Gauche 112 fo. 90.
68. Briand (?) to Laroche, 23.6.21 (Note 73), MAE Rive Gauche 111 fos 145–53.
69. McDougall, *Rhineland Diplomacy*, p. 166.

on 30 September, but the negotiations on the new inter-Allied organization to replace the Licensing Committee at Ems, which had been set up by the High Commission in April as part of the sanctions programme to issue import and export licences in the Rhineland, were bedevilled by Anglo–French differences.[70] The French manoeuvred to draw up an agreement which would enable the Allies to influence import-export licensing, and if necessary to resume control of it, while the Foreign Office, contrary to advice from Robertson who feared that this would merely give 'secret ammunition' to the Germans,[71] aimed initially to 'saboter [*sic*] the whole thing'.[72] By mid-October, however, a compromise agreement had been hammered out between the British and the French, but to the Germans, who wanted an inter-Allied committee empowered only to investigate the issue of licences, it appeared to propose too powerful a body. Protracted negotiations dragged on into 1922, and were tacitly abandoned in August 1922.[73] In the meantime the Ems Licensing Commission continued to operate on the western frontier of the occupied territory.

Parallel to this partially successful initiative to dismantle the sanctions implemented in March 1921, the British tried to weaken France's grip on the Rhineland by proposing a limit to the total costs of the military occupation of 240 million gold marks per annum.[74] Robertson was delighted at the chance to reduce Tirard's staff as 'many of them have not enough to do and so they make mischief and fuss about the behaviour of school teachers and other things of no importance at all'.[75] The Supreme Council in August agreed to set up a committee to review the costs of the occupation. Tirard had no illusions about Britain's motives and warned the Quai d'Orsay of 'le caractère nettement politique de cette intervention'.[76] The committee, which met in Paris, recommended in November 1921 that the High Commission should identify areas where it could economize and then fix an annual maximum figure for the expenses resulting from the services provided by Germany under the Rhineland Agreement. The British government was highly critical of 'the timid and tentative'[77] nature of the report and

70. DBFP Ser. 1, vol. 16 (no. 724), pp. 792–4.
71. Robertson to Hardinge, 26.8.21, Robertson Papers, Germany (The Rhine), 2.
72. DBFP Ser. 1, vol. 16 (no. 674), p. 737.
73. 'Report', 1921, pp. 34–6.
74. Wigram to Robertson, 5.8.21, Robertson Papers, Germany (The Rhine), 2.
75. Ibid., Robertson to Wigram, 15.8.21.
76. Tirard to MAE, 12.10.21 (no. 189), MAE Rive Gauche 5 fos 10–12.
77. 'Annual Report of the Inter-Allied Rhineland High Commission for 1922' (C825), p. 37, FO 371/11309 fo. 59.

attempted to have it referred back to the Conference of Ambassadors so that the committee could be instructed 'to make further enquiries'.[78] Unfortunately, the way was open for Tirard to fight an effective procedural battle when the committee rashly took the initiative to ask the High Commission to set up its own sub-committee on the reduction of expenses. Tirard pounced upon this and, in protracted arguments that lasted through to July 1922, insisted that the Paris committee was exceeding its powers and refused to set up any such sub-committee until the Allied governments themselves had authorized the instruction.[79]

By the autumn of 1921 Anglo–French relations were still poisoned by an inveterate and deeply ingrained mistrust. General Degoutte complained that 'Quand on étudie les affaires allemandes il est impossible de ne pas y apercevoir l'action continue et tenace de l'Angleterre'.[80] He warned, with reference to the growing demand in Britain for a revision of the reparation settlement, that British interests were on a direct collision course with the French. The mood of mutual Anglo–French mistrust is well illustrated by the way the French consuls at Cologne and Düsseldorf became so convinced that Ryan was conducting secret negotiations with the Oberbürgermeister of Düsseldorf in November that the French security police were authorized to exploit contacts with 'une femme de Chambre' working in the Oberbürgermeister's house in an attempt to gain information about his activities.[81]

Robertson's replacement by Lord Kilmarnock on 16 November was immediately seen by the French as a move by the Foreign Office and Lord D'Abernon, the British Ambassador in Berlin, to have at Coblenz 'un homme, qui suivit docilement leurs instructions'.[82] The French Ambassador in London observed that Robertson had irritated Curzon by an 'excess d'indépendance' and argued that his transfer to Tangier was a demotion.[83] This is clearly untrue as Robertson was transferred to Morocco with the specific task of negotiating the Tangier Treaty with the French where he exchanged

78. Ibid.
79. Ibid., pp. 37–41.
80. Rapport Mensuel, Septembre 1921, p. 44, Vincennes 7N2655.
81. E. Genoyer to MAE, 15.12.21, MAE Rive Gauche 200 fos 75–7.
82. Ibid., St Aulaire (London) to MAE, 14.11.21, fos 60–1.
83. Ibid. Major Donald Robertson, Arnold Robertson's son, informed me that Robertson was reluctant to leave Coblenz, but that it was made very clear to him that he was the right man for the job. Curzon disarmed his protests by replying that 'whenever I try to pay a man a compliment he raises difficulties'. In 1924 Arnold Robertson was given a KBE for his role in negotiating the Tangier Treaty (letter of 23.1.90 to author).

one set of complex problems for another. He continued to hold the same rank of Minister Plenipotentiary, which he had held at Coblenz. Nevertheless it would be hard to deny that many officials in the Foreign Office were pleased to see his departure from Coblenz, and that he had made an enemy of Lloyd George.[84] The Germans had been busy conducting a campaign against him on the grounds that he was too pro-French and allegedly lacked a sufficient grasp of economic issues to be effective in Coblenz.[85] It is arguable that, like Tower and Percival, Robertson became a scapegoat for the British government's own impotence in Europe. However, by following an essentially loyal yet at times highly critical policy towards the *Entente*, Robertson did remain true to the only option open to contemporary British foreign policy. This was to be the line followed by Sir Harold Stuart, when he replaced Percival in Oppeln in June 1921, but the crucial difference between Stuart and Robertson was that the former had a division of British troops to back him up! Robertson's outspoken and sometimes abrasive remarks highlighted the weakness of Britain's position on the Continent in the summer of 1921, where she could only seek to influence French policy, but could not control it. His demands for troops and visiting dignitaries annoyed the 'low profile' men in the Foreign Office, while the cleverly orchestrated campaign mounted by the Auswärtiges Amt against him weakened his credentials with those officials, like Waterlow, who advocated concession to Berlin.[86]

The Ambiguous Plebiscite: Upper Silesia, 1921–1922

By the spring of 1921 the French already had considerable vested interests in Poland. Not only was Poland an important ally, but also on 22 March a Franco–Polish convention was signed promising privileged access to French capital in private German firms in

84. For instance, at a meeting of the British Delegation to the Supreme Council of 8–13 August, Robertson had the temerity openly to criticize Lloyd George when in the 'same tone of voice as one might have used if one had been speaking of the result on one's digestion of eating an unripe peach', the latter thought aloud about what the consequences of a break-up of the *Entente* would be. 'To the amazement and horror of those present', Robertson burst out: 'It would mean chaos in Europe, the fall of the German Government, the occupation of the Ruhr and a complete break up of the Entente and war': Robertson to Wilson, 15.8.21, IWM 73/1/26 file 23.
85. Bernstorff to Reichsminister (Rosen), 17.8.21 (V.A. no. 599), FCO Lib. 3058 D602971-73.
86. K. Nelson, *Victors Divided*, p. 211.

what was assumed would shortly become Polish Upper Silesia.[87] Consequently, as so much for the French hinged on a Polish victory, the detailed preparations for the plebiscite gave rise to renewed Anglo–French recriminations as both sides manoeuvred to introduce regulations which would facilitate a result consonant with their own mutually conflicting aims.

The French first tried to argue that outvoters should be deprived of the right to vote as their presence in Silesia would endanger public order, but when it was pointed out by Lord Derby in the Ambassadors Conference that the Treaty unambiguously gave the vote to all who had been born in the area, Cambon in effect made French consent dependent on the dispatch of British troops to help keep the peace during the actual plebiscite campaign.[88] Briand then proposed a compromise[89] whereby the outvoters would vote two weeks after the residents, either in Cologne or in Upper Silesia itself, but at the end of December 1920 the Cabinet was so alarmed by the potential for trouble which a staggered vote afforded that it agreed to the dispatch of four battalions of British troops to Upper Silesia provided the French conceded a uniform polling day for both residents and outvoters.[90] Cambon rejected the proposal, but Briand overruled him when he came to London on 21 February.[91] It appeared that the British had won a significant victory. Le Rond himself felt that the prospects for a Polish majority were now 'hazardous'.[92]

British troops did not arrive in Silesia until 8 March, just nine days before the plebiscite took place.[93] Some 280 extra trains brought in 150,000 outvoters from all over the Reich;[94] to the surprise of the Germans, Korfanty instructed the Poles to adopt a policy of 'the greatest politeness'[95] towards them. British troops experienced 'no real trouble'[96] except in Beuthen where seven

---

87. See below, pp. 181–2. For a general survey of the Silesian Crisis, 1921–2, see Bertram-Libal, 'Die britische Politik in der Oberschlesienfrage', pp. 113–32; Kaiser, *Lord D' Abernon*, pp. 196–221; Gregory Campbell, 'The Struggle for Upper Silesia, 1919–22', *Journal of Modern History*, vol. 42, no. 3, 1970, pp. 367–85; Carsten, *Britain and the Weimar Republic*, pp. 68–73.
88. DBFP Ser. 1, vol. 11 (no. 78), pp. 97–8.
89. Ibid. (no. 90), p. 113.
90. Cabinet Conclusions, 30.12.20 (80 (20)), CAB 23/23 fos 349–50.
91. DBFP Ser. 1, vol. 11 (nos 151, 153), pp. 180–3.
92. Minute by E. de Peretti de La Rocca, 28.2.21, MAE Allemagne 216, fo 180.
93. Edmonds, *The Occupation*, p. 220.
94. Wambaugh, *Plebiscites*, vol. 1, p. 249.
95. Vertreter des Staatskommissars für öffentliche Ordnung in Oberschlesien, 16.3.21 (no. 158 Oberschlesien), p. 2, FCO Lib. L912 L254850-54.
96. GHQ Rhine Army to WO, 30.3.21 (C6909), FO 371/5892 fo. 141.

Germans were murdered and an army lorry attacked.[97] There was thus no opposition from the French when they were recalled to the Cologne Zone on 4 April, to replace units which had been brought back to England in response to the strike threatened by the transport workers and railwaymen in support of the miners.[98]

Although the official figures of the plebiscite were not published until 24 April, it was known within twenty-four hours that a majority of the communes, all the key cities and 60 per cent of the total vote had opted for Germany.[99] The initial British reaction to this result was to argue tentatively for the recognition of Germany's claims to the whole province,[100] yet detailed study of the figures soon revealed that this was not a practical policy. In the west and the north there were overwhelming German majorities, but in the rural areas in the east there were equally large Polish majorities. This was further complicated by the pattern of the voting in the key industrial triangle formed by Gleiwitz, Beuthen and Kattowitz where 'the result was an intricate mosaic'[101] that gave no clear guide. Headlam-Morley, the Historical Adviser to the Foreign Office, drew the conclusion 'that as regards the industrial area . . . the plebiscite has failed'.[102]

Once it was clear that the argument for the retention of the whole plebiscite zone by Germany was not viable, Percival and de Marinis put forward, with Curzon's support, a revised plan ceding Pless and Rybnik to Poland, whilst awarding the whole of the industrial region to Germany.[103] Le Rond, however, argued forcefully that as 'the industrial area . . . with its German majority form[ed] an island in a Polish sea', it should be ceded to Poland without further debate.[104] The Commission was unable to draft a unanimous report and the Allied leaders in London were presented on 30 April with two conflicting sets of recommendations.[105]

Detailed discussion of their contents was temporarily made academic by the outbreak of the third Polish uprising in Upper

97. Percival to FO, 26.3.21 (C6212), FO 371/5892 fo. 39. A graphic description of the incident is given in a letter by Capt. L.M. Preace to Col. Allen, 25.3.20 (*sic*) (from internal evidence it is clear that 1921 is meant), IWM Gedye Papers, 13.
98. DBFP Ser. 1, vol. 16 (no. 11), pp. 12–13.
99. Wambaugh, *Plebiscites*, vol. 1, pp. 248–9.
100. Cabinet Conclusions, 22.3.20 (C6303), in FO 371/5892 fos 52–3.
101. Wambaugh, *Plebiscites*, vol. 1, p. 251.
102. DBFP Ser. 1, vol. 16 (no. 13), p. 20.
103. Ibid. (no. 6), pp. 4–5.
104. Percival to Curzon, 27.4.21 (C9057), p. 1, FO 371/5896 fos 198–201.
105. Silesian Plebiscite Commission to President of the Allied Conference, London, 30.4.21 (C9210), FO 371/5897 fos 35–40.

Silesia. On the night of 2/3 May Korfanty, alarmed by rumours of the Percival–de Marinis plan, attempted to forestall an adverse decision by the Supreme Council by forcefully demonstrating 'the Polish character of Upper Silesia'.[106] Armed insurrections broke out in Pless, Rybnik and Tarnowitz. By 6 May Korfanty's forces, which were mostly composed of local foundry workers and miners 'who preferred to risk their lives rather than remain under German rule',[107] had effectively overrun the eastern two-thirds of Silesia, put the German population in the cities under siege and established a new *de facto* frontier, the Korfanty line, well west of the industrial triangle. British and Italian officials in eastern Silesia were powerless to impede Korfanty or to prevent their French colleagues from cooperating with the insurgents. In effect their power extended only 'to the four walls of their offices and occasionally to the outskirts of their towns on sufferance'.[108] Their reports gave a uniform picture of humiliating impotence and of Franco–Polish cooperation.

Lacking both the strength and the necessary will to expel the insurgents, the Commission had little option but to negotiate a cease-fire with Korfanty on 8 May,[109] but this merely provided a pause in which the German forces, strengthened by the arrival of several thousand Freikorps volunteers, could regroup. General Hoefer, the Commander of the German Selbstschutz, did initially try to pursue a defensive policy and wait for an Allied decision on Silesia, but when it became clear that the British rejected the cease-fire as a 'capitulation' to the insurgents, he lost control of the Freikorps leaders, who on 23 May, in an epic battle, captured the Annaberg from the Poles.[110] Elsewhere the situation rapidly dissolved into a series of isolated actions and counter-actions, in which British officials were often trapped. At Rosenberg, for instance, when the German forces closed in on the town, British personnel had to shelter in 'a building opposite the *Landesamt*', and were only evacuated when the Poles threatened to repeat 'the German devastation of Northern France'.[111]

106. Cienciala and Komarnicki, *From Versailles to Locarno*, p. 63.
107. Ibid., p. 63.
108. Craig to Ottley, 6.5.21 (C10952), FO 371/5905 fos 180–6. For numerous examples of the other British Kreis officers' reports see FO 890/6, 8, 10, 11.
109. DBFP Ser. 1, vol. 16 (no. 43), p. 63.
110. Cienciala and Komarnicki, *From Versailles to Locarno*, pp. 65–72; R.G.L. Waite, *Vanguard of Nazism*, Cambridge MA, 1952, pp. 228–30. For the role of Reichswehr officers in disguise see Carsten, *The Reichswehr and Politics*, pp. 149–50.
111. Diary of Capt. H. de C. Toogood (District Controller, Rosenberg), 19–25.5.21, FO 890/10 pp. 26–8.

In the area occupied by Korfanty the most pressing problem was the restoration of food, currency and water supplies. Neither the insurgents nor the German government hesitated to subject the civilian population to the very real threat of starvation in their mutual attempts to exert economic pressure upon each other. According to Moltke,[112] there were also British officials who felt that a 'ban on money and food was the only means of controlling the revolt'. The Reichsbank,[113] with the backing of Wirth and local Upper Silesian trades union leaders,[114] vetoed the transfer of 250 million Reichsmarks for fear that they would fall into the hands of the insurgents. The Commission had attempted unsuccessfully to overcome this understandable hesitancy of the Reichsbank by offering to provide military protection for the money whilst in transit, but it had refused point blank a German request to underwrite its value.[115] All transport of flour and cereals from Germany was also halted, while the local Reichsbahn staff threatened to strike should the Commission attempt to railroad supplies through.[116] On 24 May the insurgents cut off water supplies to Kattowitz, oblivious of the fact that this caused 'intensive suffering for women and children'.[117] Craig, who was one of the few British officials able to achieve anything positive during the first chaotic weeks of the insurrection, set up a 'Food Parity Committee' at Gleiwitz, on which Polish, German and Allied representatives sat, to supervise the distribution of food to the industrial zone, and managed to negotiate an agreement whereby freight trains carrying food supplies, provided they were accompanied by a British officer and marked conspicuously with a blue St Andrew's cross, would be given safe transit to Gleiwitz. Thanks to his efforts the first trains began to arrive in Upper Silesia on 22 May.[118]

In the face of the Korfanty revolt and the German backlash, the Commission at Oppeln remained so divided and impotent that Percival urged the withdrawal of the British element on 13 May.[119] Two weeks later he himself resigned because of a nervous break-

112. Moltke to AA, 16.5.21 (no. 2616), FCO Lib. K2288 K644572-75; Carsten, *Britain and the Weimar Republic*, pp. 70–1.
113. Laurent to Simons, 11.5.21 (no. 135), FCO Lib. K2288 K644559.
114. 'Sitzung der Oberschlesischen Arbeitgeber und Arbeitnehmer in der Reichskanzelei vom 21.5.21', FCO Lib. K2288 K644594-98.
115. Moltke to AA 16.5.21 (no. 2616).
116. Craig to Ottley, 19.5.21 (C11052), FO 371/5906 fos 64–5.
117. Pervival to FO, 24.5.21 (C10687), FO 371/5904 fo. 97.
118. Dept of Food Control, 'Report of the Work of the Department, 1919–22', pp. 20–3, FO 890/16 fos 167–70.
119. DBFP Ser. 1, vol. 16 (no. 56), pp. 76–7.

down. The Cabinet reluctantly accepted on 24 May the Foreign Office's advice that British influence in Silesia could only be restored by the dispatch of up to six battalions of troops,[120] even though both the CIGS and the War Minister opposed the move. Wilson warned that sending 'a small detachment, unsupported and probably unsupportable, such a distance from its base, its lines of communication being in the hands of the Germans' was 'an unwise and possibly dangerous move'.[121] Sir Harold Stuart, who had the unique reputation of being able to handle the French while remaining on good terms with them, was also persuaded to come out of retirement and take over the unfortunate Percival's post.[122]

When General Heneker, the Commander of the British Silesian Division, first arrived in Upper Silesia he found the attitude of his French colleagues 'anything but cordial',[123] while the Germans greeted the British troops as saviours, and hoped to engineer some incident that would enable them to fight shoulder to shoulder with them against the Poles.[124] Gratier was sufficiently disturbed by these German fantasies to press Le Rond to issue an official communiqué to the effect that 'the British troops were in Silesia on the same footing as the other Allied contingents'.[125] Militarily the first priority was to establish a cordon between the belligerents and then to force them to retreat back to the frontiers of Upper Silesia.[126] As a vital demonstration of Anglo–French unity, Heneker secured French cooperation in a successful operation to clear the insurgents out of Rosenberg, which by 8 June was sufficiently pacified to be handed over to the control of the local police.[127] The Poles began slowly and erratically to withdraw on 10 June. The Germans agreed not to advance any further, but were reluctant to surrender any territory until the area seized by Korfanty was back under the administration of the Commission.[128] The protracted negotiations with General Hoefer were conducted on behalf of the Commission by Heneker, who successfully managed to persuade him to evacuate

---

120. Cabinet Conclusions of 24.5.21 (40 (21)), CAB 23/25 fos 279–81.
121. Wilson to Secretary of State for War, 23.5.21, IWM Wilson Papers, 73/1/26 file 57.
122. Note by Schubert, 4.6.21, repeating telegram from Dufour-Feronce of 2.6.21, L912 L256206-207. See also Waterlow's Minute, 18.9.20 (C6604), FO 371/4805 fo. 153.
123. Heneker to WO, 3.6.21 (no. 29), FO 371/5911 fos 88–9.
124. 'Pitfalls in Silesia', *The Times*, 30.5.21.
125. Gratier to Le Rond, 11.6.21 (no. 14.006/2), Vincennes 4N101-1.
126. Heneker to Secretary, WO, July 1922 (C2034), FO 371/7470 fos 278–84.
127. Heneker to WO, 8.6.21 (file 34), FO 371/5911 fo. 96.
128. DBFP Ser. 1, vol. 16 (no. 193), pp. 214–17.

the pivotal position of the Annaberg on 23 June.[129] To the Allied units sandwiched between the belligerents this was a period of great confusion and possible danger. Colonel Jourdain, the officer commanding the 2nd Battalion of the Connaught Rangers, noted in his diary that 'all kinds of contradictory orders were showered on us, and the only thing to do was to stand quiet and do nothing but wait'.[130] By 24 June the combatants were no longer in contact and by 6 July Upper Silesia was cleared of both Polish and German forces.[131] Heneker was so delighted by the success of the operation that he optimistically believed that 'there [was] no reason why we should not be out of this by the end of July'.[132]

Sir Harold Stuart inherited from Percival a legacy of chaos and a demoralized staff, who had 'drunk the bitter cup of humiliation to the dregs',[133] but like Heneker, he believed that his stay in Upper Silesia would be brief and therefore refrained from pressing for a radical reconstruction of the Commission. In a private letter to Waterlow he described his tactics:

> I have felt and still feel, that the only possible course is to keep my eyes firmly fixed on the important and essential factors and to let the others slide; so please do not permit any carping criticism of details, however well founded the author of it may be. Compromise is in many ways a hateful thing, but on most occasions in public life a necessary one.[134]

Stuart secured a more formal system for minuting the Commission's decisions and appointed a reliable official to represent him in the *Cabinet* (executive committee) of the Commission.[135] He also persuaded the French to re-allocate Königshütte and Beuthen rural district to British controllers and Gleiwitz rural district to an Italian.[136] He failed, however, to secure any backing from London for a proposal that Heneker as the most senior serving general in Upper Silesia should become supreme commander of the Allied forces there;[137] the CIGS in an avuncular manner warned Heneker

129. Rapport du Capitaine Robien, 21.6.21, Vincennes 4N101 DOS 1.
130. Col. Jourdain's Diary, 15.6.21, vol. 1, The National Army Museum 5603/13.
131. Lt. Col. Dillon to 1st and 2nd Silesian Brigades, 6.7.21, War Diary, General Staff, July 1921 (App. XIV GOC 17.), WO 95/153.
132. Heneker to Wilson, 6.7.21, IWM 73/1/26 file 60.
133. Clark to Ottley, 10.6.21 (C12774), FO 371/5912 fos 137–9.
134. Stuart to Waterlow, 1.7.21 (C13800), FO 371/5915 fos 6–9.
135. DBFP Ser. 1, vol. 16 (no. 181), p. 207; Report on the Upper Silesian Plebiscite Commission (C9145), pp. 86–7, FO 371/8810.
136. DBFP Ser. 1, vol. 16 (no. 211), p. 235.
137. Stuart to FO, 3.7.21 (C13649), FO 371/5914 fos 167–8.

that 'it is one of those things which touch the French very nearly and which would excite them to all sorts of pinpricks both there and elsewhere'.[138] Stuart and Heneker also took great care to re-create the façade of Allied unity. British troops were informed categorically that 'by word and by deed, officers and men should show that they value and respect our French and Italian Allies'.[139] This was put into practice almost immediately at battalion level, where football matches were played with French army[140] teams and French officers entertained at British messes where they were afterwards regaled by regimental bands. According to Colonel Jourdain, the pipe band of the Connaught Rangers did 'more for consolidating the *Entente* than anything else'.[141] By July there was a new atmosphere of confidence among the British element of the Commission. When General Sir William Thwaites visited Silesia in mid-July he was so impressed that he informed Wilson that 'a happier family than Heneker and his Commission and Sir Harold Stuart I have seldom seen. The stamp of efficiency is deeply set on the British share of occupation, both military and administrative.'[142]

Curzon had hoped that Stuart's formidable talents might be able to coax the Commission into presenting a unanimous report on Upper Silesia[143] favourable to the British interpretation of the plebiscite results, but the gap between the Anglo–Italian and French proposals remained unbridgeable,[144] and it was clear that the issue would have to be fully discussed by the Supreme Council. Both sides manoeuvred for the support of the United States and attempted to defer the meeting until such a time as their protagonist was under maximum pressure. Briand tried to procrastinate until the autumn, when he hoped that Britain would be distracted by the Washington Naval Conference.[145] In the meantime he threw London into consternation by his insistence that the Allied garrison should be reinforced by at least one further French division.[146] The British suspected that the French troops would serve as *agents provocateurs* and provoke the Germans into fresh violence, which

138. Wilson to Heneker, 12.6.21, IWM 73/1/26 file 60.
139. 'Notes on Present Situation' by Col. S.E. Dillon, 3.6.21, IWM 73/1/26.
140. See *Cologne Post* (Silesian edition), 2.7.21.
141. Jourdain, Diary, vol. 1, 20.6.21, The National Army Museum 5603/13.
142. Thwaites to Wilson, 16.7.21, IWM 73/1/26 file 45.
143. DBFP Ser. 1, vol. 16 (no. 182), p. 208; Braunweiler to Meyer, 13.7.21, FCO Lib. L912 L256165-169.
144. DBFP Ser. 1, vol. 16 (nos 217 and 228), pp. 239–40 and 249–50.
145. Ibid., DBFP (no. 228), pp. 249–50; Sthamer to AA, 21.7.21 (no. 64), FCO Lib. L912 L256716-18.
146. DBFP Ser. 1, vol. 16 (no. 225), pp. 246–7.

would then provide a convenient excuse for the occupation of the Ruhr.[147] French insistence on their unilateral right to reinforce the Upper Silesian garrison rapidly became a major issue which even overshadowed the timing of the next meeting of the Supreme Council. An acute crisis in Anglo–French relations was reached when the Germans dismissed outright a French request to transport a division across Germany to Silesia, on the grounds that the Treaty of Versailles bound them only to implement demands made jointly by the Allies. In the ensuing crisis both sides practised a dangerous brinkmanship; the French sent a virtual ultimatum to Berlin while the British Cabinet seriously considered an appeal to the League, should the French act without their consent.[148] Ultimately, however, Briand shied away from a break with Britain and accepted a face-saving formula put forward by Lord Hardinge whereby the Germans would agree to transport Allied troops across to Upper Silesia whenever necessary, but that no request would be made until after the next meeting of the Supreme Council, which was now to be held in early August.[149]

The Council met in Paris on 8 August.[150] The French remained determined to hand over to the Poles the industrial triangle, which Jules Laroche, chief of the European Section in the Quai d'Orsay, pointedly described as a 'series of German islands in a Polish district',[151] and remained unmoved by Lloyd George's verbal pyrotechnics. In the course of four days' discussions during which the voting patterns in the communes and towns of the industrial triangle were studied in detail, no compromise could be agreed upon, and Lloyd George, who was desperately anxious to return to London to deal with a particularly acute crisis arising out of De Valera's rejection of British proposals for an Irish settlement, gratefully accepted an Italian proposal for referring the Upper Silesian question to the League.

The Council of the League nominated a committee to examine the question, composed of the representatives of its four non-permanent members, Belgium, China, Brazil and Spain. The British were confident[152] that the League would favour a solution

147. Ibid. (no. 236), pp. 258–9.
148. 'Draft Conclusions of a Conference of Ministers, 11.30, and . . . a meeting of representatives of the U.K., Dominions and India, 5.30', 28.7.21, Appendix 3 to CAB 64 (21), CAB 23/26 fos 223–31.
149. DBFP Ser. 1, vol. 16 (no. 273), pp. 297–8.
150. Ibid., vol. 15, ch. 6. See also Campbell, 'The Struggle for Upper Silesia', pp. 381–2.
151. DBFP Ser. 1, vol. 15 (no. 91), p. 619.
152. Cienciala and Komarnicki, *From Versailles to Locarno*, p. 80.

similar to the one it pronounced on the dispute between Finland and Sweden over the Aaland Islands, which would have left German sovereignty intact, whilst giving the Polish population autonomy, but the German Consul at Geneva was more sceptical and pointed out that only Wellington Koo, the Chinese representative, appeared to support the British line. Hymans, the Belgian, was an unambiguous 'exponent of the French view, and used the example of the economically complementary but politically divided Franco-Belgian industrial area' to justify a division of Upper Silesia.[153] The representatives of Spain and Brazil, who were both ambassadors in Paris, were potentially friendly to France, and anxious to avoid too deep an involvement in an Anglo–French quarrel.

While the diplomats were wrestling with the Upper Silesian problem in Paris and Geneva, the Commission at Oppeln continued its task of restoring some degree of normality to the area. By the end of July an uneasy peace had descended on the province and the British forces had apparently nothing more serious to report than an 'epidemic of sunburnt arms amongst the troops',[154] but Stuart had no illusions that the Commission's authority was anything but a 'very thin veneer'.[155] Unrest was endemic in the coalfields, the factories and on the railways. In early August, there were persistent rumours of another Polish uprising, which so alarmed Heneker that in Sir Harold's absence he summoned an emergency session of the Commission to draw up contingency plans.[156] It was not until 7 September that the state of siege in the zone was finally lifted.[157]

Once the semblance of law and order had been established, it was imperative to restore the economic life of the province. Cruikshank, the Director of Communications, regained the cooperation of the German railwaymen by personally visiting each station to reassure them of the Commission's impartiality. He also tried to reassure their Polish colleagues by creating a special inter-Allied tribunal to enforce equitable treatment for both Poles and Germans.[158] To alleviate a potentially explosive unemployment problem the

153. Meyer to AA, 12.9.21 (no. 9506 0/3), FCO Lib. L912 L257547-50. B. Dugdale, *Arthur James Balfour*, 2 vols, London, 1936, vol. 2, pp. 309–12.
154. *Cologne Post*, 26.7.21.
155. Stuart to FO, 16.7.21 (C14511), FO 371/5916 fos 98–9.
156. Heneker to FO, 7.8.21 (C15902), FO 371/5921 fo. 72.
157. G.S. War Diary, British Silesian Force, 7 Sept. 1921, WO 95/153.
158. 'Report of Dept. of Communications, I.A. Commission, Upper Silesia, 1920–22', pp. 12–13, FO 890/16, Appendix J fos 96–124.

Polish and Czech frontiers were reopened for Upper Silesian exports.[159]

As a legacy of the uprising, the Commission had to feed and protect in insanitary camps nearly 40,000 refugees,[160] who had fled their homes, and to administer prisons that were bursting at the seams with men awaiting trial.[161] These, however, thanks to the setting up of special courts in Tarnowitz and Gleiwitz, were emptied by early September.[162] The refugees remained a more intractable problem. In August the Commission set up a joint Polish–German committee under the chairmanship of a British colonel, Watkin Williams, to negotiate the return of the refugees to their own homes. Williams acted on the principle that if 'repatriation' was to succeed, then 'the inhabitants themselves must be made to realise that it was in their own interests that returning refugees should not be molested'.[163] In November he organized a series of reconciliation meetings amongst the miners and steel workers and tried to convince them that the Upper Silesian economy needed the return of the refugees. By January 1922, some 19,000 Poles and 16,000 Germans had returned home, leaving a hard core of some 1,200 Germans and 700 Poles in the camps.[164]

In the second week of October the Commission apprehensively awaited the League's recommendations. All troops and officials were put on the alert and plans were drawn up to circumvent the effects of a possible rail strike.[165] On 12 October the report was presented to the League Council, which unanimously accepted it and referred it to the Conference of Ambassadors. It recommended a frontier line drawn through the industrial triangle, allocating three-quarters of the coal mines, ore reserves and industrial plant to Poland. To mitigate the economic and social consequences of this, the League recommended that Poland and Germany should negotiate a fifteen-year transitional agreement safeguarding the economic unity of the area. A mixed commission composed of two Polish and two German Upper Silesians under a neutral president appointed by the League was to supervise the execution of the

159. Heneker to Curzon, 1.9.21 (C17598), FO 371/5924 fos 86–7.
160. 'Report on Refugees in Upper Silesia from August to November' by Lt. Col. E.H. Watkin Williams, 10.11.21, FO 371/5931 fos 158–60.
161. Heneker to Curzon, 1.9.21 (C17598), FO 371/5924 fos 86–7.
162. Ibid.
163. 'Report on Refugees', FO 371/5931 fos 158–60.
164. 'Final Report on Refugees in Upper Silesia', 6.1.22 (C1124), FO 371/7463 fo. 31.
165. Stuart to Curzon, 14.10.21 (C20026), FO 371/5929 fos 65–7.

economic clauses of the settlement.[166]

The British government was surprised and irritated by the League's recommendations, but weighed down with problems over Ireland, unemployment and the Middle East, it was unwilling to reopen the question.[167] Nevertheless in the Conference of Ambassadors Hardinge did oppose the French proposal that the Commission should hand over to Poland and Germany the allocated areas one month after the drawing up of the new frontier regardless of whether the economic agreement had been negotiated or the Mixed Economic Commission set up, as he feared that once the Poles had taken over they would, with the connivance of the French, refuse to negotiate an economic settlement.[168] His case was strengthened when the League recommended on 17 October that the inter-Allied Commission should continue to administer Upper Silesia until the Mixed Economic Commission was ready to function.[169] On the 19th the French agreed, and the details of the partition were formally notified to Warsaw and Berlin.[170]

Apart from token protests from left-wing intellectuals, which the Foreign Office scornfully dismissed,[171] public opinion in Britain appeared indifferent. In Germany, however, the decision was greeted with outrage. In Cologne the Commissioner, Piggott, was informed by Professor Budding, a local Centre Party politician, that 'the Germans were finished with England',[172] while in Berlin the Foreign Minister bluntly told D'Abernon that 'England by her indifference or simplicity at Geneva [had] rendered a very bad service to Europe as well as to Germany and to herself. No greater blunder has been made in History except that of Germany in 1914.'[173] Wirth resigned, but as Sir Harold Stuart had anticipated,[174] this was essentially a political demonstration and four days later he returned to power.[175]

---

166. Wambaugh, *Plebiscites*, vol. 1, pp. 258–9; Campbell, 'The Struggle for Upper Silesia, 1919–22', pp. 384–5.
167. Sthamer to AA, 20.10.21 (no. 3287) FCO Lib. L912 L258200-203.
168. DBFP Ser. 1, vol. 16 (no. 341), pp. 356–8.
169. Ibid. (no. 348), p. 366.
170. Ibid. (no. 351), p. 368.
171. Petition handed in by Raymond Beazley, Dec. 1921 (C23289), FO 371/5933 fos 90–5.
172. 'Niederschrift', 18.10.21 (unsigned), FCO Lib., L912 L258539-40.
173. DBFP Ser. 1, vol. 16 (no. 357), p. 375.
174. Deutsche Bevollmächtigter für Abstimmungsbezirk Oberschlesien to AA, 14.10.21 (no. A3346), FCO Lib. L912 L258084-85.
175. E. Eyck, *Geschichte der Weimarer Republik*, vol. 1, pp. 260–1; E. Laubach, *Die Politik der Kabinette Wirth, 1921–22*, Lübeck and Hamburg, 1968, pp. 93–107.

In Silesia itself the German population received the news with a profound and sullen disappointment. British officials fended off vociferous German accusations of betrayal by arguing that 'but for the English it would probably have been much worse'.[176] Stuart optimistically hoped that the economic convention would be concluded by mid-November and that the Commission would be able to evacuate Upper Silesia by early December,[177] but the negotiations did not start until 23 November, and there was no prospect of their finishing before the end of February.[178] Temporarily Upper Silesia was in a 'state of political lassitude', but there were 'many dangerous under-currents, which [might] at any moment gain force and cause a serious disturbance of public order'.[179] In Pless and Rybnik and parts of Ratibor and Kattowitz, the authority of the Commission existed only 'on sufferance'[180] of the local population, and there were other areas where it hardly existed at all. In Beuthen, for instance, weapon searches were discontinued for fear of antagonizing the population.[181] The clandestine war between rival Polish and German organizations also continued with the inevitable accompaniments of kidnapping and murders. Printed indelibly on the memory of the Silesian correspondent of the *Cologne Post*, was the sight at midday in Oppeln of 'a man running for his life, his face appalling in its terror'.[182] The potential for unrest was further increased by the disastrous failure of the potato crop caused by the summer's drought, and the accelerating pace of inflation, which became 'the central economic problem of the winter of 1921/22'.[183] Prices rose on average 30 per cent per month and wage increases were usually neutralized by the rise in prices before they were received by the workers. The Commission was bombarded with demands to stabilize food prices, and in the face of its inability to do so, inflation was attributed to the occupying forces' desire to exploit the favourable exchange rate.[184] With the onset of winter the danger of another *Putsch* receded, but the frequent occurrence of minor incidents and the activities of armed bands of robbers in the forests ensured that there were constant

176. Stuart to Crowe, 28.10.21 (?C21086), FO 371/5930 fo 169.
177. DBFP Ser. 1, vol. 16 (no. 356), p. 374.
178. Ibid. (no. 369), pp. 383–4.
179. Stuart to Curzon, 11.11.21 (C21862), FO 371/5931 fos 133–4.
180. Ibid.
181. Jourdain, Diary vol. 3, 16.10.21, The National Army Museum 5603/13.
182. *Cologne Post*, 7.12.21.
183. Dept. of Food Control, 'Report of the Work of the Department, 1919–22', p. 24, FO 890/16 fo. 171.
184. Ibid.

calls for patrols. An officer in the Durham Light Infantry informed the *Cologne Post* at Christmas that 'we've been so moved about lately that we shan't be very much upset if we eat our Christmas dinner in a railway truck'.[185]

British army morale was maintained by the usual mixture of sport, training and lectures. Generously stocked N.A.A.F.I.s were set up in the main garrisons where 'wonder of wonders, everything is turned out in the approved English style'.[186] The long winter and the temptations afforded by a favourable exchange rate appeared to have a more debilitating effect on many of the junior British officials on the Commission. Heneker, while deputizing for Stuart over the Christmas period, sent round a circular to the British officials reminding them that 'we are on a pedestal, so to speak, in Upper Silesia and our actions are watched by all'.[187] Privately he complained to Wilson that 'the majority of the British officials on the Commission in Silesia are about as bad and useless a type as one could well find';[188] the CIGS was hardly surprised as this confirmed his prejudices about the 'odds and ends of irregular officers . . . nine cases out of ten they are all sorts of waifs and strays – debris of war'.[189]

By mid-January the end of the Allied occupation appeared to be in sight. Calonder, the Swiss chairman of the Polish–German economic negotiations, intimated to Stuart that the economic convention would be concluded at the latest by 15 February, but Stuart continued to fear that the French would attempt to prolong the occupation in order to exert pressure on Germany if she fell behind schedule with reparation payments.[190] At the end of January just the type of incident occurred which the British feared would escalate into a major confrontation between the French and Germans. After a house-to-house search in the night of 30/31 January by French troops in Gleiwitz, where allegedly they concentrated unfairly on German householders, a band of some hundred Germans armed with bombs and rifles attacked the French barracks at Petersdorf and wounded some twenty soldiers, two of whom later died.[191] On the following day on the Commission Stuart argued forcefully that the Secret Service, run by the Sûreté and the Intelligence

185. *Cologne Post*, 28.12.21.
186. Ibid., 27.1.22.
187. Heneker to all British Officials of the Inter-Allied Commission, 18.12.21, IWM Wilson Papers, 73/1/26 file 60.
188. Ibid., Heneker to Wilson, 12.1.22.
189. Ibid., Wilson to Heneker, 24.1.22.
190. DBFP Ser. 1, vol. 16 (no. 371), pp. 386–7.
191. Ibid. (no. 373), p. 389.

bureau, Service 'H.', had deliberately ignored the Commission's instructions,[192] and made a belated attempt to place it under inter-Allied control.[193] Grudgingly the French agreed to the setting up of a new Bureau de Renseignments under Major Watts within the Department of the Interior, but some seven weeks later it was clear that, like Percival before him, he had failed to achieve effective inter-Allied control over the secret police. Watts was deprived of all vital information and his office was 'little better than a collection of clerks at the disposal of the Head of the Department of the Interior'.[194] A *tribunal extraordinaire* was set up in Gleiwitz and in early March it issued warrants for the extradition of the fourteen men who were implicated in the Petersdorf incident and who had fled over the frontier.[195] Although British officials had scant sympathy with the French[196] and doubted the validity of the warrants,[197] the British government could not dissociate itself from the French demands without precipitating, in the run-up to the Genoa Conference, a damaging row.[198] It thus grudgingly agreed that, after the Silesian Commission had reviewed the evidence, it should formally ask the German official representative in Silesia for extradition.[199] Not surprisingly the men were never found by the German government.

The German–Polish economic convention was at last concluded on 15 May and ratified by the Sejm and the Reichstag by the end of the month. On 15 June the Conference of Ambassadors notified both powers that they were free to take over their respective areas.[200] The Allied evacuation began on 19 June and was completed amidst scenes of escalating inter-racial strife and bitter incidents between French troops and German self-defence units. In anticipation of partition, German and Polish minorities were also being driven out of districts which were to be ceded respectively to Poland and Germany.[201] Up to the very end Allied troops were fully committed to peace-keeping operations. To the British troops fell the frequently dangerous task of covering the French evacuation from

192. Memorandum, 1.2.22, FO 890/2.
193. Memorandum, 6.2.22, FO 890/2.
194. 'Note from the British Commissioner' (undated draft, but early April), FO 890/2.
195. Heneker to D'Abernon, 4.3.22, FO 371/7471 fo. 46.
196. Heneker to Curzon, 23.2.22 (C2957), FO 371/7471 fos 264–5.
197. D'Abernon to Heneker, 3.3.22, FO 890/13.
198. Minute by Waterlow, 10.3.22, FO 371/7471 fos 87–8.
199. DBFP Ser. 1, vol. 16 (no. 384), pp. 400–1.
200. Wambaugh, *Plebiscites*, vol. 1, p. 260.
201. Heneker to Sec. WO July 1922 (C17176), FO 371/7470 fos 278–85.

Upper Silesia. Military discipline in some French units had broken down. At Groschowitz a British detachment had to halt a French troop train outside the station after it was learnt that the soldiers planned to avenge the murder of one of their colleagues by firing indiscriminately into the crowd on the station as they passed through. It was only with the utmost difficulty that the French commanding officer could be persuaded to restrain his men.[202]

For French policy the outcome of the Upper Silesian plebiscite was on balance a success. By acquiring most of the industrial triangle, Poland was shielded from complete economic domination by Germany, and Germany herself was made more dependent on Ruhr coal, and therefore vulnerable to French pressure on the Rhine. For the British it was an unexpected defeat and an object lesson in the folly of placing (in January 1920) a relatively inexperienced official in a sensitive post without sufficient administrative and military support. By the time Sir Harold Stuart arrived with six battalions of British troops, the consequences of Percival's failures, which in fairness were really Whitehall's, could only be mitigated, but not eradicated.

British Business and Upper Silesia:
A Postscript to the Plebiscite

Until its future was decided, British businessmen understandably viewed Upper Silesia as too risky an area for investment. They remained mere spectators when the French attempted to buy their way into the Upper Silesian coal and iron industries. In July 1920 two separate initiatives, one inspired by Laurent, the French Ambassador in Berlin, and Schneider-Creusot, which set up the Société d'études des affaires silésienses, the other by a consortium of French oil and metallurgical industries, began to negotiate the purchase of shares in Upper Silesian industry.[203] Le Rond gave every encouragement to the latter group and in a series of meetings with German officials and industrialists, the French Director of the Economic Department attempted to cajole and bludgeon the main Upper Silesian coal companies into selling their shares or accepting French capital.[204] British officials, who were quickly informed by

202. Stuart to Balfour, 31.7.22 (C10914), (FO) 371/7468 fo. 99.
203. Cienciala and Komarnicki, *From Versailles to Locarno*, pp. 84–5.
204. For a concise summary see 'Note Pour le Président du Conseil', 18.1.22, MAE Pologne 212 fos 223–5; for the German side see reports on the negotiations in FCO Lib. K2281 K642076-K642475.

the Germans of the negotiations, viewed them with detachment. Clark, the Chief Controller of Mines, informed the German mining engineer, Buntzel, that 'England was completely uninterested in Upper Silesia', although as an afterthought he conceded that the British should insist that 'the French did not receive more than was owing to them'.[205] In November Colonel Weyl of Le Creusot took over negotiations on behalf of both groups in Berlin, and in February 1921 signed a preliminary agreement with six German firms, but the efforts of the Auswärtiges Amt to make further negotiations dependent on a French guarantee that Upper Silesia should remain German effectively killed the Weyl plan.[206] Consequently a Franco–Polish economic convention was signed in March which permitted French capital to participate directly in private German firms once Upper Silesia became Polish.

There were some attempts to attract British finance as a corrective to French capital.[207] In April, for instance, Graf Henckel-Donnersmarck went to London to convince the City, but not surprisingly both he and others on similar missions failed. Not only was Britain suffering the worst economic crisis since the 1840s, but few businessmen were interested in investing in Upper Silesia until its frontier had been agreed upon.[208] The finalization of the Upper Silesian settlement by the League in October belatedly made Upper Silesia a more attractive proposition. The Quai d'Orsay was quick to sound the alarm that British economic initiatives were multiplying and 'diverses personnalités dont notamment M. Kenworthy . . . allaient à Berlin, Varsovie et Oppeln étudier la question sur place'.[209] Messrs Berwick, Moreing and Co. acquired a controlling interest in the Donnersmarck mines,[210] while Commander Kenworthy, the strongly pro–German MP, who was an important contact for the German Embassy in London, made several visits at the turn of the year[211] to negotiate a provisional agreement for setting up 'a big combine of foundries and mines, to be registered in London under the name of "the Upper Silesian

205. Bergrat Buntzel to Oberberghauptmann Althans, 18.9.20, p. 7, FCO Lib. K2281 K642105-10.
206. Cienciala and Komarnicki, *From Versailles to Locarno*, p. 85.
207. Note for G.A. Meyer, 15.12.20 (no. 820 O/S) FCO Lib. K2281 K642185-86.
208. Plessen to Meyer, 28.4.21 (no. 47471), FCO Lib. L912 L256107-110, and a note from Graf von Henckel-Donnersmarck, 28.4.21, ibid., L256180-182.
209. 'Note Pour le Président du Conseil', 18.1.22, MAE Pologne 212 fos 223–5.
210. Ibid.; see also *Dictionary of Business Biography*, vol. 4, London, 1985, p. 313.
211. For details see FCO Lib. K136 K014270-K04359.

Trust Co. Ltd.'', on behalf of John Slater's ''Amalgamated Industries Ltd.'''[212]

The Foreign Office viewed some of the businessmen interested in Upper Silesia with scarcely concealed contempt,[213] but more importantly, given the scale of Britain's diplomatic defeat over the Upper Silesian question, it was unable to offer them much real assistance. British capitalists considering investment in Upper Silesia were naturally concerned about the dangers of Polish expropriation once the fifteen-year transitional economic agreement had come to an end. To these the Foreign Office could only echo Kenworthy's advice that 'it was reasonable to suppose that . . . British financiers interesting themselves in such properties would reach some satisfying accommodation with the Polish Government'.[214] Despite this flurry of interest in Upper Silesian industry, in the end, apart from Berwick and Moreing, few British companies risked their money in Polish Upper Silesia. The Board of Trade advised strongly against investing in the Königs-und Laurahütte ironworks in February 1923 because it had 'unquestionably suffered by transfer to Poland'.[215] With the outbreak of the German–Polish tariff war in 1925 the prospects for British businessmen became still bleaker. Kimens, the British Commercial Secretary at the Warsaw Embassy warned in August that 'great care and prudence be exercised, only dealing for cash when possible'.[216]

212. Letter from H.M. Miller (Special Branch), 10.3.22 (C3764), FO 371/7562 fo. 97.
213. For instance, Waterlow observed on reading an account of an interview between Sir William Clark and a Mr W.B. Hopkins of Messrs Siemens and Co: 'Mr Hopkins was inarticulate and apparently imbecile. I suppose that he provides the money, while the German Jew [L. Kessler, his business partner] provides the brains': 12 April 1922 (C4999), FO 371/7562 fos 61–2.
214. Waterlow to R.H. Hoare, 10.5.22 (C6363), FO 371/7497 fo. 109.
215. Joynsen-Hicks to Steel Maitland, 12.2.23 (no. GS 7430/T.E.), BT 60 4/6 fos 53–5.
216. Mr Buchanan, no. 2 (30 338), 11.8.25, p. 251, Midland Bank Archives. For a list of foreign investments in the coal, iron and steel industries in 1929, see FCO Lib. 8868 E619563-68.

9

Polarization within the IAMCC, 1921–1922

By the end of 1920 it was accepted by the British government that Germany was essentially disarmed. Both Lloyd George and the War Office were inclined to dismiss any evidence to the contrary as amounting to little more than technical infringements. With the German fleet destroyed Britain was not threatened militarily by Germany; consequently the Lloyd George Cabinet subordinated disarmament to the question of reparation payments and the revival of the German economy. To the French, however, disarmament was, as Briand succinctly put it, 'a question of life and death'.[1] They explored each infringement of the Treaty meticulously and saw their suspicions confirmed when the German self-defence forces proved sufficiently strong to thwart Korfantry's attempt to seize the industrial area of Upper Silesia. The French were determined to prolong the period of direct control in Germany and kept up pressure on the German government for the absolute fulfilment of the disarmament clauses. Although the Wirth Cabinet was anxious to complete disarmament in 1921 in order to get rid of the hated Control Commissions as soon as possible, such was the hostility of the German army to control and the complexity of the disarmament clauses that Nollet had no difficulty in justifying the need for the IAMCC throughout 1921 and 1922 to remain in Germany. Bingham, of course, remained critical of Nollet's rigorous approach, but his attempts to modify it continued to be undermined by Morgan, who aligned himself with fanatical enthusiasm behind Nollet.

At the Paris Conference in January 1921 the gulf between the British and French assessments of the current state of German disarmament remained wide. Lloyd George, drawing on evidence from Bingham's reports, argued that the Germans 'substantially'[2]

1. DBFP Ser. 1, vol. 15 (no. 74), p. 489.
2. Ibid. (no. 1), p. 4.

lacked artillery, machine guns and ammunition, while Foch not only disputed the accuracy of Bingham's figures, but ominously pointed out that 'the Allies were not safe until they had received from the Germans the last machine gun and the last rifle which had to be surrendered under the Treaty'.[3] Nollet then seized the chance to emphasize that the majority opinion on the council of the IAMCC in Berlin disagreed with Bingham's calculations and that it would only take two months for Germany to produce thousands of guns. To reconcile these divergent opinions and statistics, the military experts were asked to draw up a list of what still remained to be done in Germany. This was presented to the Conference on 29 January,[4] and became the basis for the Allied disarmament note to Berlin of 29 January. Lloyd George succeeded in persuading the Conference for the time being not to couple the deadlines set in the note with an ultimatum, but instead to leak to the press rumours that sanctions would be enforced if the deadlines were not met. Foch was satisfied that this would hang 'over Germany like the sword of Damocles'.[5] The Paris notes increased the unpopularity of the Control Commission and bitterly disappointed the Germans, who had hoped for a moderating British influence. The German liaison officer in Cologne, for instance, complained to his superiors in Berlin that 'under the present conditions it takes a considerable effort of self control to listen to the arguments of *Entente* officers'.[6]

By the time German progress in disarmament was again reviewed by the Allied leaders at Lympne, insufficient progress had still been made by the Germans in executing the Paris note.[7] Lloyd George thus had little option but to agree to the inclusion of its demands in the London ultimatum, despite the opinion of the War Office that Germany was fundamentally disarmed.[8] On the day of the acceptance of the London ultimatum by the Wirth Cabinet, the Control Commission sent the Auswärtiges Amt a list of deadlines for the surrender of the remaining armaments and war materials, the dissolution of the Einwohnerwehr, the harmonization of the organization of both the army and the police forces with the demands of the Treaty of Versailles and the names of the fourteen factories to be allowed to continue the limited manufacture of arms

3. Ibid., p. 5.
4. Ibid., pp. 7–8 and Appendix 2 to no. 11, pp. 104–9.
5. Ibid. (no. 11), p. 97.
6. Nonn to Hauptverbindungsstelle, 1.2.21 (no. G.O. 4450), FCO Lib. L334 L099727-28.
7. Salewski, *Entwaffnung*, pp. 160–72.
8. DBFP Ser. 1, vol. 16 (no. 606), p. 659.

and munitions. The Germans had no choice but to agree to everything 'without reserve or condition'.[9]

Both in the Auswärtiges Amt and the Reichswehrministerium opinion gained ground that Simons had made a 'tremendous mistake in allowing France the opportunity of putting herself in the right'.[10] As part of the new fulfilment policy German liaison officers were ordered to cultivate friendly relations with their *Entente* opposite numbers.[11] Throughout the summer and autumn of 1921 considerable progress was at last made in disarmament;[12] nevertheless there still remained difficult problems concerning the reorganization of the police forces of the German states, and the inspection of Krupp and the state-owned armament factories which had been transferred into a single company called the Deutsche Werke, which comprised the former Reich arsenals. The War Office regarded the police question as 'the most important subject to be dealt with by control'.[13] At the Boulogne Conference in 1920 the Allies had agreed to a modest increase in the strength of the police, but had also ordered the dissolution of the Sicherheitspolizei and the reorganization of the police forces on a local and municipal basis, possessing an armament sanctioned only by the IAMCC. In the winter of 1920–1 a new police force, the Schutzpolizei, was organized by the Prussian and other state governments, but the IAMCC argued that in reality it represented 'a mobile military force with centralised commands and staff'.[14] Consequently, on 9 September 1921, Nollet insisted on a reduction in its personnel and several organizational reforms.[15] Lord D'Abernon, in a note in his own eccentric spelling, proposed a meeting between the IAMCC and the German Army Peace Commission to discuss 'the alledged [*sic*] infractions',[16] but no concessions were made by the IAMCC until July 1922, when Nollet grudgingly agreed that, provided excess police equipment was surrendered and several technical units were dissolved, the Schutzpolizei could be allowed to operate in a listed

9. Ibid., vol. 15 (Appendix to no. 77, Draft ultimatum submitted by M. Jaspar), p. 515.
10. Ball to Haining, 17.8.21, IWM 72/116/3.
11. Ibid.
12. Nollet was sufficiently optimistic to inform the French War Office that 'le désarmement est en bonne voie' ('Principales Questions exposées par le Général Nollet, le 23 juin 1921'), Vincennes 7N3576-1.
13. DBFP Ser. 1, vol. 16 (no. 836), p. 970.
14. Ibid., p. 973; see also Salewski, *Entwaffnung*, pp. 177 ff.
15. Salewski, *Entwaffnung*, pp. 177–78.
16. Undated note, FCO Lib. 9862, H. 319948.

number of cities.[17] This note disguised considerable differences of approach between Bingham and his colleagues. The IAMCC's reservations about the Schutzpolizei were based on Morgan's research into the Prussian Police Law and the legislation passed by the Reichstag creating the Schutzpolizei, which sought to prove that the Reichswehr and the Schutzpolizei were interchangeable.[18] Bingham, supported by D'Abernon,[19] believed that the IAMCC should be more accommodating and persuaded the War Office that the question of the Schutzpolizei should be considered town for town on its own merits. Pointedly Thwaites, the Director of Military Operations and Intelligence, observed:

> that the whole difficulty seems to resolve itself into a matter of principle, i.e. as to whether the Commission are to approach the German Government with a reasonable compromise, which, while maintaining all the safeguards we consider necessary, does still grant them some concessions, or whether the Commission are to continue to issue edicts on the police question to the German Government, as has been done for the last two years without any real results being obtained.[20]

When the Germans in September 1922 demanded further concessions, Curzon wanted the compromise proposed by the War Office, along the lines suggested by Bingham submitted to the Ambassadors' Conference as a basis for a settlement for the Schutzpolizei question, but on the advice of the Council of the Control Commission, with the single exception of Bingham, it was rejected by the Allied Military Committee of Versailles,[21] and the whole question was to remain unresolved for two more years.

By mid-1921 the majority of factories had been inspected and cleared for peace-time production. Even for smaller factories this was a lengthy and almost Kafkaesque process. Before a factory could be given a certificate clearing it for peace-time production, it was subjected to repeated visits from IAMCC officers, who would check that their original orders had been carried out.[22] These could

17. Salewski, *Entwaffnung*, p. 182.
18. DBFP Ser. 1, vol. 20, (no. 35), p. 609.
19. 'Aufzeichnung über eine Unterredung mit Lord D'Abernon in der Polizeifrage, 9.5.22', FCO Lib. 9862 H. 320304-07.
20. Thwaites to Bingham, 27.7.22 (0154 5938 M.I.3), FO 371/7561 fos 164–5.
21. Salewski, *Entwaffnung*, p. 182; DBFP Ser. 1, vol. 20 (nos 280 and 329), pp. 553–7 and 614–18.
22. For an interesting example of inspection in progress see 'Cologne District Committee. Descriptive Return of Factories dealt with during period 4–17 November, 1920', IWM 72/116/4.

suddenly be changed at short notice according to arbitrary and contradictory decisions from the IAMCC headquarters in Berlin. The fate of a whole workforce in a factory could sometimes be affected by a decision as to whether or not a particular product could be classified as war material. For instance one factory in Solingen, which produced toy and dress swords, suddenly had its export trade in these products banned by order of the IAMCC in Berlin, despite the fact that initially Bingham had given Colonel Weber, the President of the Cologne District Committee of the Armaments sub-Commission, verbal assurances that applications for small export orders were acceptable. Ball immediately wrote to Berlin pointing out that the contradictory decision 'has thrown the community at Solingen into disorder, because you cannot start working in a factory and stop it at a month's notice like a steam engine'. He also enlisted the formidable support of the British Kreis officer, who had a vested interest in avoiding the dangers that unemployment could bring in his Kreis.[23] This, of course, is a far from typical example. In unoccupied Germany, where British influence could not be brought into play in the form of a benevolent Kreis officer, the impact of the IAMCC could be both more arbitrary and more severe.

One of the most formidable tasks facing the Armaments sub-Commission was the supervision of the conversion of Krupp and the Deutsche Werke, from war- to peace-time production.[24] The Krupp Control Committee had made slow progress since May 1920. It had conducted a painstaking survey of the eighty enormous workshops in Essen. For six years five officers headed by Colonel Everett, the President of the Westphalian District Committee of the Armaments sub-Commission, were billeted in the Krupp guest house, originally designed for foreign businessmen negotiating arms contracts. The relevant directors were asked searching questions in a series of meetings with Everett's committee about the employment of their machines both before, during and after the war.[25] The Naval and Military Control Commissions authorized Krupp to produce a limited number of guns and a certain amount of armoured plating to equip the Reichswehr and the small German

23. Ball to Col. Thomson, Armaments sub-Commission, Berlin, 29.9.20, IWM 72/116/3.
24. Morgan, *Assize of Arms*, vol. 2, ch. XV (corrected in Morgan's hand to 'XIX'), 'The Munitions Industry', pp. 313–57, has much interesting information on this topic.
25. For examples of its activities and minutes of meetings, etc., see material in Vincennes (Jacobson) IK.185, especially boxes 3 and 4.

navy permitted by the Treaty. The actual number of guns was notified to the German government in October 1921, but Krupp delayed drawing up plans for their manufacture as long as possible in the hope that if it procrastinated long enough, the Control Commissions would be withdrawn. In September 1922 Everett complained to Nollet that 'unless something is done, which will have some definite result, the question will go on indefinitely'.[26]

Any specialized plant, classified as category A, not required for these contracts was to be destroyed and 'semi-specialized machinery', category B, was to be converted to peace-time production, and, if necessary, dispersed to other factories. Supervising the destruction of category A material was relatively easy, but it composed a mere 5 per cent of the equipment at Krupp which had converted to the manufacture of locomotives, agricultural machines and even typewriters, where the 'semi-specialized' machinery could be effectively adapted to new use. Inevitably this created ambiguities and interminable controversies. A *cause célèbre* was the fate of the seventy-eight heavy gun lathes in shop ten. Krupp argued, on the strength of both a contract from the Badischer Aniline Company for cylinder tubes to be used for the production of synthetic ammonia, and on the prospect of orders for equipping the new Reichsmarine, that the company needed to retain all its gun lathes. The IAMCC wanted them destroyed or dispersed, but on Bingham's insistence a compromise was proposed and Krupp was allowed to keep thirty-six of them.[27]

The IAMCC proceeded along similar lines with the Deutsche Werke, which were permitted to retain as many machines as were needed to meet 'a genuine commercial demand for "neutral" articles of manufacture'.[28] The factories then began to produce large quantities of sporting rifles and cartridges, which far exceeded the total German output for 1913 and inevitably incurred Nollet's suspicions.[29] In September 1921 the Commission decided to withdraw its authorization for the manufacture of sporting rifles and demanded that the rifling machines should be dispersed. The German government countered by whipping up a campaign in the press and trade union movement, in which it was suggested that

26. 'Future War Manufacture at Krupps', 20.9.22 (K.1438/10), ibid. box 3.
27. Morgan, *Assize of Arms*, vol. 2, pp. 321–30.
28. Ibid., p. 336.
29. Nollet visited one factory producing 100,000 shotguns a day and later observed that 'in der ganzen Welt gäbe es nicht so viel wilde Tiere, um eine derartige Produktion zu rechtfertigen'; 'Protokoll über die Unterredung zwischen . . . Nollet und dem Zentralbetriebsrat der deutschen Werke, am.14.11.21' (A.A.F.12098), pp. 14–15, FCO Lib. L377 L110334-49.

this would make tens of thousands of workers redundant.[30] On Bingham's insistence the Commission argued that they were dealing with a clear violation of the Treaty, which need not necessarily lead to mass redundancies.[31] On 14 November Bingham and Nollet met the works committees of the Haselhorst and Spandau branches of the Deutsche Werke at the headquarters of the IAMCC and sought, with some success, to put the men's fears at rest.[32]

The IAMCC pursued a policy of licensing smaller factories for armament production on the ground that they would be easier to monitor and less likely to expand their production beyond the authorized output. The relatively small firm of Simson's at Stuhl was, for example, given a licence, rather than the Erfurt branch of the Deutsche Werke. However, the complex cartelization of German industry in fact ensured that the identity of any one firm became hopelessly elusive and that the Commission's policy of limiting production to minor companies was impossible to carry out. In 1944 Morgan recalled that:

> We authorised Ehrhardt's instead of Krupp's, for the manufacture of field guns, as opposed to heavy guns, only to discover that Krupp's had a controlling interest in it. We authorised the Sommerda firm for the manufacture of fuses and then discovered that Ehrhardt's had acquired in turn the control of Sommerda. We then substituted the Dortmund Union Company for Sommerda. No sooner had we done this than the ubiquitous Herr Stinnes acquired a controlling interest in the Dortmund Union.[33]

The IAMCC was confronted with an equally intractable problem in controlling the potential production of explosives. It was not hard to destroy existing munition plants, but given the sophistication of the German chemical industry, factories producing nitrates, which are a vital ingredient of dyes and fertilizers, were potentially in a position to manufacture high explosives if they converted their plant from nitration in its secondary stage to nitration in its tertiary stage.[34] Both Bingham and, somewhat more surprisingly, the French chemical expert on the IAMCC, Colonel Muraour, were less alarmed by this possibility than Mor-

---

30. Morgan, *Assize of Arms*, vol. 2, p. 337.
31. DBFP Ser. 1, vol. 16 (no. 849 footnote 2), pp. 991–2.
32. FCO Lib. L377 L110334–49 (14.11.21).
33. Morgan, *Assize of Arms*, vol. 2, p. 341. The example of Simson's is quoted on p. 340.
34. Ibid., p. 350.

gan. Muraour was convinced that 'with such a high percentage of the population holding socialist or communistic views', any attempt to convert the plant to produce explosives would be immediately betrayed to the Allies.[35] On 13 December, 1921 Bingham, armed with material and slides supplied by Ball, gave a lecture in London, in which he argued that the German chemical industry held no military threats for Britain.[36] His somewhat facile optimism had already been indirectly criticized in *The Times* in an article which the German liaison officer in Cologne believed was orchestrated by the French section of the IAMCC, although it was arguably more likely to have been by Morgan.[37]

Inevitably the Schutzpolizei question and the intricate problem of industrial demobilization continued to exacerbate relations between the IAMCC and the Reich government, but both Bingham and Nollet agreed that by early 1922 Germany no longer represented an immediate military threat. Nollet informed the Deuxième Bureau that 'jamais la France n'avait été dans une situation meilleure qu'à l'heure actuelle, puisque l'Allemagne est au point de vue effectif et matériel désarmée à peu pres complètement',[38] but the French War Office remained obsessed by the fear of a German military revival once the IAMCC had left Germany and emphasized significantly the need for her moral disarmament.[39] In June 1921 Nollet urged a thirty-year programme to win over the minds of German youth and advised the Deuxième Bureau that a French propaganda office should be set up in Berlin 'pour changer la mentalité des jeunes générations'.[40] Apart from Ball, who floated the idea with 'various' heads of industrial concerns in the Rhineland that Germany, 'in order to convince the Continent [that she was] really out for peace', should attach British officers to Reichswehr, units, and recruit public school and university men to posts in the Gymnasien and universities to teach students football, cricket, hockey and golf, the magical qualities of which would apparently encourage the

35. Ball to Haining, 17.8.21, IWM 72/116/3.
36. The notes for the talk are in the Ball Papers, IWM 72/116/4. The talk was published in the *Journal of the Royal United Service Institution*, vol. 69, Feb. to Nov. 1924, pp. 747–63.
37. Von Stechow to Hauptverbindungsstelle, 12.12.21, FCO Lib. K138 K014536-7; see 'German Army Plot', *The Times*, 19.11.21.
38. 'Compte-Rendu, d'entretien avec Général Nollet', 26.1.22, Vincennes 7N3576-I.
39. Ibid. (Col. Fabry).
40. 'Principales Questions Exposées par le Général Nollet, le 23 juin 1921', Vincennes 7N3576-1.

Germans to 'play the game' and so liberate them from Prussianism,[41] British officials showed little interest in the concept of re-education. The War Office, in November 1921, like Lloyd George and most sections of the Labour and Liberal Parties, still placed their emphasis more on a policy of diplomatic and economic appeasement than on educational propaganda, and on the whole accepted that 'the changes in the last two years show that a policy of active repression against Germany, or even a policy of pin pricks, invariably strengthen the reactionary and military element of the population and provide a handle for all those working for a future war of recovery'.[42]

Within the British element of the IAMCC opinion on the state of German disarmament remained sharply divided. Bingham, Roddie and the Cologne District Committee remained convinced that Germany was disarmed, while Morgan was passionately committed to proving that German disarmament was a myth. It is unclear how much support he enjoyed amongst his colleagues in the British section. Morgan later claimed backing from the majority of officers on the Armaments sub-Commission working out on the district committees,[43] and that his famous exposé in the *Quarterly Review* of 1924[44] was prompted 'by a series of almost passionate appeals to me from regular officers who had served with me on the Commission'.[45] He was probably not exaggerating, as the British Control officers operating outside the Rhineland in unoccupied Germany regularly experienced the Reichswehr's guerilla war against Allied control, which at times degenerated into verbal and even physical violence.

While Morgan was prepared to intrigue with Nollet against Bingham in the interests, as he perceived them, of the *Entente*, Ball was equally active in the cause of Anglo–German trade. Both men were patriots, but differed fundamentally in their assessment of the

---

41. Ball to Haining, 11.6.21, IWM 72/116/3. Ball also wrote on this theme in the *Kölnische Zeitung* and *Deutsche Allgemeine Zeitung*: ibid., Ball to Layton, 27.7.21. Similar ideas were current in 1919: see 'Notes on the Importance of Supervision of Further Education in Germany', LSE Wise Papers, Box 1, A5, in which it was argued that 'a council of British and American Educational Authorities' should be established 'with full powers of veto and supervision for the next 25 years' over educational policy and appointments.
42. 'Germany's General Military Position and the Situation in Upper Silesia, Nov. 1921' (WO 31.10.21), WO 155/3 fo. 70.
43. Morgan, *Assize of Arms*, vol. 2, p. 291.
44. Morgan, 'The Disarmament of Germany and After', *Quarterly Review*, vol. 242, October 1924, pp. 415–57.
45. Morgan, *Assize of Arms*, vol. 2, Galley slip III (62T section II CR 166).

way their country's interests could best be served. Through his wide network of contacts with British and German businessmen and officials, Ball constantly emphasized his belief that German disarmament was completed and that British and German industry needed to cooperate. In a letter to Sir Philip Lloyd Graeme, the Parliamentary Secretary at the Board of Trade,[46] he depicted the French as dangerous economic rivals, and argued strongly that 'England and every Englishman today must cast aside all appeals to sentiment, and work individually for the best interests of his own country'. Drawing on information obtained from Thyssen, Klöckner, Lübsen, Duisberg and other leading German industrialists, he informed Graeme that 'the main French object [was] the total economic collapse of German industry' and to gain permanent control of the Ruhr and Saar.[47] He thus interpreted the imposition of the customs barrier in the Rhineland in April 1921 and French policy in Upper Silesia as steps towards realizing these aims.[48] In April 1921, through contacts with W.T. Layton, the Director of the National Federation of Iron and Steel Manufacturers, who, as a consequence of working in the Ministry of Munitions during the war, still had close contacts with Lloyd George, Ball became a remarkable two-way channel for information between the German and British governments. In April he approached von Stechow, the head of the German Military Liaison Office in Cologne, with the request for information for Lloyd George on the situation in the Saar, apparently with the aim of proving that the French occupation was ruining the Saar economy. Stechow recommended supplying him with the relevant information as he received 'through Ball much new and background material [*Stimmungsbericht*], which enabled one to see behind the scenes'.[49] Von Cramon ignored his request, but Schubert, the Undersecretary of State at the Auswärtiges Amt, welcomed his initiative and ensured that he received the necessary information.[50]

By the autumn of 1921 Lord D'Abernon was becoming increasingly impatient with what he saw as a French obsession with minor violations of the Treaty. In a celebrated memorandum in November 1921 he dismissed 'the attitude . . . assumed in certain circles'

46. Ball to Sir Philip Lloyd Graeme (undated), IWM 72/116/3. Similar sentiments are expressed in a letter to Lloyd Graeme, dated 13.4.21, ibid.
47. Ibid. (undated letter).
48. Ibid., Ball to Layton, 25.5.21.
49. Stechow to Oberst von Cramon, 18.4.21, FCO Lib. K138 K014417-18.
50. Memorandum by Schubert, 20.5.21, FCO Lib. K138 K014427-29. In return Ball communicated to him information he received from Layton et al.: see ibid., KO 14479-80 (Layton's letter of 31.5.21 to Ball).

that Germany was still or could in the immediate future become a major military power as 'a Rip van Winkle conception, totally inapplicable to present circumstances'.[51] This view was widely shared by his staff at the Berlin Embassy and helped reinforce Bingham's own assessment of the situation in Germany. In 1922, for instance, Morgan was incensed when one of D'Abernon's subordinates ironically observed that the IAMCC 'will hang on here until they have demobilized the last typewriter of the *Reichswehrministerium*'.[52]

Every fresh discovery of a cache of illegal armaments or some crafty subterfuge to disguise mobilization plans gave rise to bitter wrangles on the Control Commission, as it strengthened Nollet and Morgan, as opposed to Bingham and behind him Lord D'Abernon. Consequently, when Colonel Beasley, in response to a tip-off from a worker, found in a factory at Heidenau a cache of 587 howitzers in perfect condition in November 1921, Morgan pounced on the discovery and argued that its significance was impossible to exaggerate.[53] *The Times*, echoing Morgan, observed that 'if this sort of thing can happen in one of the many thousand factories . . . which the Commission is supposed to have inspected, it is a fair inference of fact that Germany is still in possession of an armament hugely in excess of that laid down by the Treaty of Versailles'.[54] This view was strengthened when Rockstroh, the proprietor of the Heidenau factory, admitted that all the registers of gun production were hidden in the arsenal at Spandau, but before the Commission could seize these vital documents they were removed and, despite repeated demands, never again produced. To Bingham the Heidenau incident was particularly annoying because it appeared to confirm the fears of Nollet and Morgan. Indeed, Bingham's first reaction, apparently, was to be 'simply furious'[55] with Beasley, but it did not shake his basic conviction that Germany was fundamentally disarmed, a view which continued to be shared by the War Office also until 1923.[56]

The whole question of whether the Reichswehr was a cadre army, planned with an eye to future expansion, similarly polarized opinion on the Commission. Barthélemy and Morgan produced formidable evidence, which Morgan prematurely leaked to the

51. DBFP Ser. 1, vol. 16 (no. 837), p. 981.
52. Morgan, *Assize of Arms*, vol. 2, Galley slip V (62V CR 168).
53. Ibid., pp. 292–5.
54. *The Times*, 21.2.22, quoted in Morgan, *Assize of Arms*, vol. 2, pp. 294–5.
55. Morgan, *Assize of Arms*, vol. 2, p. 294.
56. DBFP Ser. 1, vol. 20 (no. 242), pp. 497–8.

press in September 1921, to prove that the new Reichswehr was 'nothing but a cadre army',[57] but the War Office, remaining unmoved by these revelations, argued that Germany lacked the equipment to arm a mass army.[58] Indeed it attempted in June 1922 to recall Morgan, but under strong pressure from Nollet had to relent.[59] In November 1922 Morgan bypassed the War Office and began to send copies of his memoranda directly to the Foreign Office, which had initially shared the War Office's suspicions of Morgan as a 'temporary gentleman', primarily concerned with extending his tenure in Germany,[60] but in December 1922 after studying his work on the pension legislation, both Crowe and Lampson[61] conceded that he was probably right. Crowe minuted that Morgan had placed 'himself in the wrong by reporting behind the back of his chief to us in the obvious hope that we shall not readily accept the War Office views based on General Bingham's reports', but advised that 'careful note' should be made of Morgan's reports although the Foreign Office should keep out of 'personal questions'. Lampson also found them 'very convincing', but, rather than challenge the War Office, he observed: 'I would personally much rather that they did not reach us at all . . . the really unsatisfactory feature of the whole business is that we are "*nolens volens*" being forced to believe that our representative on the IAMCC is inefficient, but the War Office will not for a moment admit that'.

Incidents like the Heidenau discovery strengthened French arguments against a premature withdrawal of control from Germany. By the summer of 1921 the question of monitoring German disarmament, once the Control Commissions had been withdrawn, was being considered by both the British and the French governments. Curzon rejected a proposal made originally by Bingham[62] for handing over the task to the League of Nations, and instead proposed[63] a troika of military, aeronautical and naval committees of guarantee which would each be composed of a small inter-Allied

57. J.H. Morgan, 'Report on the Armed Forces of Germany and the Work of the Effectives sub-Commission of Control', April 1922, pp. 1–58, ADM 116 1937. For the 'leak' see *The Times*, 26.9.21, 'New German Army'.

58. See for example the Memorandum communicated unofficially by the War Office to the Foreign Office: '*The Times* Article on the New German Army', 26.9.21, FO 371/5858 fos 58–61.

59. Morgan, *Assize of Arms*, vol. 1, p. 277.

60. Minute by Wigram, 27.9.21 (18716), FO 371/5858 fos 56–7.

61. Minutes (C17141), 27.12.22, FO 371/7561 fos 251–2.

62. DBFP Ser. 1, vol. 10 (no. 317), pp. 433–4.

63. Ibid., vol. 16 (no. 815), pp. 922–4.

staff, normally stationed in their own capitals, but which could be dispatched to Germany if the Allied governments became suspicious of any German military activity. As the Peace Treaty made no allowance for these bodies, Curzon proposed to win German consent to such a step by an immediate Allied promise 'to dissolve the existing Commissions of Control by fixed dates'.[64] When the question was discussed by the Supreme Council in Paris in August 1921,[65] Curzon secured outright agreement for the withdrawal of the Aeronautical Commission by the end of the year and considerable reductions in the IAMCC involving the withdrawal of the Fortifications sub-Commission and a reduction of 50 per cent in the Armaments sub-Commission, but Admirals Charlton and de Marguerye opposed a premature dissolution of the IANCC,[66] although they had already conceded substantial cuts in personnel.[67] There was no agreement where the proposed Committees of Guarantee should sit, as the French continued to insist on Berlin. In the autumn of 1921 the Foreign Office in consultation with the Admiralty, War Office and Air Ministry drew up a compromise scheme,[68] which was discussed at the Conference of Ambassadors in March 1922.[69] The Germans were to be presented with a list of outstanding disarmament measures, which still needed to be executed; when this was done, they would be asked to accept the new Committees of Guarantee, which would consist of small intelligence-collecting bodies in Berlin and a larger body of personnel, employed on routine duties at home, who could be summoned to Germany to carry out inspections if necessary. The Guarantee Committees would initially be provisional and their future would be reviewed when the northern Rhineland zone was due to be evacuated in 1925.

The French reluctantly agreed to the proposal[70] and the acceptance by the German government of the Aeronautical Committee of Guarantee in May 1922[71] appeared to augur well for a similar solution for military and naval disarmament, but in practice only very slow progress was made towards this goal in the remaining months of 1922. There was sharp disagreement between Nollet and

64. Ibid., p. 924.
65. Hardinge to FO, 13.8.21 (C16356), FO 371/5864 fos 143–5.
66. Extract from 'British Secretary's Notes of an Allied Conference held at the Quai d'Orsay, 13.8.21', ADM 116 1935.
67. Ibid., Charlton to Admiralty, 24.6.21 (no. 369/8/A/20).
68. DBFP Ser. 1, vol. 16 (no. 836), pp. 976–7.
69. Ibid., vol. 20 (no. 180), pp. 396–8.
70. Ibid. (no. 199), pp. 422–3.
71. Ibid. (no. 221), p. 459.

the British War Office on the relative importance of the outstanding questions which still needed to be cleared up before Germany could be judged to be effectively disarmed. The War Office argued that the only matters of prime importance were the completion of the reorganization of the police forces, the transformation of the munitions factories and the surrender of all the remaining unauthorized war material, as well as the key documents giving the details of armament production during the war, although later it conceded the need to ban the import and export of war material and to regulate military recruitment more strictly. The French, on the other hand, had a much longer list of priorities which opened up the prospect of endless haggling with Berlin.[72] Both sets of these demands were then grouped into five main points, which formed the basis of the Allied note of 29 September to Berlin.[73] The German government was prepared to negotiate on the military Committee of Guarantee,[74] but on 10 December argued[75] that Germany had already disarmed completely and that total compliance with the five points would endanger both the Reich's economy and its security.

By the end of December 1922 negotiations on the future of control appeared to be blocked. Simultaneously relations between the Control Commissions and the German authorities were exacerbated by incidents at Passau and Ingolstadt where mobs attacked IAMCC officers and stoned their cars.[76] The tenacious determination of Nollet to probe every aspect of German disarmament at the end of 1922 held out the prospect of a prolonged period of tension and friction both between the IAMCC and German authorities, and, within the Council of the IAMCC, between Bingham and Nollet, although in practice the Ruhr occupation of January 1923 was to prevent any effective control for another year. By the end of 1922 the repeated assurances by D'Abernon and Bingham that Germany was virtually disarmed were being challenged by the embarrassing revelations that the Reichswehr was a cadre army and by the discovery of caches of weapons, of which the howitzers at Heidenau was the most dramatic. Yet viewed from London, where Germany's continued existence as a great power was a basic assumption of British policy and whose economic revival was deemed essential for European recovery, these revelations were of

72. Ibid. (no. 238), pp. 482–4.
73. Ibid. (nos 270 and 277), pp. 541–3 and 549.
74. Ibid. (no. 287), pp. 565–6.
75. Ibid. (no. 351), pp. 639–42.
76. Ibid. (nos 309 and 318), pp. 593–4 and 602–4.

marginal importance and did not affect the basic British argument that German disarmament was as good as complete. Germany's helpless reaction in January 1923 to the Franco–Belgian invasion of the Ruhr seemed to confirm this assessment of the situation.

–10–

The Rhineland under the Shadow of Poincaré, 1922

Kilmarnock arrived in the Rhineland on 16 December 1921 to take up the post of British High Commissioner with a reputation of being dour and taciturn,[1] but in the aftermath of the sanctions crisis, tenacity and a degree of bloody-mindedness was essential for any British High Commissioner if he were to counter successfully French machinations in the Rhineland. Kilmarnock took over a small garrison of nearly 5,000 troops and an effective and experienced team of administrators, who enjoyed the trust of the local German population and knew how to differentiate 'between firmness and harshness'.[2] Not being agents of a power with political ambitions on the Rhine, they were able to display, with the odd inevitable exception, an admirable impartiality and attempted 'truly and indifferently to administer justice within the terms of the Armistice and Treaty'.[3]

Like his predecessors, Kilmarnock was hindered in the constant struggle to assert British influence at Coblenz by the penny-pinching policy of the Treasury, which in December 1921 even suggested cutting his salary by half[4] and which continued to exercise constant pressure on the Foreign Office to keep British expenses in the Rhineland to a minimum. While Tirard successfully blocked all attempts to cut down the overblown French bureaucracy in the Rhineland,[5] Robertson in one of his last decisions as Commissioner had abolished some ten posts in the British section.[6] The British element also faced the prospect of increasing isolation in the Rhineland, as the American Army of Occupation was

1. St Aulaire to MAE, 14.11.21, MAE Rive Gauche 200 fos 60–1.
2. Minute by Lampson, 26.4.22 (C4528), FO 371/7520 fo. 149.
3. Minute by A. Cadogan, 25.9.22 (C12842), FO 371/7521 fos 218–19.
4. Minute by Headlam Morley, 23.12.21, FO 371/5855 fo. 178.
5. Kilmarnock to Curzon, 17.1.22 (C899), FO 371/7542 fo. 24.
6. Robertson to Curzon, 12.11.21 (C21825), FO 371/5885 fos 153–5.

progressively cut.[7] On 20 March 1922, orders were issued by the State Department in Washington for the complete evacuation of the American contingent. All the Allies were anxious to keep an American presence on the Rhine, as were the Germans, who dreaded that the vacuum left would be filled by French troops. Consequently, as a result of both Allied and German representations at Washington, Allen was permitted, for the time being, to remain at Coblenz with a token number of 1,000 troops, and withdrawal was averted until February 1923. To offset the reductions in the American forces, Rathenau, the German Foreign Minister, actually appealed to Kilmarnock for British troop reinforcements,[8] but the British garrison could not be brought up to strength until Silesia was evacuated in July. In April Morland and Kilmarnock did, however, press for the extension of the British Zone to include the Kreise of Bonn, Siegburg, Euskirchen and Rheinbach, which had been handed over to the French in October 1919, on the ground that it would give the British army access to the manoeuvre grounds at Wahn and more barrack space,[9] as well as going some way to balance the imminent absorption by the French of the American Zone, but the proposal was vetoed by Foch in July.[10]

Both the Germans and the British greeted Poincaré's appointment with apprehension, but initially his impact on the Rhineland was milder than expected.[11] Nevertheless, against a background of deteriorating Anglo–French relations at international level the Rhineland High Commission increasingly became dominated by what amounted to a stubborn trench war between the British and French Commissioners and their staff. Kilmarnock's first major clash with Tirard in the Commission came over the Smeets affair. Joseph Smeets, the editor and proprietor of the *Rheinische Republik*, a separatist journal, was summoned on 5 December 1921 to appear before the Cologne Landgericht for slandering a German official. He insisted on being taken to Colonel Birch, the acting Chief Delegate of the High Commission in Cologne, to plead for release on the grounds that he was being persecuted for his political beliefs. Birch informed the police that the execution of the warrant could proceed provided that Smeets was not taken into unoccupied

7. 'Annual Report of the Inter-Allied High Commission for 1922', pp. 33–6.
8. Kilmarnock to Curzon, 21.2.22 (C2724), FO 371/7520 fos 124–7.
9. WO to Undersec., FO 24.5.22 (C7598), FO 371/7521 fo. 38; 'Report', 1922, pp. 36–7.
10. Ibid., 17.7.22 (C10251), fo. 136.
11. Kilmarnock to Curzon, 21.2.22 (C2724), FO 371/7520 fos 124–7.

territory. Smeets then appealed directly to the High Commission, where he was guaranteed a more favourable hearing. His case was then discussed at successive sittings 'from every point of view with keenness and at times with acrimony'.[12] Kilmarnock attempted to take a purely *laissez-faire* line and argue that it was a domestic German quarrel, but Tirard, conscious that several articles had already appeared in the French press on Smeets, and that twenty-five French deputies had already sent a petition to Briand urging Smeets' release, surprised both General Allen and Lord Kilmarnock by insisting that if the High Commission refused to intervene on behalf of Smeets, 'his Government would be obliged to change the whole basis of its policy in the Rhineland, and that the solidarity of the Allies in the Rhineland would be shattered'.[13] Kilmarnock was unimpressed and forced a vote, which caused the Belgian Commissioner to desert Tirard and propose a temporary compromise whereby Smeets would be released pending further assessment of the case.

The Smeets case rumbled on throughout 1922.[14] Smeets was tried by German courts in February, March and June, and in August the affair came before the High Commission again when the Germans requested confirmation by the High Commission of his eight months' prison sentence. Kilmarnock had to steer a difficult course between showing public loyalty to the Commission, while privately opposing Tirard's attempts to secure Smeets' release. In September Kilmarnock received instructions from the Foreign Office which were based on Sir William Tyrrel's crisp minute: 'We should on no account give way . . . The French have made perfect fools of themselves over this miserable creature.'[15] When the High Commission met on 28 September Ryan, acting in Kilmarnock's absence, forced a vote, which he lost but which publicly demonstrated the deep divisions between the Allies in the Rhineland. In the words of the annual report of the British element of the High Commission, 'M. Tirard was visibly upset . . . and it was only with the greatest reluctance, after having proposed compromise after compromise, different in form but identical in substance, that he finally resigned himself to putting the question to the vote.'[16]

While the Smeets affair was a *cause célèbre*, Anglo–French dis-

12. 'Report', 1921, p. 25.
13. Ibid., p. 25.
14. 'Report', 1922, pp. 12–17.
15. Minute, 4.9.22 (C12507), FO 371/7521 fo. 214.
16. 'Report', 1922, p. 15.

agreement was evident over all decisions which could in any way, however indirectly, influence the political future of the Rhineland. Thus Kilmarnock initially had considerable reservations about the setting up of a committee in January 1922 to examine whether teachers were inculcating their pupils with nationalist propaganda, as this might lead to active French interference in education and the appointment of teachers. It was only when Colonel Stone, the American representative, enthusiastically welcomed it that Kilmarnock gave it his grudging support.[17] The report of the Intelligence Committee of the IARHC on the Republican demonstrations in Wiesbaden on 4 July marking Rathenau's assassination, which escalated into a riot, again divided the Commission.[18] The French demanded the removal of both the Regierungspräsident and the Police Commissioner, while Kilmarnock was satisfied with the measures taken by the police and suspected that the French were anxious to remove known opponents of the Rhineland separatist movement. Deadlock was prevented only by another American compromise, which proposed that after a short period of time the two officials should be transferred by the Prussian government to some other post. Only when the Prussian government rejected this compromise did Kilmarnock agree to the suspension of the Regierungspräsident. Even the perennial question of introducing western European time on the railways to facilitate troop movements, where previously the British High Commissioners had allowed themselves to be overruled, now led to a further clash between the British and the French.[19] On 26 September, two days before the Smeets *dénouement*, Ryan made history by forcing a vote for the first time on this question.

Throughout 1922 the French tenaciously maintained their support for separatism. In June the Rhineland question again came into sharp focus when, in a series of speeches by both Prussian and Reich politicians, French-backed separatism was bitterly attacked. Braun, the Prussian Prime Minister, declared in the Landtag that 'the Franc was rolling in the occupied territories as the roubles of the Tsar used to roll in the Balkans to corrupt the population'.[20] Thurstan, the British Consul in Cologne, warned that the French were successfully exploiting the inflationary crisis to win over the peasantry in the Eifel and the rural districts west of Cologne. He feared that the more the French were thwarted in their designs on

17. Ibid., p. 24; Tirard to MAE (no. 3), 5.1.22, MAE Rive Gauche 5 fos 120–2.
18. 'Report', 1922, pp. 7–8.
19. Ibid., pp. 30–2.
20. Ibid., 1922, p. 6.

the Ruhr, the more they would try to encourage Smeets to risk a coup in the Rhineland.[21] In practice neither policy excluded the other. In May Dariac, the president of the Finance Commission of the French Chamber, visited the Rhineland and put forward a coherent programme for the separation of the Rhineland, involving customs barriers on its eastern frontiers, a separate budget and currency, the elimination of Prussian officials and 'la convocation d'une assemblée élue'.[22] But the French were also casting their net even wider. On 24 June General Mangin dispatched confidential information to Paris from Dannenberg, the Guelph separatist leader, on plans for an independent Lower Saxony, in the event of a French occupation of the Ruhr.[23] Kilmarnock's staff did not, however, rate the chances of success for Rhineland separatism very highly, unless there was 'another great crisis' which would force the Rhinelanders to act in self-preservation 'or that the principle of water in continual action against stone [might] create in the Rhinelander such a stage [*sic*] of political apathy as would bring him at length to such a mind that he would only exhibit resignation when faced with a *fait accompli*'.[24] By the autumn of 1922 'the principle of water in continual action against stone' had been in operation for three years without much effect, but the prospect of a Ruhr occupation offered the French an opportunity of exploiting a suitably 'great crisis'.

The Foreign Office recognized that without a general settlement with France, British officials were powerless to check French initiatives in the Rhineland. Thus throughout 1922 all the outstanding Anglo–French differences in the Rhineland remained unresolved. Waterlow, for instance, observed in April that unless it was within the context of a larger settlement there was little point in attempting to cut Tirard's budget 'for the problem [was] one of that group of subordinate issues which, however important, are insusceptible of any real settlement so long as we have no large political settlement with France. To attack in isolation is merely to irritate one exceptionally sensitive part of a diseased surface.'[25]

As a consequence of French policy, German nationalist attacks on the High Commission increased. Lectures and rallies were held

21. DBFP Ser. 1, vol. 20 (no. 219), pp. 456–8.
22. 'Rapport sur une Mission De Contrôle A L'Armée Du Rhin, presenté par M. Adrien Dariac, 23.5.22', MAE Rive Gauche 6 fos 192–219; see also McDougall *Rhineland Diplomacy*, pp. 205–6.
23. 'Note pour le Président Du Conseil, 24.6.22', MAE Rive Gauche 6 fo. 272; McDougall, *Rhineland Diplomacy*, p. 117.
24. 'General Report on the Rhineland' (C12842), p. 22, FO 371/7521 fos 220–30.
25. Minute, 10.4.22 (C5201), FO 371/7543 fos 276–7.

just outside the occupied territories by such war heroes as General Liman von Sanders, Admiral von Scheer and Kapitän von Müller of the Emden.[26] In March 1922 a Belgian Lieutenant was severely wounded in a tram in Aachen as a reprisal for an earlier incident in which a German policeman had been shot.[27] The main target of this agitation was the French, but the British were also attacked particularly for their billeting policy, which at a time of acute housing shortages in Cologne was a major source of friction between the Rhine Army and the population.[28]

Industrial relations, however, remained peaceful. In the autumn of 1921 escalating inflation seemed to be about to precipitate a general financial collapse, but the falling mark triggered off an export boom, and by April 1922 the unemployment figure in the British Zone had touched a post-war low of nine per thousand.[29] Then, just as the boom appeared to be over in June, the value of the mark began to decline rapidly again and the frenetic pace of industrial output could therefore be maintained. The British authorities were uncomfortably aware of the fragile nature of the boom and of how it had 'been brought about by abnormal conditions which may collapse as suddenly as they appeared'.[30]

At the end of December 1921,[31] the Reichsbahn personnel staged a series of selective strikes in the key railway districts of Essen, Elberfeld and Cologne, hoping thereby to paralyse the Ruhr coalfield traffic and the Rhenish-Westphalian industrial market on both sides of the Rhine. The High Commission ordered the strikers in the Cologne district back immediately. In practice both the strike leaders and the British officials moved with considerable circumspection. Colonel Manton, the president of the Inter-Allied Railway sub-Commission at Cologne, conducted talks with the railwaymen in a deliberately low key; he overlooked the fact that they had not immediately obeyed the orders of the High Commission and conceded that economic conditions had driven them into strike action. He also stressed that the High Commission was attempting to put the railwaymen's case for wage increases to the German government. The French, on the other hand, pressed for more decisive action. Payot, who was responsible for the French army's

26. 'Report', 1922, p. 3.
27. Ibid., p. 4.
28. Williamson, 'Cologne and The British', p. 701.
29. 'Report', 1922, p. 10; Edmonds, *The Occupation*, p. 227.
30. 'Summary of the Most Important Chapters of the Annual Report', March 1922 (C4528), FO 371/7520 fos 150–3.
31. 'Report', 1921, pp. 16–19; 'Report', 1922, pp. 1–2.

lines of communication, created a momentary crisis on the commission by exceeding his instructions and sending out an order for the collective requisitioning of the personnel in the Cologne district. Morland pointed out that such instructions presupposed a state of siege, which at that point had not yet been called. The order was modified, but before it could be applied negotiations between the German government and the rail unions led to a return to work on 1 January. To avoid a similar muddle in the future, the High Commission passed a new ordinance, which defined more precisely the powers of the military authorities to intervene in future rail strikes. Kilmarnock worked harmoniously with Tirard over this issue and agreed that while in theory a rail strike might be permitted, 'the High Commission should supply such machinery as would make it almost impossible in practice for a strike to occur legally'.[32] When a second rail strike broke out on the night of 1/2 February, this ordinance was successfully put into operation.

The problems caused by accelerating inflation were compounded in early 1922 by the Berlin government's withdrawal of the bread subsidy, which 'increased the cost of bread for a family of four to the equivalent of 46 pfennigs per hour on a man's wages'.[33] In February the monthly report of the Labour Department of the High Commission warned that 'movements to secure higher wages with which to meet this increased cost of living, are on foot in almost all branches of industry'. Wage agreements became out of date almost as soon as they were made, but the crucial key to industrial peace lay in the fact that 'in the majority of cases the men's demands [were] being reasonably dealt with by employers'.[34]

By late summer and autumn accelerating inflation had almost reached the stage of hyper-inflation. In August the value of the mark to the pound was about 5,000; in September it was about 6,500 and it then suddenly jumped in October to 14,000 and in November more than doubled to 32,000.[35] Inflation on this scale was beginning to cause a currency shortage, which was compounded by a strike of note printers in Berlin in the autumn. Several firms in the British Zone resorted to the expedient of using coupons, and emergency notes were issued by the local authorities under licence by the Reich Finance Minister.[36] To alleviate

32. Ibid., 1922, p. 2.
33. Labour Report No. 33, ending 24.2.22, p. 2, FO 371/7550 fos 132–5.
34. Ibid.
35. 'Report', 1922, p. 10.
36. Thurstan to Addison, 14.9.22 (no. 104 (80/22)), FO 371/7522 fos 8–9, and Kilmarnock to Curzon, 15.11.22 (C15790), ibid., fos 187–8.

difficulties for the armies of occupation, the local branches of the Reichsbank promised to accept emergency currency for all occupation personnel.[37]

For the majority of the population a race developed between the price of food and basic commodities and wages. In November at a time when the shops were posting up hourly changes of price, bread riots broke out in Kalk, Ehrenfeld and Solingen. German police backed by British troops quickly had the situation under control.[38] The riots in themselves were no real threat to the security of the zone, but they were an indication of the unrest that hyper-inflation would bring. In his report to Curzon, Kilmarnock ominously remarked that for the future he could not 'but feel considerable anxiety'.[39]

Kilmarnock's sentiments were shared in December by both the British and the Germans in the Rhineland. In early November rumours began to circulate amongst British officials that the new Prime Minister, Bonar Law, was 'inclined to let France have her way here and in Germany generally'.[40] Piggott was so alarmed at this prospect, which he feared would 'result in turmoil on the Continent for years',[41] that he asked Lampson to inform him of what policy Bonar Law was likely to follow. Lampson was unable to provide any firm guidelines; he could only warn that 'a crisis between Germany and the Allies . . . [was] . . . fast approaching' over both reparations and disarmament. 'The net result of all this is that H.M.G. are getting restive and losing patience; and I shouldn't be at all surprised if their attitude on such things as, say, for example, French policy in the Rhineland underwent a change.'[42] The new government was undoubtedly anxious to reach an overall European settlement with France in order to secure French cooperation in the Near East. Significantly, a Foreign Office Minute on 23 November played down the dangers of a Ruhr occupation, while Sthamer, the German Ambassador in London, reported rumours of an Anglo–French compromise at the cost of Germany and 'the constantly repeated remark that England initially will be able to do nothing if France should proceed unilaterally against Germany'.[43] Both industrialists and German officials in the Cologne Zone were

37. Ibid. (C15790).
38. Garrett to Piggott, 13.11.22, FO 371/7522 fos 184–5; 'Report', 1922, p. 11.
39. Kilmarnock to Curzon, 4.12.22 (C16732), FO 371/7523 fo. 26.
40. Piggott to Lampson, 8.11.22 (C15786), FO 371/7522 fo. 173.
41. Ibid.
42. Ibid., Lampson to Piggott, 20.11.22 (C15786), fos 176–7.
43. FO Minute 'British Policy in Germany', 23.11.22 (C16157), FO 371/7487 fos 217–19; Sthamer to AA, 1.11.22 (no. A. 2284), FCO Lib. 3058 D603039-40.

aghast at this apparent softening of the British attitude. In early December the German Reichskommissar for the Occupied Territories reported that 'he had never met such a depressed mood amongst the leading business and trade union circles of the occupied territories before'.[44] Taking their line from London Piggott, and his deputy Garrett, had thoroughly disabused the Rhinelanders of any possibility of the British being able to prevent a Ruhr occupation. Piggott had indeed advised trade union leaders in December[45] that the Germans would have 'to adapt themselves more to the mentality of the French' and try to see the problems of reparations from the perspective of Paris. When the union leaders attempted to alarm Piggott by stressing the dangerous consequences of an occupation and hinting at the possibility of large-scale unrest, Piggott called their bluff by brutally asking: 'What do you want to do . . . You can not do anything. What would you do if a plebiscite over a buffer or separate state was held?' They were surprised by the apparent *volte face* in Piggott's opinions and assumed that this indicated 'a *fait accompli* and an already accomplished U-turn by the English'. Privately, however, British officials in Cologne and Coblenz dreaded the prospect of a French occupation of the Ruhr. Troughton, Kilmarnock's Economic Adviser,[46] warned of the threat it would bring to British trade through competition from Ruhr coal and French manipulation of a new import licence scheme. Piggott took a more apocalyptic view, and informed Lampson that

> We can't sit still and see Germany dissolve into fragments, which is what will happen sooner or later if the French have a free hand – some of the fragments will only unite again with the help of some evil smelling Russian cement and we shall have turmoil on the Continent for years – to say nothing of the ruin of our markets.[47]

He also feared, despite what he had said to the trade union leaders, that the French would be confronted by some form of passive resistance, and pertinently asked what would be the role of the British army in the event of isolated French action.[48] Ryan, on the other hand, felt that 'the masses were much too worried by

---

44. Brügger to Reichskanzler, 4.12.22 (IV.12425), FCO Lib. L1711 L502596–602.
45. Ibid., Der Staatssekretär in der Reichskanzlei: 'Aus einer Besprechung mit Herrn Staatssekretär Dr Brügger, 4.12.22' (RK 10079), L1711 L502603–05.
46. Memorandum by Troughton, 10.12.22 (C17445), FO 371/7490 fos 230–1.
47. Piggott to Lampson, 8.11.22 (C15786), FO 371/7522 fo. 173.
48. Piggott to Lampson, 7.12.22 (C17050), FO 371/7489 fos 233–8.

economic anxieties to offer anything but feeble resistance to whatever measures might eventually be adopted'.[49]

In December reports from the Rhineland, Paris and Brussels all suggested that the long-awaited occupation of the Ruhr was imminent. Military confirmation of this came from Colonel Daubeny, Godley's (the new GOC, Cologne) representative at Wiesbaden, who reported that 'whatever office I go into, the occupants are all busy with railway marches, maps of the Ruhr etc. . . .'[50]

49. Ibid., Ryan to Curzon, 11.12.22 (C17111), fo. 244.
50. Daubeny to Godley, 2.12.22 (C16815), FO 371/7523 fo. 36.

The British in Cologne, 1920–1923

The Rhine Army officially prided itself on its good relations with the German population. In the bombastic language of its journal, the *Cologne Post*, it saw itself as the 'humble ambassador for the eternal principles which a five year wanton war had failed to abrogate'.[1] Was it in practice only grudgingly tolerated in Cologne as an inescapable consequence of the lost war, or did it enjoy a special and unique relationship with the local population, and help bring about an Anglo–German reconciliation?

The British army in the 1920s was an inward-looking organization on the defensive against a post-war world at home where it was often both mocked and criticized. It has been described 'as the perfect vehicle for an *émigration intérieure'*,[2] in that it provided its officers with a comfortable and undemanding life, which shielded them from the harsh post-war world. Apart from a few ambitious intelligence officers, the average regular regimental officer in Cologne, unlike his French counterpart,[3] showed little interest in German affairs. Life in Cologne was like any other posting, except more comfortable. One officer later wrote: 'I need not have been concerned with the problem of whether to avoid Germans or not; there was no question of any contact with them.'[4] Both officers and men were firmly tied to the regimental system: their battalion was their world. Much of their leisure time was taken up with games; cricket pitches 'were made on every space of green that could be

---

1. J.W.N., 'First Anniversary of The Cologne Post', *Cologne Post*, 31.3.20.
2. Michael Howard, quoted in Bond, *British Military Policy*, p. 60.
3. See for instance Tuohy, *Occupied, 1918–30*, p. 277. Tirard sent Georges Leygues on 25.10.20 an interesting summary of a report on the British Officers' Corps by the French Ambassador in Berlin: AN AJ9 3210.
4. 'Apex' (R.G. Coulson), *The Uneasy Triangle. Four Years of Occupation as seen by 'Apex'*, London, 1931, p. 7.

found'[5] and there were regular race meetings, football matches and boxing.

In and around Cologne in early 1921 there were some 1,600 army families, which in addition to the 10,000 strong garrison accounted for a further 5,000 Britons.[6] The army families were catered for by the provision of a comprehensive network of supportive organizations. There were Scouts and Guides, a mothers' union and of course, the garrison schools. In the Frankstrasse the Central School catered for all children over the age of nine, while there were two other schools in Solingen, and several infant schools in the zone. Although the ethos of the army was 'sports orientated' there was a considerable demand for places in the Opera, and two theatres and a cinema were requisitioned for army use. The Rhine Army Dramatic Company put on impressive productions; in August 1920, for instance, it produced Galsworthy's *Skin Game* almost concurrently with the West End production. A number of shops sprang up to meet the need of the Rhine Army. There was a British military store in the Höhestrasse, Quantocks and Roberts, the *Cologne Post* bookshop, an off-licence and even a bakery which specialized in scones, crumpets and white bread. There is no doubt that life in Cologne in the years 1920–3 was pleasant and, thanks to German inflation, very cheap. Champagne could be bought for 2d a bottle and an overcoat for 3s in late 1922.[7]

While the majority of the British garrison lived in its own world, it did inevitably, as an army of occupation under the Rhineland Agreement, impinge on the German population. The local military Commanders were invested with the power to arrest anybody who attacked or appeared to threaten the officials of the High Commission, the army or relatives of servicemen. Sometimes this led to abuses by over-zealous officers. In May 1921, for example, a well-meaning civilian separated three children fighting in the street, only to find that he himself was immediately apprehended for assaulting a British sergeant's boy, who made up one of the trio, and in the Summary Court he was confronted with either paying a

5. J.H.H., 'Eleven Years in Occupation', *Cologne Post* and *Wiesbaden Times*, 3.11.29. M. Henniker's *Memoirs of a Junior Officer*, London, 1951, provides a good account of an officer's life in the inter-war period.
6. Bericht (f.217), HA d SK 902/241/1. The report is on a briefing given to a visiting parliamentary delegation of the Italian Populari Party in Berlin; it is undated. Becker, 'Sieben Jahre', pp. 140–1 (HA d SK, Chron. u. Darst. 501) contains a detailed list of British civil and military institutions in Cologne.
7. The best guide to army life in Cologne is in the reports and advertisements of the *Cologne Post*. The facts on the schools came from the edition of 2.8.24.

stiff fine or going to Klingelputz jail.[8]

The most serious cause of friction between the British army and the civilian population was domestic rather than official. In July 1919, once the Peace was signed, wives were allowed out to join their husbands, and whole families were billeted in generous suites of rooms in private houses. The officers were allowed to choose their own rooms and demand accommodation for servants. The women, long exposed to Lord Northcliffe's war-time anti–German propaganda, were suspicious of the Germans, and they in turn appeared to many of the more educated natives as brash and aggressive. The city's Occupation Bureau was flooded with complaints from irate German *Hausfrauen* about the way in which British families maltreated the pristine cleanliness of their kitchens, bathrooms and furniture. At a time when there were 12,000 homeless awaiting accommodation in Cologne, the billeting of British army families was a considerable burden for the city. In November 1920 the City Council began a comprehensive housing programme to provide housing for the British and by 1923 the great majority of married soldiers were no longer billeted on Germans.[9]

Although the restrictions on fraternization between soldiers and German women were lifted with the signing of the Peace, intermarriage was emphatically not encouraged by the British authorities. General Morland, for instance, made a point of transferring any officer who married a German.[10] Nevertheless, by September 1921, 150 serving men and seven officers had married Germans and by 1925 the total had risen to 700.[11] The German wife of a British soldier immediately became a member of the occupation forces and was thus exempted from most German regulations.

The British military authorities in Cologne were, however, more concerned by those inevitable concomitants of army life, prostitution and venereal desease. Undoubtedly the inflated German mark made prostitution a profitable two-way business. Morland claimed that there were 30,000 'loose women' in Cologne.[12] In December 1922, as a result of a public outcry at home, Mrs Corbett Ashby was sent out to investigate the situation. She found

8. D.G. Williamson, 'Cologne and the British', p. 700.
9. Ibid., p. 701; Bericht (f.217) HA d SK 902/241/1; 'On the Rhine in 1923', *Cologne Post Annual*, 1923.
10. Morland to Wilson, 25.6.20, IWM 73/1/26 file 57.
11. E. Gordon (Gedye), 'Tommy's German Wife', *Sunday Chronicle*, 25.9.21. See also *Rheinzeitung* 29.12.25, on an article in the *Observer* by Sir William Beach Thomas.
12. Morland to Wilson, 25.6.20, IWM 73/1/26 file 57.

that the 'streets seemed no worse than elsewhere, but very narrow and crowded with very slow crowds, easy for new acquaintances to be found. In the cafés the soldiers seemed very young and nearly all seemed to have had too much to drink, flushed, sleepy or excitable faces, not really drunk'.[13] She proposed that a joint Anglo–German team of women police should patrol the streets. In July 1923 six British policewomen were dispatched, but they had little effect and were sent home in March 1925.[14]

From the summer of 1919 onwards a sizeable British civilian population grew up in Cologne. By 1922 there were 2,500 British civilians in Cologne,[15] most of whom were ex–officers and soldiers who, when faced with demobilization and unemployment, decided to stay in Cologne. Not all of those who wanted to remain managed to find jobs; Gedye painted an ironic but sympathetic picture of demobilized officers 'going from Commission to Commission and from British bank to British business house' in search of work.[16] One or two led dramatic lives which deserve a novelist's pen. The correspondence of Thurstan, the British Consul at Cologne, with the Foreign Office is briefly enlivened by the story of one Robert Eunson, who had been a clerk at Cox and Co.'s Shipping Agency. He murdered his pregnant German mistress and was handed over by the British authorities to the German police. He was imprisoned over the frontier in Elberfeld, but escaped in March 1920 when the Spartacists attacked the jail and was then hidden by a British officer in Cologne. When this officer discussed the case confidentially at the Consulate, Thurstan deliberately refrained from taking his address and advised officials in London that Eunson should be sent home on the grounds that he could not expect a fair trial in Germany. The Foreign Office was prepared to turn a blind eye, but Eunson ran away from Cologne and was reported killed in the street fighting in the Ruhr. In June it emerged that he was still alive, but he apparently vanished without trace.[17]

The British colony was further supplemented by the forced repatriation from England of German immigrants who had been interned in Britain during the war. As many of them were in

13. Mrs Corbett Ashby's visit to Cologne, 7–11 December 1922 (A.B.A2), Ashby Papers, IWM, P. 63.
14. Edmonds, *The Occupation*, p. 209.
15. 'The British Occupation of the Cologne Bridgehead and its importance in relation to British Commercial Interests', 16.2.23 (C 3858), FO 371/8718 fos 83–95.
16. *Bystander*, 24.3.20.
17. Thurstan to Curzon, 24.2.20 (188651) and 8.4.20 (191505); Rechtsanwalt von Coellen to Thurstan 7.6.20 (204977); all in FO 371/4351 fos 182–202.

essence more British than German they gravitated to Cologne, where they could be found running barber's shops and bakeries, or operating as bookies at Cologne race meetings. In many ways their plight was comparable to that of the Eurasians under the British Raj. They clung passionately to a culture which rejected them; for instance they delighted in talking to the occupying forces of 'home' and found, according to one observer, 'a happiness in using the old names and talking of the old spots: "Go to Brighton at all? Any luck at Goodwood? Did you dine at the Carlton? Where's Robey now?" They roll the familiar names lovingly round their tongues and we suppress the smile that comes involuntarily at hearing them from a German.' There was even a barber's shop in Cologne where the Anglo–German assistants spoke English amongst themselves![18]

The majority of British subjects remained in Cologne essentially because it was a 'distinctly lovable City'[19] where living was cheap. There were also excellent commercial possibilities. While Danzig and Upper Silesia were unstable areas which were not attractive to British capital investment, Cologne, on the other hand, with a British garrison stationed there for at least five years, and an industrious and moderate workforce, presented a very different picture. By late summer 1919 British traders had begun to appreciate the potential significance of Cologne as the major commercial centre of Western Germany. Efforts were made to reconstitute the former British Rhine shipping company, Drughorn, to exploit the coal-carrying trade on the Rhine.[20] The *Cologne Post* fully understood the economic importance of Cologne and from October 1919 onwards began to publish a regular column 'for businessmen in the Rhineland'. By early 1920 the British business community in Cologne was large enough to support three banks 'employing between a hundred and a hundred and fifty clerks' and a Chamber of Commerce.[21] In April one of the more powerful arguments General Morland put forward against a precipitate evacuation was that 'commercially it would be bad. Cologne is becoming more and more the trade centre of Western Germany. With the French here our traders would find barriers of all sorts against them.'[22]

The Ball Papers provide the historian with a detailed example of how one ambitious and exceptionally energetic businessman, still

18. 'Exiled Home', *Bystander*, 1.9.20.
19. *Bystander*, 24.3.20.
20. 'Travail du Cdt. Berger', p. 7, Vincennes 7N2664–1.
21. E. Gedye, 'Rhineland Jobs for Englishmen', *Nash's Illustrated Weekly*, 14.2.20.
22. Morland to Wilson, 22.4.20, IWM 73/1/26 file 57.

in khaki, was able to build up a formidable import-export business. For him, as a consequence of his contacts with the trading company F.A. Hughes, Cologne was indeed what the French called 'l'Eldorado des Commerçants britanniques'.[23] Through his official visits as a member of the Armaments sub-Commission to former munitions factories he was able to hold the industrialists whose factories he inspected 'absolutely in the palm of [his] hand'.[24] The German industrialists were desperate to rebuild their export trade and thus 'knowing each one of us personally, they are out to back us all they can'.[25] To exploit these excellent commercial opportunities F.A. Hughes became a limited company in the summer of 1920 and also opened up offices in Cologne.[26] Ball rapidly drew up plans, which were realized a few years later at Feltham, for building a factory to act as a store for celluloid and the manufacture of celluloid buttons,[27] but as his correspondence shows, his business activities embraced a wide range of activities such as importing into the Rhineland khaki cloth, chocolate, cocoa and fuel oil, and arranging for the export of railway material from Krupp to Brazil and detonators to India and 'the rest of the Colonies'.[28] Ball was the most successful and articulate of the new generation of British traders in Cologne, but as the minutes of the local branch of Lloyds (France) and National Provincial Bank (France) show, he was not unique.[29]

In January 1921 it was accepted by French public opinion, 'comme un dogma indiscutable', that the British had established a complete economic domination over the Cologne region.[30] French officials in Cologne were rather more sceptical,[31] and certainly the sanctions of March and April 1921 temporarily, but severely, damaged British trade with Germany and opened the door to a flood of Belgian and French goods;[32] but with the lifting of the customs sanctions on 30 September British business was able to recapture its markets. In 1922 there were forty-seven firms in the

23. 'Une note d'un agent bien informé sur la question rhénane vue du point de vue britannique', (Sent to President du Conseil, MAE, 4.4.21), MAE Rive Gauche 3 fos. 227–41.
24. Ball to father, 6.6.20, IWM 72/116/4.
25. Ibid.
26. Ibid., Ball to Jackie (Downs), 31.5.20.
27. Ibid., Ball to Boone, 28.9.20; Anon., *F.A.Hughes Centenary Year*, Epsom, 1968.
28. Ibid., Ball to Hethey, 8.1.20 and 17.7.20.
29. See for instance Lloyds Bank (France) and National Provincial Bank (France) Ltd, Minute Books 5, no. 2983; 6, no. 3944; 7, no. 4451.
30. 'Une note d'un agent', 4.4.21.
31. Ibid.
32. See for instance Ball to Haining, 11.6.21, IWM 72/116/3.

British Chamber of Commerce in Cologne, and a quarter of the 2,500 British subjects in the Cologne district were engaged in business.[33] By the end of 1922 the bulk of British exports in manufactured and semi-manufactured goods to Germany went through Cologne rather than the North Sea ports, as they did before the war. This switch was primarily brought about by the enormous advantage that the presence of a British representative at the Bad Ems Licensing Office afforded British trade, as he could, together with his Allied colleagues, ensure that the German officials interpreted their government's import regulations liberally: the British were being granted licences for the import of goods at the rate of 200 per day, as compared to a mere 90 for the French.[34] The London and Cologne Steamship Company ran regular weekly steamers which carried some 35,000 to 37,000 tons per annum. The general trade done by the British merchants in Cologne consisted in the export to Britain of toys, fancy goods, textiles, hardware and cutlery, iron, steel and celluloid, while they imported into Germany textiles, foodstuffs, chemicals and semi–raw products and coal. In 1922 nearly 19 million kilograms of cotton fabric were imported through Cologne.[35] It is thus not surprising that the Department of Overseas Trade was implacably hostile in 1923 to any suggestion of a premature withdrawal of British forces from Cologne as a consequence of the French occupation of the Ruhr, and stressed that:

> the fact must not be lost sight of that Cologne is, for this country, not merely the key to the British Zone, but to all the occupied territory, for, once goods have been imported into any part of the occupied territory, they can, without further formalities, be moved from one part of that territory to another. If this country loses its footing in Cologne, it loses its footing in the occupied territory as a whole; and the occupied territory is that part of Germany which consumes British manufactured goods rather than British raw materials.[36]

By the end of 1922 the British occupation had brought Cologne some real material benefits by making it an attractive and stable entrepôt for British trade with Germany. The army of occupation did, of course, weigh heavily on the population and remained a symbol of defeat, but in 1923 when the French occupied the Ruhr,

33. 'The British Occupation of the Cologne Bridgehead', fos 93–5, p. 2.
34. Ibid., p. 3.
35. Ibid., p. 2.
36. Ibid., p. 3.

the British garrison by merely being in Cologne protected the city from the French. The British were as popular there as the Americans were in West Berlin in 1948–9 during the airlift. A delegation of British Labour MPs was astonished in March 1923 when some German trade union officials in Cologne summarized the attitude of the working classes to the Army of the Rhine by saying: 'We give our daughters to them.' From the tenor of further remarks they deduced that 'there is no reason to believe that the ladies in question were reluctant wives'.[37]

37. 'Report of Labour Delegation to Ruhr District', Labour Party Archives, Minutes of the National Executive Committee, vol. 26.

PART IV

The Ruhr Crisis, January 1923–January 1924

Introduction: The Turning Point

When the Brussels Conference broke up and French and Belgian troops were poised to occupy the Ruhr in January 1923, *The Times* declared that 'something as far reaching in its effects as the declaration of war in 1914 or the conclusion of the armistice'[1] had occurred. The frequently bitter Anglo–French dialogue over the interpretation of the Treaty of Versailles and the role of Germany in post-war Europe had at last reached a decisive stage. The French staked their claim to European hegemony on the successful outcome of the occupation. They gambled on its weakening Germany and tipping the balance of power decisively towards Paris; they also hoped that the possession of productive pledges in the Ruhr would enable France in any future reparation settlement to extract favourable terms from Britain and America. By refusing to join in the occupation of the Ruhr, the British government demonstrated its belief that the economic restoration of Germany was the key to a general economic revival. The ultimate French failure in the Ruhr marked the end of French military hegemony in Europe and the re-emergence of Germany as a great power within Europe.[2]

1. *The Times*, 6.1.23.
2. L. Kochan, *The Struggle for Germany, 1914–45*, Edinburgh, 1963, p. 29. For studies of the Ruhr crisis see J. Bariéty, *Les relations franco-allemandes après la première guerre mondiale, 10 November 1918–10 Janvier 1925. De l'exécution à la négociation*, Paris, 1977, chs 16–20; McDougall, *Rhineland Diplomacy*, chs 7 and 8; Krüger, *die Außenpolitik der Republik von Weimar*, pp. 199–247.

–12–

Benevolent Passivity and Passive Resistance, January–September 1923

The Policy of Benevolent Passivity

When French and Belgian troops moved into the Ruhr, the British government wished to avoid the two extremes of either breaking entirely with France or of cooperating with her, and so adopted a policy of 'benevolent passivity',[1] which consisted of 'minimizing . . . the adverse effects upon Anglo-French relations of French action and [of] reducing to a minimum the opportunities for friction upon the several inter-Allied bodies'.[2] Kilmarnock was thus instructed to abstain from voting on the High Commission when issues concerning the Ruhr occupation were raised.[3] This was sharply criticized by the unions and the Labour Party which argued that it was as bad as 'actual cooperation',[4] although the Party's demands for the withdrawal of British troops were stilled when Rudolf Breitscheid visited London in February on behalf of the German Social Democratic Party and impressed on it 'with all the force he could'[5] that British troops should remain in the Rhineland as a counter to the French. D'Abernon was the only important British official to urge the total evacuation of the Cologne Zone as he feared the vulnerability of British forces 'at a moment when large scale operations [were] not improbable'.[6] He

---

1. See Williamson, 'Great Britain and the Ruhr Crisis, 1923–24', *British Journal of International Studies*, vol. 3, no. 1, 1977, p. 70.
2. Cabinet Conclusions of 11.1.23 (1(23)), p. 3, CAB 23/45 fos 5–6.
3. Ibid.
4. TUC and Labour Party Joint Executive Minutes, 24.1.23, TUC Archives, T. 39 fo. 114.
5. Minute by Lampson, 13.2.23 (C2808), FO 371/8712 fo. 213.
6. D'Abernon to FO, 24.1.23 (C1567), FO 371/8707 fos 105–7; D'Abernon, *Ambassador of Peace*, vol. 2 (25.1.23), pp. 160–2. Shortly after he conceded to Georgi that there were equally strong reasons for staying put: D'Abernon to Georgi, 2.2.23, D'Abernon Papers, BL 48927A fos 193–4.

argued strongly that Britain would eventually have much more influence as a mediator if she were not so directly involved in the Rhineland, but neither the Foreign Office nor the majority of the British officials in the Rhineland agreed with him as they feared that a sudden withdrawal would not only be construed by the French as an 'unfriendly act',[7] but would also weaken British prestige and destroy any hope of extracting reparation payments from Germany. There were also strong commercial reasons for the army of occupation to remain as a guarantee of stability in the important trading centre of Cologne.[8] The Cabinet accepted this advice and the Rhine Army remained in the zone with strict instructions to do its 'utmost to avert any incident which might necessitate [its] withdrawal'.[9]

Poincaré's assessment that the German government had no plans to counter a French occupation were initially proved correct. Opposition to the occupation began with a locally inspired general strike; once it became clear that this had popular backing, only then did the Berlin Government officially support it.[10] While passive resistance in the longer term significantly increased the cost of the Ruhr occupation, thereby weakening the franc, it also destroyed the mark through hyper-inflation and gave Poincaré the opportunity to take coercive measures, which went far beyond seizing control of productive pledges. There was initially nothing that the British government could do to break the deadlock in the Ruhr. Any hint of mediation between France and Germany was counter-productive and provoked a sharp reaction from Paris. Essentially Poincaré was determined 'first and foremost to create in Germany by a seizure of pledges and by coercion the will to pay'.[11] Thus any British initiative based on accepting an American proposal first made in December 1922 for setting up a committee of experts to assess Germany's capacity to pay was blocked until either French coercion worked or the cost of the Ruhr occupation began to damage the franc. This deadlock was to last until the new Strese-

7. Quarry to Kilmarnock, 22.1.23 (C1535), FO 371/8707 fos 14–15; see also Carsten, *Britain and the Weimar Republic*, p. 126.
8. 'The British Occupation of the Cologne Bridgehead and its Importance in Relation to British Commercial Interests' (Dept. of Overseas Trade, FO 2.3.23) (C3858), FO 371/8718 fos 93–5.
9. Cabinet Conclusions of 26.1.23 (3(23)), p. 6, CAB 23/45 fo. 22.
10. McDougall, *Rhineland Diplomacy*, p. 269; D'Abernon, *Ambassador of Peace*, vol. 2 (20.1.23), p. 158.
11. Toynbee, *Survey of International Affairs*, vol. 2, p. 333; K. Middlemas and J. Barnes, *Baldwin*, London, 1969, pp. 154–5.

mann government called off passive resistance on 26 September 1923.[12]

Cologne: 'Die Insel der Seligen' ('The Island of the Blest'). The British Occupation during the Period of Passive Resistance, January–September 1923

The doctrine of 'benevolent passivity' ensured that during the Ruhr occupation British officials at Coblenz and Cologne trod a constant tightrope between active cooperation with the French, and a hostile, pro-German neutrality. Significant differences in emphasis existed between Cologne and Coblenz. One disgruntled official complained that 'for the sake of this easy and over paid life the British in Cologne annoy the French and those in Coblenz repulse the Germans. Both nations understand and despise us and our opportunities for mediation are lost.'[13] While this was a jaundiced view, it was true that officials in Cologne were used to working closely with the Germans and were often at the receiving end of French policy. Piggott was known to be 'a trifle pro German',[14] while Kilmarnock, despite his anti-French reputation, believed, like Robertson two years earlier, that the French ultimately needed to be supported. He wrote to Curzon in January 1923:

> much as we disapprove of French action, we cannot afford to let them be defeated. If, as I anticipate, [the] struggle proves to be long and bitter [the] time will come when we shall have to decide what would be the position if [the] Germans were to win. The last shot of the Allies would have been fired and would have failed in its effects.[15]

In practice in the early stages of the Ruhr crisis the British, French and Belgian authorities cooperated to ensure that potentially embarrassing incidents would be avoided. When, for example, Poincaré notified the British government of the decision to seize the German customs receipts in the whole of the occupied territory including the British Zone, Bonar Law consented, provided that there was 'no question of the use of British troops'.[16] A more

12. Earl of Ronaldshay, *The Life of Lord Curzon*, 3 vols, London, 1928, vol. 3, ch. 21; H. Nicolson, *Curzon, The Last Phase, 1919–25*, London, 1934, pp. 360–8; Krüger, *Die Außenpolitik der Republik von Weimar*, p. 206.
13. Huddleston to Lampson, 23.10.23 (C18483), FO 371/8685 fos 135–6.
14. See Minute by Lampson, 24.2.23, FO 371/8716 fo. 80.
15. Kilmarnock to FO, 22.1.23 (C1300), FO 371/8706 fos 55–6.
16. FO to Kilmarnock, 17.1.23 (no. 5D), FO 371/8704 fos 63–4.

complex problem arose when the German government as part of its passive resistance campaign ordered firms and officials in the occupied territories to cease delivering reparations in kind to France and Belgium. Those who obeyed were liable to suffer arrest and to be tried in Allied military courts for carrying out instructions which had not first been cleared by the High Commission. There thus existed the danger that German officials might be arrested in the British Zone and be tried in British military courts, thereby implicating Britain in the Ruhr occupation.[17] To avoid this Kilmarnock was instructed to let the French make the necessary arrests in the British Zone, 'provided always that there can be no question of employment of either British troops or officials'.[18]

'Benevolent passivity' was strained to its utmost limits when the French, attempting to counter the passive resistance of the German railwaymen, demanded control of the railways in the British Zone. The vast junction at Cologne was in Foch's words an 'essential nodal point for the safety of French troops'[19] and equally crucial for the transport of reparation material out of Germany. Such a move by the French would almost certainly have led to a strike by German railwaymen within the British Zone, forcing the British either to evacuate Cologne or to abandon benevolent passivity.[20] The French rejected an initial British proposal for re-routing all reparation traffic around the west of the zone via Jülich, Düren and Euskirchen, but then Degoutte suggested a compromise that was ultimately to solve the problem by proposing that the French should take over the section of the British Zone through which the Grevenbroich–Düren line ran.[21] Piggott unofficially sounded out Chancellor Cuno through Silverberg[22] to see whether the German government would consider this 'an infringement of the neutrality declared by Britain'. The next day Rosenberg, anxious to keep the British in Cologne, wired the German Embassy in London that Berlin approved the compromise.[23] On 15 February Le Trocquer, the French Minister of Public Works, General Payot and the French

17. Kilmarnock to WO, 19.1.23 (C1167), FO 371/8705 fo. 32.
18. FO to Kilmarnock, 22.1.23 (C1167), FO 371/8705 fo. 34.
19. Quoted in 'Rough Notes of a Conversation held at 10 Downing Street' on 16 Feb. 1923, p. 4 (C2945), FO 371/8713 fos 156–8. See Williamson, 'Great Britain and the Ruhr Crisis', pp. 75–6; see also D'Abernon Papers, BL 48927A, fos 206–28.
20. Der Reichsverkehrsminister to Rosenberg, 11.2.23, FCO Lib. 3058 D603240–43.
21. Kilmarnock to FO, 7.2.23 (C32393), FO 371/8711 fo. 73.
22. Silverberg to Cuno, 10.2.23 (433), FCO Lib. 3058 D603263–65.
23. Rosenberg to German Embassy (no. 148), 11.2.23, FCO Lib. 3058 D603234–36.

Ambassador met Bonar Law, Curzon and Derby.[24] The French delegation had strict instructions from Poincaré 'ni sacrifier la sécurité de nos troupes, ni renoncer à nos réparations'.[25] The French were offered the Düren–Grevenbroich strip, but they also insisted on the right to use the other main lines running right through the British Zone. Bonar Law was at first inclined to fall back on the ultimate threat of withdrawing the Rhine Army, but the following day, after consulting the Cabinet, he made considerable concessions. Provided that the trains were worked by German personnel, he would allow through the British Zone the same number of French troop trains as ran before the Ruhr occupation began. The French were aghast at 'handing themselves over to the goodwill of the Germans' and at one juncture Payot, much to the embarrassment of the French delegation, crudely threatened that France could 'cut off Cologne entirely on every side should she so desire', but Bonar Law sharply retaliated by warning the French that any rash move would merely strengthen the hand of the Labour Party, which wished to submit the whole question of the Ruhr occupation to the League of Nations.[26]

Poincaré grudgingly accepted this compromise[27] and the British Zone was excluded from the Franco-Belgian Railway Régie, which was set up to control the railways in occupied Germany on 1 March.[28] It was left to General Godley to make the necessary arrangements with Payot, although these were to be subject to confirmation by the Foreign Office. On 19 February Godley met Degoutte and Payot, who initially pitched their demands as high as possible. It was only with the greatest difficulty that he managed to persuade them to agree to limit French troop trains to the Ruhr to five a day on each of the two main lines running across the British Zone.[29] Curzon only grudgingly accepted this total,[30] which Godley felt was in practice reasonable and acceptable to the Germans.[31] On 26 February Colonel Manton, the British representative of the Railway sub-Commission at Cologne, and Georgi, Kilmarnock's technical adviser, had a successful and thoroughly amiable meeting

24. 'Rough Notes', 15.2.23 (C2922 and C2945), FO 371/8713 fos 108–11 and 156–8.
25. Poincaré to French Embassy, 15.2.23, Tels 571–72, Copy in AN AJ9 3324.
26. 'Rough Notes', 16.2.23 (C2945), pp. 2 and 5, FO 371/8713 fos 156–8.
27. Crewe to FO, 18.2.23 (C3013), FO 371/8714 fos 32–4.
28. 'Memorandum on the Franco-Belgian Railway Régie', Jan. 1924 (C1362), FO 371/9738 fos 24–8.
29. GOC Rhine Army to WO, 20.2.23 (C3265), FO 371/8715 fos 77–8.
30. DBFP Ser. 1, vol. 21 (no. 111), pp. 120–1.
31. Godley to CIGS, 22.2.23 (C3601), FO 371/8716 fos 168–70.

with General Groener, the Reich Minister for Transport, at Frankfurt. The British officials stressed the many 'concrete instances of [their] benevolent attitude to Germany', whilst emphasizing 'that legitimate French demands must be met', but they also threatened that their government might be moved to withdraw its troops from Cologne if faced with either 'excessive demands by the French or undue restrictions of the facilities by the Germans'. Groener was sceptical about the evacuation threat, but he did not conceal that Berlin wished British forces to remain in the Rhineland and so readily conceded the adequate but 'strictly limited facilities to the French' of a total of ten trains per day, provided that British officials supervised the changeover between French and German railway personnel at the frontiers of the British Zone.[32]

The French reluctantly endorsed this agreement, although they managed to extract a further concession from the British that two extra trains – *les trains journaliers* – carrying rations only should be allowed to run across the British Zone.[33] Inevitably the Germans protested that this exceeded the agreed total of French trains, but hints of a British withdrawal from Cologne were sufficient to secure their consent and the Frankfurt agreement came into force on 29 March.[34] By April the movement of the specified number of French troop trains was proceeding relatively smoothly. The occasional minor incidents '[were] invariably settled in a tactful manner by the British R.T.O. [Railway Officer] on duty at the frontier stations'.[35] Outside the British Zone the railwaymen remained on strike. The Régie, with the help of an inadequate number of specially recruited Belgian and French railwaymen, just about managed to keep a skeleton passenger service functioning besides the military traffic. It was not until the cessation of passive resistance that it was able to exercise effective pressure on the British Zone.[36]

The introduction of customs sanctions both in the newly occupied and the 'old' occupied territories and the refusal by the Germans to recognize the licences issued at Bad Ems inevitably hit British trade with Germany, a considerable volume of which passed through Cologne.[37] In early February the British Chamber

32. 'Report of Conference of 26.2.23' (C4656), FO 371/8721 fos 163–70.
33. 'Inter-Allied Rhineland High Commission. Annual Report, 1923', pp. 57–8 (C198), FO 371/12130 fos 2–56.
34. Ibid., p. 59; Kilmarnock to FO, 29.3.23 (C5895), FO 371/8725 fo. 220.
35. Kilmarnock to Curzon, 18.4.23 (C7079), FO 371/8728 fos 100–1.
36. 'Report', 1923, pp. 59–63.
37. 'The British Occupation of the Cologne Bridgehead', 16.2.23 (C3858), FO 371/8718 fos 93–5.

of Commerce at Cologne drew the attention of the Foreign Office to the dilemma confronting any British businessman obeying German instructions when applying for import-export licences from unoccupied Germany, since he could well end up by being fined or even imprisoned by the Allied authorities. British exports bound for the Ruhr and Rhineland were also held up on the German waterways and in the marshalling yards, where it was 'difficult to imagine the reign of chaos'.[38]

By the end of February the French and Belgians had reorganized the Bad Ems Office and created a line of customs posts around the perimeter of the occupied territories. Goods could cross through into unoccupied territory only on the payment of a 10 per cent *ad valorem* duty. The export of coal, coke, pig iron and rails were forbidden. British officials at Coblenz could only concentrate on trying to mitigate the impact of these measures on British trade. In early March they managed to extract several apparently important concessions from the French; it was agreed, for instance, that German export contracts signed with Allied firms before 25 January should be treated as special cases for a period of three months and that the purchasing companies be allowed to apply to Bad Ems for the necessary licences. Also, of particular importance to the growing volume of British coal exports was the agreement that foreign coal could enter the occupied territories if covered by a licence issued without charge by the Coal Committee of the High Commission.[39] However, many of these concessions remained theoretical, as orders issued at Coblenz were not necessarily carried out by French officials in the Ruhr and on the customs frontiers. Kilmarnock, for instance, complained that the customs officials at both Ruhrort and Düsseldorf seemed 'to ignore the High Commission's decision in regard to the freedom of foreign coal from any import duty or tax',[40] while Georgi reported that the 'Coste Mission [MICUM], through its agents in occupied territory [was] seizing English coal on the Rhine and forcibly distributing it to whom it pleases'.[41] Renewed pressure on the French authorities in Coblenz and Paris and on the German government in Berlin appeared by the end of April to produce workable compromises,[42]

38. Chairman of British Chamber of Commerce, 3.2.23 (no. 240/23), FO 371/8711 fos 104–5; Kavanagh to D'Abernon (no. 18/3/23), 24.2.23, FO 371/8719 fos 36–8.
39. 'Report', 1923, pp. 32–3.
40. Kilmarnock to Curzon, 13.3.23 (C4842), FO 371/8722 fo. 160.
41. 'Coal Situation in Occupied Territory', 9.3.23 (C4842), p. 5, FO 371/8722 fos 160–4.
42. 'Report', 1923, pp. 34–5.

but ultimately British trade was caught not only in the cross-fire between the French and the Germans, but also between Degoutte and Tirard. According to the Annual Report on the Rhineland for 1923 the French army 'chafed at being influenced by decisions made by the civil body at Coblenz. They considered that the policy pursued there was the wrong one and were firmly convinced that every concession made to British trade lengthened the period of Germany's resistance.'[43] The army's view was shared by French officials at the Licensing Offices at Essen and Düsseldorf, who were determined to prevent the export of steel and the import of coal. It appeared that these officials adopted an attitude 'just short of completely exasperating His Majesty's Government in the hope that the majority of British traders would become so discouraged at the difficulties and delays with which they were faced as to regard their position as hopeless'.[44] Yet the unremitting pressure exercised by British officials in Paris, Coblenz and Cologne succeeded in keeping the Ruhr export trade in steel to Britain viable and above all in opening up the occupied territories to British coal imports, which more than trebled between January and July 1923.[45]

While the defence of British trading interests and the complexities of 'benevolent passivity' spoilt the British Zone 'as a pleasant military station',[46] British officials and troops continued to enjoy the great advantage of being popular with the Germans as they were a guarantee that in the turmoil of the Ruhr crisis Cologne would remain 'an island of peace'.[47] In February, Piggott reported back to the Foreign Office that 'all classes have vied with each other in making things easy for us'.[48] The local trade union leaders, for instance, used their authority to impress upon their members the importance of avoiding any strikes or disturbances in the Cologne bridgehead.[49] Although the British Zone remained dangerously dependent on both the French and the Germans for food and raw materials, nevertheless supplies of coal and food were regularly dispatched from unoccupied Germany and allowed through the frontiers by the Belgian and French authorities. In April Kilmarnock

43. Ibid., p. 35.
44. Ibid., p. 39.
45. Ibid., p. 39; 'Memorandum on the Effect on British Trade of the Ruhr Occupation', 26.7.23 (C13324), FO 371/8737 fos 51–2.
46. 'Report', 1923, p. 20.
47. Gedye, *The Revolver Republic*, p. 126. see also Godley to D'Abernon, 16.2.23, D'Abernon Papers, BL 48927A, fos 208–9.
48. Piggott to Lampson, 13.2.23 (C2944), FO 371/8713 fos 152–4.
49. 'Report No. 40 on the Labour Situation in German Territory, occupied by the British for the period ending 31.1.23', FO 371/8793 fos 230–6.

was sufficiently confident that 'whatever crisis may ultimately threaten the French and Belgian zones, I feel justified in hoping that the British will not be affected, at any rate not to the extent of endangering the maintenance of public order'.[50]

However, the potential shortage of bank notes, the result of accelerating inflation, remained of constant concern to both British and German officials, who feared that the French would seize the opportunity to create a new franc currency in the Rhineland.[51] As the daily requirements of bank notes for the British army and the German population in the Cologne Zone were between eight and ten (American) billions, and the Reichsbank branch in Cologne had a reserve of only twenty-two billions, it was essential that a constant supply should be maintained from Berlin.[52] Inevitably, and with some justification, the French suspected that at least a part of this money was earmarked for financing passive resistance. In March they seized thirteen billions' worth of bank notes at the border post of Hengstei;[53] the Germans retaliated by announcing that the money was destined solely for the use by the British army, in an attempt to exacerbate relations between the British and the French.[54] In the interests of the *Entente* Kilmarnock and Godley attempted to minimize the incident,[55] but Gedye, who was now *The Times* correspondent in the Ruhr, seized upon it and gave it maximum publicity.[56] The President of the Reichsbank also personally took up the incident with Montagu Norman at the Bank of England, who on his behalf protested strongly to the Foreign Office.[57] Curzon did not make a formal complaint, but Crowe forwarded Norman's letter to Lord Crewe in Paris with instructions 'to use his discretion as to the best method of letting the French government know why the High Finance circles in this country must view such proceedings with the gravest misgivings'.[58]

50. Kilmarnock to Curzon, 7.4.23 (C6432), FO 371/8726 fo. 166. It is interesting that in the recollections of two veterans of the Rhine Army it was the inflation and not the Ruhr occupation that was remembered; the Ruhr occupation hardly affected the ordinary British soldier. (Interview by the author with Corporal C. Painter and Sergeant J. McLellan at the Royal Hospital, Chelsea, 28.3.83.)
51. Reichsarbeitsminister to Reichskanzler, 12.2.23 (XR 1/23), FCO Lib. L1711 L502643-4.
52. Piggott to Kilmarnock, 26.2.23 (C3821), FO 371/8718 fos 49–51.
53. Ibid.
54. Kilmarnock to Curzon, 4.3.23 (C4104), FO 371/8719 fos 65–71.
55. Ibid.; and Godley to Lord Cavan, 1.3.23, FO 371/8722 fo. 214.
56. 'Report', 1923, pp. 20–1.
57. Havenstein to Montague Norman (no. 11458), 18.4.23, Bank of England OV 34/71 fo. 132[A]. M. Norman to Crowe, 2.5.23, ibid. fo. 138.
58. See Crowe's reply to Norman, 8.5.23 (C8083), ibid. fo. 142.

In July and August the shortage in bank notes became steadily more acute and threatened the political and economic stability of the British Zone. The problem was aggravated both by a printers' strike and by Franco–Belgian determination to cut the supply of notes from Cologne financing passive resistance in the Ruhr. On several occasions[59] in July and August extra supplies of notes could be obtained to pay the workers only after urgent appeals were made by Kilmarnock to the French and Belgians to allow them to cross the frontier from unoccupied Germany. On 10 August permission was granted after Kilmarnock threatened that 'in the event of a refusal' he would inform Curzon 'that the entire responsibility for any disturbance which might occur in Cologne must rest on the shoulders of the French and Belgian authorities'.[60] Much then to the embarrassment of the British authorities, it was discovered in September that the German government was paying the British-owned Instone Airlines to fly in crates of notes to Cologne from Berlin via Amsterdam and London. The money was then transferred through business accounts to Trier, Coblenz and Aachen to finance passive resistance by German officials.[61] Pressure was put on Instone Airlines to end this lucrative business with the German government by a threat from the High Commission to ban its flights over occupied territory.[62]

To the French, Cologne was a 'Trojan horse' within the occupied territories and 'benevolent passivity' was a shield behind which German resistance to the Ruhr occupation and separatism could be organized and financed. French fears appeared to be confirmed when Smeets was wounded and his secretary shot by a German nationalist in Cologne on 17 March. Tirard immediately pressed for the arrest of the Cologne Police President, the imposition of a curfew, the trial of Smeets' assassins by an Allied tribunal and rigorous control of circulation between occupied and unoccupied Germany.[63] Kilmarnock, fearing the impact of these measures on public opinion in Cologne, managed to delay decisions on the first three demands, but was unable to prevent the High Commission from promulgating Ordinance 167 banning all circulation between occupied and unoccupied Germany between 8 p.m. and 5 a.m., except by train. The Foreign Office refused to consent to its

---

59. See for example Kilmarnock to FO, 16.7.23 (C12492), FO 371/8682 fos 139–42.
60. Kilmarnock to Curzon, 11.8.23 (C13835), FO 371/8683 fos 60–2.
61. 'Immigration Officer's Report' (HO no. 448 735), FO 371/8683 fo. 70; Ryan to Curzon, 10.9.23 (C15790), FO 371/8684 fos 34–41.
62. FO to Air Ministry, 19.9.23 (C15793), FO 371/8684 fos 53–5.
63. 'Memorandum on the Smeets' Case', 25.5.23 (C9504), FO 371/8681 fos 110–18.

application along the borders of the British Zone on the grounds that to do so would be a *de facto* recognition of the French occupation of the Ruhr. Finally, however, in May the French proposed an acceptable compromise, whereby visas would be issued by the German authorities in the British Zone and then stamped by an intelligence officer of the British army.[64] This appeared to square the circle and represented, according to Lampson, 'a reasonable way out of the difficulty' and 'shows incidentally that the French authorities in the Rhineland appreciate our difficulties and are anxious to meet us as far as they can'.[65]

The British authorities in Cologne were sensitive to accusations that the Cologne Zone was a refuge for nationalist terrorists and agitators, which to a certain extent it was bound to be.[66] They were therefore meticulous in their attempts to track down active nationalists in Cologne, even though this could lead to awkward questions in the press and the Commons at home. Shortly after the attack on Smeets, British military police raided the house of Professor Moldenhauer, a member of the Reichstag, who in April 1922 had been reprimanded for making inflammatory speeches against France and attacking the costs of the British occupation.[67] They were also active in searching for anti-French propaganda and saboteurs; on 26 June four men were arrested at Ohligs in possession of two hundredweight of explosives for destroying a bridge near Düsseldorf.[68] Four days later[69] 'benevolent passivity' was again severely tested when a bomb exploded on a Belgian military train at Duisburg, killing ten Belgians and wounding forty others. The High Commission decided immediately to ban all circulation for fourteen days between occupied and unoccupied Germany. As this whole incident was a direct consequence of the Ruhr occupation, Kilmarnock abstained from voting, but the Foreign Office advised making some concession to Tirard by restricting visas 'to persons whose character is above suspicion'.[70] Gedye, relying on information from Piggott, compiled another sensational story for *The Times*[71] in which it was alleged that the British Zone was severed

---

64. 'Annual Report', 1923, p. 11.
65. Lampson's Minute, 18.5.23, FO 371/8681 fos 71–2.
66. 'Endgültiger Bericht des Reichministers a.D. Koch aus dem altbesetzten Gebiet', 12.2.23, FCO Lib. L.1711 L502645-48.
67. Kilmarnock to Curzon, 9.4.23 (C6557), FO 371/8727 fo. 2.
68. 'Report', 1923, p. 14.
69. Ibid., p. 14.
70. Minute by Lampson, 2.7.23 (C11402), FO 371/8682 fo. 35.
71. 'Report', 1923, p. 19.

from its food and coal supplies by the French closure of the frontier. This led to embarrassing questions in Parliament[72] and had specifically to be contradicted by the Rhine Army. Godley had been privately reassured by Degoutte that 'he would do his utmost to meet any wish [he] might express'.[73] There had admittedly been some delays in the transport of food, but British officials on the Railway sub-Commission were convinced that this was merely another attempt by local German officials at the Elberfeld district offices of the Reichsbahn to ferment trouble between the British and French.[74]

On 13 July, when a French patrol was captured by a detachment of German police on the wrong side of the frontier, the High Commission decided to keep the frontier closed for a further fifteen days. This time the British did not cooperate[75] and reverted back to the policy agreed upon in April of issuing passes 'to all persons who were previously in possession of them unless they see any objection on the grounds of security'.[76] Further incidents were to ensure that the frontier remained closed until September, albeit without British cooperation.[77] It was at this stage that considerable friction began to take place between the French border sentries and junior British officials in Cologne. The French were convinced that as a result of laxness in the British Zone German nationalists in the Ruhr were able to obtain British passes; French officials therefore subjected trains leaving the British Zone to stringent checks and actually tore up British passes issued at Cologne to Germans resident outside the British Zone.[78] One Nottingham University student passing through the Ruhr on the way to Berlin described these checks as 'worthy of the purest "Prussianism"',[79] but in fact it did emerge later that some passes had been forged by the Germans and others issued far too casually. One Kreis officer 'would hand a packet of passes, together with the British seal bearing a reproduction of his signature, either to a German interpreter . . . or to a German policeman. These . . . would stamp and take away the blank sheets

72. Morel in the Commons on 9.7.23 (C12006), FO 371/8682 fo. 105.
73. Note to C.-in-C. from Col. Wright, 5.7.23, FO 371/8735 fos 102–3.
74. Ibid.
75. Kilmarnock to FO 14.7.23 (C12259), and FO to Kilmarnock, 17.7.23 (C12259), FO 371/8682 fos 123 and 125.
76. Kilmarnock to FO 18.7.23 (C12445), FO 371/8682 fo. 133.
77. See, for example, Rhine Army to WO, 8.8.23 (C13739), FO 371/8683 fo. 36.
78. Ryan to British Consul, Cologne, 11.9.23, FO 371/8684 fos 88–90.
79. C. Osborne, 'In Berlin', *The Gong* (Christmas, 1923), pp. 5–6, Nottingham University Archives.

upon which any falsehood might be written above a British signature.'[80] Consequently instructions had to be sent to the British officials to issue no passes without a strict enquiry into their application.[81]

During the summer the economic situation in Cologne deteriorated sharply. In June the Kreis officers reported 'increasing anxiety and discontent amongst the working classes on account of the high costs of foodstuffs and the shortage of potatoes'.[82] In the first two weeks of August there were widespread outbreaks of strikes and rioting throughout the occupied territories. In Solingen police had to be strengthened by a company of British troops,[83] and in Opladen workers in four factories surrounded the houses of their employees and forced them to make immediate payments.[84] At Bayer's dye works an unofficially elected Betriebsrat and a crowd of 10,000 people also demanded an immediate payment of 50 million marks and then took over the factory.[85] The disturbances were a direct consequence of the tardy adjustment of wages to the rising rate of inflation. In the calamitous week of 4–11 August too many firms, as a result of the shortage in notes, had to delay the payment of wages until the following week. The local British Kreis officer also blamed the German Landrat for being slow to secure emergency food supplies.[86] At the end of August Kilmarnock summoned the Kreis officers to meet him, and in answer to the question of how long they thought law and order could be maintained, they replied that they 'could only see a fortnight ahead; if there was another slump in the mark, there would inevitably be increased rioting'.[87]

By late summer the occupied territories were at breaking point. Outside the British Zone separatism was gaining ground, and even in Cologne rumours were circulating that the city was about to follow Danzig's example and become a free city.[88] In mid-September production had practically ceased and the British Kreis

---

80. N.C. Huddleston to Lampson, 23.10.23 (C18483), FO 371/8685 fos 135–6.
81. 'Report', 1923, p. 20.
82. 'Labour Report No. 41 for the Period ending 30 June; p. 1, FO 371/8793 fos 247–56.
83. Kilmarnock to FO 7.8.23 (C13540), FO 371/8683 fo. 5.
84. 'Report on Exceptional Unrest in Kreis Opladen', 20.8.23, p. 3 (Capt. Lawson), FO 371/8683 fos 177–87.
85. Ibid., pp. 3–4.
86. Ibid., p. 7.
87. Minute by Lampson, 25.8.23, FO 371/8683, fos 153–4.
88. Telegram from Dirksen, (?) 30.8.23 FCO Lib. 3058 D603613.

officers were unanimously reporting that 'the struggle [against the French] now appears to be nearing its close'.[89] Kilmarnock and his colleagues had to brace themselves to face the challenge from an apparently victorious and invincible France.

89. Ryan to Curzon, 8.9.23 (C15723), FO 371/8741 fo. 10.

The Dual Challenge of Economic and Political Separatism, October 1923–January 1924

Although Poincaré had won a considerable victory, when Stresemann called off passive resistance France was not completely free to exploit her success in the Ruhr. A total break with Britain would almost certainly have had disastrous consequences for the franc, already suffering from the protracted deadlock in the Ruhr. Poincaré was therefore ready to accept the long-canvassed proposal for setting up a committee of experts to investigate the German economy and devise a practical scale of reparation payments, especially because by continuing to occupy the Ruhr, France appeared to hold sufficient productive pledges to prevent the sacrifice of her interests. On 9 October President Coolidge renewed an offer, first made in December 1922, to convene an expert committee, provided there was initial Allied agreement. It took a further two months to define its brief, but by Christmas agreement had been achieved that the Reparation Commission should set up a commission under the American financier Charles G. Dawes, composed of two expert committees, one to enquire into ways for stabilizing the German economy, the other to draw up proposals for attracting exported capital back to Germany.[1]

French agreement to cooperate with the Dawes Commission was not accompanied by any lessening of tension in the Ruhr and the Rhineland. While the Expert Committees undoubtedly offered the prospect of an eventual solution to the Ruhr crisis, in the short term the collapse of passive resistance created a new and potentially more dangerous situation for Britain. The French were engaged in a race against time to impose their will on the Rhineland and Ruhr partly through locally negotiated agreements between the industrialists and MICUM, the joint Franco–Belgian industrial commission,

1. McDougall, *Rhineland Diplomacy*, pp. 295–9.

which had been sent into the Ruhr in January to supervise the production of the mines and factories there, and also, if possible, partly by separatist coups before France's own economic weakness became too crippling and Anglo-American influence could be decisively brought to bear through the Experts Committees.

MICUM, the Régie and the Rhenish Notenbank

The cessation of passive resistance created an entirely new situation in the occupied territories, and compelled the British government to review its policy of benevolent passivity. It was initially assumed in both London and Berlin that Poincaré would negotiate directly with Stresemann on the immediate resumption of reparation payments but he chose, instead, to approach the local industrialists and bankers individually through Tirard, Degoutte and Bréaud, the director of the Régie. He hoped by a series of bilateral negotiations to secure the local payment of reparations, the creation of a Rhenish bank of issue and an autonomous Rhine-Ruhr railway company.[2]

In the short term Poincaré's policy secured an impressive series of agreements with the industrialists as sheer economic pressure forced them one by one to seek an accommodation with MICUM in the Ruhr and with the High Commission in the old occupied territories. Otto Wolff concluded an agreement with MICUM on 17 October and Krupp followed suit on 1 November. On 23 November the German Mining Federation concluded an agreement with MICUM whereby it consented to make full deliveries of reparation coke and coal, to pay the coal tax and a special levy on all coal sold locally or sent to unoccupied Germany. The French also approached individual manufacturers in the British Zone and bribed them into negotiations by the prospect of a cut in export duties on their products.[3]

Parallel to these negotiations, discussions took place between Tirard and Hagen and Schröder, the Cologne bankers, on the establishment of a Rhenish Notenbank or bank of issue in which the French would have a 30 per cent holding.[4] Tirard had long harboured the ambition of introducing a Rhineland currency and sought to build on local initiatives to bring this about. Thus when in late October Hagen offered to take the lead in setting up a

2. Ibid., p. 293.
3. 'Memorandum on the MICUM Agreements', 13.6.24 (C9407), FO 371/9766 fos 6–9; Kilmarnock to Curzon, 2.11.23 (C19025), FO 371/8748 fo. 31.
4. Piggott to Lampson, 5.11.23 (C19277), FO 371/8687 fos 101–2.

gold-based Rhenish currency, both Poincaré and Tirard welcomed the idea as a key step towards creating an independent Rhineland,[5] and strove, ultimately unsuccessfully, to facilitate its introduction before the new Rentenmark, which the Reichsbank put into circulation on 15 November, could restore confidence in a unified German currency.

In the meantime Bréaud, aiming to set up an autonomous Rhine-Ruhr railway company which would be capitalized by the Allies, attempted to force the Germans into recognizing the Régie and into handing over to it the administration of the rail network within the British Zone.[6] The German government refused to recognize the Régie, but it did order its personnel in the occupied territories to cooperate with it and to supply it with the necessary rolling stock and locomotives to enable the Ruhr industries to resume work.[7]

French policy in the Ruhr in the autumn of 1923 represented a major economic threat to British industrial and commercial interests. The British Iron and Steel industry was, however, initially less worried by the 'old bogey' of a Franco–German metallurgical combine than by the more immediate danger of where the great accumulation of steel stocks, which had built up since January, would be dumped.[8] The French readily agreed not to flood the British market, but the worry remained that these stocks would be dumped in foreign markets, so undercutting British industry.[9] The Board of Trade, on the other hand, was alarmed by the consequences of a possible combination of Ruhr coke and Lorraine ore, to which it feared the MICUM agreements might eventually lead. 'Discreet and unofficial enquiries'[10] were made in Paris, but not surprisingly the situation remained 'very far from clear, despite all our efforts to obtain authoritative information'.[11]

Even though the situation in the Ruhr was rapidly changing, the British government refused to participate in any form in a policy of productive pledges. At times this seemed incomprehensible folly to both the Germans and the British officials in the Rhineland. 'Bitter

5. McDougall, *Rhineland Diplomacy*, p. 325.
6. 'Inter-Allied Rhineland High Commission Annual Report', 1923, p. 63.
7. Ibid., p. 69.
8. Bradbury to Niemeyer, 28.9.23, FO 371/8748 fos 46–8. See also Cabinet Conclusions of 15.10.23 (48(23)), p. 6, CAB 23/46 fo. 274.
9. Kilmarnock to Curzon, 2.11.23 (C19024), FO 371/8748 fo. 29.
10. Curzon to Crewe, 29.10.23 (with Enclosure no. 1, BT to FO, 26.10.23) (C18388), FO 371/8747 fo. 45.
11. Memorandum by Lampson, 8.11.23 (C19428), FO 371/8748 fos 142–5.

complaints'[12] were made in German banking circles in Cologne about the lack of British participation in plans for a Rhineland Notenbank. Piggott reported that 'the reasons for the abstention of Great Britain from political matters affecting the future of the Rhineland is understood, but as the Gold Note Bank is regarded first and foremost as a first class financial undertaking, astonishment is felt that more interest is not being displayed by British official quarters'.[13] Silverberg was also shocked by Britain's apparently defeatist attitude towards MICUM. After a discussion with leading British officials in Cologne, he was convinced that 'the British had completely surrendered to the French'.[14]

Both in the Rhineland and in the Foreign Office there were British officials urging an element of British participation in productive pledges. Manton, Godley and Kilmarnock pressed for British participation in the Régie, arguing that the control of the Cologne nodal point would ensure that its policy could be nudged in the direction of British wishes.[15] Within the Foreign Office a memorandum was written shortly after the cessation of passive resistance stressing that some measure of British participation in productive pledges, provided that this was done in such a way as not 'to entail undue interference with the German economy', would be consonant with Curzon's expressed aim of keeping the *Entente* 'as the one solid and stable factor in a world of flux'.[16] This policy was, however, categorically rejected by Curzon, who minuted: 'I do not believe in cooperation in the exploitation policy. We should give away our whole case, become dangerously entangled and find ourselves the catspaw of France.'[17] On 1 October McLachlan, Manton and Georgi arrived to brief the Foreign Office more thoroughly on the new situation in the Rhineland. Curzon, Crowe and Wigram were convinced that the possession of Cologne gave the British 'a trump card', which would ultimately ensure them a decisive say in the railway question.[18] On the strength of these discussions, instructions were then sent to Kilmarnock informing him categorically that 'we could not in any circumstances admit French or Belgian interference in administration of railways,

12. Piggott to Curzon, 17.11.23 (C20177), 21.11.23, FO 371/8689 fos 112–13.
13. Ibid.
14. Silverberg to Adenauer, 18.10.23, BA.KO, *Nachlaß* Silverberg, /408.
15. Godley to Sec. WO, 24.9.23 (no. 17140(Q)), FO 371/8744 fos 34–5; Kilmarnock to Curzon, 25.9.23 (C16883) (enclosing Note by Colonel Manton), FO 371/8743 fo. 33.
16. DBFP Ser. 1, vol. 21 (no. 382), pp. 552–3.
17. Ibid., p. 554.
18. Minutes, 1.10.23, FO 371/8743 fos 26–30.

mines or other concerns in our zone or agree to any change of regime except as part of a general settlement'.[19] At the same time pressure was put on Berlin not to 'enter into any separate arrangements with France to [the] disadvantage of His Majesty's Government or calculated to make difficulties for the position of His Majesty's Government in the British zone'.[20]

British non-cooperation was inevitably resented by the French; Tirard observed that Britain was proceeding to active resistance at the very point when Germany was abandoning passive resistance.[21] Pressure was put on the Germans to include Cologne in the Régie. Kilmarnock informed Curzon that Bréaud had threatened 'to adopt certain aggressive tactics, having isolation of our zone as [the] objective'[22] and by 16 October reports were already reaching Kilmarnock of 'delay and bad management of our troop trains taking reliefs to and from England'.[23] On 19 October the French Ambassador in London made a formal request for the incorporation of the Cologne Railway Directorate into the Régie.[24]

Kilmarnock and his advisers were unhappy with the instructions issued by the Foreign Office. On 20 October[25] he again reviewed the situation as it appeared to British officials in the Rhineland. He was convinced that 'from the point of view of British interests, commercial and economic, in the Rhineland and the Ruhr – the importance of which is greater than is perhaps realised – the greatest advantage which could be drawn from the position would be by means of immediate participation in the exploitation of productive pledges'. The memorandum led to renewed discussion within the Foreign Office about British participation. On 22 October another conference[26] was held to which Kilmarnock was summoned. While it was axiomatic that under no circumstances should the French 'be allowed to give orders in our zone without our consent', it was conceded that some sort of *modus vivendi* would have to be reached with the Régie, whereby it could use the railway lines in the zone for passenger traffic. To avoid the intrusion of

19. FO to Kilmarnock, 4.10.23 (no. 199), FO 371/8743 fo. 45.
20. DBFP Ser. 1, vol. 21 (no. 396), pp. 568–9.
21. Kilmarnock to FO, 13.10.23 (C17711), FO 371/8745 fos 72–3.
22. Kilmarnock to FO, 16.10.23 (C17893), ibid. fo. 160.
23. Ibid.
24. DBFP Ser. 1, vol. 21 (no. 404), pp. 576–7.
25. 'Memorandum by Lord Kilmarnock on the situation in the Occupied Territories', 20.10.20 (C18170), FO 371/8746 fos 120–1. Attached are memoranda from Georgi and Troughton (fos 121–2) which advised negotiations with the Régie and the appointment of a British observer to MICUM.
26. DBFP Ser. 1, vol. 21 (nos 405 and 406), pp. 577–82.

French officials a small number of British railwaymen would be sent to liaise between the Régie and the Reichsbahn and to ensure that the trains ran effectively. The Germans accepted this compromise and the Reichsbahn was ordered to facilitate the task of the British railway officials.

On 9 November Georgi met the Régie directors, who accepted that the railways in the British Zone should remain under German control, but proposed that the Régie should pay the salaries and wages of all the Reichsbahn personnel in the zone. When this was rejected by Godley and the Railway sub-Commission at Cologne on the grounds that it would give the Régie 'an unhealthy influence' at Cologne, an effective *modus vivendi* appeared to be arrived at on 16 November when the Régie at last conceded that the German railway authorities should remain financially and administratively independent under British control, but that, as far as the actual running of the railways went, the internal frontiers between the Régie and the Zone would be abolished.[27]

Against a background of unemployment, hyper-inflation and separatist uprisings in the neighbouring French and Belgian Zones, Kilmarnock was primarily interested in getting the Rhineland economy moving again even if this meant a degree of British participation in the policy of productive pledges. The urgency of the problem was emphasized when the Cologne and Solingen Chambers of Commerce informed Piggott on 22 October that the majority of the works in the British Zone would be forced to close down before Christmas, unless the economy could be revived.[28]

Berlin had terminated all emergency financial assistance to the occupied territories in October, and in November adjusted the rates of unemployment relief down to the same level as those in unoccupied Germany.[29] By the third week of November Thurston reported that there were 350,000 'necessitous persons' in Cologne.[30] In Opladen, Ohligs and Solingen there were rioting and attempts to seize the local Town Halls.[31] Across the border the new currency, the Rentenmark, was beginning to become a viable currency, but its introduction to the occupied territories was craftily delayed by Tirard, who insisted that the High Commission should subject the *Rentenmarkgesetz*, the law legalizing its introduc-

27. 'Report', 1923, pp. 66–7.
28. Ryan to Curzon, 24.10.23 (C18414), FO 371/8747 fo. 58.
29. 'Report', 1923, p. 23.
30. Thurstan to D'Abernon, 21.11.23 (C20577), FO 371/8690 fo. 40.
31. Kilmarnock to Curzon, 24.11.23 (C20436), FO 371/8689 fo. 248.

tion, to detailed scrutiny:[32] consequently the circulation of practically worthless emergency paper marks continued. Unlike the Foreign Office, which essentially wanted to wait until the Expert Committees had reported, Kilmarnock and his staff were more immediately preoccupied by the time bomb of unemployment and hunger ticking away in the British Zone. He informed Curzon that 'it is essential in the interests of public order, and therefore of the maintenance, safety and requirements of the armies of occupation, that everything possible should be done to facilitate the recommencement of work'.[33] He continued to favour a more interventionist policy in the Rhineland and believed that Britain should support, in the short term, attempts by the High Commission to regulate the issue of emergency marks by insisting on strict conditions of issue that would make them acceptable both in the occupied territories and to the Reichsbank.[34] He was also sympathetic to British participation in the establishment of a Rhenish Notenbank on the grounds that it would stabilize the currency, revive commerce and thereby avert disorder.[35] A completely opposing view was taken by Sir John Bradbury, the British representative of the Reparation Commission, who argued strongly that any cooperation with French policies in the Ruhr and Rhineland would merely temporarily postpone their inevitable failure and ensure the ultimate crash of the whole Ruhr economy. He advised that Britain should, instead, subsidize the population in the Cologne Zone and negotiate with the German government 'an agreement supplementary to the . . . Rhineland Agreement, for the purpose of investing the British Commander-in-Chief with wide general powers of emergency legislation'.[36]

Once again the whole question of British policy in the Rhineland was re-examined in two further meetings in the Foreign Office on 27 and 28 November.[37] The problems facing Kilmarnock in the Rhineland were reviewed and, for the most part, his cautious pragmatic policy was approved. His compromise with the Régie was endorsed, and despite the warning from Bradbury that the Franco–German seizure of the customs duties 'amounted in fact technically to malversation', it was agreed, after pleas from both

32. 'Report', 1923, p. 25.
33. Kilmarnock to Curzon, 21.11.23 (C20343), FO 371/8749 fo. 193
34. 'Minutes of a Meeting held at the Foreign Office on Wed. 28.11.23' (C20743), FO 371/8750 fos 133–4.
35. Kilmarnock to Curzon, 29.10.23 (C18908), FO 371/8686 fo. 119.
36. Bradbury to Treasury, 3.11.23 (C19028), FO 371/8748 fo. 42.
37. 'Minutes of a Meeting held at the FO . . . on 27 and 28.11.23' (C20574 and C20743), FO 371/8750 fos 70–2 and 133–4.

the Board of Trade and the Coblenz officials on the absolute necessity of reviving the Ruhr economy, that the *de facto* situation already tolerated by Kilmarnock whereby individual firms could make their own agreements with the French on the payment of customs duties or coal tax should be continued, even if it enabled the French to send in officials to the British Zone. Commercial arguments weighed heavily when the proposed Rhenish Notenbank was considered. Crowe 'was convinced that we should be well advised to keep out', but conceded that 'the question was how far the interests of British trade and commerce outweighed political reasons'.[38] It was consequently decided to set up a small committee of bankers to sound out the City. No opinion was passed on the validity of the MICUM agreements, as it was decided to wait until the Reparation Commission had itself assessed their legality. It was also appreciated that the British in Cologne were potentially in danger of being marginalized by the French appealing directly over their heads to the Germans to carry out decisions taken by the High Commission on a majority vote, from which Kilmarnock had abstained. There was little option but to advise Kilmarnock to seek a 'gentleman's agreement' whereby 'he could get the French to agree [as a result of the concessions which he had been authorized to make in the customs question] not in fact to enforce such decisions in our zone over our heads through the medium of the German officials'.[39] The following day, 28 November, the Treasury, anxious to back the Rentenmark, strongly opposed Kilmarnock's arguments in support of the High Commission's attempts to regulate the issue of temporary paper money [Notgeld] by the local municipalities. As with the payment of customs duties, it was again decided to adopt a *laissez-faire* attitude and leave it to individual firms or municipal councils to conform to the ordinances on Notgeld if they so wished. Cynically Crowe observed: 'It did not appear that any hardship was by our not adhering inflicted upon anybody. We merely take no responsibility in the matter and get any benefit there may be.'[40]

The British government thus continued to maintain its policy of official non-participation in productive pledges. The City backed the Treasury's advice to boycott the discussions between Hagen, Schröder and Tirard on the Rhenish Notenbank. On 13 December the Committee of Clearing Banks decisively vetoed partici-

38. Ibid. (27.11.23), p. 5.
39. Ibid., p. 6.
40. Ibid. (28.11.23), p. 3.

pation,[41] while in early January 1924 Montagu Norman turned down pleas from the Banque de Paris et des Pays Bas to participate, informing Schacht, the new President of the Reichsbank, that he had 'now killed the Rhenish Bank'.[42] Convinced by Schacht that only the creation of a central Note and Discount Bank in Berlin as a subsidiary of the Reichsbank would make the foundation of the Rhenish Bank both unnecessary and financially impossible,[43] Norman agreed to raise and invest five million pounds in the project and played a key role in persuading other central banks to advance funds.[44] At the end of January Hagen and Schröder admitted defeat and broke off negotiations with the French.[45]

Throughout December and January Kilmarnock had no option but to continue the complex task of minimizing the harmful economic effects on the British Zone of the policy of non-participation. He personally[46] intervened to secure a reduction in the tariff for the Solingen cutlery industry, and managed to reduce unemployment there by nearly 50 per cent. He reported back to Curzon:

> In normal times it would be considered dangerous as one sixth of the whole population in Solingen town is still in receipt of relief. Bad conditions are expected to continue throughout the winter and the support of the unemployed will probably mean heavy taxation, which in this *Kreis* is equivalent to a heavy burden on industry. The present mood, however, is one of relief. The workman is working quietly, if not contentedly for £1 a week and his wages will always be cheap compared with English standards.[47]

Pressure on the Cologne Zone was further relaxed when Adenauer managed to persuade the Reichsbank to accept Notgeld as legal tender until January 1924.[48] The subsequent improvement in the exchange rate also encouraged hoarders of food to release their

41. M. Norman to Phillips, 14.12.23, FO 371/8961 fo. 106.
42. Besuch des Herrn Reichsbankpräsidenten Dr Schacht (Report by Sthamer), 2.1.24 (no. A. 34), p. 10, FCO Lib. L1620 L491589-599, pp. 1–11.
43. Memorandum 'Private and Confidential', 11.1.24, Bank of England OV 34/117 fo. 18.
44. See Norman to Reisch, 9.4.24, Bank of England OV 34/113 fo. 17; Norman to Vissering, 5.1.24, OV 34/117 fo. 4; also subsequent letters to central banks in South Africa, Switzerland and elsewhere in OV 34/117; and also Schacht to Norman, 3.11.24, ibid., fo. 111.
45. McDougall, *Rhineland Diplomacy*, p. 351.
46. Kilmarnock to Curzon, 21.11.23 (C20343), FO 371/8749 fo. 198.
47. Kilmarnock to Curzon, 22.12.23 (C22105), FO 371/8691 fo. 95.
48. Kilmarnock to Curzon, 15.12.23 (C21640), ibid. fo. 100.

stocks.[49] By 15 December Kilmarnock was sufficiently confident of the economic situation to advise Curzon that a possible loan to Cologne by a consortium of British banks was no longer necessary.

On 12 December Kilmarnock reached agreement with the French and Belgians on the key question of executing majority decisions within the British Zone. Both Tirard and Rolin-Jaequemyns agreed to 'abstain in practice from taking decisions which would lead to the execution in the British zone without [Kilmarnock's] consent of decisions and ordinances of the High Commission'.[50] This conciliatory attitude did not, however, lead to a speedy resolution of the negotiations with the Régie, which began at Mainz on 8 December.[51] On 14 December Régie officials accepted an agreement, which would have enabled the German Railway Directorate at Cologne to continue to work the rail system within the British Zone under British supervision, but Tirard himself rejected this outright on the grounds that it still left the vital nodal point of Cologne under the control of the Germans.[52] He clearly hoped that the threat of unemployment and pressure from trade and industry within the British Zone would force the British to concede control to the Régie,[53] and on 21 December made fresh proposals to merge the Cologne Directorate into the Régie. Through leaked reports and interviews in the local press French officials tried to bring indirect pressure to bear on the British by suggesting that an obstructive British attitude was damaging trade and causing unemployment.[54] In mid-January a diplomatic incident was caused when a Régie circular was published in the German press announcing that, in view of the deadlock in the negotiations with the British authorities, only military goods and foodstuffs would be accepted for consignment to Cologne. It created a considerable sensation when it was reported in *The Times*. Godley advised against overreaction by the British government as he feared that this would provoke a real blockade and strengthen the Régie just at a time when the French army was becoming increasingly critical of it.[55] Nevertheless Curzon instructed Crowe to enquire into whether what at first sight appeared to be 'a deliberately unfriendly act',[56] in

49. Ibid.
50. DBFP Ser. 1, vol. 21 (no. 492), p. 710.
51. 'Report', 1923, pp. 67–8.
52. Tirard to MAE, 14.12.23 (no. 664), AN AJR 3324.
53. Ibid.
54. 'Annual Report of the Inter-Allied Rhineland Commission for 1924' (C5051), p. 65, FO 371/12916 fos 39–99.
55. Rhine Army to WO, 21.1.24 (50010 Cipher 21/1), FO 371/9738 fos 6–7.
56. DBFP Ser. 1, vol. 26 (no. 335), p. 505.

fact had the backing of the French government. He was assured rapidly that the whole incident was merely an attempt by the Germans to 'create ill feeling' between the Allies, by publishing an old circular from March 1923, although it was later to emerge that it had in fact been published by the Régie Office on 9 January 1924.[57]

Arguably the months September 1923 to January 1924 were the most testing time for the British in the Rhineland since the occupation began. French economic pressure through MICUM, the Régie and the proposed Notenbank was relentless but an even more acute threat to British policy in the Rhineland were the separatist movements, which for a time threatened to confront both London and Berlin with *de facto* French buffer states on the Rhine.

The Separatist Challenge, September 1923–January 1924

Within the British Zone separatists, deprived of French support, had little chance of success. There was not even a majority for a federal Rhineland State within the German Reich.[58] The separatists looked upon Cologne 'as a thorn in their flesh' and hoped by building up the movement elsewhere gradually 'to squeeze Cologne into agreement'.[59] From the end of July until the collapse of passive resistance the separatist leaders, Dorten, Smeets and Friedrich Matthes, held a series of rallies in the main Rhineland cities, the enthusiastic attendance at which surprised even the French. While Poincaré was anxious to avoid overt French support, Tirard was less circumspect and organized the leasing of halls and arranged the necessary security.[60] On 17 September, when all three leaders shared the same platform at a meeting in Aachen, rumours began to circulate in both Paris and the Rhineland that a separatist republic would shortly be proclaimed in Düsseldorf. Kilmarnock was sufficiently worried to ask the Foreign Office for instruction as to what attitude he should take, if this were to take place. He was advised to

57. Ibid., p. 505.
58. When Professor Webster visited Cologne to canvass this on behalf of British League of Nations' supporters, he was told by the Cardinal Archbishop of Cologne that 'not 10 per cent' would vote for it; Note by von Janson, 3.6.23, FCO Lib. L1711 L502758–62.
59. 'Extract from a letter to a General' (received 25.6.23) (C11264), FO 371/8682 fo. 14.
60. McDougall, *Rhineland Diplomacy*, pp. 299–302.

adopt a non-interventionist policy and to use British troops merely to keep order until the Cabinet had the opportunity to assess the situation and the prospects of the new regime.[61]

However, the expected coup did not occur at the separatist rally at Düsseldorf on 30 September, where, instead, German police clashed with armed separatists and order was only restored by the intervention of French cavalry. Twelve separatists and five police were killed and about four hundred people were wounded.[62] Inevitably this *Blutbad* increased tension still further, but it was not until 21 October that 'the expected event happened'[63] and a Rhineland Republic was declared at Aachen by the 'Free Rhineland Movement' under Leo Deckers. It forced the hands of Matthes and Dorten, who hastily ordered their followers to seize key public buildings in a large number of towns including Trier, Bonn and Coblenz itself, where posters were put up announcing that with Tirard's approval the Provisional Government of the Rhineland had been constituted. Faced with this *fait accompli* and the impotence of the Reich, Adenauer and the other political and economic leaders of the Rhineland informed Berlin that they had no option but to talk directly with the French, not in order to agree to a complete separation, but, as the industrialists were doing with MICUM, to negotiate a *modus vivendi* which would enable the occupied territories to feed their population and avert revolution. Facing open challenges from Bavaria, Thuringia and Saxony, Stresemann could only play for time and conduct a *Verschleppungspolitik* or policy of procrastination. He thus met Adenauer and his colleagues at Hagen on 25 October where he agreed to allow them 'a limited negotiating autonomy'[64] to sound out Tirard on French intentions. Two committees, one political and the other economic, headed respectively by Adenauer and Louis Hagen the banker, were set up. Initially their approaches were rejected by Tirard, but he was persuaded by Poincaré after a visit to Paris at the end of October that only important leaders like Adenauer could win over Cologne to separatism. Over the next month, as a series of inconclusive negotiations took place with Tirard, 'the issues of Germany's future wavered like sea water caught between the tide and the opposing winds'.[65] Adenauer held out to Tirard on 14 Novem-

61. 'Report', 1923, pp. 73–4.
62. Ibid.
63. Ibid., p. 75.
64. McDougall, *Rhineland Diplomacy*, p. 318; see also Erdmann, *Adenauer in der Rheinlandpolitik*, pp. 107–86.
65. McDougall, *Rhineland Diplomacy*, p. 319.

ber the tantalizing possibility of setting up an autonomous Rhineland state within the Reich, but the proposal remained a mirage
which at the crucial meeting on 23 November was replaced by
Moldenhauer's more limited plan for creating a Rhineland direc-
torium for administering the local affairs of the Rhineland for five
years. Not surprisingly this was summarily dismissed by an irate
Tirard.[66]

Cologne itself remained an island of relative calm, despite the
War Office's fears of clashes between British troops and separatists.[67] Godley was unperturbed and was confident that the local
police would be able to disarm any separatists who crossed the
frontier. He optimistically told the War Office that there was 'no
likelihood of any clash with the civil population as the majority of
people here are all for a quiet life'.[68] Piggott, however, was less
sanguine and foresaw only chaos and misery resulting from French
policies, which would in the end engulf Cologne.[69] The official
British reaction to the separatist revolts was contained in a speech
by Baldwin at Plymouth on 28 October when he unambiguously
opposed 'the breaking off of any part of Germany into a separate
state'.[70] On 25 October Kilmarnock was given strict instructions to
give no encouragement to any variation of separatism whether
directed 'to the establishment of a separate Rhineland state independent of the *Reich* or of a federal Rhineland state within the *Reich*',[71]
and to press for the disarming of the separatists and the withdrawal
of French support for them.

On the following day Ryan asked Tirard for a full report on the
irregularities which had occurred when the separatists took over
Coblenz.[72] Tirard refused point blank, and as a retaliatory measure
demanded that disciplinary measures should be taken against the
Regierungspräsident of Cologne who 'had acted in respect of the
town of Bonn in an unsupportable manner and in direct opposition
to the French authorities'.[73] Owing to Tirard's absence it was not
possible to convene a plenary session of the High Commission until
5 November. The meeting witnessed a dramatic confrontation

---

66. 'Aufzeichnung' by von Friedberg, 30.11.23 (no. 9070), FCO Lib. 3058
D603890-94.
67. Edmonds, *The Occupation*, p. 257.
68. GOC, Rhine Army, Cologne to WO, 23.10.23 (C18312), FO 371/8685 fo. 64.
69. Piggot (*sic*) to Kilmarnock, 26.10.23 (C19031), FO 371/8686 fo. 223; Piggott to
Lampson, 30.10.23 (C19198), FO 371/8687 fos 77–8.
70. DBFP Ser. 1, vol. 21 (no. 418), p. 603.
71. Ibid. (no. 422), p. 607.
72. 'Report', 1923, p. 81.
73. Ibid., p. 81.

between Kilmarnock and Tirard, at whose request no shorthand minutes were taken.[74] Tirard again refused to consent to any enquiry into the separatist activities in the French Zone and was able to ignore Kilmarnock's criticisms. When Kilmarnock returned to the attack on 13 November[75] and accused Tirard of breaking the Rhineland Agreement, Tirard evaded action by arguing that the whole question was now being considered at ambassadorial level and, as neither British nor French troops were in any danger, he could make no further observations.

While Kilmarnock attacked the grosser irregularities of French-backed separatism, he was not convinced that the British government should distance itself from all the separatist options being canvassed in the autumn of 1923. As a High Commissioner, he was aware of the paramount need to grapple with the mounting economic crisis in the Rhineland and of the appalling incompetence of the Provisional Separatist Government, and therefore wanted permission to participate in Tirard's negotiations with Adenauer and Hagen, as he believed that these might lead to a competent administration acceptable to the majority of the Rhinelanders, particularly if Britain was able to exert any influence on the discussions.[76] Piggott was equally critical of official British policy and urged the convocation of a conference of states interested in the Rhineland, even though he feared that Poincaré would refuse 'till the gaol birds have completed their task'. Nevertheless, he was convinced that even if such an action were abortive 'we shall have done our best and not cut quite such a poor figure, as if we had merely watched our wishes being ignored for the nth. time'.[77] Curzon, however, refused to modify his instructions even though Kilmarnock again pressed his argument at the Foreign Office at the end of November.[78] The British government remained fundamentally convinced that the separatist movement came into being 'not in virtue of any legal title, nor because of its efficiency, nor because it enjoys any measure of popular support, but simply because the French authorities have allowed it to come into existence in open contravention of their obligations, and now interpret these obligations in such a manner as to secure its continuance'.[79]

74. Kilmarnock to Curzon, 6.11.23 (C19292), FO 371/8687 fo. 133.
75. 'Report', 1923, p. 83.
76. Kilmarnock to Curzon, 6.11.23 (C19242), FO 371/8687 fos 90–1.
77. Piggott to Lampson, 30.10.23 (C19198), FO 371/8687 fos 77–8.
78. 'Minutes of a Meeting held at F.O. on . . . 28.11.23' (C20743), FO 371/8650 fos 133–4.
79. DBFP Ser. 1, vol. 21 (no. 485), p. 697.

By early December this assessment seemed at least partially confirmed by events in Berlin and Coblenz. Adenauer's Committee of Fifteen was replaced by an evasive Committee of Sixty chosen from the Rhenish-Westphalian Reichstag deputies. On 4 December the new Chancellor Marx categorically pledged his government to maintain the unity of the Reich. The separatist government in Coblenz was weakened by the 'battle' of Honnef where a marauding party of separatists were set upon by the local peasantry and fourteen of them killed in revenge for earlier incidents. Matthes and Dorten, the two 'Chiefs of the Executive',[80] began to quarrel, and by the second week in December the movement was virtually moribund in the Rhineland Province. One by one the towns and villages which they had seized in October were evacuated.[81]

This was obviously a severe blow to Tirard's plans, but separatism remained a force in the Palatinate, where on 5 November Hoffmann, Kleefost and Wagner, again with overt French assistance, had taken over Kaiserslautern.[82] Crewe had delivered a strong protest in Paris, but Poincaré insisted that the movement had genuine support.[83] By December the whole Palatinate had fallen to the separatists and the legal Bavarian administration had retreated over the border to Heidelberg. Just before Christmas a deputation came to Coblenz and informed Kilmarnock that declarations of adherence to the new regime had been extracted by the separatists through threats of deportation and violence. He raised this at the next High Commission meeting, where Tirard adroitly avoided further discussion by referring it to the Intelligence Committee.[84]

Early in the new year the crisis in Anglo–French relations came to a head when Heinz-Orbis, the Head of the new 'autonomous government' in the Palatinate, submitted laws for raising taxes and the creation of an unemployment fund for registration by the High Commission, thereby immediately raising the question of whether his regime should be officially recognized. Kilmarnock naturally opposed registration but was outvoted by both Tirard and Rolin-Jaequemyns, the latter supporting Tirard on the grounds that the security of the occupying forces required immediate registration. The decrees were then referred to the legal sub-Committee for

80. 'Report', 1923, p. 84.
81. McDougall, *Rhineland Diplomacy*, pp. 322–3 and 328–31.
82. Ibid., pp. 331–5; 'Report', 1923, pp. 88–91; 'Report', 1924, pp. 27–64.
83. DBFP Ser. 1, vol. 21 (nos 455 and 461), pp. 647–8 and 652.
84. Ibid. (no. 513), pp. 736–8; Carsten, *Britain and the Weimar Republic*, pp. 163–4.

examination and were due to come back before the High Commission for review on 10 January. Curzon ordered Kilmarnock to press 'for a postponement pending representation at Paris and Brussels'[85] and to dispatch one of his officials to the Palatinate to assess the reality of the situation 'as the matter may possibly become one of acute controversy with [the] French government'.[86] Tirard inevitably refused to agree to this on the grounds that it reflected badly on the competence of his own official there, General de Metz, the French delegate-General in Speyer, and would consequently be seen as a British investigation into French methods; the most that he conceded was to summon de Metz to Coblenz.[87] Curzon was adamant that the fact-finding mission should take place, but, as a small concession to French susceptibilities, he agreed that R.H. Clive, the Consul General at Munich in whose 'parish' the Palatinate was, should be dispatched, instead of Major Quarry from the High Commission.[88]

On 9 January, when a group of German nationalists assassinated Heinz-Orbis and four other members of the autonomous government in Speyer, Tirard argued strongly that the registration of the decrees had become even more urgent in order to calm the situation, but on instructions from Poincaré, who had bowed to representations from the British and Belgian Ambassadors, he consented to postpone their implementation for another week.[89] Kilmarnock had gained a brief respite, but remained under intense pressure as he feared 'falling into some trap which looks innocent at the moment, but which subsequently assumes portentous shapes'.[90] The British government redoubled its campaign to ensure the rejection of the decrees and the disavowal of the separatist regime. On 12 January Crowe acidly informed the French Ambassador, St. Aulaire, that the British position on the High Commission was rapidly becoming intolerable,

> for whilst under the Treaty of Versailles and the Rhineland Agreement, they remained saddled with their share of responsibility for everything done by the High Commission, the latter had by a misuse of the

85. FO to Kilmarnock, 3.1.24 (C91), FO 371/9770 fo. 206; 'Report', 1924, pp. 28–9.
86. FO to Kilmarnock, 4.1.24 (C91), FO 371/9770 fo. 223.
87. 'Report', 1924, p. 30.
88. FO to Clive, 9.1.24 (no. 2), FO 371/9771 fo. 56.
89. 'Report', 1924, p. 37.
90. Kilmarnock to Lampson, 11.1.24 (C723), FO 371/9771 fo. 224.

majority votes become an organisation for registering decisions taken in opposition to the British government, solely in the interests of a separate Franco-Belgian policy and lying altogether outside the powers conferred on the High Commission by the Rhineland Agreement.[91]

In the Foreign Office the possibility of ordering Kilmarnock to boycott the High Commission sessions until the decrees were decisively rejected by the Commissioners was considered.[92] Crowe played with the idea of advising the ejection of the French officials attached to Piggott's office in Cologne, although his advice was criticized by Sir Cecil Hurst, the Foreign Office legal adviser, who feared that it would lead to embarrassing comparisons in the Paris press 'of the way in which Great Britain will not have French officials working with the British in the Cologne area, while they themselves are only too ready to attach a French official to help Mr Clive in his investigations in the Palatinate'. Ultimately Hurst felt that if the High Commission did take a majority decision to recognize the autonomous government, the British government could do little but lay the dispute before the International Court at the Hague, even though this might not 'seem a very heroic measure'.[93] Another official, Selby, emphasized Britain's powerlessness: 'Our position is uncomfortable in the extreme. It seems that where we cannot assume any responsibility for certain proceedings of the High Commission, we have no means at present of effectively retaliating upon the French or checking their nefarious proceedings.' He advised that the British could only 'tread water and wait for the Dawes Committee to report'.[94]

Clive reached Speyer on 16 January where he dined with General de Metz, who afterwards confided to him 'en gentleman à gentleman' that while an independent Palatinate was not viable, if a future war was to be avoided, 'there must be a Rhineland state within the *Reich*, but yet capable of declaring itself neutral if there was danger of war'. To this Clive observed ironically that whilst it was admissible in theory, it 'presumed the possibility of creating a state so far unknown to political science'.[95] He then spent the next four days travelling through the Palatinate and gathering evidence for his

91. FO to Crewe, 12.1.24 (no. 28R Amended Copy), FO 371/9771 fos 98–103.
92. 'Memorandum respecting friction with French Government over Registration by Rhineland High Commission of certain Decrees of Autonomous Government of the Palatinate' (C704), FO 371/9771 fos 209–10.
93. 'Memorandum by Sir C. Hurst, 14 Jan. 1924' (C705), p. 4, FO 371/9771 fos 212–13.
94. Memorandum by G. W. Selby, 15.1.24 (C884), FO 371/9772 fos 93–4.
95. Clive to Curzon, 16.1.24 (C1300), FO 371/9773 fo. 91.

report to Curzon.[96] When the French retaliated by insisting on sending their own fact-finding mission to the British Zone to enquire into allegations that the Regierungspräsident in Cologne had deliberately caused problems for the French in Bonn, Kilmarnock consented provided it was in a 'non executive capacity'.[97]

Meanwhile, in an attempt to secure registration of the decrees Tirard proposed that the High Commission should add a rider specifically declaring that the process of registration did not involve *de jure* recognition of the Autonomous government.[98] Curzon, however, refused to compromise, and informed Kilmarnock that if the decrees were not postponed or cancelled, he must declare them *ultra vires*.[99] A further temporary postponement was gained, which enabled Clive to send a preliminary report to Curzon unambiguously stating that the 'overwhelming mass of population [were] opposed to the autonomous government'. This report was then read out to the Commons on 21 January in answer to a question by Kenworthy in what was virtually the last act of the Conservative government before handing over power to Labour.[100]

Emboldened by Clive's report, a signed declaration by the councils and mayors of 410 towns and villages in the Palatinate was sent to the High Commission in protest against the separatist regime. Only further subsidies from France could now have prolonged the life of the autonomous government, but the rapidly collapsing franc, which needed assistance from London and Washington, forced a French retreat. A temporary inter-Allied control committee was set up in February to supervise the return of the Palatinate to Bavarian administration; on 17 February the illegal government of the Palatinate was finally dissolved.[101] The collapse of the separatist movement was a decisive defeat for the French on the Rhine and effectively marked the end of their attempts to create a buffer state.

96. 'Report', 1924, p. 44.
97. Kilmarnock to FO, 13.1.24 (C594), FO 371/9771 fos 192–3.
98. Kilmarnock to FO, 15.1.24 (C753), FO 371/9772 fo. 33.
99. FO to Kilmarnock, 16.1.24 (no. 31), ibid., fo. 35.
100. 'Questions asked in the House of Commons, 21.1.24' (C1225), FO 371/9773 fo. 64A.
101. McDougall, *Rhineland Diplomacy*, p. 351; 'Report', 1924, pp. 43–51. For details of the collapse of the franc see T. Kemp, *The French Economy, 1913–39. The History of a Decline*, London, 1972, pp. 76–7.

–14–

The Impact of the Ruhr Crisis on the Control Commissions

The Ruhr crisis made inspections virtually impossible to carry out. The wave of intense hatred for France and Belgium that swept Germany turned the Control Commissions into 'a besieged fortress in the middle of enemy territory'.[1] There were assaults on officers and demonstrations outside the hotels where Allied officers were billeted.[2] Bingham was understating the situation when he wrote that 'life in unoccupied Germany is far from pleasant for any French or Belgian officer at the present . . .'.[3]

The Reichswehr was quick to exploit the outbreak of passive resistance on the Ruhr to break off relations with the IAMCC. Reichskanzler Cuno attempted to compromise by proposing to Nollet that inspections should be carried out only by British and Italian officers, but Nollet, determined to preserve Allied unity at a time when it had ceased to exist in the Rhineland, was adamant that 'the Commission formed one solid block and that any obstacles in the way of Franco-Belgian control therefore meant the suspension of the whole control'.[4] He stubbornly persisted in resuming control, but in practice a total German lack of cooperation made the few visits that took place in January and February abortive.[5] The British government was reluctant to support Nollet as it was anxious to avoid incidents which could exacerbate the situation in the Ruhr. The Foreign Office was therefore irritated when Bingham, without referring back to London, agreed to the dispatch of 'an ill judged'[6] letter by Nollet to the German government

---

1. Salewski, *Entwaffnung*, p. 217.
2. Report on the incident which occurred on 24.1.23 in front of Bremer Hof Hotel (no. 760655), ADM 116 1941, Pack no. 44/A1.
3. Bingham to DMO, 20.3.23 (C5770), FO 371/8778 fos 99–100.
4. Nollet to Foch, 19.1.23 (no. 2296), ADM 116 1941, Pack no. 44/A/1.
5. For details see Enclosure no. 2 in no. 1, Addison to Curzon, 27.6.23 (C11556), FO 371/8780 fo. 58; also Carsten, *The Reichswehr and Politics*, pp. 155–63.
6. Minute by Lampson, 6.5.23, FO 371/8778 fos 121–6.

demanding the resumption of unimpeded control. When the Germans refused on the grounds that they could not guarantee the safety of the Belgian and French personnel, the question was referred to the Allied Military Committee of Versailles, where it was agreed, in the absence of the British member, to send another letter insisting on further inspections despite the danger of incidents. Its dispatch was only prevented by the urgent intervention of Phipps of the Embassy who insisted on referring to London for instructions.[7] Reluctantly Curzon conceded that the resumption of control was 'a duty which we cannot evade',[8] and Phipps was instructed to agree, provided that everything was done to avoid incidents.[9]

When control began again on 27 March the Foreign Office could only hold its breath and hope for the best.[10] Nollet ordered a preliminary control visit to take place in each sub-Commission district, but in eight out of ten inspections the results were 'fiascos',[11] although there were no serious incidents. Both the Foreign Office and the War Office were in agreement[12] that the situation in the Ruhr effectively prevented further control, and Bingham was specifically forbidden to attach British officers to the inspection team going to Königsbrücke for fear that 'even the simplest visit might give rise at this juncture to some unfortunate situation',[13] although in fact these instructions arrived too late to have any effect. Ironically, despite Bingham's initial confidence that the Ruhr crisis had proved beyond doubt that Germany was disarmed,[14] this inspection revealed the illegal training of a considerable number of Reichswehr reserve officers and caused the British government to lift its ban on British participation,[15] although Lord D'Abernon and his staff were surprised at this *volte face* and doubted its effectiveness.[16] Bingham was accordingly instructed to:

7. Salewski, *Entwaffnung*, p. 219; DBFP Ser. 1, vol. 21 (nos 534 and 535), pp. 764–6.
8. Crowe's Minute, 12.3.23, FO 371/8777 fos 204–6. Curzon commented: 'I dislike the whole position, but assume that we must do as proposed.'
9. DBFP Ser. 1, vol. 21 (no. 541), p. 771.
10. See Minute by Lampson, 22.3.23: 'It lies in their hands', FO 371/8778 fo. 29.
11. Lampson's Minute of 6.5.23, FO 371/8778 fos 121–6.
12. Cubitt to Undersecretary of State, 5.4.23 (C6203), FO 371/8778 fo. 139.
13. WO to Control, 5.5.23 (M.I.3/5315), FO 371/8779 fo. 44.
14. Bingham to WO, 15.1.23, 'Where is Northcliffe's secret army?' (C990), FO 371/8704 fo. 79.
15. WO to Undersecretary of State, 18.5.23 (0154/6181 M.I.3), FO 371/8779 fo. 116, and Minute by Wigram, 26.5.23, ibid., fo. 131; Rosenberg to London Embassy, 23.5.23 (no. 406), FCO Lib. 2368 490325-27.
16. Addison to Lampson, 14.6.23 (C10702), FO 371/8780 fo. 20.

do everything in your control to bring to bear upon your Allied colleagues the most moderating influences so as to reduce to a minimum the chances of further incidents between German and Allied officers . . . For example, it might be as well at first to refrain from insisting upon visits to certain disaffected factories, whilst at the same time you could be quite firm in regard to visits to military and police units.[17]

Predictably the new programme of visits ended in failure, and throughout August there was a virtual standstill in the activities of the IAMCC.[18] The end of passive resistance on 26 September led to hopes that the deadlock could be broken. On 3 October the Ambassadors' Conference delivered what amounted to an ultimatum to Berlin insisting on the renewal of control, but it arrived at the crucial moment when the Stresemann government was dependent on the Reichswehr to preserve the unity of the Reich. Stresemann was therefore in no position to order the army to comply with Nollet's instructions.[19] It was Bingham's 'considered opinion that if Stresemann were to give a definite order to von Seeckt . . . the military would depose the Republican Government and establish a dictatorship'.[20] Despite renewed advice from the War Office that the resumption of control would be counter-productive, the Foreign Office initially conceded that it had little practical option but to support France in the exercise of her legitimate rights,[21] but when it became clear that this was leading to yet another major confrontation in which the French would resort to further sanctions, it frantically sought to moderate French policy. Fundamentally the British government at this stage only wanted to re-establish the principle that the Allies had the right to control, but it was ready to exercise it with discretion. Stresemann, on the other hand, had little option but to delay making any concessions until his government was no longer directly dependent on the army. He consequently attempted to defer visits by the IAMCC on the grounds that Allied security could not be guaranteed.[22]

French anger was further exacerbated by the German government's refusal to ban the return of the Crown Prince to German territory. On 13 November the French even threatened more

---

17. Burnett Stuart to Bingham (0154/6242 M.I.3), 30.5.23, FO 371/8779 fo. 199.
18. Bingham to FO, 11.7.23 (I/W.O./86), FO 371/8780 fos 86–7.
19. Salewski, *Entwaffnung*, p. 223.
20. Bingham to DMO & I, 13.11.23 (C19892), FO 371/8782 fos 78–9.
21. Memorandum by Crowe, 8.10.23 (C17501), FO 371/8781 fo. 86.
22. DBFP Ser. 1, vol. 21 (no. 639), pp. 896–7.

sanctions if the Crown Prince was not surrendered and control resumed.[23] Crewe, referring back to London for instructions, warned Curzon that 'if His Majesty's Government are unable to support French action or to suggest some alternative methods of applying strong pressure to Germany without delay, they must be prepared . . . to face an estrangement here which will endanger the whole of the *Entente*'.[24] Curzon, however, preferred to listen to advice from the War Office, which argued that the French were deliberately provoking a crisis 'to justify, in the eyes of the world, the maintenance of their hold on the Ruhr and the Rhineland'.[25] The French were therefore sharply informed that Britain would not support the unilateral application of sanctions, as such a step 'would make an individual Power both the interpreter and the executant of the Treaty'.[26] He recommended instead a more pragmatic approach as outlined by the War Office, whereby inspection should only proceed when and where it was safe to do so. In the face of British threats to withdraw from the Ambassadors' Conference, and 'possibly'[27] from the Control Commission itself, the French grudgingly gave way and agreed on 21 November that control operations should not go ahead unless the Allied officers in charge of the IAMCC first consulted with their Embassies in Berlin 'as to the possibility of the particular operation being conducted with safety'.[28]

A new and damaging confrontation between the French and Germans, which would have strengthened the French position in the Ruhr, had, at least temporarily, been averted, but the arrest of Major Hennessy, for allegedly spying on German military manoeuvres at Limbach in October, and a month later of a Belgian officer and a French sergeant for doing the same in Saxony, created fresh sources of friction between the IAMCC and the Reichswehr, which threatened to escalate into a major political row.[29] On 2 November the IAMCC took the law into its own hands. Despite ineffectual attempts by the British representative, who in Bingham's absence was Colonel Longhurst, to refer the matter back to the Conference of Ambassadors, it demanded a personal apology to

23. Ibid.
24. Crewe to FO, 12.11.23 (C19569), FO 371/8781 fo. 286.
25. WO to Undersecretary of State (0154/6242 M.I.3), 13.11.23, FO 371/8782 fos 26–7.
26. DBFP Ser. 1, vol. 21 (no. 639), p. 897.
27. Ibid. (nos 650 and 656), pp. 913 and 919.
28. Ibid. (nos 660 and 663), pp. 926–9 and 931–2.
29. WO to Undersecretary of State, 7.11.23 (C19237), FO 371/8781 fos 218–21; D'Abernon to FO, 21.11.23 (C20227), FO 371/8783 fo. 50.

Hennessy and immediate steps to be taken by the German government to ensure the complete liberty of movement for all members
of the Allied members of the Control Commissions. The unfortunate Longhurst was pilloried by the Foreign Office for lacking 'the
guts to stand up to the French',[30] and ordered in the future to insist
on such issues first being referred back to the Conference of
Ambassadors.[31] On 16 November the German officer responsible
for Hennessy's arrest apologized in writing to him,[32] and D'Abernon assumed that, as far as the British went, the matter was settled.
The German Undersecretary of State, Carl von Schubert, confided
in him that Hennessy was 'not a very pleasant person', and had
deliberately provoked the Reichswehr by bringing *The Times*
journalist, Barker, with him. He even urged D'Abernon to use his
influence to have Hennessy sent on leave 'so that we could be
temporarily rid of him'.[33] There was little sympathy for Hennessy
in the Foreign Office and considerable irritation when Nollet found
the German apology to Hennessy inadequate and referred the
whole matter to the Conference of Ambassadors.[34] Nevertheless,
on calmer reflection it was conceded that Hennessy and the other
two Allied soldiers were in fact doing their duty and acting on
Nollet's orders, and that therefore some sort of punishment for the
German troops who seized them would have to be insisted on.
Consequently in Paris Crewe was authorized to consent to French
demands for the dismissal of the relevant German soldiers.[35] Both
D'Abernon and Crowe diplomatically impressed upon the Germans the importance of meting out some symbolic act of punishment to these men if the British were to have any success in
restraining the French from exacerbating the whole incident.[36]

Just at this delicate stage when the Foreign Office and D'Abernon
were attempting behind the scenes to put pressure on the Germans,
whilst restraining the French, Reuters published a list, which was
reprinted in all the main British papers, giving alarmist details of
German breaches of the disarmament clauses.[37] It was assumed
immediately by both Britain's allies and the Germans that the

30. Minute by Wigram, 10.11.23, FO 371/8781 fo. 246.
31. WO to Longhurst, 16.11.23 (0154/6242 M.I.3), FO 371/8782 fo. 222.
32. Schubert to Moraht, 16.11.23, FCO Lib. 9483 H276929-30.
33. Ibid.
34. See Wigram's Minute of 22.11.23 on D'Abernon's Telegram of 21.11.23
(C20227), FO 371/8783 fos 48–9.
35. DBFP Ser. 1, vol. 21 (no. 671), pp. 942–4.
36. Sthamer to AA, no. 613, 29.11.23, FCO Lib. 9483 H277030; 'Aufzeichnung',
29.11.23 (Maltzan?), FCO Lib. 9483 H277034-35.
37. Released 29.11.23; see *The Times*, 30.11.23.

Baldwin government, in the middle of a general election and smarting from a series of attacks in the *Daily Mail*, which were also directed at Bingham, was attempting to convince the electorate that it was not pro-German.[38] The article was officially disowned by the Foreign Office in a statement in *The Times*,[39] and *The Times* itself in a leading article regretted 'that there should have been accumulated lately a good deal of evidence of a disingenuous attack on General Bingham, who is creditably performing a most difficult task in Berlin'.[40] Bingham hastily compiled a list of evidence largely refuting the Reuter's article.[41] The information on which the article was based was probably inspired by Morgan, although he himself denied it.[42]

The French were determined to press on with control as soon as possible. On 15 December Nollet urged a programme of visits, but Bingham, bound by his new instructions, had first to consult both D'Abernon and the War Office.[43] Eventually it was agreed that initially visits should be confined to areas where least opposition was to be expected and that all visiting parties must consist of officers 'of at least four of the nationalities represented on the Control Commission'.[44] Privately the Germans 'through an English contact' in the Commission were told that 'the non-French and non-Belgian officers are actually against the continuation of control as the participation of officers of the other powers is designed [*nur dazu dienen solle*] to pull the chestnuts out of the fire for France and "sauver la peau des Français"'.[45] Von Seeckt was bitterly hostile to further control, but the German Cabinet finally secured his grudging consent after Schubert was reassured by Bingham and D'Abernon that control personnel would not come into direct contact with the German rank and file.[46] The visits took place on 18 January and passed off satisfactorily except for one minor incident.[47] At Stuttgart it was noticed by a local police officer that 'only the French and Belgians showed any interest in

38. Vermerk (Zu 11F 3306 and 3354), 12.12.23, FCO Lib. 9490 H279344–46; DBFP Ser. 1, vol. 21 (no. 673), p. 946.
39. *The Times*, 30.11.23.
40. Ibid.
41. Enclosure in Berlin dispatch no. 911 of 30.11.23, FO 371/8785 fo. 9.
42. Finlayson to Lampson, 3.12.22, and Curzon's Minute of 5.12.22, FO 371/8785 fos 82–3.
43. Control to WO, 16.12.23 (C21775), FO 371/8785 fo. 225.
44. DBFP Ser. 1, vol. 21 (no. 690), pp. 960–1.
45. Note by Moraht, 28.12.23 (no. 11F 3079), FCO Lib. 9490 H279402–403.
46. Note by Schubert, 5.1.24, FCO Lib. 4530 E138557–558.
47. DBFP Ser. 1, vol. 26 (no. 620), pp. 983–4 (footnote 3).

control, while the Italian and British representatives behaved with complete indifference'.[48] The German government was determined that these visits should be the last attempt to inspect military units and installations. In a note on 9 January addressed to Nollet, it argued that, as most of the disarmament clauses had already been fulfilled, any remaining problems such as those enumerated in the five points in the Allied note of 29 September 1922 could be resolved through negotiations.[49] Inevitably the majority of the IAMCC viewed the German proposals with suspicion and sent what Bingham called an 'alarmist' letter to the Conference of Ambassadors arguing that Germany still constituted a serious danger and was actually attempting to re-arm.[50] Acting on instructions from Foch the Commission also answered the German note itself without referring back for further instructions.[51] Although its tone was mild in that it merely affirmed its right to control and pointed out that it had not yet been able to check the German enlistment returns, the Foreign Office was highly critical of Bingham for permitting yet another letter with potentially important political implications go forward. Crowe acidly observed that 'this General is always bungling'; he 'is even by the War Office's admissions hopelessly incompetent, and we are in hope that he will before long be replaced by a less inefficient officer'.[52]

While, by the end of January 1924 for British officials on the Rhineland High Commission the worst of the crises precipitated by the Ruhr occupation appeared to have been surmounted, for Bingham and his colleagues the resumption of control after a year of virtual inactivity was to create fresh problems, which were to become increasingly more difficult to solve as the adoption of the Dawes Plan restored Germany's self-confidence and guaranteed her territorial integrity.

48. Württ.Polizeipräsidium, Stuttgart, 15.1.24 (Nr.IV Z.ST 85/24) to Ministerium des Innens, 15.1.24, FCO Lib. 9490 H279717-20.
49. Communicated to FO by German Embassy, 11.1.24 (C696), FO 371/9722 fos 167–8.
50. DBFP Ser. 1, vol. 26 (no. 622), p. 985; Bingham to Nollet (Enclosure 4 in no. 1), FO 371/9723 fos 16–16A.
51. DBFP Ser. 1, vol. 26 (no. 622).
52. Minute by Crowe, 6.2.24 (C2050), FO 371/9723 fo. 115.

PART V

From Dawes to Locarno,
February 1924–January 1926

Introduction

The collapse of the franc, the failure of separatism and Poincaré's grudging agreement to the setting up of the Dawes Commission marked the beginning of the end of the post-war era of sanctions and German isolation. France had failed to revise the Versailles Treaty forcibly and now had no option but to pursue, in cooperation with London, and tacitly also with Washington, a new policy of negotiation and gradual appeasement of Germany. The Treaty still provided the framework in which Germany and the former war-time allies operated. In January 1925, despite the new atmosphere of *détente*, the evacuation of the Cologne Zone by British troops was delayed for a year on French insistence, and with reluctant British agreement, on the incontrovertible evidence that Germany had not sufficiently carried out the disarmament clauses of the Treaty. Nevertheless it was becoming possible for Germany, in cooperation with the other powers, to influence the *de facto* revision of the Versailles Treaty through the negotiation of new treaties. Between April 1924, when the Dawes Commission published its recommendations, and the Locarno Treaties of October 1925, there occurred what can arguably be described as a diplomatic revolution. Not only was German economic and territorial unity assured at the London Conference in August 1924, when the Dawes Plan was adopted, but a year later the intractable problem of French security was apparently solved by the Locarno agreements.

Liquidating the Ruhr Crisis, 1924

By early 1924 in Britain the sense of fair play, residual Gladstonian Liberalism and self-interest were all united in desiring an end to the Ruhr crisis and the reconstruction of Germany. Not only did businessmen and industrialists yearn after economic stability, but the constant news of the distress and hunger caused by the Franco–Belgian occupation and the inflation were powerful factors working for the German cause in Britain in 1923/4.[1] In the spring of 1924 Professor Kantorowicz of Freiburg University noted after a visit to Britain that 'as far as Germany goes the English today are undoubtedly most interested in the charitable aspect. Almost every conversation begins with enquiries about the suffering in Germany and keeps returning to the theme.'[2] The University Committee of the Imperial War Relief Fund, for instance, enlisted the active support of the ecclesiastical, literary and academic establishments on behalf of impoverished German students and teachers. Galsworthy, in a classic appeal to the spirit of fair play in his countrymen, stressed

1. See Williamson, 'Great Britain and the Ruhr Crisis, 1923–24', from which most of the information below is taken.
2. 'Bericht über eine Reise nach England (Frühjahr, 1924)', FCO Lib. K2002 K516208. The experiences of the British occupation were probably only marginal in bringing about this awareness of Germany's plight in 1923. The various charities, like the Save the Children Fund, and the Quakers' Friends Emergency and War Victims Relief Committee were concerned with the situation in the whole of Central Europe. Nevertheless the British involvement in the Rhineland, Upper Silesia and Danzig must have helped focus public opinion on German suffering. Miss Tower was instrumental in involving the Save The Children Fund in Danzig, while the Quakers cooperated with Piggott in Cologne (see above, ch. 6). In Silesia the revulsion at French complicity in the Korfanty revolts led to at least one British official, Lt Col. Graham Hutchison, who resigned from the Upper Silesian Commission in May 1921, combining self-interest with moral outrage by offering the services of his newly founded PR agency to the German government for the fee of £20,000, to launch a propaganda campaign on behalf of German policy (FCO Lib. K128 KO13430-39 and KO13503-05). Gedye also used his experience as Col. Ryan's secretary on the IARHC after he had resigned in 1922 to cover the Ruhr crisis and the separatist uprisings as *The Times'* special correspondent in a series of articles which were highly critical of the French. (These later formed the basis of his book *The Revolver Republic*.)

the 'great meaning in the expression to be British; and I feel that here is a chance for the real humanity, the generosity to a foe, the rising above pettiness . . .'.[3] While the Labour Party, most intellectuals and politically active students were pro-German, the majority of the British people were neither pro-German nor pro-French and wanted a European settlement which would usher in an era of real peace and economic stability. Germans visiting Britain confirmed this mood of war weariness. Kantorowicz was struck by the feeling of exhaustion in Britain and aptly observed that 'John Bull has become an old man who wants his rest after the enormous efforts of the last few years.'[4]

Despite this overwhelming desire for peace on the Rhine, the entry into office of a minority Labour government in January 1924 did not lead to a dramatic break with Poincaré. MacDonald, who combined the post of Prime Minister with that of Foreign Secretary, soon realized like his predecessors that there was no real alternative to cooperation with France and that only by working within the *Entente* could France be prised out of the Ruhr and eventually the Rhineland.[5]

The Dawes Plan and the London Conference, April–August 1924

The Dawes Commission presented its plan for the eventual resumption of reparation payments by Germany in early April. Despite considerable reservations from the trade unions and many Labour MPs,[6] the Treasury informed Snowden, the new Chancellor of the Exchequer, that acceptance was unavoidable 'even if it had been much less sound than it is', as it was 'the only constructive suggestion for escape from the present position, which if left must inevitably lead to war, open or concealed, between France and Germany'.[7] MacDonald needed no such advice. He seized upon the report as the key to his plans for the pacification of Europe, since by recommending the evacuation of the Ruhr, German economic

3. Galsworthy, quoted in Williamson, 'Great Britain and the Ruhr Crisis, 1923–24', pp. 78–9.
4. 'Bericht'.
5. R. Lyman, *The First Labour Government of 1924*, New York, 1975; R. Marquand, *Ramsay MacDonald,* London, 1977, ch. 15.
6. See Joint Meeting of TUC General Council and Executive Committee of the Labour Party, 27.3.24, NEC vol. 30, Labour Party Archives.
7. Memorandum by Mr Niemeyer on the Reparation Experts Report, 14.4.24 (C6331), p. 1, FO 371/9740 fos 234–6. See Bariéty, *Les relations franco-allemandes.*

unity, a large foreign loan, a four-year partial moratorium and the financing of reparations from railway bonds, industrial debentures, taxes and customs duties, it offered a real solution to the reparation problem.

MacDonald was able to persuade the Labour Party to support it despite the fact that it entailed the acceptance of the principle of reparations and the conversion of the German Reichsbahn into a private corporation.[8] Poincaré remained a formidable hindrance to a quick realization of the Dawes Plan. Although dependence of the franc on Anglo-American support ensured that France would ultimately have 'to swallow anything on which the Americans chose to insist',[9] both the Treasury and the Foreign Office feared that the French would skilfully goad the Germans into rejecting the report outright or else so enmesh it in a 'mass of tangled discussion on matters of detail'[10] that the whole plan would be ruined. Mac-Donald was therefore determined to keep the discussion of the plan 'as far away as possible' from the Reparation Commission, negotiate with Germany as 'a voluntary contracting party' and secure 'the maximum cooperation from America'.[11]

It was clear, however, that 'short of being a victorious power imposing terms on a beaten France',[12] Britain would have to offer at least the prospects of concessions to France on inter-Allied debts and move some way to meeting her wishes on security and demands for a system of sanctions should the Germans again default on reparation payments. Yet this placed MacDonald in an awkward dilemma. The Treasury, convinced that 'debts are our only weapon if the Allies seek to disturb the settlement unduly',[13] advised against concessions on debts for at least five years. The Foreign Office grudgingly conceded that there would have to be provision for 'some sort of sanctions or penalties' against Germany in the case of a default in reparation payments[14] if the French were ever to be eased out of the Ruhr, but they were to be so hedged around with safeguards aimed at preventing unilateral French action, that MacDonald could only assure his allies that in the event

8. Williamson, 'Great Britain and the Ruhr Crisis', p. 86. I have drawn heavily on pp. 86–91 of the above article for this section.
9. Bradbury to Snowden, 12.3.24 (C4525), FO 371/9739 fos 2–3.
10. Minute by Lampson, 11.4.24, FO 371/9740 fo. 101.
11. 'The Objects of His Majesty's Government', 23.4.24, FO 371/9741 (C6671) fo. 185.
12. See FO Minute (unsigned) on 'An Outline Agreement drafted by Sir John Bradbury', 3.5.24 (C7239), FO 371/9743 fo. 89.
13. Memorandum by Niemeyer (C6331), p. 5.
14. 'Objects of H.M.G.' (C6671).

of a future German default, 'she would find herself confronted by England, Belgium and France inflexibly united as they were during the war'.[15] It was more difficult to find a similarly vague and imprecise formula which would encourage the French without irrevocably committing the British when Poincaré raised the question of an Anglo–French security pact in May. MacDonald had an imprecise vision of a comprehensive policy of pacification and reconstruction guaranteed by the League of Nations, but under no circumstances was he ready to consider a simple defensive alliance with France. British policy was to persuade the Belgians, French and Germans to implement the Dawes Plan and then repose their trust in subsequent British generosity. MacDonald was convinced that the Dawes Plan would prepare the way for a general European settlement.

Once the Germans agreed in principle to accept the Plan on 16 April, MacDonald had to tread a delicate path between discouraging Germany from expecting too much too quickly from France,[16] and persuading the French to couple their acceptance of the Plan with some real concessions to Germany. Yet in leading both France and Germany towards a settlement, MacDonald could not afford to appear too blatantly a mediator. The key to a reparation settlement continued to lie in Paris and consequently concessions could only be extracted from France behind the façade of the *Entente Cordiale*. MacDonald's task was considerably eased by Poincaré's defeat in the French elections in May and his replacement on 13 June after a prolonged political crisis by the Radical Herriot, the leader of the Radical–Socialist alliance, the 'Cartel des Gauches'.

MacDonald, anxious to implement the Dawes Plan as soon as possible, invited Herriot to Chequers for informal talks on 21–22 June.[17] It became clear on the first day of the talks that as far as the technical details of the implementations of the report were concerned, an Anglo–French agreement was possible. MacDonald promised to make a 'full exploration of the whole question of security' once the Dawes Plan was implemented, but he warned Herriot against expecting any major concessions: 'I cannot take an easy way and participate in the offer made to France of a military guarantee of security . . . None of the Dominions would support

15. Quoted in Poincaré to MacDonald, 14.5.23 (C7960), p. 2, FO 371/9745 fos 6–7.
16. MacDonald to D'Abernon, 29.5.24 (C8478), FO 371/9746 fos 99–100; DBFP Ser. 1, vol. 26 (no. 431), p. 638.
17. 'Notes taken during a Conversation between M. Edouard Herriot . . . and Mr. Ramsay MacDonald, at Chequers, 21 and 22 June 1924', pp. 1–21 (C12270), FO 371/9749 fos 85–95.

me, a reactionary government would replace mine, and finally France would only have false security.'[18]

The London Conference opened on 16 July. After the Allies had secured agreement amongst themselves, Germany was invited to attend. By 18 August agreement on the application of the Plan and written pledges from France and Belgium to evacuate the Ruhr within twelve months had been obtained.[19] There is no doubt that it was a 'crushing defeat'[20] for the French. Any future resort by a French government to sanctions over reparations was effectively blocked by Anglo–American insistence that if a majority on the Reparation Commission, as in January 1923, decided on sanctions, the minority, by which was meant Britain, could appeal ultimately to the International Court at the Hague. To reinforce this right it was agreed that an American representative would join the Reparation Commission if a German default occurred. The London Agreement was warmly welcomed by the Conservative Party; indeed Austen Chamberlain's vigorous defence of it in a letter to the *Birmingham Post* was later published as an election pamphlet by the Conservative Central Office.[21] When the Agreement was ratified by Parliament in the autumn after the Conservatives' return to power, only the minuscule Independent Labour Party voted against it.

The Slow Return to Normality: The Cologne Zone, 1924

When Ramsay MacDonald moved into Downing Street, in January, the French were already in retreat in the Rhineland. Not only had they accepted the setting up of the Experts Committees, but they had failed to create either an independent railway system or an independent Rhineland currency, while the separatist movement in the Palatinate had been convincingly shown by Clive to lack any popular support and was on the verge of collapse. The Conservative government had fought Poincaré to a halt. Paradoxically, therefore, the new Labour government was in a position, despite its Germanophil preferences, to improve relations with the French. Summing up the policy of the new government, the Foreign Office informed Kilmarnock in March that 'the direction in which the tide

18. Ibid., pp. 19–20.
19. Williamson, 'Great Britain and the Ruhr Crisis', p. 89.
20. McDougall, *Rhineland Diplomacy*, p. 369.
21. Williamson, 'Great Britain and the Ruhr Crisis', p. 90.

is setting here' was to use every opportunity to be friendly to France, but also to evince 'an iron determination to oppose any further abuse of the Rhineland Agreement'.[22] However, in attempting to normalize the situation in the British Zone MacDonald, like Baldwin before him, could only hope to mark time until the Dawes Plan enabled the whole apparatus of French control in the Ruhr to be wound up.

Inevitably the mutual distrust which had poisoned Anglo–French relations since the beginning of the Ruhr crisis was still active in the Rhineland, but the growing weakness of the French position made compromises easier to negotiate. By appealing to Poincaré MacDonald was able to exert pressure on Tirard to accept the agreement of 14 December 1923 which provided a *modus vivendi* between the Régie and the German-controlled railways in the Cologne Zone.[23] In the technical discussions held at Mainz two weeks later Colonel Manton noted that 'the atmosphere of the whole meeting was business-like and friendly'.[24] By 23 March the enmeshing of the Régie and the Reichsbahn timetables for the Cologne Zone was accomplished for all local and Reich traffic,[25] although the timetables for international expresses created a problem of principle, as Bréaud attempted to seize the chance to gain international recognition for the Régie by insisting that its name should appear on the international tariff on sale to the public, bracketed with the relevant European rail companies. This raised the question of international recognition and was vetoed by the Germans on principle. It became a case of 'the immovable object and the irresistible force',[26] and was not solved until the Régie was dissolved.[27]

While their plans for creating the economic and political infrastructure for a separate Rhineland were in evident disarray, in the MICUM Agreements and in the customs barriers between occupied and unoccupied Germany the French still possessed cards of considerable potential. On 18 January alarming reports were sent to London by Kilmarnock of French plans for raising a levy on 'the actual production in kind' in the Rhineland and Ruhr and of

22. FO to Kilmarnock, 15.3.24 (C4590), FO 371/9832 fo. 16.
23. 'Annual Report of the Inter-Allied High Commission for 1924', p. 66; Kilmarnock to FO, 7.2.24 (C2154), FO 371/9738 fo. 74.
24. 'Report on the Technical Conference held at Mainz, 14 and 16 Feb. 1924' (C3007), FO 371/9738 fos 95–6.
25. 'Report', 1924, p. 66.
26. Manton, 'Report on Progress of Through Railway Arrangements in the British Zone', p. 2, 1.3.24 (C3752), FO 371/9738 fos 112–13.
27. 'Report', 1924, pp. 67–8.

maintaining a permanent customs cordon on the eastern boundaries of the occupied territories, whereby it was hoped to placate local manufacturers by creating a protected home market.[28] Silverberg had warned Kilmarnock's economic adviser that 'it was beyond question that the French would never abandon their eastern customs line, which is the keystone of their present economic plans, and this fact would necessitate a complete readjustment of manufacturing conditions and industrial development in [the] occupied territory and the Ruhr'.[29]

In early February the French began a series of abortive and acrimonious discussions with the Ruhr industrialists for the renewal of the MICUM Agreements, due to lapse in April.[30] The Agreements had come under increasing criticism from the British mining industry and Parliament, where Lloyd George had delivered a blistering attack on the French.[31] The British were particularly worried about rumours that German mine owners would have to deposit with the French, as collateral security, shares in their own mines.[32] As before Christmas, the British government remained aloof, but discreetly attempted to monitor the progress of the negotiations, pinning its faith on the Dawes Report and a rapid settlement of the Ruhr crisis.[33] Even when the French in early April threatened that a breakdown in the negotiations would inevitably lead to more sanctions, MacDonald was not ready to intervene. He turned a deaf ear to appeals from Sthamer and merely observed 'that Britain had already too often given warnings but always without success'.[34] Thus the Rhineland and Ruhr industrialists had little option but to renew the Agreement for a further two months in the hope that the Dawes Plan would already be in force by then.[35]

By May 1924 the process of re-integrating the Ruhr and the Rhineland administratively and economically back into Germany was under way, despite dogged attempts by the French to block it. In March[36] the High Commission had been threatened with

28. Memorandum by W.C.H.M. Georgi, 16.1.24 (C1127), FO 371/9763 fos 30–1.
29. Ibid., p. 1.
30. 'Memorandum on the MICUM Agreements', 13.6.24 (C9407), FO 371/9766 fos 6–9.
31. Quoted in Kilmarnock to MacDonald, 4.2.24 (C2238), FO 371/9763 fos 74–6.
32. Sthamer to AA, 14.2.24 (A501), FCO Lib. 9426 H270803-08.
33. 'As the Experts report is coming so soon we can wait . . .'; Ramsay MacDonald's Minute, 3.4.24 (on C5510), FO 371/9764 fo. 144.
34. Sthamer to AA, 8.4.24 (no. 144), FCO Lib. 2368 490846-47; D'Abernon, *Ambassador of Peace*, vol. 3 (30.6.24), p. 7.
35. 'Memorandum on the MICUM Agreements' (C9407).
36. 'Report', 1924, pp. 9–10, 19.

paralysis when Tirard and Baron Rolin-Jaequemyns attempted systematically to block the registration of key Reich legislation introducing into the occupied territory the Rentenmark, new taxation and a law for turning the Reichsbahn into an independent corporation. Kilmarnock was instructed not only to abstain from vetoing these laws and to record his protests in the minutes of the Commission's proceedings, but also to announce that his government was prepared to take any decisions which they considered to be *ultra vires* according to the Rhineland Agreement, to the Permanent Court of International Justice at the Hague. Kilmarnock successfully persuaded the Commission to accept the Reichsbahn law on 3 April, but the Emergency Taxation Laws were sanctioned in early May only after pressure had been brought to bear by MacDonald directly on the French and Belgian governments. The application of the *Rentenmarkgesetz* still remained to be considered, but Tirard managed to procrastinate until 12 September on the grounds that he was awaiting instructions from Paris.

The potentially catastrophic effects on the economy of the British Zone of this prolonged delay in the application of the *Rentenmarkgesetz* were mitigated both by Schacht's decision to allow the depreciated currency to run down to the exchange rate of one billion to the gold mark, so that it could on that basis still be used as legal tender, and by the Reichsbank's continued acceptance of the *Notgeld* issued by the majority of the Rhineland cities as legal exchange, provided that it was backed by sufficient securities.[37] This ensured that at least the majority of the workmen could be paid. Confidence in money returned and the price of food fell dramatically; by the end of January the number of people fed by municipal soup kitchens in Cologne was halved.[38] Apart from a strike in the brown coal mines in January 1924,[39] where the miners avoided a clash with the High Commission by agreeing to continue to supply the British occupying forces and essential services with coal, there was little labour militancy in the British Zone in the first quarter of 1924.

The fear of communist-inspired unrest spreading across from the Ruhr was always uppermost in the minds of British officials, particularly during the Ruhr coal strikes of May, especially as Schacht's drastic credit restrictions in April forced many weaker firms into liquidation,[40] but in fact the activities of nationalist

37. Ibid., pp. 97–8.
38. Ibid., p. 100.
39. *The Times*, 22.1.24.
40. Ibid., 23.5.24; 'Report', 1924, p. 99.

groups posed at least as great a threat. As an inevitable reaction to the collapse of passive resistance and the separatist revolt in the Palatinate, there was a marked increase in nationalist groups all over Germany. In Cologne a series of largely abortive raids were carried out by military police on nationalist associations in February.[41] A month later the Intelligence Committee of the High Commission reported that the Jungdeutsche Orden was active there in recruiting young men of military age for short-term training with the Reichswehr.[42] Although the consensus of opinion amongst British officials was that over-reaction would be counter-productive and would merely drive these societies underground, Kilmarnock supported the promulgation of Ordinances 245 and 257 which gave the Allied authorities specific power to prohibit societies in the occupied territories from carrying out activities which threatened the armies of occupation or were tantamount to illegal military training.[43] The British delegate in Cologne used these powers sparingly. For instance, when the Völkisch–Sozialer bloc, which had absorbed many of the right-wing organizations banned by the Prussian government, such as the Nazis, applied for recognition in May, so that it could disguise its illegal activities more effectively, he avoided falling into the trap of declaring a group with representation in the Reichstag illegal and agreed to recognize it as a legitimate political force as long as it conformed to the ordinances of the High Commission.[44]

The British viewed the increase in nationalist agitation as an inevitable response to French policy in the Ruhr and Palatinate, and hoped that the formation of the Herriot government on 13 June would herald further French concessions in the Rhineland and Ruhr. In this respect they were not disappointed. A few days before the Chequers talks Tirard, on instructions from Herriot, announced the reinstatement of the majority of the officials who had been expelled from the Palatinate, and by the end of June an amnesty had been granted to all but a few hundred of the nearly 40,000 Germans deported from the Ruhr.[45] Nevertheless, as the date of the London Conference approached, Bréaud, Frantzen and Tirard tried desperately to salvage something from the imminent collapse of MICUM and the Régie. Bréaud first proposed a scheme

41. Minutes of 221st Sitting of the IARHC, 18, 20, 22 and 23 Feb. 1924, Annex No. 4615, p. 81, FO 894/18 fo. 44.
42. 'Report', 1924, p. 104.
43. Ibid., pp. 104–5.
44. Ibid.
45. Ibid., pp. 14–15.

for perpetuating the control of the Régie over the Rhineland railways, but when this was blocked by the British, Tirard suggested that either ten battalions of Allied railway troops should be stationed in the Rhineland as a guarantee against renewed German efforts to paralyse the railways, or that the Rhineland Railways Directorate, while remaining under the control of the *Reichsbahn*, should employ a limited number of Allied experts and personnel to work together with the German railwaymen and officials.[46] There were similar plans put forward by Frantzen, the President of MICUM, to perpetuate MICUM by transforming it into an inter-Allied organization 'to serve as an intermediary between the Reparation Commission and the German industrialists in the application of the scheme for deliveries in kind recommended in the report of the Dawes Committee'.[47] Both proposals inevitably alarmed the British, but Frantzen's initiative was killed even before the London Conference,[48] while Tirard's proposal was eventually withdrawn in the face of British and German opposition at the Conference.[49]

The adoption of the Dawes Plan had a profound effect on the occupation. Not only did it give the *coup de grâce* to both the Régie and MICUM, which were finally liquidated in November, and ensure the repeal of all the ordinances passed on a majority vote,[50] but it also inaugurated an attempt by the High Commission to create a new atmosphere of conciliation and appeasement in the Rhineland. Shortly after the London Conference MacDonald emphasized to Kilmarnock the need to respond to an observation by the German delegation that all ordinances prior to 11 January 1923 should be reviewed to ensure that German fiscal and economic unity should no longer be subject to any restrictions which were not essential to the maintenance, safety and requirements of the troops of occupation.[51] In November the High Commission set up a revisory Committee with the aim of encouraging 'mutual conciliation in the occupied Territory and to wipe out the past to the utmost possible extent'.[52] Austen Chamberlain, the new Conservative Foreign Minister, in one of his first dispatches to Coblenz on 26 November, after Baldwin's return to power in the election of October 1924, welcomed the committee and reiterated that it

46. Ibid., pp. 69–71.
47. Ibid., p. 80.
48. Ibid., p. 80.
49. Ibid., pp. 71–2.
50. Ibid., p. 88.
51. DBFP Ser. 1, vol. 26 (no. 550), p. 851.
52. Ibid. (no. 594), p. 918.

should recommend that any ordinances 'which run counter to, or are not covered by, the letter or the spirit of the Rhineland Agreement, in other words, which do not conduce in some shape or form to the maintenance, safety and requirements of the troops should be repealed'.[53] In an attempt to influence the coming election in Germany, the cancellation of several ordinances and the modifications of others were published in the German press on 4 December. Altogether they added up to some quite significant alleviations.[54] For instance, among them were provisions in almost all cases for German laws to come into force simultaneously in both the occupied and unoccupied territories, and for those German officials whom the High Commission desired to dismiss to have the right to defend themselves first. The High Commission was also prohibited from encouraging non-German insurance companies or private postal firms, and committed to granting permission for displaying flags or holding national, sporting or religious festivals in as 'liberal' a spirit as possible. Colonel Ryan's attempts to modify the 'Protective Ordinances', particularly No. 90, which enabled the Commission to protect legally any person who was penalized by the German authorities for cooperating with the Allies, proved more contentious. However, by early February 1925, an agreement was reached, whereby all appeals for the application of Ordinance 90 would first be scrutinized by an examining committee composed of British, French and Belgian representatives.[55]

The Dawes Plan also imposed a new financial discipline on the High Commission and the Rhineland garrisons, as the costs of the occupation were now to be credited to Germany as a first charge on her reparation payments, or to put it more succinctly in the words of the quasi-official historian of the Rhineland occupation: 'the more . . . the Armies spent, the less reparation money there would be to divide'.[56] While the Treasury was anxious to cut overall military and administrative expenditure in the Rhineland, care had to be exercised that the economies were evenly spread, so that Tirard's formidable bureaucratic apparatus was not left unpruned. The British government was also anxious to ensure that of the money made available to cover occupation costs, the British gained a fair share, which the Treasury estimated to be about 20 per cent.[57]

53. Ibid. (no. 600), p. 940.
54. 'Report', 1924, pp. 89–93.
55. Ibid., p. 93.
56. Edmonds, *The Occupation*, p. 267.
57. 'Treasury Memorandum on Army of Occupation Costs', 23.12.24 (C19183), FO 371/9797.

Through the Conference of Ambassadors, the British were able to block a proposal by Tirard to delegate to a sub-committee of the High Commission the task of assessing the financial requirements of the armies of occupation, and to insist that an independent committee should be set up.[58] Ultimately the question was settled over the heads of both the Foreign Office and the High Commission at the Conference of Finance Ministers on 6 January 1925. The Treasury did not invite any British High Commission officials to act as advisers and infuriated Kilmarnock by making concessions to 'inflated'[59] French claims. The finance ministers agreed that the normal charge on the Dawes annuities for the High Commission should be not more than ten million gold marks per annum and should be allocated between the French, British and Belgians at the rate of 62:22:16. Given these new financial restraints the British Department at Coblenz was cut to the bone and by the spring of 1925 consisted merely of nine officials and twenty-one clerks, typists and chauffeurs.[60]

Paradoxically the Dawes Plan and the new policy of conciliation it introduced made life more difficult for the British occupying forces. The easy days of the strong pound were over, as the exchange rate for one pound sterling was only sixteen marks. Army families had to struggle to keep within their means and make most of their purchases at military canteens.[61] The military authorities economized by handing back theatres, playing fields and club premises to the Germans; it is thus not surprising that the *Cologne Post* was complaining in December that life was 'routine and without adventure'.[62] The Aüswartiges Amt, strengthened by success in the London Conference and uneasily aware of the increase in support for the nationalists in Germany, was more vigorous in its efforts to defend the rights of the Germans in the occupied territory. It vigorously backed Baron Guillaume's attempt to prevent General Ducane, who succeeded Godley in June, from requisitioning his house, and it also sharply criticized the continued military use of school buildings in Cologne and Solingen.[63] British officials and soldiers accused the Germans of a new truculence, which was attributed to the psychological effect on the population

58. 'Report', 1924, pp. 111–12.
59. 'IARHC Annual Report for 1925' (C2306), p. 58, FO 371/13640 fos 199–207.
60. Ibid., pp. 57–61.
61. 'Eleven Years in Occupation', *Cologne Post and Wiesbaden Times*, 3.11.29; Edmonds, *The Occupation*, p. 267.
62. *Cologne Post*, 11.12.24.
63. Aide Memoire from the German Embassy, 19.9.24 (C14937) and complaint from the German Chargé d'Affaires, 29.9.24 (C15573), FO 371/9817 fos 163–203.

of the stabilization of the mark: the 1924 Annual Report of the British element of the Rhineland High Commission noted that 'cases of insolent behaviour were not infrequent. Germany had now become a *"hochvaluta"* land, with a currency which could hold its own with the dollar; her sons adopted a patronising attitude and made contemptuous remarks about the weakness of sterling and the depreciation of the French and Belgian franc.'[64] It was perhaps resentment at this new mood which led to an uncharacteristically bitter incident in September at Möderath, near Cologne, when a four-year-old child threw a stone at a British officer's car. After a fight when the officer attempted to drag the child from its parents' house, the incident escalated into the arrest of two hundred villagers and the imposition of a ten-day curfew.[65]

Although this sudden change of mood towards the British in the summer of 1924 may have been exaggerated, it does nevertheless provide an indication of the coming difficulties of occupying the Rhineland in the Dawes and Locarno era. As Germany re-entered the European concert of powers, the occupation became increasingly hard to justify and became a nagging source of friction between Berlin and the capitals of the former Allies.

The Struggle to Resume Control, January–November 1924

The French position in the Rhineland was irreparably weakened by August 1924. Inevitably this re-emphasized France's need for security and focused attention on the progress of the IAMCC in Germany. In September 1922 the Allies had reduced Germany's outstanding disarmament obligations to five key points.[66] As soon as control could be resumed after the virtual standstill caused by the Ruhr occupation, it was essential to check that Germany had not exploited the absence of inspections in order to re-arm. The extreme German reluctance to agree to further visits after the perfunctory inspections of 10 January 1924 seemed to confirm French, and increasingly the War Office's, suspicions about the Reichswehr and to emphasize the need for a thorough general inspection.

The change of government in London led to a joint review of the

64. 'Report', 1924, p. 97.
65. Minutes of 251st sitting of the IARHC, 3.10.24, § XXXIII, Min. 8900, FO 894 fo. 27; *Frankfurter Zeitung*, 13.10.24.
66. See above, ch. 9.

whole disarmament problem by the Foreign Office and War Office on 5 January. The War Office officials and Bingham, who had been recalled from Berlin to attend the meeting, argued unequivocally that, as Germany had never formally accepted the Allied demands in the five points, 'the situation had changed and the Allies [should] not now be ready to renew the offer until they were satisfied that the disarmament of Germany in matters other than the five points was in the same degree of completion as on the day when the offer was originally made'. Sir Cecil Hurst's objection that 'a court of arbitration' might well support the German contention that by their offer of September 1922 the Allies had in fact waived their rights to any control measures outside the five points, was quickly rejected by Lampson and Bingham, who argued strongly that, as full control had existed up to January 1923, its resumption was not legally in doubt. Finally Bingham and the War Office official, Colonel Finlayson, urged that the Ambassadors' Conference should write to the German government defining the current Allied policy on control.[67]

As a first step in this direction, the War Office carefully rethought its own policy on control in a memorandum on 31 January.[68] It reconfirmed the Allies' right to exercise full control, but nevertheless advised against turning the clock back to January 1923 'as they consider, firstly, that such would be a retrograde movement, and secondly, that whatever steps are now taken should be such as will lead towards some finality upon this vexed question, which they have no doubt tends to hold Germany back as well as to create disaffection amongst the people of Europe'. It therefore suggested that the Germans should both execute the five points and grant facilities for a final and effective general inspection, after which plans for the withdrawal of the IAMCC and the creation of a Committee of Guarantee could be considered. Crowe welcomed the proposal warmly,[69] while Cambon saw it as 'a golden bridge' for the French 'to retire over gracefully',[70] and it became the basis for the Allied note to the German government[71] of 5 March. While waiting for the German reply, the Ambassadors instructed Nollet to draw up plans for a general inspection.[72] These, however, proved to be contrary to the spirit of the War Office's advice, as

67. Meeting in Sir Cecil Hurst's Room, 25.1.24 (C11461), FO 371/9723 fos 42–4.
68. War Office to Foreign Office, 31.1.4 (C1725), FO 371/9723 fos 96–7.
69. See Crowe's Minutes of 9 and 12.2.24, on C1725, FO 371/9723 fos 93–4.
70. Phipps to Crowe, 21.2.24 (C2998), FO 371/9723 fos 223–4.
71. DBFP Ser. 1, vol. 26 (no. 640), p. 1007.
72. Ibid. (no. 642), pp. 1008–9.

according to Bingham, they would merely ensure 'that the whole of the work that we have done during the last four years is to be repeated'.[73] Further debate was temporarily made academic by the German rejection of a general inspection on 31 March coupled with a counter-proposal that the Commission should give way to some method of supervision by the League of Nations.[74]

To avoid giving the nationalists any encouragement, the Allied response was delayed until after the German election of 4 May.[75] MacDonald instructed Crewe to ensure that the new note would 'be temperate and courteous; it should avoid all dictatorial plans; its general tone should not be one of Allied imposition'.[76] MacDonald also stressed that in effect the Dawes Report created a new situation by destroying 'one of the chief forms of pressure which the Allies can bring to bear upon Germany, namely, the fact that Germany has to pay for the Commission of Control, so long as it remains'.[77] The costs of the Commissions of Control, like those of the occupation, now became a first charge on the Dawes annuities. A joint note was hammered out in the Ambassadors' Conference and delivered to the German Embassy on 28 May.[78] Behind the scenes the British attempted to secure its acceptance by the German government. Wauchope, who took over from Bingham in May, called on the German Embassy in London before leaving for Berlin and assured Sthamer that he was ready to do 'everything in his power and within the parameters of his duty to mitigate control in any practical way'. Sthamer was quite won over by his charm and informed the Auswärtiges Amt that 'we are dealing with a benevolent man, well disposed towards Germany';[79] while D'Abernon was instructed specifically by MacDonald to convince the Germans both of the dangers of opposing Allied demands and that 'the Allied offer is honestly intended'.[80]

The German government realized that it would eventually have to agree to the inspection. In a seminal memorandum the Auswärtiges Amt recognized that 'the control question had become the pivot of foreign policy. If we understand how to exploit the situation by

73. Bingham to Nollet (Enclosure 2 in no. 1), 22.3.24 (C5327), FO 371/9724 fo. 181.
74. Salewski, *Entwaffnung*, p. 245.
75. DBFP Ser. 1, vol. 26 (no. 652), pp. 1031–4.
76. MacDonald to Crewe, 3.5.24 (C6886), FO 371/9725 fos 106–7.
77. Ibid.
78. DBFP Ser. 1, vol. 26 (nos 661 and 663), pp. 1053–6 and 1060.
79. Sthamer's Report of 25.4.24, quoted by Schubert, 5.5.24, FCO Lib. 4530 E138944-45.
80. MacDonald to D'Abernon, 27.5.24 (C7802), FO 371/9725 fo. 184.

conceding a general inspection, not only will military control be dismantled, but in all probability a tolerable solution will also be found for the reparation and occupation problems.'[81] Strong opposition to such concessions came from the Reichswehr, which saw its struggle against the resumption of control as '*Ehrensache*'.[82] In Paris Kessler, the German writer, suggested to General Clive that the Allies should send a general to Berlin to negotiate with von Seeckt as one military man with another.[83] This advice received short shrift in London where Crowe acidly dismissed it by observing: 'Our military men always want to play the part of diplomats and meddle with foreign policy. Their interference has always been disastrous.'[84] Stresemann's efforts to gain von Seeckt's cooperation were complicated by the publication of an interview in the *Morning Post* with Nollet, who had just been appointed Minister of War by Herriot, in which Nollet claimed that Europe was witnessing the revival of German military power.[85] In an effort to calm the '*envenimée*'[86] atmosphere, MacDonald and Herriot agreed[87] to send identical notes to Berlin balancing their remonstrations about the increase in nationalist agitation with a plea for German cooperation in bringing about the end of military control. They stressed particularly that once the Allied demands had been met, they were 'ready and anxious to see the machinery of the Control Commission replaced by the rights of investigation conferred on the Council of the League of Nations by Article 213 of the Treaty'.[88] The notes were well received in Berlin and on 30 June the Germans, 'in a strangely satisfactory document', agreed to a general inspection as a mark of the new spirit introduced by the Dawes Plan, provided that it was executed after consultation with the German authorities and finished by 30 September.[89]

The IAMCC completed its plans for the inspection by 16 July.

81. 'Pro Memoria', 15.6.24, FCO Lib. 4530 E138885-92.
82. Maltzan to German Embassy, London, 3.6.24 (3u 11 F 1614 Ang. 2), FCO Lib. 4530 (?) E138909-10.
83. Clive to DMO & I, 28.5.24 (no. 33A/11/1295), FO 371/9725 fos 219–21.
84. Minute by Crowe, 6.6.24, FO 371/9725 fo. 216.
85. *Morning Post*, 20.6.24; DBFP Ser. 1, vol. 26 (no. 669), pp. 1071–2.
86. Forster, 'Unterredung mit General Marietti über die Militärkontrollfrage', 19.6.24 (zu 11 Nr. 1856/24), p. 1, FCO Lib. 9490 H280362-66.
87. 'Notes taken during a Conversation between M. Edouard Herriot . . . and Mr. Ramsay MacDonald, at Chequers, 21 and 22 June 1924' (C12270), pp. 20–2, FO 371/9749 fos 85–95.
88. DBFP Ser. 1, vol. 26 (no. 670), p. 1073.
89. 'Memorandum Respecting the Present State of German Disarmament', 16.6.25 (C8109), p. 4, FO 371/10709 fos 233–7. For text see Enclosure 1, Crewe to MacDonald, 30.6.24 (C10438), FO 371/9726 fos 114–15.

The French showed a new willingness to accommodate British proposals; for instance, the programme of visits was cut from four to three months and officers were to carry out inspections in plain clothes.[90] The inspection was initially planned to start on 22 July, but a recrudescence of Anglo–French differences over surprise visits delayed it until 8 September.[91] Initially there was a pleasing spirit of mutual cooperation, but despite Wauchope's at times frantic attempts to foster 'that new spirit of goodwill',[92] by the end of the month the old animosities were resurfacing. The key issue which caused the spirit of reconciliation to founder was the IAMCC's insistence on trying to find out what the German army had been doing during 1923 when effective inspections had been impossible to mount.[93] The Reichswehr remained adamant that only the current state of their actual armaments was open to investigation and even Wauchope's entreaties fell upon deaf ears.[94] The increasingly frustrated and sour atmosphere was further compounded by another incident at Ingolstadt where British officers were again insulted by a large crowd.[95]

The renewed deadlock between the IAMCC and the German Army Peace Commission did not, however, prevent the withdrawal of the IANCC in September. By 1924 the IANCC was too small to be effective and the Admiralty was anxious to hand over its remaining responsibilities for stock-checking in the dockyards to the IAMCC.[96] Despite the initial reservations of the German Naval Peace Commission, agreement was secured in September and the IANCC left Germany at the end of the month.[97]

90. D'Abernon to FO, 16.7.24 (C11192), FO 371/9726 fo. 213.
91. 'Memorandum' (C8109), p. 5.
92. Notes no. 8 by Wauchope, 8.8.24 (C12936), FO 371/9727 fos 133–5.
93. Salewski, *Entwaffnung*, p. 273.
94. Wauchope to DMO & I, 22.10.24 (C16631), FO 371/9728 fo. 149.
95. Wauchope to WO, 7.11.24 (C16915), FO 371/9727 fo. 184.
96. Capt. Drax, 'Statement of the Situation', 4.8.24, ADM 116 1998, Pack no. 8/A/20.
97. Morath to Reichswehrministerium, Marinefriedenskommission, 21.9.24 (zu 14 F 2923), FCO Lib. L128 L025958-59; DBFP Ser. 1, vol. 26 (no. 701), p. 1110 (footnote 1).

-16-

Locarno and Evacuation

Introduction

The Dawes Plan may have led to the abolition of economic sanctions against Germany, but paradoxically by weakening the French it was directly instrumental in delaying the punctual evacuation by Allied troops of the whole northern section of the Rhineland, of which the British Cologne Zone was so important a part. In the absence of a security pact Herriot had little option but to argue that the blatant German violation of the disarmament clauses of the Treaty made a continued occupation of Cologne unavoidable. Only some form of security pact could uncouple this link between disarmament and evacuation.

The Decision to Defer Evacuation of the Northern Zone, January 1925

In November 1922 Poincaré, on the strength of Article 429 of the Versailles Treaty, which gave the occupying powers the right to delay the evacuation of any of the Rhineland zones if they were convinced that 'the guarantees against unprovoked aggression by Germany' were still not sufficient, insisted that the five-year period for the occupation of the northern zone had not even begun to run. The British dismissed this interpretation and argued that the occupation began officially on the day the Treaty came into force – 10 January 1920. However, the Foreign Office refrained from pressing the issue at a time when the Ruhr occupation was imminent. In April 1924 the Berlin government raised the question of evacuation, but, following D'Abernon's advice, MacDonald pushed the matter to one side until after the London Conference. The Foreign Office wanted to avoid linking the question of German disarmament with the evacuation of the northern zone, but by November 1924 it was becoming clear that the defaults in German disarmament, while not individually serious, added up to 'a formidable aggregate'[1] and would threaten the punctual evacuation of the Cologne Zone by the Rhine Army.[2] Wauchope's report to the War Office on 30 November confirmed that Germany had not 'carried out the military clauses of the Treaty of Versailles either in the spirit or in the letter', although he was in no doubt 'that Germany [was] sufficiently disarmed at the present moment to prevent her going to war with a civilized power on a modern scale'.[3]

Fundamentally Chamberlain was sceptical about ever really achieving complete German disarmament; paradoxically he used Morgan's article in the *Quarterly Review*[4] to prove his point. He argued that Morgan, a professed supporter of Nollet, and critic of 'the War Office and the other British members of Control', in fact by his arguments succeeded in proving only 'that disarmament cannot be enforced and that those who think that the Allies or the League of Nations can keep effective watch over Germany or any other nation's vital preparation for the wars of the future are living in a fools' paradise'.[5] Nevertheless such was the evidence from the IAMCC that the French had an unanswerable case in their insistence on delaying the evacuation. On 17 December the Cabinet resigned itself to delaying evacuation, as it realized that even if the IAMCC had been able to show that Germany had substantially fulfilled the Treaty, 'we should recognise that the Cologne area could not be evacuated while the French were still in the Ruhr'.[6] Although the detailed report from the IAMCC had not yet been compiled, as its programme of visits was scheduled to end in January, there was sufficient preliminary evidence already available for the Allies to be able to demonstrate in their note of 5 January 1925[7] that Germany had not yet effectively disarmed and had therefore forfeited the right to demand the punctual evacuation of Cologne and the northern zone.

1. Warburton to Baxton, 12.11.24 (C17183), FO 371/9728 fo. 206; See also Kaiser, *Lord D'Abernon*, pp. 287–8.
2. See Lampson's discussion with Schubert, 24.11.24 (C17812), FO 371/9833 fos 101–3.
3. Wauchope to WO, 30.11.24 (C18122), p. 8, FO 371/9729 fos 53–6.
4. J.H. Morgan, 'The Disarmament of Germany And After', *Quarterly Review*, vol. 242, October 1924, pp. 415–57.
5. Austen Chamberlain's Minute, 26.11.24 (C17812), FO 371/9833 fo. 100.
6. Extract from CAB 67 (24), FO 371/9833 fo. 212.
7. DBFP Ser. 1, vol. 27 (no. 553), pp. 896–7 (footnote 4); 'Memorandum Respecting the Present State of German Disarmament' (C8109), pp. 7–8, FO 371/10709 fos 233–7.

Chamberlain's Diplomatic Offensive

The Allied note of 5 January 1925 was met with a predictable storm of rage in the German press,[8] while in Britain there was a real fear in the City[9] that it would undo the work of the London Conference. Sthamer reported that 'almost everywhere there was a gloomy feeling that an injustice has been perpetrated on Germany for a bagatelle . . .'.[10] This unease was fully shared by Austen Chamberlain and many of the officials at the Foreign Office who felt that the chances of a European settlement had received a considerable setback.[11] The non-evacuation of the northern zone created a vicious circle which was hard to break: essentially only German goodwill could guarantee that the infractions noted by the IAMCC would be effectively remedied, but this in turn depended on the evacuation. The British desired to uncouple the question of evacuation from disarmament but this was not practical politics, unless in some way French security could be guaranteed.[12] In October 1924 MacDonald had hoped that this might be achieved through the Geneva Protocol, which ambitiously contained clauses covering security, universal disarmament and Germany's entry into the League, but the incoming Conservative government, fearful of the commitments that this would entail, was determined to reject it. It thus became all the more essential to offer the French a more concrete guarantee. Initially Chamberlain considered a straight Anglo–French–Belgian tripartite defensive agreement, but in face of stiff Cabinet opposition, he had to abandon this solution.[13] He had no option but to fall back on a proposal made by Stresemann, who, alerted by D'Abernon to the dangers of an Anglo–French alliance, had written to London on 20 January outlining a plan for a multilateral non-aggression pact between France, Germany, Belgium, Italy and Britain.[14] Potentially it

8. Tirard commented sourly: 'cette campaigne est organisée selon le rythme ordinaire et les modalités de la propaganda allemande en pareille matière', Tirard to Herriot, 9.1.25, MAE Rive Gauche 80 fo. 85.
9. Montague Norman to J.P. Morgan, 12.2.25, Bank of England OV 34/108 fo. 31A.
10. Sthamer to AA, 8.1.25 (A41/25), FCO Lib. 9518 H282760-65, p.2.
11. See Minutes by Sterndale Bennett, 26.1.25 (C11362), FO 371/10370 fos 17–26. Lampson was rather more sceptical (ibid.). For a general survey of Chamberlain's policy see C. Petrie, *The Life and Letters of the Right Honourable Sir Austen Chamberlain*, vol. 2, London 1939–40, ch. 6.
12. J. Jacobson, *Locarno Diplomacy. Germany and the West, 1925–29*, Princeton, 1972, pp. 48ff.
13. Ibid., pp. 15–20.
14. DBFP Ser. 1, vol. 27 (no. 189), pp. 282–4; D'Abernon, *Ambassador of Peace*, vol. 3, 21 and 23.1.25, pp. 125–7; F.G Stambrook, 'Das Kind. Lord D'Abernon and the

offered Chamberlain the opportunity to square the circle by achieving both French security and the evacuation of Cologne without committing Britain to a military pact with France. Although he had at first suspected the proposal of being an attempt to divide France and Britain, he now seized upon it enthusiastically and made it very clear to the French that 'it was on these lines and none other that we could offer any additional guarantees for French security'.[15] By early May Cecil Hurst had drawn up a draft security pact[16] and a month later Chamberlain was able to inform the House of Commons that Britain and France had reached agreement on 'certain basic principles'.[17] Their remaining differences were then ironed out at a meeting in London on 11 and 12 August. Chamberlain defined precisely the conditions under which Britain would militarily assist France as coming into force only if Germany reoccupied the demilitarized zone in the Rhineland or launched an unprovoked attack against France. The Germans were then invited to discuss the adoption of the Stresemann proposal at a conference which was to meet at Locarno on 5 October.[18]

The Occupation in Suspended Animation, January–November 1925

The Allied decision to delay the evacuation of the northern area of the Rhineland inevitably intensified the impatience of the local population.[19] General Ducane feared rioting when the main political parties decided to hold simultaneous protest meetings, which would have coincided with the start of the carnival season. The British authorities insisted that the meetings should be strictly limited to card carriers, and the press was forbidden to publish any inflammatory material. In fact the meetings passed off entirely without incidents and any popular anger that existed was directed at the City Council for closing all the municipal halls and forcing

Origins of the Locarno Pact', *Central European History* vol. 1, 1968, pp. 233–63; Jacobson, *Locarno Diplomacy*, pp. 12–13; A. Kaiser, 'Lord D'Abernon und die Entstehungsgeschichte der Locarno-Verträge', *Vierteljahrshefte fur Zeitgeschichte*, vol. 34, Jan. 1986, pp. 85–104. For a general survey of Lord D'Abernon's role see Kaiser, *Lord D'Abernon*, ch. 6.
15. DBFP Ser. 1, vol. 27 (no. 283), p. 437.
16. Ibid. (no. 316), pp. 488–9.
17. Ibid. (no. 370), p. 594.
18. Jacobson, *Locarno Diplomacy*, p. 33.
19. Tirard to Herriot, 9.1.25, MAE Rive Gauche 80 fo. 85. See also Victor Basch, 'La Nouvelle Europe', 13.1.25, ibid. fo. 112.

the cancellation of numerous *Fasching* (carnival) balls.[20] Until the decision to evacuate was taken in November, the British authorities in Cologne were in a state of suspended animation. By March 1925 the garrison and the British colony were already in the throes of preparing for the eventual move. An army school and four canteens were closed and both Lloyds and Barclays Banks had asked their clients to liquidate their accounts.[21] Nevertheless, the routine duties of the occupation had to be performed; summary courts were still held and when a municipal strike threatened the security of the occupation, British officials still intervened to restrain the strikers and push the employers into a more flexible attitude.[22]

In this twilight period of the occupation of the Cologne Zone, both Chamberlain and Kilmarnock were anxious to avoid any provocative action which might damage the prospects for a non-aggression pact between Germany and the Allies. Thus despite the fact that the greatest challenge to the authority of the High Commission in the Rhineland came from nationalist associations, particularly the Nazi Party, which began to establish itself in Cologne when the Prussian government lifted the ban on its organization in January 1925, the High Commission decided to cancel its own ban of July 1923 in response to requests from the German government; but far from appeasing the nationalists this merely encouraged them in such activities as illegally recruiting short-term volunteers for the Reichswehr.[23]

It was against this background that the High Commission viewed with alarm plans to hold celebrations in Cologne in the summer of 1925 to celebrate the millennium of the Rhineland's union with Germany. Ducane and Kilmarnock were particularly concerned by plans for the newly elected Reich President, Hindenburg, whose name was still technically on the Allied list of war criminals, to visit the celebrations, as they feared that this would encourage nationalist demonstrations.[24] Efforts were made by Chamberlain to persuade the Germans to stop the celebrations altogether on the grounds that they rendered British support in the evacuation and security questions 'almost impossible'.[25] Although

20. 'IARHC Annual Report for 1925' (C2306) pp. 2–3, FO 371/13640 fos 199–207.
21. Chastand to Raynaud (no. 58), 2.4.25, MAE Rive Gauche 81 fo. 60.
22. Minutes of 291st Sitting of the IARHC, 20.8.25, Annex no. 7049a, b and c, FO, 894/22 fos 33–4.
23. 'Report', 1925, pp. 3–4.
24. DBFP Ser. 1, vol. 27 (no. 629), pp. 1031-2.
25. Schubert to German Embassy, 16.5.25 (no. 184), FCO Lib. 3058 D60517070-71.

Hindenburg's visit was discreetly cancelled,[26] Schubert *in energischer Weise* pointed out to Lord D'Abernon that 'one could not easily prevent the population after a long period of repression from organizing harmless festivities'.[27] The High Commission had therefore no option but to entrust its Kreis officers with the task of 'arranging amicably' with the Germans the programmes which were to be carried out. They were also given special powers under Ordinance 173, which was passed during the Ruhr crisis, to prohibit assemblies likely to cause disturbances and to impose restrictions on free circulation.[28] The millenary celebrations were opened on 16 May by the Reich Chancellor and passed off without incident, although temporarily they undoubtedly damaged Franco–German relations.[29] The mood of the Rhinelanders was summed up somewhat cynically by Quarry in the Annual Report:

> The ordinary Rhinelander saw no great reason for a general demonstration of loyalty to the *Reich*; of those who came from non-occupied territory to make patriotic speeches and indignant gestures over a 'Rhineland in chains', his reception was not enthusiastic – it resembled somewhat that given to officers who visited in full daylight forward posts, which were enjoying an absence of attention from the enemy. There had been enough trouble already in 1923 and 1924, and nothing was to be gained by asking for more.[30]

Nevertheless, despite the cool reception towards visiting nationalists, the old friendliness born of a desperate dependence on British goodwill as protection against the French had evaporated. By the autumn, as one officer in the military police wrote, 'the impression that the army was out of place in Cologne grew more pronounced'.[31]

The Wauchope–D'Abernon Axis, January–November 1925

While Chamberlain was attempting to break the link between disarmament and evacuation through direct negotiations with Briand, who had accepted the post of Foreign Minister in the Painlevé

26. 'Report', 1925, p. 23.
27. Schubert to German Embassy, 16.5.25 (no. 184).
28. DBFP Ser. 1, vol. 27 (no. 618), pp. 1012–14.
29. Col. Ryan, 'Notes on the Rhenish Celebrations', 10.7.25 (C9321), FO 371/10758 fos 177–80.
30. 'Report', 1925, p. 11.
31. 'Apex', *The Uneasy Triangle. Four Years of Occupation*, p. 159.

government formed in April 1925, Wauchope's role in Berlin was to ensure that the French did not exaggerate Germany's defaults in disarmament. Arguably he became a diplomat rather than remaining a soldier, and in his actions he identified more closely with the Foreign Office's policy of appeasement than with the War Office's increasingly more cautious attitude towards the slow pace of German disarmament.[32] Wauchope was politically more adroit than Bingham and had the considerable advantage of not having, as a colleague, Morgan who had returned to the Bar in 1923.[33] Wauchope formed an effective team with D'Abernon and proved a doughty warrior in the cause of Locarno and appeasement.

The general inspection that began in September 1924 was only completed on 25 January.[34] In the ensuing discussions on drafting the report for the Inter-Allied Military Committee at Versailles, Wauchope rapidly became suspicious that Walch, Nollet's successor, was attempting to put pressure on him to depict a more serious situation than in reality existed in order to justify 'un ajournement indéfini de l'évacuation'.[35] Chamberlain immediately protested strongly in Paris and Brussels and threatened to instruct Wauchope to produce a minority report.[36] His threats were successful and the Commission was able to agree and sign the report on 15 February. On balance Wauchope felt that it presented an accurate picture, although he warned the War Office that:

> when five artists set to work on one canvas it is not unnatural to find that their views on perspective or on light and shade are apt to differ . . . General Walch, as a draughtsman, tends towards the Romantic school, and it has been a real pain to my colleagues to see the darkest shadows in the picture relieved by some white splotches from my brush.[37]

The Versailles Committee received the report on 18 February, and then officially communicated it to the Ambassadors' Conference on 28 February accompanied by an appreciation of the military situation in Germany, the gist of which was that Germany was potentially capable of mobilizing at short notice an army 'of the

32. Fox, 'Britain and the Inter-Allied Military Commission of Control', p. 149.
33. Morgan, *Assize of Arms*, vol. 2, Galley Slip III (62T CR p. 166 deleted).
34. 'Memorandum' (C8109), p. 7.
35. Herriot to French Ambassador, London, 5.2.25 (2959 3D), MAE Rive Gauche 80 fos 242–6.
36. Ibid., and 'Memorandum' (C8109), p. 9; D'Abernon, *Ambassador of Peace*, vol. 3, 7.1.25, p. 318.
37. Notes no. 18, Wauchope, 16.2.25 (Enclosure 2 in C2407), FO 371/10708 fo. 132.

highest fighting capacity'.[38] At Crewe's request the Versailles Committee was then asked to formulate a precise statement of German defaults, but this exercise did not even begin until 28 March as a compromise had to be reached with the French, who wanted a sharp differentiation between what Germany needed to accomplish to secure the evacuation of the whole northern zone and the actual withdrawal of the Commission itself. It was agreed that the Committee should look carefully at whether the findings of the general inspection of September 1924 to January 1925 warranted future operations of the Commission being limited to the original five points, or whether they ought to continue to deal with a wide number of other infractions. On 10 April the Versailles Committee reported back, adding to the original five points three new ones dealing with fortifications.

Chamberlain initially hoped to solve the intricate disarmament problem by holding a conference in London. The Foreign Office had a touching faith in the conference procedure; Lampson, for instance, was convinced that a full conference in London chaired by Chamberlain would soon 'get the French into line'.[39] However, the French proved not so easy to bulldoze and insisted on the communication of Allied demands in the form of a note, which despite growing German impatience was not dispatched to Berlin until 4 June 1925.[40] The Allies stressed their intention to evacuate the northern zone as soon as the Germans had satisfied their demands on what were now expanded into thirteen key points, which included the question of the organization of the police, the completion of the transformation of certain factories, depots and workshops into peace-time production and the organization of the army along the lines laid down by the Treaty of Versailles.[41] The note was relatively well received in Berlin, but the German government took nearly six weeks before officially reacting to it.[42] Behind the scenes Wauchope and D'Abernon attempted to advise the Germans on how to respond to it. On 10 June Wauchope met Kessler and advised him confidentially that while 'the German Government in the coming struggle over the disarmament note should make the *Schutzpolizei* its sticking point [*am meisten Rückgrat zeigen sollte*]', it

38. 'Memorandum' (C8109), p. 9.
39. See his Minute of 11.2.25 (C2030), FO 371/10703 fos 91–3.
40. For a concise summary of the drafting of the note see 'Memorandum' (C8109), pp. 10–15.
41. Ibid., pp. 14–15.
42. 'Memorandum Respecting German Disarmament and the Evacuation of Cologne, 4 June–16 November, 1925', 30.11.25, p. 1 (C15299), FO 371/10711 fos 80–3.

should concede to Allied demands for the abolition of the post of Chief of Staff and the completion of the process of transforming armaments factories to peace-time production.[43] Three days later Knox, the first Secretary of the British Embassy, handed over to the Auswärtiges Amt 'quite unofficially' the report of the IAMCC of 18 February.[44]

A month later the Germans set up a committee under General Pawelsz with special powers to negotiate with the IAMCC and to implement the necessary disarmament measures.[45] Initially in the absence of General Walch, the French members boycotted the committee on the grounds that the Germans had not formally accepted the note of 5 June. On Walch's return from Paris, the IAMCC under pressure from Wauchope grudgingly agreed to consider Pawelsz's proposals, but it was not until specific instructions were issued by the Ambassadors' Conference to speed up the execution of the Allied demands and to consider the Pawelsz Committee as 'a starting point'[46] that real progress began to be made. By the middle of September negotiations had entered into their 'most acute stage'.[47] Daily discussions took place on the key problems of the status of the police, industrial disarmament and the import and export of weapons between the relevant German officials and the IAMCC. Both Lord D'Abernon and the British officers did all they could to lubricate the machinery of these negotiations. The main thrust of their efforts was aimed at cutting corners and persuading the Germans to agree to certain symbolic gestures, which would appease the French and enable the vital meeting at Locarno to take place in early October. Thus Lord D'Abernon sought to solve the police question by trying to persuade the Germans to drop military titles for the higher police officials,[48] while General Wauchope and Colonel Gosset, his deputy, attempted to break the deadlock at Krupp over the destruction of twenty-four *Spezialmaschinen* by proposing a compromise whereby they would be removed and 'dispersed'.[49] Gosset stressed 'that the dispersal of even 24 machines carried out quickly . . .

---

43. Kessler to Karl Köpke, 10.6.25, FCO Lib. 4530 E139844–47. See also note by Treudenberg, 10.6.25, ibid., E139843.
44. Note, 13.6.25 ('Herrn Geh. Rat Nord Vorgelegt'), FCO Lib. 9627 H 292081.
45. 'Memorandum' (C15299), p. 1.
46. Ibid., p. 2.
47. 'Aufzeichnung' by Köpke, 11.9.25, FCO Lib. 4530 E139897–8.
48. Note by Schubert, 14.8.25, FCO Lib. 4530 E139884–5.
49. Gosset to Dr Nord, 12.9.25 (II 3198), FCO Lib. L120 L022476.

would tend to create a good impression'.[50] Under direct orders from Paris Walch genuinely strove to speed up negotiations,[51] but some of his junior officers resented British attempts to cut corners. For instance, Major Henniquin openly disagreed with his British colleague, Major Wright, in front of German officials and businessmen at the Deutsches Werk in Haselhorst about whether they had themselves seen the scrapped remains of 205 *Spezialmaschinen*.[52] The unease of the French element was shared by the *Morning Post*,[53] which revealed in an article written by its German correspondent that only a third of the machines in Krupp's notorious number 10 workshop, where the great guns which bombarded Paris were made, had been dismantled.

Shortly before the Locarno Conference Wauchope sent a guardedly optimistic report[54] to London in which he argued that over the last two months the Germans had demonstrated a willingness to carry out Allied demands, such as they had never shown before. Nevertheless he did not foresee the work of the Control Commission finishing before Easter 1926.

Locarno

To Stresemann a key object of the Locarno Conference was to facilitate agreements leading to the evacuation of Cologne and the final settlement of the disarmament question, but publicly the British government refused to be drawn on this, and argued that 'these questions have, in fact, no relation to the negotiations for a security Pact, and have formed no part of the preliminary exchange of views'.[55] The Conference proceeded without a hitch, as the main issues concerning the pact had effectively already been resolved.[56] The arguments began when the Reichskanzler, Dr Luther, and Stresemann in a series of informal discussions raised

50. Ibid., 9.9.25 (II 3127), FCO Lib. L120 L022469.
51. 'Memorandum' (C15299), p. 2.
52. Bericht II, 22.8.25 (zu 22521), 'über den Besuch der I.W.K.K.-Mitglieder im Werke Haselhorst', FCO Lib. L377 L110509-511.
53. *Morning Post*, 2.10.25.
54. 'Memorandum' (C15299), p. 3.
55. British reply of 29.9.25 to German note accepting invitation to Locarno, quoted in 'Memorandum Respecting German Disarmament' (C15299), p. 3, FO 371/10711 fos 80–3. For the documentary background to Stresemann's Locarno policy see G. Stresemann, *Diaries, Letters and Papers*, edited by E. Sutton, vol. 2, London, 1935–40.
56. Jacobson, *Locarno Diplomacy*, p. 60.

the question of the *quid pro quo* Germany would receive for accepting the Locarno Agreements. On 12 October Stresemann argued strongly for a more lenient interpretation[57] of some of the German disarmament defaults listed by the Conference of Ambassadors, and for a definite commitment both to evacuate the northern zone and to modify the terms of the occupation in the remaining two zones. Briand refused to commit himself beyond stressing that: 'If the pact went through, there were many such possibilities as Stresemann had foreseen. Once signed and in force there would be an immediate *détente*. This would render impossible a state of affairs, which was possible before. Quite certainly a modification would follow in the conditions of occupation.'[58]

Despite determined and sometimes acrimonious attempts by the Germans to gain immediate concrete concessions, Briand and Chamberlain remained adamant that until further progress had been made in German disarmament, they could not commit themselves to a date for the evacuation of the northern zone. Briand did, however, send instructions to General Walch to settle all outstanding points as quickly as possible and urged the Germans to send in a detailed account of the current progress in disarmament to the Ambassadors' Conference in answer to the Allied note of 4 June.[59] On 23 October the Germans obliged,[60] but they had to concede that what Wauchope called 'the five dangerous points',[61] involving the police, the High Command, military training, the fortress of Königsberg and the disbanding of the paramilitary associations, still awaited solutions. Behind the scenes Briand did everything he could to smooth the way to evacuation. He even informed Hoesch that he would resign if he met significant opposition.[62]

On 6 November the Ambassadors' Conference requested further clarification on how the Germans intended to settle the five points.[63] In Berlin Wauchope and D'Abernon worked feverishly in numerous meetings with Pawelsz and Schubert to effect a compromise. Wauchope and his staff completely won the confidence of Pawelsz and convinced him that 'England has placed herself emphatically on our side and is absolutely ready to help us'.[64] Their

57. DBFP Ser. 1, vol. 27 (no. 11), p. 1138.
58. Ibid., p. 1139.
59. 'Memorandum' (C15299), pp. 3–4.
60. Ibid., p. 4.
61. Pawelsz to Luther, 14.10.25 (RK no. 178/10.25 geh), FCO Lib. 9627 H292338-39.
62. Hoesch to AA 23.10.25 (no. 749), p. 3, FCO Lib. 9627 H292371-78.
63. 'Memorandum' (C15299), p. 5.
64. Note by Schubert, 31.10.25, FCO Lib. 4530 E14055-57, p. 1.

efforts were rewarded when in two further notes of 11 and 13 November the Germans at last reassured the French that solutions were possible and the way was cleared for the evacuation of Cologne.[65] On 16 November the Conference of Ambassadors finally informed the German government that evacuation of the Cologne Zone would begin on 1 December.[66]

The 'Hors d'oeuvres of Locarno'

Although Chamberlain and Briand maintained the fiction that the Locarno Agreement and the evacuation of the northern zone were two distinct issues, in reality the new Locarno spirit created the necessary climate of *détente* which made a prolongation of the Allied occupation there inconceivable. Indeed Locarno marked the point where even the occupation of the two remaining zones became increasingly anachronistic. From now on until the final evacuation in 1930 the 'ex-Allies', as they significantly became called, found it each year harder morally to justify their presence to the Germans, while in Britain it became increasingly difficult to persuade public opinion of the continued need to keep British troops on the Rhine.[67]

In the immediate aftermath of the Locarno Conference Chamberlain spelt out in a telegram to Ryan at Coblenz the implications of the agreements for the Allied occupation. Not only would the Allies agree to the re-appointment of a German Reich Commissioner to Coblenz after the post had been abolished in 1923, but existing legislation of the High Commission would be subjected to further scrutiny with the intention of deleting anything that could not be justified by the need to secure the 'safety and requirements of [the] troops of occupation'.[68] Ryan was sceptical about the degree of cooperation he would secure from his French colleagues whose 'gospel was the *Écho de Paris* and . . . Prophet Poincaré',[69] but Briand himself intervened and summoned Tirard and General Guillaumat, the new French Commander-in-Chief in the Rhineland, and impressed upon them the need for concessions.[70]

65. 'Memorandum' (C15299), p. 6.
66. 'Report', 1925, p. 15.
67. Jacobson, *Locarno Diplomacy*, pp. 60–7.
68. DBFP Ser. 1A, vol. 1 (no. 3), p. 19.
69. Ibid. (no. 12), p.33.
70. Kirchholtes to AA, 22.10.25 (no. 740), FCO Lib. 9627 H292354; Hoesch to AA, 23.10.25 (no. 749), ibid. H29371-78.

Initially there was some confusion about how the modifications to the Rhineland regime would be negotiated. Hoesch, the German Ambassador in Paris, was given a formidable shopping list by the Auswärtiges Amt and instructions to negotiate directly with Briand since the High Commission had to be bypassed 'in view of the mentality of its existing members'.[71] Chamberlain, however, envisaged preliminary negotiations taking place between the High Commission and the new Reich Commissioner,[72] but as he was not appointed until December the High Commissioners at first discussed possible concessions amongst themselves before sending in their recommendations to the Conference of Ambassadors.[73] Tirard, who had been lucky not to be removed from Coblenz,[74] showed a new flexibility and moderation: indeed in some respects he was ready to go further than his British colleagues. He was ready to sweep away the whole system of Kreis officers which Ryan considered to be a useful buffer between the occupying armies and the German civilians. In an appeal to Chamberlain Ryan argued that their abolition would simply open up the way for interference by the French military authorities and accordingly proposed the retention of one Allied civilian official in each zone.[75] Chamberlain scrupulously referred the problem to Hoesch in Paris, who after consulting Berlin, insisted on the total abolition of the system of local representatives of the High Commission.[76]

The Rhine Army also had serious reservations about the sweeping nature of the alleviations proposed by the High Commission. It strongly opposed plans for transferring certain categories of offences, which had hitherto been tried in the Allied Summary Courts, back to the German courts on the grounds that military justice was a real deterrent to the Germans who had 'a wholesome regard' for it.[77] This argument was rejected by both Chamberlain and Ryan, who appreciated the political advantages of limiting the powers of the French courts whose 'judgements have been rough and ready, severe and in German eyes, often unjust'.[78]

The High Commission sent its recommendations, which liberally extended the alleviations of December 1924, to the Conference

71. Schubert to German Embassy, Paris, 27.10.25 (no. 6089[1]), FCO Lib. 3058 605545-50.
72. DBFP Ser. 1a, vol. 1 (no. 15), pp. 40–1.
73. 'Report', 1925, pp. 48–9.
74. Ibid., p. 48; DBFP Ser. 1A, vol. 1 (no. 3), pp. 19–20.
75. Ryan to Chamberlain, 7.11.25 (C14230), FO 371 10760 fo. 35.
76. 'Rhineland Alleviations', 30.11.25 (C15577), p. 19, FO 371/10761 fos 67–79.
77. Col. Maxwell Scott to WO, 9.11.25 (C14532), FO 371/10760 fo. 127.
78. Ryan to Chamberlain, 12.11.25 (C14593), FO 371/10760 fo. 153.

of Ambassadors on 6 November. Confidentially Ryan advised Chamberlain that the whole programme of concessions should not be implemented at once as:

> the German mentality is such that as soon as one concession is given, the tendency is to demand another, and I therefore feel that from a tactical point of view it will be better to adapt a few ordinances only as tangible evidence of our intentions to alleviate conditions in the Rhineland and only to indicate the majority of the concessions, which we have decided to make.[79]

Ryan's machiavellian advice was disregarded by the Ambassadors' Conference, which wanted the concessions to make an immediate impact on German public opinion. After consultation with Stresemann it decided to communicate the concessions to Hoesch on 14 November. Three days later the High Commission published the full details in a press communiqué, and on 18 November those concessions which did not require any further negotiations with the Germans were implemented through Ordinance 308.[80] Besides the immediate abolition of the Kreis officers and the transfer of certain categories of cases to the German courts, the Commission announced the abolition of its rights to scrutinize German laws before these came into force in the Rhineland, although it still kept reserve powers to modify or suspend any enactment which might threaten the armies of occupation. The number of German officials whose appointments had to be approved by the High Commission was also drastically revised, while censorship of the press and restrictions on circulation between occupied and unoccupied Germany were relaxed and postal censorship abolished. The ordinances dealing with such matters as the display of flags, marking prices on food and the banning of wireless receiving sets would also all be abolished.[81]

Two days after the announcement of Ordinance 308, General Ducane was finally given the order to evacuate Cologne for Wiesbaden.[82] For the past year the army had lobbied hard to secure the Coblenz bridgehead as the new British Zone, as this would shorten its lines of communication with the channel ports.[83] To overcome

79. Quoted in WO to FO, 10.11.25 (C14379), FO 371/10760 fo. 72.
80. 'Rhineland Alleviations', pp. 15–18.
81. 'Report', 1925, p. 50.
82. WO to GOC, 20.11.25 (C14946), FO 371/10704 fo. 206.
83. 'Memorandum on the Re-Allocation of Zones in the Rhineland', 11.2.25 (C12020), FO 371/10750 fos 111–22.

French reluctance to hand over Coblenz, which was second only to Cologne as an administrative and communications centre, the War Office had alarmed the Foreign Office in December 1924 by proposing that jointly with the French and Belgian general staffs they should work out plans for reinforcing the Rhine armies in a time of rising tension with Germany.[84] Inevitably this smacked of the Anglo–French staff talks which began during the first Moroccan crisis in 1905, and the War Office proposal was dismissed testily as 'a foolish letter'.[85] Nevertheless the Foreign Office agreed that Britain needed to occupy a zone 'compatible with the dignity and prestige of this country' and that only Coblenz would 'give us similar advantages to those which we enjoy in Cologne'.[86] The French were, however, determined not to repeat the mistake they had made in November 1918 when they had absentmindedly allowed the vital 'nodal point' of Cologne to fall into British hands. Foch hammered home the lessons of the last six years when on 7 October 1925 at a meeting chaired by the French Prime Minister, Painlevé, he stressed that not only the small size of the British army of occupation justified its move to Wiesbaden, but also 'la nécessité absolue' of controlling the Coblenz Railway system and of avoiding 'le retour des difficultés graves qu'a révélées le contrôle britannique pendant les opérations de la Ruhr'.[87] Chamberlain had already made it clear that he was not prepared to insist on Coblenz and consequently Ducane and the War Office had to accept Wiesbaden.[88]

Before the British evacuated Cologne, they had, according to the Peace Treaty, to ensure that the former zone of occupation was fully demilitarized. This entailed checking on the manpower levels of the police and the demolition of certain strategic railways. Since 1918 the number of police in Cologne had risen from 990 to 2,168 in order to minimize the danger of British military involvement in civilian policing operations.[89] In January 1925 Nollet had already warned dramatically that the presence of a 'numerous and well armed' police force in Cologne 'would constitute a very severe danger for our security',[90] while Tirard had floated the idea of an international police force.[91] A decision on the size of the Rhineland

84. Creedy to Undersec. of State, December 1924 (19106), FO 371/9833 fo. 245.
85. Minute by Lampson, 24.12.24 (C19109), FO 371/9833 fos 243–4.
86. 'Memorandum on the Re-allocation of Zones' (C12020).
87. 'Projet de Procès Verbal de la Séance tenue à la Présidence du Conseil, le 7 October 1925 à 15 heures', MAE Rive Gauche 82 fos 24–32.
88. FO to WO, 14.7.25 (C9015), FO 371/10750 fos 138–9.
89. Kilmarnock to Chamberlain, 1.8.25 (C10195), FO 371/10704 fos 26–9.
90. Minute by Nollet, 15.1.25 (no. 053), Vincennes 7N3577-2.
91. Ibid., 'Proposition Tirard', 23.12.24.

police force was delayed until the Allies fixed a global total for the number of police effectives in Germany in November 1925; out of a total number of 150,000 police for the whole Reich, the occupied territories were allowed a force of ten thousand which would be divided between the three zones by agreement between the German government and the High Commission.[92] The question of the strategic railways was tacitly ignored. Colonel Manton, with the concurrence of General Ducane, pointed out in October 1925 that not only were these particular railways of dubious military value, but that their demolition would cost the Allies enormous sums as well as damage the local economy. In the words of a Foreign Office official, 'it [was] quite obviously not a practical proposition. You cannot usher in a new era of peace with one hand and destroy railway lines of indisputed commercial value with the other.'[93] The question was thus allowed to remain 'indefinitely in abeyance'.[94]

To protect Germans who had helped the British during the occupation of the Cologne Zone, it was also vital to negotiate an amnesty with the German government. Kilmarnock advised a settlement similar to the amnesty provisions of the London Agreement of August 1924, which would ensure that the German government would take no legal action against any German citizen who had assisted Allied officials or troops in the Cologne Zone.[95] In its turn as part of the package of Rhineland alleviations the High Commission was ready to grant an amnesty for offences against Allied property and the ordinances of the High Commission as long as this did not involve 'infractions of common law or espionage'.[96] German legal experts met the legal advisers of the High Commission at Coblenz in early December and proposed that the German courts and administrative authorities should be issued with instructions 'to prevent direct or indirect reprisals against any persons by reason of their obedience to the orders of the authorities of the occupation'. Significantly, however, the Germans exempted those who had committed acts of treason or espionage.[97] Nevertheless the High Commissioners and the Belgian Commander in Chief accepted the German assurances, as did General Ducane who

92. 'Report', 1925, pp. 37–8.
93. Troutbeck's Minute on Manton's report, 22.10.25 (C13134), FO 371/10704 fos 92–3.
94. 'Report', 1925, p. 39.
95. Kilmarnock to Chamberlain, 1.8.25 (C10195), FO 371/10704 fos 26–9.
96. 'Rhineland Alleviations', p. 20.
97. See Draft Protocol (Annex 1 to Enclosure 2), Ryan to Chamberlain 14.12.25 (C16111), FO 371/10761 fos 101–101A.

added the proviso that acts of treason and espionage should not be interpreted to cover civilians and policemen who had helped the occupying authorities by reporting to them cases of the illegal possession of arms or illegal meetings, but General Guillaumat was more critical and argued that the Germans were merely making a promise in return for a precise undertaking by the Allies. By the time the German proposals reached the Conference of Ambassadors, French opposition had hardened and no agreement on an amnesty was concluded until September 1926.[98]

The evacuation of the Cologne Zone faced the British Rhine Army with difficult logistical problems. Since the Rhine Army was a force of regular troops, many of whom were accompanied by their families, it needed to requisition many more houses and public buildings than had the conscript French Army, which it was replacing. The problem was further compounded by Ducane's plans to replace the French corps headquarters in Wiesbaden by an army headquarters, which inevitably involved a need for more offices and billets in the centre of the town.[99] The billets that were to be handed over by the French to the British Army were not sufficient in either Wiesbaden or Königstein, and in Bingen initially every hotel was taken over by the British.[100] This inevitably had embarrassing political implications[101] for Chamberlain's attempt to breath life into the Locarno *détente*, and he complained testily that it was 'really intolerable that the effect of substituting a British for a French force should be to render the situation harder for the civil population'.[102] The obvious solution was to cut the number of British troops, particularly as both the French and Belgians were planning quite substantial reductions, but because there was an acute shortage of barracks in Britain as a result of the loss of buildings in the new Irish Free State, the War Office was only willing at the very most to withdraw one infantry battalion, a battery of field artillery and to send 342 army families back to England.[103]

The problem of securing sufficient billets delayed the British

98. 'Report', 1925, p. 41.

99. GOC Rhine Army to WO 23.11.25 (C15105), FO 371/10704 fo. 212; Creedy to Undersec. of State, FO 16.12.25 (C16118), FO 371/10705 fos 68–9.

100. 'Requisitioning by the British Army of Occupation in the Wiesbaden Area', 27.2.26, FO 371/11255 fos 151–8.

101. See Aide Memoire, German Embassy, 28.11.25 (C15385), FO 371/10704 fo. 222.

102. Chamberlain's Minute, 2.12.25, on C15502, FO 371/10761 fo. 55.

103. Edmonds, *The Occupation*, p. 283; Creedy to Undersec. of State, 16.12.25 (C16118), FO 371/10705 fos 68–9; 'Rhineland Alleviations', p. 22.

departure from Cologne, and both the French and the Germans became increasingly impatient with Ducane's procrastination.[104] The first reconnaissance party was dispatched to Wiesbaden on 31 October,[105] and from early December to the end of January a steady stream of troops and army families moved south. The last party left on 30 January 1926, except for a few 'liquidating elements'.[106] The civilian staff of the High Commission in Cologne were all discharged except for Colonel Birch, who was appointed liaison officer between the military headquarters at Wiesbaden and the High Commission offices at Coblenz.[107] The British civilians, or 'Colognials' as they were nicknamed, who had initially been part of the Second Army in 1918 and after demobilization had stayed on to work in messes or army workshops, were repatriated back to Britain, which in many respects was an alien world to them. Many of the mushrooming import–export businesses, which had flourished in the early 1920s had collapsed in 1923–24 when, first the Ruhr occupation, and then the subsequent stabilization of the mark made trade less profitable. The dismantling of the customs sanctions in September 1924 and the Anglo-German trade Agreement of December 1924, which granted to British imports 'the most favoured nation' status, rendered Cologne dispensable for British traders.

How many British citizens were left in Cologne is impossible to assess, but the great majority had left by January 1926. Twenty years later there were some tantalizing glimpses of the fate of some of the original 'Colognials' who stayed on. A former quartermaster sergeant of the Coldstream Guards was elected mayor of Siegburg in 1946 as it was assumed that he would be the best man to deal with the British authorities. The orphaned daughter of another 'Colognial', who together with his German wife had died during the Second World War in Germany, was delivered dramatically by an American soldier to her British godfather serving with the British occupying forces in Berlin. He had not seen her since his regiment had left Cologne in 1926.[108]

104. DBFP Ser. 1A, vol. 1 (no. 103), pp. 152–4; Hoesch to Schubert, 16.11.25 (no. 843), FCO Lib. 4501 E114659-62.
105. *The Times*, 30.10.25.
106. FO to D'Abernon, 28.1.26 (C1091), FO 371/11307 fo. 48.
107. Edmonds, *The Occupation*, p. 295; FO Minutes, 5 and 6.1.26 (C16720), FO 371/10761 fo. 162.
108. *The Times*, 10.12.25; *The Cologne Post Annual, 1923*, p. 15; Krüger, *die Außenpolitik der Republik von Weimar*, pp. 257–8. The official statistics published by the city of Cologne give for the year 1926 no information about the number of British citizens in Cologne; for this information I am grateful to Dr Verscharen of

The evacuation naturally led the Kölner to draw up a balance sheet of the seven years of occupation. With the exception of the Nationalist *Rheinische Tageszeitung*, the local press willingly conceded that the British had been conciliatory occupiers. The *Rheinzeitung* even went as far as to say that they had 'done much in the general service of international peace'.[109] Adenauer himself, while not hesitating to stress the impact of 'the hard fist of the victor for seven long years',[110] recognized that politically the British had always been scrupulously fair. It was this aspect of the occupation that impressed itself most on the people of Cologne and perhaps accounted for the strictly unofficial farewell, which the General Staff Intelligence report described:

> On the evening of 29 January many of the N.C.O.'s in Cologne availed themselves of their last opportunity to visit local cafés. They received an effusive welcome . . . Almost every party of Germans asked the N.C.O.'s to do them the honour of coming to their table for refreshment . . . In at least one café the Germans locked the door so that the N.C.O.'s whom they seemed to delight in entertaining, should not depart too early.[111]

Although the friction engendered by the Wiesbaden occupation to some extent erased memories both in Germany and in Britain of the very real popularity of the British garrison in Cologne in 1923, it is nevertheless arguable that the legacy of the Cologne occupation was an improvement, on the personal level at least, in Anglo–German relations. Thanks to Ball, F.A. Hughes and Co. Ltd built up a major business with the Germans and by 1927 was one of the main distributors of German chemical products in Britain.[112] Both Julian Piggott and General Hutchison, the former Quartermaster-General of the Rhine Army, joined the Anglo–German Association.[113] After the Second World War Piggott became director and secretary of a revived Anglo–German Society and was decorated by the Federal Republic.[114] In 1935 General Clive, formerly Fergusson's Chief of Staff and then Military Governor of Cologne,

109. Quoted in Williamson, 'Cologne and the British', p. 702.
110. Ibid.
111. Weekly Report, GS Intelligence, 5.2.26, FO 371/11307 fos 95–100; quoted in Williamson ibid. p. 702.
112. Anon, *F.A. Hughes Centenary Year*.
113. 'Anglo–German Association', 16.8.32, FCO Lib. 5742 H032787-91. Col. Stewart Roddie was also a member.
114. *Who's Who*, 1962, pp. 2419–20.

actively intervened through the German Embassy in London on behalf of Adenauer, who was virtually outlawed by the Nazi regime because of his alleged separatist activities in 1919 and 1923, and was apparently successful in having him exonerated and granted a pension.[115] These links were no doubt mirrored at more humble but anonymous levels.

115. H.G. Lehmann, 'Clives Unterredung mit Adenauer und ihre Folgen', in R. Morsey and K. Repgen (eds), *Untersuchungen und Dokumente zur Ostpolitik und Biographie*, Adenauer-Studien III, Mainz, 1974. pp. 216–19.

PART VI

The Occupation and the Locarno Spirit, 1926–1927

Introduction

The 'Locarno Spirit' was an elusive concept which was interpreted very differently in London, Paris and Berlin. All sides were agreed that it involved concessions, yet inevitably the scope and spread of these concessions were a matter of constant and acrimonious debate. It still took until January 1927 before the IAMCC could be wound up, and even then its ghostly presence lingered on in the military experts attached to the ex-Allied embassies. In the two years following Locarno the Rhineland occupation remained a festering source of friction between Germany and the Western powers, as Stresemann pressed persistently for the implementation of the troop cuts promised by the Allies in their note of 14 November 1925 and attempted, whenever the possibility seemed favourable, to argue for a total evacuation of the Rhineland.[1]

On his visit to Cologne to celebrate the British evacuation he pointedly announced that 'if the spirit of Locarno was to be a symbol of future European policy, then its final and visible expression must be the withdrawal of troops from the Rhineland'.[2] Over the next two years he lost no opportunity to press both his maximum and minimum demands. When Germany was admitted to the League of Nations in October 1926, he seized the chance to meet Briand at Thoiry and unsuccessfully attempted to exploit France's financial weakness to offer him a deal whereby 'the French government would obtain immediate financial assistance through the sale of its assets, which they [held] in respect of Germany'.[3] When this failed he fell back on a policy of wresting piecemeal

---

1. The Conference of Ambassadors assured the German government that the occupying troops would be 'sensiblement réduits' and brought down to 'chiffres normaux': 'IARHC Annual Report for 1925' (C2306), p. 17, FO 371/13640 fos 199–207. For a summary of Stresemann's foreign policy see G. Niedhart, 'Stresemanns Außenpolitik und die Grenzen der Entspannung', in W. Michalka and M. Lee (eds), *Gustav Stresemann*, Darmstadt, 1982, pp. 416–28.
2. Stresemann's speech in Cologne, 21.2.26 (C2441), FO 371/11307 fos 106–8.
3. 'The Rhineland: its Occupation by the Allied Forces and its eventual Evacuation', 18.8.28 (C6400), p. 10, FO 371/12903 fos 5–5i; J. Jacobson and J.T. Walker, 'The Impulse for the Franco-German Entente: The Origins of the Thoiry Conference, 1926', *Journal of Contemporary History*, vol. 10, no. 1, 1975, pp. 157–75.

concessions from the ex-Allies, which ultimately in August 1927 amounted to the modest cut of only 10,000 troops.

In 1926 Chamberlain was anxious to withdraw the IAMCC from Germany,[4] and honour the pledges given to cut the occupation forces on the Rhine, but by 1927 the Rhineland was not a major priority in British foreign policy, which was more concerned with threats to the Empire from Soviet Russia and the Kuomintang.[5] This sense of detachment from German affairs was also strengthened by the growing warmth between London and Paris, which alarmed not only Berlin but also the British Left. Despite an understandable unwillingness to become involved in the first Anglo–Soviet 'cold war',[6] Stresemann was only able to secure British support for troop cuts in June 1927 by first tacitly agreeing to warn Russia not to take retaliatory action against Poland after the Russian envoy in Warsaw had been murdered.

4. Fox, 'Britain and the Inter-Allied Military Commission of Control', p. 164.
5. Chamberlain to Crewe, 6.5.25 (C5238), FO 371/11301 fos 82–4; also Petrie, *Chamberlain*, ch. 7, and Niedhart, 'Multipolares Gleichgewicht und Weltwirtschaftliche Verflechtung', p. 122.
6. Jacobson, *Locarno Diplomacy*, p. 132.

–17–

The Problems of Occupation in the Locarno Era: The British in the Wiesbaden Bridgehead, 1926–1927

In December 1918 Germany had been in a state of chaos and the British had been welcomed in the Rhineland as protectors from anarchy and revolution. In the years up to 1924 their presence in Cologne was appreciated as a formidable obstacle against French-inspired separatism. In Wiesbaden, however, the situation could not have been more different. Anglo–French relations were as cordial as they had ever been since 1914, and the British occupation was actively resented by the population. In Cologne the British controlled the metropolis of the Rhineland and their officials were in close daily touch with trade union officials, businessmen and local politicians. The Wiesbaden bridgehead was, on the other hand, essentially a rural backwater, apart from the *Kurstadt* of Wiesbaden itself, and the alleviations made to the Rhineland Agreement after the Locarno Agreement cut down obligatory official contact between the British and the Germans to a minimum.

As a result of the abolition of the Kreis officers, the army regained some of the powers it lost under the Rhineland Agreement. Ducane set up a Civil Affairs Branch within his general staff. Initially it had the delicate task of interpreting the mood of Locarno, as some of the concessions agreed upon in principle in Paris and Coblenz had still not been formulated. When officers of the Department first interviewed the Regierungspräsident, they told him that 'whenever the ordinances gave the Commander in Chief powers to refuse or permit certain things, they would in principle be permitted', but also significantly stressed that the German authorities were responsible that this liberality was not 'abused'.[1] Inevitably this led to a paradox, which was later succinctly ex-

---

1. 'Apex', *The Uneasy Triangle*, pp. 209–10.

pressed by a British officer on the Civil Affairs Branch of the General Staff at Wiesbaden:

> . . . it made the smooth working of the whole machine in occupied territory to a far greater extent than ever before dependent on their goodwill. It seemed to me that this produced a strange anomaly. The genuine goodwill of the Germans was demanded in order to ensure the successful running of the occupation, which at the same time they were essentially bound to dislike, however liberal it was . . . To occupy a country and treat the population as an enemy was one thing. It was a definite attitude. To be in occupation and try to behave as visitors was an anomaly.[2]

Despite Locarno, 1926 was therefore a difficult year for the British authorities. The goodwill created by the evacuation of Cologne was neutralized by the controversies stirred up by the move to Wiesbaden. The accommodation shortage caused by the requisitioning of houses, schools and hotels was given maximum publicity by the German press, and in the absence of immediate and drastic troop cuts the inhabitants were encouraged to complain, arguably with some justice, that their burdens had been made heavier rather than lighter. One wealthy Frankfurter woman, who had influential contacts in Britain, had her complaints about British requisitioning in Königstein sent directly to the Foreign Office. Her assertion that 'we are faring worse than in 1918, when the French arrived',[3] considerably embarrassed the Foreign Office, despite attempts by D'Abernon to make light of it by arguing that the majority of the Königstein villas 'belong largely to Frankfurt Jews and there is no power on earth or Heaven which will stop these gentlemen from making trouble when their interests are affected',[4] Resentment of the British requisitioning policies inevitably made itself felt in the attitude of the German officials towards the High Commission as a whole. The negotiations between the High Commission and the German legal experts over the Amnesty were protracted and difficult. In February the German legal team suddenly disrupted negotiations by apparently arguing that the High Commission no longer had the right to intervene in German legal or administrative decisions.[5] In interview after interview Tirard and Kilmarnock appealed to Langwerth, the German Com-

2. Ibid., pp. 203–4.
3. Kanzellbogen to Butler, 8.4.26 (C4800), FO 371/11255 fos 164–5.
4. D'Abernon to Chamberlain, 30.4.26 (C5238), FO 371/11301 fos 77–8.
5. 'Annual Report for 1926 on the Inter-Allied Rhineland High Commission' (C7260), p. 39, FO 371/13640 fo. 212.

missioner, to inspire his countrymen with the Locarno spirit. On 27 February, for instance, Kilmarnock, according to Langwerth, complained that 'since Locarno the Allies are constantly giving and we [in Germany] keep demanding more'.[6] Each time Langwerth replied by stressing the need to reconcile German public opinion to the continued occupation by making some generous troop cuts.[7] By April relations between the Germans and the High Commission were rapidly deteriorating. In a dispatch, which was circulated to the Cabinet, Kilmarnock went to the heart of the problem, as it was perceived in London and Coblenz:

> The German understands only two methods of conduct – how to browbeat or to be browbeaten; for him there is no happy mean. Up to Locarno he found it natural to receive orders from the occupation. Now he argues that since Germany has been received into the comity of nations the system has been fundamentally altered. He feels that henceforth the occupation should be run on the principle that the requirements of the armies should be notified to the German authorities, who themselves should give the orders necessary to satisfy them. In other words he demands the revision of the Rhineland Agreement. His pride is accordingly injured when orders continue to be issued to him under that agreement.[8]

Kilmarnock's complaints were taken up with the Auswärtiges Amt by D'Abernon, but Schubert defiantly argued that in the absence of troop cuts 'the debts on the other side are far higher'. D'Abernon could only reply that although Chamberlain was fundamentally in sympathy with this demand, he would have to wait for the bad impression to pass, which had been created in London and Paris by the signature of the Berlin Treaty with Soviet Russia, before being able to take any action. This treaty secured Germany's neutrality in the event of a war between Russia and a third power and was most unwelcome in London at a time of rapidly deteriorating Anglo–Soviet relations.[9]

Privately, Chamberlain was uneasily aware that British public opinion was becoming more critical of the occupation and that the Allies had in fact promised cuts. He was therefore anxious not to

6. Langwerth to AA, 27.2.26 (no. 6), FCO Lib. 3058 D605971–73; see too Tirard, reported as saying: 'man vermisse in Besprechung durchaus vorhanden Geist von Locarno entsprechenden Ton': Langwerth to AA, 17.3.26 (no. 7), ibid., D606004–005.
7. For instance, Langwerth to AA, 2.4.26 (no. 9), p. 2, ibid., D606027–30.
8. Kilmarnock to Chamberlain, 15.4.26 (C4703), p. 1, FO 371/11301 fo. 39.
9. Schubert, 28.4.26, FCO Lib. 4501 E115257–58.

run the risk of endangering the whole Locarno Agreement by giving Stresemann 'just cause of complaint'.[10] His efforts to create the necessary climate of goodwill as a preliminary to persuading Briand to agree to troop cuts, were, however, seriously threatened by a series of incidents in the Rhineland during the summer of 1926. To celebrate the visit of the German Board of Agriculture to Bingen, the town council decided to illuminate the Niederwalddenkmal, or the Germania as it was known, which commemorated the German victories of 1870–1. Inevitably this was seen by Tirard and Guillaumat as an unnecessary provocation. Kilmarnock dissuaded them from issuing a direct order banning the illuminations for fear of provoking a nationalist backlash; instead he advised Langwerth to bring pressure to bear on Bingen Council to cancel the illuminations, but after one abortive telephone call, Langwerth diplomatically withdrew to an allegedly important engagement in Düsseldorf.[11] Ducane then sent two officers to remonstrate with the mayor, who asked the officers point blank whether they were ready to ban the illuminations. When they refused, he replied that neither was he.[12] The illuminations therefore went ahead.

Chamberlain was so incensed that he banged the table in rage in front of Sthamer.[13] Seeking to justify his behaviour later, he informed D'Abernon that he had spoken so strongly because:

> there were times when I could almost weep that stupidity of this kind should endanger the progress of appeasement. No doubt each of the incidents was petty in itself. That only made them more aggravating. . . . They were grains of sand heedlessly or maliciously cast into the machinery causing a friction which would not indeed reverse our policy, but most seriously hinder its progress.[14]

Although Stresemann countered British complaints with a catalogue of his own,[15] he did nevertheless restrain the Mayor of Bingen from persisting with further plans for illuminating the Germania one day a week throughout the summer.[16]

10. Chamberlain to Crewe, 6.5.26 (C5238), FO 371/11301 fos 82–4.
11. Kilmarnock to Chamberlain, 12.5.26 (Enclosure no. 1 in C5890), FO 371/11301 fos 111–12.
12. Ibid.
13. 'Aufzeichnung', Stresemann, 22.5.26 (RM946), FCO Lib. 3058 D606090-093.
14. Chamberlain to D'Abernon, 19.5.26 (C5890), FO 371/11301 fo. 111.
15. 'Aufzeichnung'.
16. Ryan to Chamberlain, 11.6.26 (C6709), FO 371/11301 fo. 208; 'Report', 1926, p. 7.

In early July another incident occurred which again threatened the fragile process of appeasement, when the Germersheimer Soldiers and Ex-Servicemen's Club (*Krieger- und Veteranerverein*) held a festival at Germersheim, where some 3,000 French troops were quartered.[17] During the two days of the festival inevitably there occurred a series of incidents between the French garrison and the veterans. Technically the French were in the wrong as flags were torn down and posters vandalized, but they were provoked by what was in essence a nationalist demonstration. Tirard felt that the French garrison was the victim of deliberate acts of provocation and wanted the High Commission to retaliate by banning any such meetings in the future.[18] The Foreign Office, on the other hand, was anxious to avoid blowing the whole incident up. Kilmarnock, echoing this sentiment, informed Langwerth that 'we should let the matter rest in the interests of great objectives'.[19] Although Stresemann, under pressure from the Reichstag, could not 'just close the book',[20] he did in fact connive at setting up an enquiry that worked at so leisurely a pace that the whole crisis was guaranteed to go off the boil.[21]

Nevertheless these incidents did strengthen French opposition to troop cuts on the Rhine, which both Chamberlain and Stresemann were so anxious to obtain. In answer to a personal appeal from Chamberlain on 29 July 1926, Briand was able to offer a cosmetic cut of a mere 6,000.[22] The Foreign Office unofficially floated the possibility of a unilateral British military evacuation, leaving Kilmarnock with little more than a personal bodyguard;[23] Schubert welcomed the proposal, but Stresemann was wary of so complete a British withdrawal and urged instead a cut of 5,000 in the Rhine Army, as this would obviate the dangers of a complete takeover of the Wiesbaden Zone by the French.[24] Ironically it was opposition within the Treasury and War Office that prevented the implementation of these cuts. The Treasury pointed out that if a disproportionate percentage of British troops were withdrawn, the

17. 'Report', 1926, p. 7.
18. Langwerth to AA, 28.7.26 (no. 28), FCO Lib. 3058 D606211-13; and Dufour to AA, 4.8.26 (no. 585), FCO Lib. 4501 E115548-50.
19. Langwerth to AA, 6.8.26 (no. 26), FCO Lib. 4501 E115571-73.
20. 'Auszug-aus einem Gespräch zwischen dem Herrn Reichsminister und Lord D'Abernon von 10.8.26', ibid. E115581-82.
21. 'Report', 1926, p. 9.
22. 'Report', 1926, pp. 17–19.
23. Report of meeting between Schubert and D'Abernon, 20.8.26, FCO Lib. 4501 E115658-59.
24. D'Abernon to AA, 25.8.26 (C9463), FO 371/11299 fo. 22.

Exchequer would lose eight million gold marks per annum. The sum would not be transferred to Britain's reparation account as increased Belgian and French troop costs would inevitably soak it up.[25] The War Office argued strongly that the Rhine Army needed to be able to defend itself and have some reserves for an emergency, 'however remote that possibility may be'; it also stressed that drastic unilateral cuts would weaken British prestige 'in the eyes of the rest of Europe and shake their faith in the solidarity of the Franco–British *Entente*'.[26] Inevitably the embarrassingly pre-Locarno arguments of the War Office were pilloried by officials in the Foreign Office. Troutbeck minuted, for instance, that they were 'written in entire disregard of the Locarno Treaty',[27] but Chamberlain cynically observed what was common knowledge in Berlin and Paris: 'The truth is that most of this letter is camouflage put up to protect the War Office in its receipt of a grant in aid from Germany'.[28] It was thus clear that only a Cabinet decision could overcome the War Office's opposition,[29] and consequently Chamberlain was forced temporarily to abandon his proposals for drastic troop cuts. The Foreign Office had to content itself with dispatching to the War office a pedantic, schoolmasterly letter emphasizing that:

> while it is [Chamberlain's] firm belief that the foreign policy of this country should be based on an entente with France, it is certainly no longer correct to speak of an alliance. . . . It was indeed the very essence of the Locarno policy to bring to an end the war time alliance and to put in its place a system of cooperation in which Germany should be included. Such indeed is the character of the Treaty that this country might conceivably find itself ranged in alliance with France against Germany or with Germany against France . . .[30]

Theoretically Locarno placed the British Rhine Army in an impossible situation. In General Guillaumat's overall defence scheme for the Rhine, British forces were allotted the key role of covering the Mainz road bridge which, according to General Thwaites, Ducane's successor in the Rhineland, 'entailed a scuttle back to the French frontier there to hold [*sic*] until the main French

25. Treasury to FO, 30.9.26 (C10555), FO 371/11299 fo. 98.
26. WO to FO, 26.8.26 (C9472), FO 371/11299 fo. 28.
27. Ibid., Minute by Troutbeck (on C9472), 27.8.26, fos 23–5.
28. Ibid., Minute by Chamberlain, 30.8.26, fo. 26.
29. Ibid., Minute by Howard Smith, 27.8.26, fo. 25.
30. FO (Orme Sargent) to WO, 8.9.26 (C9472), FO 371/11299 fo. 37.

armies were ready to advance'.[31] This was a formidable task, which would have involved the defence of the defile of the River Nahe at Kreuznach, just south of Bingen. Responsibility for defending the rearguard would have fallen on the British Army, which was 'like a nut in a nutcracker between Germany and its French ally'.[32] In practice the contingency of an alliance with Germany against France was never envisaged by the War Office, and, given the army's vital role in Guillaumat's overall defence plan, it is not surprising that the War Office opposed further cuts.

Despite Chamberlain's failure to secure any dramatic manpower reductions on the Rhine, Stresemann's plan to negotiate an overall deal on reparations and the Rhineland with Briand at Thoiry led to the conclusion of the protracted negotiations over the Amnesty on 10 September. The protective Ordinances, whereby the High Commission could shield Germans who had cooperated with it from legal action by the German courts, were dropped in exchange for reassurances from the German government that there would be no witch-hunts against such individuals. It was agreed that any Germans, with the sole exception of those found guilty of murder, who were sentenced by military tribunals should be handed over to the Reich authorities, who would supervise the execution of their sentences.[33]

Throughout the summer the High Commission had been attempting to build on the *détente* created by the Locarno Treaty by recodifying and revising the ordinances. The mass of ordinances covering the period 1920–6 were reorganized and simplified into seven new 'organic ordinances' and handed over to the German government on 6 October for a preliminary perusal before being officially published by the Commission.[34] While recodification was intended to further the spirit of Locarno and removed some offensive anomalies dating from the early 1920s, the whole operation was arguably a psychological error because, as one German official in the Auswärtiges Amt minuted, 'the codification repeats most of the earlier severe penalties, which have largely been forgotten in occupied and unoccupied Germany, but naturally if they are republished in the present political climate, the impression will be

31. 'Lt. General Sir William Thwaites' Period of Command, Rhine Army', p. 2, WO 106/463 fos 3–34.
32. Ibid., p. 2.
33. 'Amnesty Provisions on Evacuation of the Rhineland', 22.7.29 (C5586), pp. 1–2, FO 371/13618 fos 153–5.
34. 'Report', 1926, pp. 49–50.

created amongst the public that there can be no talk of a policy of détente within the Rhineland'.[35]

The recodified ordinances were received by the Auswärtiges Amt just at the point when yet another and more serious incident at Germersheim forced the High Commission to exercise its still considerable legal powers. A French officer, Rouzier, killed one German and wounded two others, allegedly in self-defence. The French inflamed German public opinion by arresting the two wounded men.[36] Local papers which dared criticize French action were promptly threatened with suspension.[37] On 22 December a French military court acquitted Rouzier and sentenced six Germans to terms of imprisonment ranging from two years to two months; the verdict caused a storm of protest in Germany, which united both the Left and the Right. Visibly shaken, Tirard called a special meeting of the High Commission. The British and Belgian Commissioners suggested a re-trial, whereas Tirard favoured a pardon, which on the advice of Briand was granted by the French President. The storm appeared to die down 'as quickly as it had arisen, leaving only rumblings on the necessity of evacuation as the only effective means of avoiding the recurrence of conflicts in the occupied territories'.[38]

These rumblings continued throughout 1927. The German press gave maximum coverage to every incident involving occupation troops. Even the Germanophil *Manchester Guardian* commented that 'the smallest public house brawl is served up as another incident'.[39] Exasperated by what he regarded as the carping attitude of the German officials, Ryan contrasted in an interview with Langwerth the 'sincere effort' by the ex-Allies to 'further the spirit of reconciliation', with Germany's negative record 'in what could only be a mutual task'.[40] Inevitably this was not an interpretation that appealed to the German government. In a memorandum dated 28 February 1927[41] the German Chancellor, Marx, drew up a list of concessions, which he wanted Stresemann to secure at the next meeting of the League Council in March. He conceded that com-

35. Friedberg to 'Germadiplo', 27.10.26 (3725), FCO Lib. 4502 E117532-33.
36. 'Report', 1926, p. 12.
37. Minutes of 325th Sitting of the IARHC, 26, 28 and 29 Oct., 3, 9 and 12 Nov. 1926, §LXIV, Min. 11934, FO 894/27 fos 43–4.
38. 'Report', 1926, p. 13.
39. *Manchester Guardian*, 5.1.27.
40. DBFP Ser. lA, vol. 3 (no. 1), p. 4
41. 'Der Reichsminister für die besetzten Gebiete', 28.2.27, FCO Lib. 4501 E116156-63.

plete evacuation was temporarily 'difficult to achieve', but instructed Stresemann to negotiate troop cuts totalling some one-third to half of the overall forces. He was also to make it plain that the 'organic' ordinances represented an unsatisfactory codification of existing laws rather than a radical revision. In words that mirrored Chamberlain's and Ryan's he complained that while the Rhineland Commission and the army commanders were attempting to adapt to the new spirit, this had not yet permeated through to the rank and file of the occupation. 'The soldiers, N.C.O.'s, gendarmes and subalterns, who in the final analysis are in immediate contact with the population must be certain that they will be seriously punished if they are guilty of . . . [any] transgressions.'

In the course of the summer Stresemann had only modest success. It was not until June that he managed to secure from Chamberlain a definite statement that troop reductions would be considered by the ex-Allies.[42] In the meantime prolonged discussion continued on the codification of the ordinances. Tirard accused the Germans of proposing amendments 'which they themselves knew could not be granted'.[43] By July the High Commission impatiently decided that once the clauses on railway disputes, civil jurisdiction and taxes were finalized, the ordinances 'would be drawn up and communicated to Langwerth'.[44] Largely thanks to Chamberlain, who was anxious to remove a propaganda weapon from the Germans,[45] real progress was made in the question of troop cuts. Initially Chamberlain hoped to secure cuts of about 14,000 troops, virtually all of which would be French, by setting an overall ceiling of 56,000 soldiers in the Rhineland,[46] but Briand insisted that the ex-Allies should share the cuts, which should not total more than 10,000.[47] Reluctantly Chamberlain had to accept this. The Treasury put forward a proposal for cutting the British force by 2,000 and despite its earlier reservations, managed to devise a way of transferring the money saved to the reparation account,[48] but the War Office stubbornly opposed, on grounds of

42. DBFP Ser. 1A, vol. 3 (no. 244), pp. 391–3.
43. 333rd Sitting of the IARHC, 26 and 28 March and 1 Apr. 1927, §XXIV, Min. 12343, FO 894/28 fo. 588.
44. 339th Sitting of the IARHC, 4, 6, 11, 13 and 15 July 1927, §XIX, Min. 12653, FO 894/29 fo. 221.
45. DBFP Ser. 1A, vol. 3 (no. 280), pp. 467–74.
46. 'Annual Report for 1927 on the Inter-Allied High Commission' (C2782), p. 25, FO 371/14375 fos 164–8.
47. Minute by Howard Smith, 12.8.27 (C6776), FO 371/12149 fos 14–16; 'Report', 1927, p. 25.
48. Treasury to FO, 12.8.27 (C6789), FO 371/12149 fo. 30.

operational necessity, such a swingeing cut. Its arguments were strengthened by a decision taken by the League of Nations in early 1927 to replace French troops in the Saar by an international contingent to which the Rhine Army was committed to contribute a hundred men every three months.[49] The most, therefore, it was ready to countenance was a reduction of 900. The Cabinet supported the army's arguments and agreed to cuts in the Rhine Army 'in proportion to the total reduction of 10,000, provided that the French and Belgian governments will make the same proportionate reduction in their armies of occupation'. That would amount to 1,060 British troops.[50] 'After considerable discussion'[51] this proved acceptable to Briand and was duly communicated to Stresemann at Geneva on 5 September.

The cuts were regarded by the Germans as the absolute minimum, and did not appreciably change the atmosphere in the Rhineland. As long as the High Commission wielded an ultimate veto over political life in the Rhineland, friction was inevitable. In September, for instance, when the German Scientific Society for Air Travel chose Wiesbaden for its annual congress and asked Thwaites' permission for ten Reichswehr officers to attend, he refused since two of them were involved as liaison officers with nationalist societies. When Prince Heinrich of Prussia opened the Congress, he crudely attacked the High Commission's ban 'coming as it did years after the end of the war', and touched a popular chord by quoting the well-known and obscene words of defiance, 'which Goethe placed in the mouth of Goetz von Berlichingen'.[52]

In December after touring the occupied areas Marx attempted to draw up a balance sheet on the occupation for the Reichstag. On the one hand there had been troop reductions, and a tightening up of military discipline. The number of deportations from the occupied territory had also decreased and there had been less interference with the press. On the other hand the burden of military manoeuvres, and particularly the French mustering ordinance, which made the Franco-Belgian zones exploitable for military purposes, were increasingly resented, as was the existence of the gendarmerie and the secret police.[53] The High Commission, of

49. 'Reduction of Armies of Occupation', 22.8.27 (CP224 (27)), FO 371/12149 fos 57–8. For a brief account of the British garrison in the Saar see Edmonds, *The Occupation*, p. 301.
50. Extract from Conclusions of Cabinet Meeting on 25.8.27 (C7412), FO 371/12149 fos 144–7.
51. DBFP Ser. 1A, vol. 3 (no. 312), p. 537.
52. 'Report', 1927, pp. 14–15.
53. Ibid., p. 17.

course, thought that it was incumbent on the German press 'to emphasise the scope and favourable effects of the decisions taken . . . rather than to minimise systematically what had been achieved',[54] but the Germans, and increasingly the British public, were becoming impatient with even the vestigial powers of the High Commission.

For the majority of the Rhine Army these rancorous arguments about the consequences of Locarno were academic. The British garrison, as it had been in Cologne, was self-sufficient. It ran its own schools, Scout and Guide troops for army children, and organized small arms meetings, horse shows and balls.[55] For officers, life was not so different from that in any other foreign posting. Their social life was limited and fraternization between officers and German women was strongly discouraged by the British 'memsahibs'. Paradoxically the NCOs and the private soldiers had greater freedom to meet Germans in cafés and popular dance halls and many learnt to speak German during their two-year tours of duty.[56] Some, as we have seen, even married German women!

54. 347th Sitting of the IARHC, 18 and 24 Nov. 1927, §IV, Min 12995, FO 894/29 fos 609–10.
55. A good impression of army life at Wiesbaden can be gained from Thwaites' collection of photographs, etc. in 5 vols, IWM Library, 416.311, no. 38145.
56. 'Apex', *The Uneasy Triangle*, pp. 252–3; *The Times*, 18.9.29.

18

The Withdrawal of the IAMCC

It was hoped in London that the evacuation of Cologne and the new Locarno spirit would rapidly lead to the recall of the IAMCC, the sole remaining task of which was to monitor German progress towards fulfilling the five outstanding points in List 4 of the German note of 23 October 1925.[1] Wauchope was instructed to do all he could to speed up negotiations and bring control to an end,[2] but any hopes that the IAMCC would be wound up quickly were soon dispelled.

On 12 January 1926 at a meeting of the council of the IAMCC Wauchope suggested several technical concessions which could be made to the Germans, but he found himself in a minority of one, as the council appeared to be immune to the appeals of the Locarno spirit.[3] On reading Wauchope's dispatch General Burnett-Stuart, the Director of Military Intelligence, commented that 'if this situation is allowed to continue, there is little likelihood of control ever coming to an end'.[4] Privately Wauchope confided to Pawelsz that certain French circles were attempting to delay the termination of control until the question of the institution of investigations by the League of Nations had been settled.[5] Wauchope pressed for clear instructions from the Conference of Ambassadors to be issued to the IAMCC to make concessions on 'non-essential matters',[6] but what actually constituted 'non-essential matters' had been the sub-

1. See above, ch. 16, pp. 292–3.
2. Schubert's report of a discussion with D'Abernon, 5.2.26, FCO Lib. 9627 H292740-43.
3. 'Notes No. 49 by Major General A.G. Wauchope', 12.1.26 (C776), and 'Remarks made by me at our Council Meeting held on 12 January' (C973), FO 371/11286 fos 134–7 and 149–51.
4. Minute by Burnett-Stuart, 18.1.26, on 'Notes No. 49' (0154/6675 M.I.3), FO 371/11286.
5. Köpke to German Embassy, London, 13.2.26 (no. 110), FCO Lib. 9627 H292761-62.
6. 'Notes No. 50', 13.2.26 (C2084), FO 371/11286 fos 37–40.

ject of recurring and often rancorous debates between Britain and France since the start of control in January 1920. In the spring of 1926 the mood was not favourable to compromise. Briand sought to establish links between troop cuts on the Rhine and German disarmament,[7] while the German government pinned its hopes on the change that German membership of the League of Nations might be reasonably expected to bring about, and consequently marked time in the expectation that it might gain some important concessions at the League Council meeting in September.[8]

British desire to terminate control as quickly as possible cast Wauchope in the role of mediator between the French and the Germans. He had to contend with 'the difficulty of persuading our French allies and our German ex-enemies to deem as non-essential things which they in their different ways deem essential'.[9] He advised strongly against fixing a deadline for the withdrawal of control on the grounds that this would encourage the Germans to procrastinate and irritate the French. He also vigorously opposed the resumption of surprise visits in July when General Walch received a tip-off about hidden stores of arms and factories that were still manufacturing war material, as he suspected that, if a search failed to find any incriminating evidence, there would be an explosion of rage throughout Germany.[10] Wauchope's gentlemanly fair play was the object of considerable criticism by the German Left, which after the Pilsudski coup in Poland in May 1926, followed the paramilitary activities of the right-wing associations with increasing anxiety.[11] *Das Tagebuch*, for instance, complained that Wauchope after his appointment in 1924:

> very soon cut adrift from the well tried system of 'surprise' and unannounced controls. He did not consider it fair – as an officer dealing with officers – to surprise his partner. Here he really showed true British sporting spirit. 'Hide what you want, can and would like to, I'll look for it. But I'll give you a chance by announcing beforehand when and where and what I am looking for'.[12]

With the entry of Germany into the League of Nations, Chamberlain was determined to wind up the IAMCC as quickly as

7. Jacobson, *Locarno Diplomacy*, p. 78.
8. 'Notes No. 53 by . . . Wauchope', 19.5.26 (C6113), FO 371/1127 fo. 110.
9. Ibid.
10. 'Notes by . . . Wauchope', 26.7.26 (C8704), FO 371/11289 fo. 243.
11. Ibid., 'Notes No. 53' (C6113).
12. See extract from *Das Tagebuch*, 12.6.26, FO 371/11288 fos 222–3.

possible,[13] and a series of 'semi-official discussions' with the War Office on the best procedure for doing this took place in October.[14] The key lay in avoiding becoming bogged down in what Pawelsz called 'Bagatellen'[15] and to revise the original instructions of June 1925, so that the new test 'as far as H.M.G. are concerned should be not the technical military importance of military demands, but whether the failure of the German Government to conform to the requests of the Commission of Control would constitute a real and immediate danger to British security'.[16] The War Office warned the Foreign Office that for this policy to work, identical instructions would have to be issued by France, Italy and Belgium to their representatives on the IAMCC. Wauchope made the same point in a more light-hearted manner:

> As it is the duty of the reaper to reap, of the Jew to exact his pound of flesh, or of the Treasury official to save, so it is the task of an officer of a commission of control to enforce the demands made by 'la haute Assemblée' in Paris. Consequently, when that high and august body wishes its executive organ in Berlin to adopt an attitude consonant to the year 1926, then it must metaphorically give that organ so well directed a kick as will speed it on its way, if not rejoicingly, at least with understanding.[17]

On 5 November Chamberlain proposed to France, Italy and Belgium that out of the four main issues which still remained unresolved – illegal enlistments, the police, import and export of war materials and the paramilitary associations – compromises could be reached on every point except on the import-export questions. Once this was solved the IAMCC should be withdrawn. To avoid any hiatus before a proper system of League investigations could be devised, the Germans would have to agree to the occasional inspection carried out under the existing League scheme set up to deal with aeronautical questions in the Aeronautical Agreement of 22 May 1926. The French grudgingly agreed to withdrawing the IAMCC as soon as possible, but took a more pessimistic view on the possibility of solving the outstanding points. On 27 November, the Ambassadors' Conference invited the Germans to send Pawelsz

13. FO to WO, 21.9.26 (C9950), FO 371/11290 fo. 123.
14. Minute by Troutbeck, 1.11.26 (C11460), FO 371/11291 fo. 106.
15. Note by Clodius, 7.9.26 (no. illegible), FCO Lib. 9627 H293020.
16. FO to WO, 21.9.26 (C9950).
17. 'Notes No. 71 by . . . Wauchope', 2.11.26 (C11795), FO 371/11292 fo. 219.

and a team of military experts to Paris to begin negotiations on the four outstanding points.[18]

Behind the scenes Wauchope gave Dufour, over breakfast at the German Embassy in London, advice on how the Germans should proceed. He told him that it would be more practical and more helpful 'not to demand that all the disputed points should be negotiated as a whole, but that single points should be picked out, which it could be assumed with reasonable certainty could be solved before the December meeting [of the League Council]'.[19] His advice bore fruit as negotiations between the experts and the Ambassadors' Conference managed to solve all the outstanding points except for the prohibition of the export of war material and a matter which particularly worried the French, the demolition of the eastern fortifications. At Geneva Stresemann at last secured agreement for the termination of the IAMCC on 31 January 1927. Negotiations on the outstanding points were scheduled to continue up to that date after which they would be taken over by the League. As a concession to the French, Stresemann also conceded that each Allied power could appoint a special military expert to their Berlin embassies to liaise with the German authorities on any outstanding disarmament problems after the withdrawal of the IAMCC.[20]

In the six weeks remaining before the withdrawal of the IAMCC the War Office was anxious to negotiate a settlement of the export question as it feared that, once transferred to the League, the issue would cease to be of primary importance, or indeed that British objections might even be overruled.[21] Wauchope himself was adamant that 'the date when Germany would feel herself capable of waging war will be brought very much nearer', if she were permitted to produce war material for export.[22] Nevertheless in the complex negotiations in early January 1927 Wauchope was ready to compromise as he was aware that both British and French legal experts were sceptical as to whether the Allied case would stand up to arbitration by the League and that 'instead of gaining half, we might gain nothing'.[23] An acceptable compromise was finally

18. For a concise summary of events from 5 to 27.11.26 see 'Memorandum regarding the Present Position of German Disarmament', 29.11.26 (C12572), FO 371/11293 fo. 95.
19. Dufour to AA, 24.11.26 (AA. II.F. 3516), FCO Lib. 9627 H293133.
20. Jacobson, *Locarno Diplomacy*, pp. 95–7.
21. 'Opinion de l'état-Major Britannique sur l'accord de Genève du 12 Décembre an sujet du désarmement de l'Allemagne', Londres le 22.12.26, no. 1057, Vincennes 7N3577-3.
22. 'Notes No. 78 by . . . Wauchope', 22.12.26 (C13665), FO 371/11296 fo. 241.
23. 'Notes No. 81 . . .', 15.1.27 (C594), FO 371/12116 fos 147–8.

reached on 22 January much to the relief of the Foreign Office, where Wauchope was the hero of the hour.[24]

The question of the eastern fortifications was solved in negotiations at Paris where it was agreed at the Conference of Ambassadors on 1 February that the Germans would choose seventeen gun shelters to destroy, and the Allies five.[25] The last task facing Wauchope was to ensure that the final report on the whole history of the IAMCC in Germany did not open old wounds and overtly criticize either the Ambassadors' Conference or the Allied Committee of Versailles for conceding too much to the Germans. The Foreign Office wanted it to be 'entirely and solely a statement of facts',[26] and Wauchope managed so to influence its tone that it resembled 'an official war history, that relates events but assigns neither praise nor blame to anyone'.[27]

The remaining tasks of verification were carried out by the experts attached now to the ex-Allied embassies. Despite suggestions emanating from Wickham Steed, the former editor of *The Times*, that Morgan should become the British expert, the post was filled by Colonel Gosset, Wauchope's former second-in-command.[28] The experts rapidly became immersed in a wrangle with the German government over the legality of the proposed visits to confirm the destruction of the East Prussian fortifications; initially the Germans were adamant that such measures, smacking of control, should never be permitted.[29] The deadlock was only broken at Geneva when Stresemann realized that a cut in the number of Rhineland troops would be more likely if the Germans made concessions over disarmament. Consequently he offered to invite a couple of Allied experts to view the demolition work in Königsberg, Cüstrin and Glogau.[30] In the autumn of 1927 Gosset was allowed to visit the police barracks in Breslau, whilst his French colleague was pointedly not invited. How effective Gosset's inspection was remains open to debate as he later recorded, 'we sat

24. DBFP Ser. 1A, vol. 2 (no. 420), pp. 760–76; Minute by Sargent, 24.1.27 (C656), FO 371/12117 fos 1–2.
25. DBFP Ser. 1A, vol. 2 (no. 438), pp. 800–2.
26. Sargent to Undersecretary of State, WO, 30.12.26 (C13445), FO 371/11296 fo. 73.
27. 'Notes No. 79 by . . . Wauchope', 9.1.27 (C342), FO 371/12115 fos 162–3; for the eventual report see 'Rapport Final de la Commission Militaire interalliée de Contrôle en Allemagne', WO 155/63.
28. Wauchope to McGrath, 20.12.26 (C13445), FO 371/11296 fos 69–70.
29. Note by Schubert, 24.3.27 (AA II.F. 1016), FCO Lib. 9622 H291564–6; ibid., 31.3.27 (zu II, I 1074), H291571–72.
30. DBFP Ser. 1A, vol. 3 (no. 234), pp. 359–63.

down to an enormous lunch given by the Police President . . . After that I was glad to get into the train about 3.15 and do a bit of quiet thinking.'[31] By the end of the year in the opinion of one Foreign Office official the experts had ceased to be an inflammatory issue and should be left to vegetate a while.[32]

The experts remained in Berlin until March 1930 as ghostly reminders of the old IAMCC. Gosset was kept there more as a concession to the French than as a specific act of policy, but in January 1928 the War Office wanted to withdraw him as it was convinced that the experts 'were doing no good of any sort'.[33] They could make visits only on sufferance of the German government and their very presence tended to create 'alarms and excursions'[34] in the German press. By the time the Hague Conference met, British officials openly conceded that the 'integral fulfilment by Germany of the disarmament clauses of the Treaty of Versailles [was] not today a practical possibility'.[35] Gosset himself, like his predecessors ten years earlier, felt that the only safeguard against a German military renaissance was 'to maintain in power a government in Germany depending in the main on the republican parties'.[36] After a compromise had been reached on the perennial questions of paramilitary associations and the training of General Staff officers in January 1930, the experts were finally withdrawn three months later.[37]

31. Gosset to McGrath, 23.11.27 (C9689), FO 371/12124 fo. 195.

32. Lindsay to FO, 30.11.27 (C9712), FO 371/12124 fo. 201.

33. Minute by Perowne, 12.1.28 (C409), FO 371/12895 fo. 184.

34. Memorandum by Perowne, 18.4.28 (C3031), FO 371/12896 fos 54–9.

35. Nicolson to Henderson, 9.9.29 (C6267), FO 371/13622 fo. 195.

36. Ibid., Gosset, 'Notes on the Situation as regards German Disarmament', 10.8.29 (enclosure in C6267), fo. 195.

37. 'Agreement for the Withdrawal from Berlin of the ex-Allied Military Experts' (C611), FO 371/14366 fos 216–17.

PART VII

The Final Phase, 1928–1930

Introduction

The Dawes Plan, Locarno and the termination of control all made the continuation of the occupation increasingly anachronistic. By 1928 the growing consensus amongst the international banking community that the Dawes Plan would have to be revised after the American presidential election coincided with a determined initiative by the new Müller government to secure a final evacuation. Briand, with tacit backing from Chamberlain, was determined to link reparations and provisions for guaranteeing the demilitarization of the Rhineland with evacuation. Consequently, as a compromise it was agreed at Geneva in September 1928 that two parallel but separate sets of negotiations on reparation and evacuation would take place. By the time the British general election took place in May 1929 the occupation was obviously dying, but the new Labour government, through a unilateral decision to recall the Rhine Army by Christmas 1929, hastened its end.

19

The 'Dying Occupation'

The Beleaguered Rhine Army, January 1928–July 1929

On 20 February 1928 Lord Erroll (Kilmarnock) died suddenly in the night from a heart attack.[1] Although the Quai d'Orsay was resigned to Ryan replacing him, the Foreign Office decided to move William Seeds from Albania to Coblenz on the strength of his previous experience as Consul in Munich.[2] The French Ambassador in London interpreted this, predictably, as a sure indication of the secondary importance of the High Commission in the eyes of the Foreign Office.[3]

Seeds, an amusing if somewhat supercilious man who delighted in writing in dismissive terms not only about the Germans but also his French colleagues and Ducane's successor, General Thwaites, inherited a 'dying occupation'.[4] Tirard was more often in Paris than in Coblenz, only returning for formal meetings of the High Commission.[5] At home British participation was subject to hostile scrutiny in both Parliament and the press. In March 1928, for instance, in a debate on the army estimates,[6] Kenworthy launched into a detailed and damaging attack on the Rhine Army which he described as 'the lost legion'. He tellingly asked: 'what on earth is the use of an army of two weak brigades in the middle of a nation of 60,000,000 people, a nation which is allowed, under the Peace Treaty, 100,000 troops and which has millions of trained men of good military value . . .?' He went on to argue that it was an

---

1. 'Annual Report for the Year 1928' (C3836), p. 3, FO 371/14375 fo. 172. Kilmarnock had succeeded to the Erroll title in 1927.
2. MAE to Tirard, 28.2.28 (nos 146–147), MAE Rive Gauche 203 fo. 127.
3. Ibid., French Ambassador to MAE, 26.3.28 (no. 187), fo. 142.
4. Seeds to Cushendun, 22.9.28 (C7249), p. 2, FO 371/12904 fos 123–6.
5. 'I had this morning a conversation on the subject of the evacuation of the Rhineland with M. Tirard, who is paying one of his rare visits to Coblenz': Ryan to Cushendun, 25.8.28 (C6499), FO 371/12903 fo. 80.
6. Extract from House of Commons Debates, 20.3.28 (C2298), FO 371/12909 fos 187–9.

expensive anachronism, quoting as evidence that the annual cost of the headquarters staff in Wiesbaden was £31,750, whereas the staff of the far larger Northern Command in Britain cost a mere £23,600. Surprisingly, perhaps, as a Germanophil internationalist, he even criticized the intermarriage occurring between British troops and German girls, arguing that 'he would rather see these young soldiers in England . . . marrying English girls'. Chamberlain was disturbed by Kenworthy's financial statistics and testily minuted that 'if true, surely a scandal. Let us ask the Metropolitan Police to do the job or the West African Frontier Force.'[7] Research by the Foreign Office showed that the cost of the High Commission was even higher, although it was met from a prior charge out of the Dawes annuities. Nevertheless it seemed to one official 'ridiculously swollen and absurdly overpaid; the volume of work at Coblenz is now small and there can be practically no use for legal advisers, or financial, technical and administrative advisers'.[8]

The Foreign Office was, of course, right. The work of both the military and civil authorities in the occupied Rhineland had declined dramatically since 1926. For the average Rhinelander, as the German delegation conceded at the international Socialist meeting in Luxemburg, the occupation was 'barely noticeable'.[9] According to the Annual Report of 1928, the Rhinelander

> could travel freely by rail or air in and out of the occupied territories; he could hoist his national flag and sing his *Deutschland über alles* when and where he pleased so long as he did not do so in a provocative manner: he could if he liked persist in flying the old *schwarz-weiss-rot* colours, for the occupying authorities took the view that such an act was a purely German affair so long as it did not cause a riot.[10]

In practice, within the British Zone liberty was only curtailed through a degree of censorship, involving the banning of films and the occasional newspaper article or a potentially inflammatory nationalist meeting. Householders, however, were still liable to have troops billeted upon them, although they were given a fair rent.[11] The occupation bore slightly more heavily on the local German officials, who continued to have to notify the military authorities of police promotions and appointments, the dates and

7. Minute by Chamberlain, 21.3.28 (C2478), FO 371/12909 fo. 193.
8. Minute by Perowne, 23.3.28 (C2478), ibid. fos 194–7.
9. 'Report', 1928, p. 13.
10. Ibid., p. 13.
11. Ibid., p. 13.

venues of political rallies and aviation meetings, and so forth.[12]

Overall the atmosphere in the occupied territory was peaceful, but inevitably the very existence of the occupation ensured that 'the grains of sand'[13] that Chamberlain had so bitterly complained about in 1926 still continued to act as an irritant in Anglo–German and Franco–German relations. Significantly in the elections of May 1928 the Nazi vote rose to 5.6 per cent in the Palatinate, and the *Vossische Zeitung* pointedly observed that the 'extreme wave, which has subsided in Bavaria whence it started, is now rising on the further bank of the Rhine', and drew the conclusion that 'the sooner the occupation comes to an end, the sooner will the campaign of the ultra-Nationalists die of inanition'.[14] Each new incident involving a clash between the Allied authorities and the Germans threatened to exacerbate the situation. In May, for example, Guillaumat vetoed the construction of a new bridge at Zeltingen on the Mosel on the grounds that it was a breach of Article 43 of the Treaty and could eventually facilitate the mobilization of German forces. He lifted his ban in July under pressure from Seeds, but only after the nationalists had been given a superb propaganda opportunity. Plans for enlarging the station at Russelheim and of improving the connection with Bischofsheim were banned for similar reasons until permission was granted in September. To the *Manchester Guardian* these incidents were 'food for the Junkers'.[15]

As the occupation became harder to justify in the post-Locarno climate, the more anachronistic and offensive to German – and much of British – public opinion did the periodic displays of ex-Allied military power become. Even the routine annual manoeuvres of the Rhine Army threatened to create fresh misunderstandings between London and Berlin. The participation of the 8th Hussars in the French summer manoeuvres of 1928 was interpreted by the German press to be tangible evidence of the new Franco–British *Entente*, and according to Harold Nicolson threatened to 'flare up into a real fuss'.[16] He had been told in no uncertain terms by an official in the Auswärtiges Amt that 'such manoeuvres at the present moment . . . are for anybody with a normal sensitivity an

---

12. See 'Erläuterung zur Aufzeichnung über die deutschen Rheinlandforderungen', August 1928, FCO Lib. 3058 D607149-70.
13. Chamberlain to D'Abernon, 19.5.26 (C5890), FO 371/11307 fo. 111; see also ch. 16 above.
14. DBFP Ser. 1A, vol. 5 (no. 64), p. 126.
15. 'Report', 1928, p. 4; *Manchester Guardian*, 3.7.28.
16. H. Nicolson to 'Moley' (Sargent), 15.8.28 (C6306), FO 371/12902 fo. 229.

outrage [*Ungeheuerlichkeit*]'.[17] Both Thwaites and Ryan were irritated by the German attitude as British military cooperation had been a regular feature of manoeuvres since 1926. Ryan dismissed the German protest as part of the general campaign against the High Commission and 'a lever to remove the occupation'.[18] A more emotive crisis blew up on Armistice Day, which in 1928 fell on a Sunday. Thwaites arranged for four churches in Wiesbaden to be made available on the Sunday morning and for the striking of the clock on the Ringkirche to be stilled at eleven o'clock. These arrangements were accepted by the Germans, but then on 17 November, after strong complaints from the Nationalists in the Reichstag, Langwerth was instructed by the Auswärtiges Amt to make a formal complaint about the ostentatious British celebration of Armistice Day.[19] Stresemann referred to the incident in the Reichstag, where he bitterly remarked that 'the progress of pacification and friendly relations was not assisted by the parades of foreign troops in the occupied territory to make it plain to the German people that they were vanquished in the Great War'.[20]

By the spring of 1929 it was clear that a British evacuation of the Rhineland was not far off. In anticipation of this, the War Office had already sent out experts to discuss technical details with Thwaites, and was actively pushing for the recall of the British contingent, as it now had sufficient barrack accomodation on British soil available.[21] Seeds himself was convinced that Britain would withdraw by the end of the year, and in private talks with his colleagues kept 'harping in an airy fashion on [his] almost feminine intuition'[22] which led him to this conclusion. Politically he believed that it was a mistake to evacuate the Rhineland prematurely as it distracted the Germans from opening up such new questions as the rectification of the eastern frontiers or the return of colonies, but as he wrote to Orme Sargent, 'your 'umble [*sic*] is prepared to witness at any time without undue regret, the great historical pageant of Great Britain marching out of the Rhineland'.[23]

This 'pageant' moved inexorably nearer when the Labour Party

17. 'Aufzeichnung' by O.W. Wachendorf, 16.8.28 (no. 1890), FCO Lib. 4502 E119312-13.
18. Ryan to Chamberlain, 15.8.28 (C6308), FO 371/12902 fos 238–9.
19. 'Report', 1928, pp. 9–10.
20. Ibid., p. 10.
21. Minute by Perowne, 6.3.29 (C1866), FO 371/13617 fos 15–19.
22. Seeds to Sargent, 29.4.29 (C3115), ibid. fos 96–8.
23. Ibid.

won power in June 1929. The first indication of the change of mood in London was when Henderson, the new Foreign Secretary, attempted unsuccessfully to veto plans for the annual early autumn manoeuvres on the grounds that they were politically highly undesirable 'at the time when public opinion expects us to be making arrangements for withdrawing our forces'.[24] The Foreign Office was furious when the War Office refused to halt the manoeuvres for the technical reason that they were 'essential unit and brigade exercises' rather than full-blown manoeuvres.[25] By July plans for evacuation were so far advanced that Seeds was already thinking about the future of the archives of the British departments.[26]

The Re-emergence of the Evacuation Question

It was not until the end of January 1928 that a call by Parker Gilbert, the Agent General for Reparation Payments, for a final reparation settlement, and a scheme floated by Paul-Boncour, the French Socialist politician, for the creation of an international body to guarantee the demilitarization of the Rhineland, enabled Stresemann once again to demand the end of the Rhineland occupation. Briand, irritated that Stresemann had reopened the issue before the German elections, nevertheless announced in a speech to the Senate that once these elections were out of the way, negotiations could be opened, provided that the Germans were ready to offer something in exchange.[27] The British Conservative government was happy to leave the initiative to Briand, and as it made clear in the Commons, did not contemplate a premature unilateral withdrawal from the Rhineland.[28] As a result of the German election campaign in May and the priority given to negotiations for the formation of the Great Coalition under Müller, the Rhineland question was not formally raised until early July 1928, when Müller in his first speech to the new Reichstag emphasized the need for a reparations settlement and evacuation of the Rhine.[29] The British reaction was cautious and sceptical. Chamberlain stressed to Sthamer the need for proceeding step by step to a solution,[30] while privately the Foreign

24. Henderson to Shaw, 21.6.29 (C4437), FO 371/13617 fos 219–20.
25. Sargent to Nicolson, 12.7.29 (C5179), FO 371/13618 fos 106–8.
26. Seeds to Sargent, 16.7.29 (C5563), FO 371/13618 fos 140–1.
27. Jacobson, *Locarno Diplomacy*, pp. 143–9.
28. See Locker Lampson's reply to Buxton's question in the Commons (C1067), FO 371/12902 fo. 40.
29. DBFP Ser. 1A, vol. 5 (no. 80), pp. 159–61.
30. Sthamer to AA, 4.7.28 (no. 1307), FCO Lib. 4502 E119104-106.

Office was pessimistic about the prospect of an agreement as Briand's insistence on a *quid pro quo* could not be reconciled with Germany's determination to make no further concessions.[31]

To the Germans Britain had ceased to be 'the honest broker'. They suspected that her 'cold war' against Moscow influenced her policy in the Rhineland, as a premature evacuation would inevitably have repercussions on the security of Poland, which for Britain was now an important front-line state against Soviet Russia. Chamberlain's reply to a question by a Labour MP in the Commons on the prospects for evacuation electrified the Germans when, after the well-rehearsed answer that 'earlier evacuation can only be the result of an arrangement between the occupying powers . . . and the German Government', he added, 'and other powers besides occupying powers must be consulted'.[32] The Anglo–French disarmament compromise announced at the end of July also fuelled German suspicions of Britain, because in exchange for a French acceptance of an increase in British naval tonnage, the British agreed tacitly on the League's Preparatory Commission on Disarmament to acquiesce in the French refusal to include trained reserves, which the French system of conscription produced in abundance, among the numbers of effectives to be permitted under the land disarmament clauses of the draft convention.[33] Inevitably the new Anglo–French *détente* was believed in Germany to be the reason behind the deadlock on the evacuation of the Rhine. Sthamer reported in August that 'the Foreign Office and Quai d'Orsay are closer than at any other time . . . No step is undertaken without previous agreement or at least contact between both governments.'[34]

Despite Stresemann's illness, the new German government was determined to demand evacuation at the League Council in September. Müller was ready to act on an incisive *Denkschrift* drawn up by Schubert on 20 July 1928, advising that as Germany had fulfilled every demand of the Treaty of Versailles, only an unconditional Allied evacuation of the Rhineland could now pacify Europe.[35] Bilateral discussions were held between the French and Germans in Paris in August, but so little progress was made that Stresemann

31. Minute by Huxley, 10.7.28 (C5325), FO 371/12902 fo. 134.
32. Reply in FO 371/12902 fo. 145; see also Hoesch to AA, 20.7.28 (no. 785), FCO Lib. 4502 E119141, and article in *Kölnische Zeitung* of 20.7.28 (trans.), FO 371/12902 fos 150–2.
33. Northedge, *The Troubled Giant*, pp. 335–6.
34. Sthamer to AA, 20.8.28 (no. 541), FCO Lib. 4502 E119321-24.
35. Jacobson, *Locarno Diplomacy*, pp. 175–83.

privately advised that it might be wiser to accept 'a minor success in lieu of a major victory',[36] and aim more modestly at the evacuation of the second zone only. Müller, however, was not to be deterred, and in Geneva raised the whole question. Only when it became clear that Briand insisted on linking evacuation with reparations and security did Müller fall back on a compromise already foreseen by Schubert, and propose two separate but parallel negotiations on evacuation and reparation. On Briand's insistence he included a third set of negotiations, on the establishment of a Rhineland Commission of Verification and Conciliation, provided that it would be withdrawn in 1935. Briand accepted this compromise and in the final communiqué of the Conference it was announced that the three parallel sets of negotiations would begin in the reasonably near future.[37]

The reaction in Britain to this was mixed. The Liberal and Labour parties argued that British troops should be pulled out immediately.[38] The Treasury was at first hostile to the negotiations of a new reparation settlement as it believed that it would 'impoverish Germany without enriching us'.[39] Churchill, the Chancellor of the Exchequer, had also wanted to delay negotiations until after the American presidential elections and retain a British occupation on the Rhine as some guarantee for extracting concessions from the Germans on reparations.[40] The Foreign Office, while anxious to avoid linking evacuation and reparations in principle, nevertheless stressed 'the practical connection between the two questions'.[41] It was thus aghast when Churchill inadvertently, in reply to a supplementary question from Hore-Belisha as to whether the reparation settlement was bound up with the question of the evacuation of the Rhine territory, replied: 'No. That is an entirely separate matter, and it is also a desirable object.'[42] Churchill's answer encouraged the campaign both in Germany and amongst the British Left for unilateral evacuation. In a debate on 19 November, Lloyd George seized upon it and virtually accused the government of violating Article 431 of the Versailles Treaty. Chamberlain defended himself clumsily by arguing accurately but tactlessly that

---

36. Ibid., p. 195.
37. Ibid., pp. 195–201; 'Summary of meetings at Geneva to discuss Evacuation of the Rhineland, and questions related thereto, Sept. 11th–16th 1928' (C7160), FO 371/12904 fos 83–91.
38. See, for example, *Manchester Guardian*, 24.9.28.
39. Leith Ross quoted in Jacobson, *Locarno Diplomacy*, p. 203.
40. DBFP Ser. 1A, vol. 5 (nos 155 and 159), pp. 311–12, 324–5.
41. Foreign Office Minute, 5.12.28 (C9105), FO 371/12905 fos 223–9.
42. Ibid.

Germany had in fact not discharged her obligations under the Treaty.[43] This intensified opposition to the government's foreign policy, and on the Left unconditional evacuation became 'a sort of Ark of the Covenant'.[44]

An experts committee was selected in January 1929 and began its work on drawing up recommendations for a revision of the Dawes Plan in February under the chairmanship of the American, Owen Young.[45] Despite constant pressure from the Parliamentary opposition right up to the British general election in May, Chamberlain was unwilling to force the pace on evacuation. The attitude of the Foreign Office was summed up by Tyrell in a letter to Sargent at the Paris Embassy in which he argued that 'precipitate and independent action by the British government in the matter of withdrawal would, far from inducing the French to evacuate, strengthen them in their resolve to remain'.[46]

It is difficult to judge whether Chamberlain's foreign policy actually cost the Conservatives the election. Labour and the Liberals campaigned resolutely for an immediate and unconditional evacuation. The apparent revival of the pre-war *Entente* and secret diplomacy symbolized by the anachronistic occupation of the Rhineland did not assist the Conservatives. In the opinion of *The Observer*, 'beyond all doubt the Army on the Rhine cost the Government votes . . .'.[47]

43. Ibid.
44. FO Minute by J.V. Perowne, 7.12.28 (C9141), FO 371/12906 fos 22–3.
45. Jacobson, *Locarno Diplomacy*, p. 239.
46. Tyrell to Sargent, 15.5.29 (C3502), FO 371/13617 fos 131–2.
47. *The Observer*, 30.6.29.

-20-

The End of the Occupation

The Hague Conference and the Decision to Withdraw the Rhine Army

When the Labour Party won the General Election of 31 May 1929, there was a marked change in British policy. Henderson, the new Foreign Secretary, went out of his way to reassure Sthamer about the government's intentions to evacuate the Rhineland and promised to make himself available whenever he wished to speak to him.[1] The Cabinet's Rhineland policy was announced in the speech from the Throne, when the Parliament met on 2 July. It was unequivocally stated that Britain desired to evacuate the Rhineland, but a slightly ambiguous note was struck when it was stressed that it was hoped that this would be in conjunction with the French and Belgians.[2] A week later Henderson was more specific. Although he parried a question from Wedgwood about whether the French would exploit 'our reluctance to act without France as a weapon to enforce such modifications of the Young scheme as may suit the French exchequer', and conceded that evacuation was 'to some extent' bound up with the settlement of the Young Report, he assured Hore-Belisha that ultimately evacuation did not depend on a reparation settlement.[3] On 24 July the Cabinet decided to withdraw the British Rhine Army unilaterally, even if there was no agreement with the French at the coming conference.[4] Henderson was determined to have the troops home by Christmas.

The Committee of Experts completed their report on 6 June. After a refusal by the French to meet in London, the neutral Hague was agreed upon as a venue for the Conference to consider the report's recommendations and the possible measures for

1. Sthamer to AA, 9.7.29 (no. 406), FCO Lib. 2368 D 492811–13.
2. Jacobson, *Locarno Diplomacy*, p. 283.
3. Sthamer to AA, 9.7.29 (no. 471), FCO Lib. 3058 D607542–44.
4. Jacobson, *Locarno Diplomacy*, p. 284.

implementing them.[5] There appeared initially to be every chance that Britain and France would not agree on the share of reparations to be allotted to them. Snowden, the Chancellor of the Exchequer, was determined to seek a revision of the report's proposals by demanding compensation for the £200 million war debt payments the British Treasury had already made to the Americans; he presented his demands within six hours of the commencement of the conference and caused a crisis which was not resolved until 28 August.[6] Inevitably this had repercussions on the parallel negotiations on evacuation. Briand was prepared to begin evacuation of the second zone on 15 September, but he refused to agree to a final evacuation of the third zone until the financial settlement was completed. By threatening not to sign the reparation agreement, Stresemann managed to force Briand into conceding October 1930 as a deadline for evacuation, but this still did not break the deadlock as the former insisted on 1 April 1930. Briand was forced to give up his plans for a Commission of Verification under joint pressure from both Henderson and Stresemann, when on 21 August he reluctantly agreed to refer disputes over the demilitarized zone to the Conciliation Commission provided for in Article 3 of the Locarno Treaty of Mutual Guarantee. Anglo–French agreement on the division of reparations had to wait until the dramatic meeting at midnight on 27 August when Snowden finally agreed to compromise and accept only 75 per cent of his original demands. Even then Stresemann attempted to withhold his agreement to the reparation clauses, until Briand had conceded 1 April 1930 as the final evacuation date, but Briand stubbornly clung to a fresh compromise date of 30 June, which Stresemann grudgingly accepted at 2 a.m. on 29 August. On the following day notes were exchanged providing for the complete evacuation of the Rhineland by 30 June 1930.[7]

The War Office then immediately ordered General Thwaites to complete the evacuation of the Wiesbaden Zone by early December.[8] Seeds was anxious to leave with the troops as he feared that he would otherwise be seen by the Germans as a French puppet.[9] This was initially also the view of Henderson,[10] but the French managed to convince him of the desirability of keeping Seeds in Coblenz in order to maintain the inter-Allied character of the occupation. As

5. DBFP Ser. 1A, vol. 6 (nos 250–261), pp. 442–3, 449–50.
6. Jacobson, *Locarno Diplomacy*, pp. 284 and 309.
7. Ibid., pp. 309–43.
8. WO to GOC, 30.8.29 (C6860), FO 371/13619 fo. 221.
9. Seeds to Sargent, 16.8.29 (C6453), ibid., fos 82–4.
10. Howard Smith to Sargent, 21.8.29 (C6557), ibid., fos 98–9.

the Belgians had already decided to keep their Commissioner, the British Delegation advised 'giving into Briand . . . if he insists, as public opinion in England will not bother about the High Commission. What they are interested in is the withdrawal of the troops.'[11] In London, Sargent strongly supported this line, as it minimized the adverse effect on Anglo–French relations of the unilateral British military withdrawal.[12] Thus on 24 August Henderson agreed that Seeds should remain 'without any staff or troops at Coblenz'.[13]

The Evacuation, September 1929–June 1930

The contrast between the evacuation of the Rhine Army in 1929 with the advance of the Second Army in 1918 into Cologne could not have been more marked. In 1918 the Second Army was part of a victorious force enforcing the Armistice. Its advance was followed at home with interest and pride. In 1929 its successor, the Rhine Army, was an embarrassment, and the final stages of its evacuation in December bordered on the farcical.

The evacuations began on 14 September and continued by rail and barge over the next three months.[14] The administrative measures attendant on the evacuation of the second zone were quickly agreed upon. The boundaries of the third zone, to which the High Commission would move from Coblenz, were fixed by 18 September and an amnesty signed on 5 October.[15] The Foreign Office modified its decision of 24 August and allowed Seeds two assistants, a typist and a messenger. The rest of his staff were given one month's notice.[16] The British military evacuation went without a hitch, although behind the scenes there was considerable disagreement between the Foreign Office and Thwaites over the planning of the farewell ceremony. The Foreign Office was anxious to avoid holding a joint ceremony with the French in which the Union Jack would be hauled down and the tricolour raised at the same time, as

11. Ibid.
12. Sargent to Howard Smith, 22.8.29 (C6557), ibid., fos 103–7.
13. Phipps to Sargent, 25.8.29 (C6559), ibid., fo. 111.
14. WO to GOC Rhine Army, 30.8.29 (C6860), FO 371/13619 fo. 221; Thwaites, pp. 23–4, WO 106/463. The small force in the Saar was withdrawn in September. Edmonds, *The Occupation*, pp. 315–16.
15. 'Annual Report for 1929 and 1930 on the Inter-Allied Rhineland High Commission' (C5053), p. 15, FO 371/14375 fo. 178.
16. Seeds to Sargent, 30.8.29 (C6795), FO 371/13619 fos 200–3.

it feared that this would hurt German susceptibilities.[17] In the end Seeds, who was uneasy at being 'rude to the French',[18] devised an innocuous farewell ceremony whereby the High Commission and the French generals would watch the proceedings out of the windows of the British GHQ, while 'away round the corner, and completely out of sight' a French cavalry squadron would wait to escort Thwaites' car to the station.[19] According to Seeds Thwaites also made considerable difficulties about the move of the High Commission's offices to Wiesbaden as he felt 'himself no longer cock of the walk and seems to imagine that he would lose face'.[20] Tirard, however, tactfully promised to put the French troops needed to guard the High Commission nominally under Thwaites' command and thereby managed to create a 'sunlight atmosphere'.[21] However prickly Thwaites might have seemed to Seeds and the Foreign Office, his behaviour to the Germans was faultlessly correct. In his Armistice Day address to the troops, he stressed the significance of the evacuation for European peace[22] and won considerable local popularity by releasing the requisitioned playing fields in early December in time for Sarasani's travelling circus. The last week of the occupation was 'employed by the C. in C. and staff eating their way out of Wiesbaden through a wall of food at numbers of banquets given in their honour'.[23]

On 12 December the final contingent of British troops left Wiesbaden. Apart from Seeds and a skeleton staff, a small number of ex-soldiers who had married Germans stayed behind, and one unfortunate military policeman lay terminally ill in hospital.[24] Seeds commented that 'the occasion indeed was not calculated to stir the pride of a sensitive British onlooker. In the eyes of the Frenchmen he read resentment at what seemed desertion at the eleventh hour; in the eyes of the Germans inability to fathom our motives and a determination to show no gratitude for something of little worth.'[25] Nothing demonstrated more accurately that the Rhine Army was indeed an anachronism than the low-key reception given to Thwaites and his troops when they arrived at Victoria

17. Lindsay to Seeds, 25.9.29 (C8235), FO 371/13620 fo. 143.
18. Seeds to Lindsay, 10.10.29 (C8236), FO 371/13620 fos 148–50.
19. Seeds to Lindsay, 26.11.29 (C9264), FO 371/13621 fos 17–19.
20. Seeds to Lindsay, 10.10.29 (C8236), FO 371/13620 fos 148–50.
21. Seeds to Lindsay, 15.10.29 (C8236), FO 371/13620 fo. 151.
22. 'Armistice Day Address, 1929', p. 3, Thwaites Collection vol. 5, IWM Library.
23. Thwaites, pp. 26–7, WO 106/463.
24. Thwaites to Seeds, 1.11.29 (S/45765), FO 371/13620 fos 189–90; 'Report', 1929, p. 20.
25. Seeds to Henderson, 13.12.29 (C9678), FO 371/13621 fo. 55.

Station in London. Bitterly Thwaites later observed: 'It seemed a suitable end to what may be said to have been a historical event, namely the completion of evacuation of the Rhineland by British troops after eleven years of occupation, that the G.O.C. in C. was obliged to drive to his private residence in London in a taxi-cab . . .'.[26] Unknown to Thwaites the insult was compounded by the Foreign Office's determination not to lavish any undue praise on him as 'he had been rather pernickety in his dealings with the High Commission'.[27] He was therefore sent a suitably vague letter congratulating him on the tact and efficiency of the Rhine Army![28]

Christmas and the New Year passed quietly in Wiesbaden. At the end of January Seeds was moved on to Rio de Janeiro and his political officer, Herbertson, took over the post of High Commissioner until June. Even at this late date Tirard lamented that Britain had not appointed 'une personalité de rang plus élevé'.[29] By April, with the final evacuation under three months away, serious doubts were beginning to surface in London whether the French would in fact evacuate punctually. The Young Plan had still not been ratified by the German government, while neither had the question of the future police strength in the third zone been agreed upon nor the destruction of various zeppelin sheds and other aeronautical installations been carried out.[30] At the end of April Henderson was beginning to contemplate his options should the French decide to remain in Wiesbaden. In the Foreign Office E.H. Carr pointed out that 'there will be something like an explosion in Germany and the situation, particularly with a government in power which is maintained by nationalist votes and contains nationalist ministers, may become distinctly unpleasant'. He argued strongly that Britain had no option but to withdraw Herbertson punctually on 30 June.[31] However, despite pessimistic hints from Tirard and Guillaumat that preparations for withdrawal had hardly started, the essential preconditions for evacuation were fulfilled when on 12 May all the ratifications of the Young Plan by the national parliaments were finally deposited in Paris. On 19 May Tardieu, the French Prime Minister, informed the German

26. Thwaites, p. 30, WO 106/463.
27. Minute by Sargent, 14.12.29, FO 371/1361 fo. 50.
28. FO to Thwaites, 27.12.29 (C9546), IWM Thwaites Collection vol. 5.
29. Tirard to MAE, 10.12.29 (Tel. no. 52), MAE Rive Gauche 203 fo. 261.
30. 'Report', 1929–30, p. 22.
31. 'Date of Evacuation of the Rhineland', 25.4.30 (C3211), FO 371/14354 fos 243–6; see also Herbertson to Henderson, 5.5.30 (C3536), FO 371/14355 fos 7–8.

Ambassador that orders had been given to begin evacuation.[32] By the end of May Herbertson had sorted out the archives and given notice to his staff.[33] The Commission left punctually at 9.30 a.m. on 30 June. Herbertson, after sending the remaining confidential documents to the Consulate in Cologne and the combination safe to the Consulate at Antwerp, departed inconspicuously for London,[34] bringing to an end eleven and a half years of British occupation of the Rhineland.

32. 'Report', 1929–30, p. 23.
33. Herbertson to Sargent, 31.5.30 (C4430), FO 371/14355 fo. 28.
34. Herbertson to Henderson, 20.6.30 (C5013), FO 371/14355 fos 42–3.

Conclusion

Between December 1918 and June 1930, British participation in the Allied occupation of key regions of Germany evolved through five distinct phases.

1. In December 1918 the Cologne Zone was occupied by twelve divisions of first-class fighting troops and eighteen squadrons of the RAF for what was assumed in London and at Haig's Head-quarters to be a short interim period until the signature of the peace. The military government hastily set up under General Fergusson was charged with the ultimate responsibility for the welfare of a major city and over a million and a quarter Germans at a time when Germany was teetering on the verge of revolution. By March 1919 the Second and Fourth Armies had melted away and were replaced by inexperienced 'young soldier' battalions. From that point on Britain ceased to be a great military power on the Continent and had to revert to her traditional policy of holding the balance of power in order to assert her interests.

2. The second phase began in January 1920 with the ratification of the Treaty of Versailles and ended in the Ruhr occupation of January 1923. The British were trapped into participating in the various Allied occupying forces in Germany by the very success of Lloyd George's efforts to moderate the terms of the Treaty. Not only was there to be a British element in the Rhineland, but British troops and administrators were sent to the plebiscite areas and Danzig. In the three years between January 1920 and December 1922 Britain's interpretation of how the Treaty should be executed was bitterly challenged by France, and her bluff was almost called. Up to the autumn of 1920 Britain could exploit her near-monopoly of coal to force her interpretation of the Treaty on Paris. She had little difficulty in blocking last-minute attempts by the French to reinterpret the Treaty clauses on Marienwerder and Schleswig or in forcing Millerand to evacuate Darmstadt, Frankfurt, Hanau and Homburg in May 1920, while she herself was able to extract considerable concessions for Danzig, which significantly modified Article 104.

When, however, the bottom dropped out of the British coal export trade in the winter of 1920–1, British leverage on France was decisively weakened. In Upper Silesia she signally failed to secure a pro-German interpretation of the plebiscite results, and in March 1920 had reluctantly to consent to a series of sanctions in the Rhineland, which appeared to strengthen the prospects of success there for French-inspired separatism. The year 1921, even more than 1923, was the *annus terribilis* for British officials in Germany. They were left in the Rhineland and Upper Silesia without adequate force to safeguard British interests. There were moments, such as during the initial stages of the implementation of the economic sanctions in the Rhineland, the Korfanty revolt in May 1921 or the Loucheur–Rathenau discussions at Wiesbaden, when Britain's bluff appeared to be called and her influence marginalized. While the underlying balance of power in Europe was more favourable to Britain than in 1945, nevertheless the limits of British power were painfully clear to those entrusted with its defence in the Rhineland and Upper Silesia. There would have been few British officials in Berlin, Oppeln, Cologne or Coblenz who would not have agreed with Kettenacker's observation that 'the endeavour to exert influence without an adequate basis of power is always a risky undertaking'.[1] With the collapse of Wirth's fulfilment policy at the end of 1921, Lloyd George was temporarily able to reassert his influence over Paris, but the fall of Briand in January 1922 and the formation of the Poincaré administration ensured that Paris would continue to follow in 1922 a line independent of London.

3. The third phase covered the acute stage of the Ruhr crisis between January 1923 and February 1924. In retrospect it is perhaps possible to argue, like Maier, that the occupation 'changed little that would not have otherwise occurred',[2] but the operation was a direct challenge to British policy on Germany. Had the long drawn out economic war of attrition between France and Germany not delayed the acceptance by the Rhenish and Ruhr industrialists of the MICUM Agreements until November 1923, French influence would have been greatly strengthened on the Rhine. Britain was reduced to a policy of impotent 'benevolent passivity' for nine months, and then from

1. L. Kettenacker, *Krieg zur Friedenssicherung. Die Deutschland-Plannung der britischen Regierung während des zweiten Weltkrieges*, Publications of the German History Institute, London, vol. 22, Göttingen and Zürich, 1989, p. 519 (my translation).
2. Maier, *Recasting Bourgeois Europe*, p. 580.

September 1923 until February 1924 she could only conduct a stubborn delaying action against French initiatives to create the economic infrastructure of an independent Rhineland until the decline of the franc and the consequent French dependence on loans from the City of London and New York created a new malleability in Paris.

4. The fourth stage of the occupation bridged the period from February 1924 to December 1925 when the Versailles settlement was modified by the Dawes Plan and the Locarno pacts. The failure of the Ruhr operation and the subsequent underwriting of German fiscal and political union by the Dawes Plan finally destroyed the capacity of the French to threaten German unity by detaching the Rhineland from the Reich. As a corollary of this weakness they placed even greater emphasis on German disarmament and made the evacuation of the first zone in the Rhineland dependent on the progress reports coming from the IAMCC. It was thus an apparent paradox that only four months after the London Conference, which Ramsay MacDonald firmly believed marked the beginning of a new era, the Allies refused to evacuate the northern zone punctually in January 1925, as stipulated in Article 429 of the Treaty, on the indisputable grounds that progress in German disarmament had been minimal since 1922. The deadlock was broken by the Locarno Agreements which, by providing an Anglo–Italian guarantee of the Franco–German borders, went some way towards meeting French demands for security and so opened up the way for the evacuation of the northern zone and the withdrawal of the IAMCC fifteen months later.

5. The surprising aspect of the fifth and final phase of the occupation was that it lasted so long. Dawes, Locarno and Germany's entry into the League of Nations removed the moral, if not legal, justification for the occupation, yet Chamberlain, having established Britain as an arbiter between France and Germany through Locarno, and increasingly distracted by threats to the Empire from Moscow and the Kuomintang, was happy to let the occupation run its course. Indeed, both the War Office and the Treasury perceived solid advantages in its continuation: the former had until 1928 no surplus barracks space for the men of the Rhine Army, while the latter appreciated that ultimately the occupation provided them with some bargaining counters when the Dawes Plan came up for revision. The end of the occupation was signalled when, in response to a determined initiative by Müller, Briand agreed in September 1928 to the

convocation of the Experts Committee and eventually to parallel negotiations on reparations and evacuation. The election of a Labour government in June 1929 hastened the final evacuation of the Rhine Army, but given Chamberlain's assent to the setting up of an Experts Committee, it is unlikely that its withdrawal was greatly accelerated.

Viewed from the perspective of the inter-war period, the maintenance of British troops in Germany for eleven years was unprecedented. Did the occupation in its various forms assist British diplomacy to keep French revisionism in check? Unlike 1945, when Britain was the junior partner of an Allied coalition, in 1919, as a consequence of the pivotal role played by Haig's forces on the Western Front in 1917–18, and the opportune ending of hostilities before the full potential of American military power could be brought into play, Lloyd George commanded sufficient prestige at the Peace Conference to enforce a compromise settlement on Clemenceau, which ultimately enabled Britain to hold the balance of power in Europe until 1936. However, up to 1924, as a result of British economic and military weakness, as well as her worldwide Imperial commitments, the execution of the compromise Treaty of Versailles provided France with repeated opportunities to attempt a *de facto* Treaty revision.

Although Britain relied upon her seat at the Conference of Ambassadors and ultimately on the Supreme Council to mobilize diplomatic support to block hostile French initiatives, the front line against the French was held by British officials in the Rhineland and Danzig and on the Plebiscite and Control Commissions. In Schleswig, Marienwerder and Allenstein their presence was probably only of marginal importance, as the results of the plebiscites were a foregone conclusion, but in Danzig the uneasy Haking–Tower partnership facilitated the execution of a compromise favourable to Britain. The absence of a British garrison in Upper Silesia may not have been the main reason for the failure of the British government to enforce its interpretation of the plebiscite on France, but it is undeniable that the lack of a British military presence in the first seventeen months of the Upper Silesian Administrative Commission gravely weakened Percival's prestige and subsequent ability to control Le Rond.

Up to 1927 British officials both on the IAMCC and in Cologne and Coblenz played, with mixed success, a crucial role in acting as a brake on the French. Bingham, undermined by Morgan and faced by the single-mindedness of Nollet, was frequently outwitted, but by cooperating closely with Lord D'Abernon his very existence on the IAMCC acted as a tripwire which ensured that Nollet's decisions were usually challenged and referred back to the Conference of Ambassadors. In the different diplomatic climate of 1925–7 Wauchope played a key role in liaising with Pawelsz to secure the necessary compromises to enable the IAMCC to withdraw. In Cologne, the Rhine Army blocked repeated attempts by the French to create a separatist Rhineland by simply being there and protecting the capital of the Rhineland from French pressure. The hesitant and passive British occupation of Cologne played a major role in the eventual defeat of the Ruhr occupation by initially providing a haven for the local organization of passive resistance, and secondly by depriving the French of the banking, political and communications capital of the Rhineland. An accidental but valuable consequence of the occupation was to provide a secure entrepôt for British trade into the Rhineland during a period of chaos in Germany.

Once the London Conference of 1924 and the Locarno Pacts had established Britain as 'the honest broker' between Germany and France, the occupation ceased to have much value for Britain, except as a depreciating asset to be used to clinch a favourable settlement when the Dawes Plan came to be renegotiated, or as a temporary source of surplus barrack space to replace what had been lost in the Irish Free State.

By 1930 British participation in the Plebiscite Commissions of 1920–2, Danzig and the Control Commissions was virtually forgotten in Britain except by the odd former participant or specialized body in international affairs.[3] Even the occupation of the Rhineland was perceived to be a 'postscript to the Western front'[4] that went on for too long. British involvement in Germany did, however, leave amongst the British public a reservoir of goodwill towards the Germans and the gut reaction that Germany had been treated unfairly by the Versailles Treaty. Hitler's accession to power led to questions being raised in some quarters whether the Allies should not have occupied the whole of Germany in 1919,[5]

3. See for instance G.S. Hutchinson, *Silesia Revisited, 1929. An Examination of the Problems Arising from the Plebiscite and the Partitions, and the Relations between the British Coal Problem and Silesia*, London, 1929; it was published with a grant from the German government (Hutchison to Bernsdorff, 26.1.29, FCO Lib. 1572 380919–20). See also above, ch. 15, footnote 2.
4. Tuohy, *Occupied, 1918–30*.
5. 'The mistake, as personally I have never ceased to think was not to have crossed the Rhine in full massiveness in 1919'; J.L. Garvin, quoted in M. Gilbert, *The Roots of Appeasement*, London, 1966, p. 141.

but rapidly the consensus of informed opinion in Britain came to accept that Hitler was essentially the product of Versailles, of which the occupation of the Rhineland was a particularly humiliating part.[6] There was a marked absence of opinion suggesting that premature evacuation in 1929 was an error. Almost certainly had British forces still been in the Rhineland in 1933, Hitler's takeover of power would have merely strengthened the arguments for evacuation. It was, for instance, with the greatest reluctance that the British sent troops in 1935 to police the Saar plebiscite. The Cabinet was only persuaded to agree to their dispatch in order to avoid provoking Berlin by the use of French troops.[7] Even the German military re-occupation of the Rhineland in 1936 failed to provoke a decisive stand. Neither the government nor the Labour opposition wished to travel again down the road of military and economic sanctions against Germany. Only gradually, as Hitler's aggressive foreign policy and repressive domestic policy exhausted the legacy of sympathy in Britain for Germany, did British public opinion lose its pro-German bias and join with the new 'realists' to force Neville Chamberlain, after the Nazi occupation of Prague, to abandon the traditional British policy of appeasement.

In the Second World War the dual question of the disarmament and re-occupation of Germany again became relevant. The solutions of 1919 were rejected out of hand by both the academic experts at Chatham House and by the Research Department of the Foreign Office, who were determined not to repeat the crucial error made by the Treaty of Versailles, which forced on Germany a punitive peace without the initial destruction of her *Machtpotential*.[8] Morgan had the satisfaction of seeing his biting criticisms of Bingham and D'Abernon vindicated. He was invited to advise the Post-war Policy Group of members of both Houses of Parliament on the disarmament of Germany,[9] and became something of a cult figure. His battle against the appeasers was described in a book by the German refugee Leopold Schwarzschild, and was even the subject of a broadcast 'of a semi-dramatic character'[10] on the BBC.

---

6. Ibid., pp. 142–50. Significantly, one former British official of the IARHC (B.T. Reynolds) published his reminiscences in 1933 (London) under the title *Prelude to Hitler. A Personal Record of Ten Postwar Years in Germany*. See also Fraenkel, *Military Occupation*, p. 3.
7. C.J. Hill, 'Great Britain and the Saar Plebiscite of 13 January, 1935', *Journal of Contemporary History*, vol. 9, no. 2, 1974, pp. 131–42.
8. Kettenacker, *Krieg zur Friedenssicherung*, pp. 523–4.
9. Morgan, *Assize of Arms*, vol. 1, p. xvii.
10. L. Schwarzschild, *World in Trance*, London, 1943; Morgan, *Assize of Arms*, vol. 1, p. xiii; ibid., vol. 2, Galley slip III (62T CR). The broadcast was on 12.11.43.

Eight hundred copies of the first volume of *Assize of Arms* were ordered by the War Office when it was published in 1945![11]

In March 1943 the German experts in the Foreign Office presented the Cabinet with a memorandum on post-war Germany.[12] It was still assumed that the Germans would, as in 1918, overthrow their government and request an armistice to avoid the destruction of their homeland, but this time the Cabinet was emphatically advised to insist on the total occupation of Germany. In the words of a memorandum written in July 1945, from a position of strength the Allies would then be able to insist on 'a drastic policy over a selected field of German industry with a view to eliminating the basis of Germany's war potential'.[13]

It was British policy neither to dismember Germany nor to destroy her economically. As in 1919 it was recognized that Germany was an essential motor of the European economy. The crucial difference between the two occupations, apart from the enormous contrast in scale, lay in the change in Britain's status. In 1945 Britain was a junior partner whose power was fast ebbing away, while in 1919 in the final analysis she still possessed sufficient power to protect her interests and to restrain the French. Paradoxically, in 1945 the Foreign Office positively welcomed an occupation of Germany as it would keep the war-time alliance together and guarantee Britain a major role in the shaping of the post-war settlement. Despite the huge discrepancy in power between Britain and her major allies, the Foreign Office was convinced of Britain's innate ability based on her 'political maturity, . . . diplomatic experience; the confidence which the solidarity of our democratic institutions inspires in western Europe – and our incomparable war record',[14] to seize the leadership in the post-war world. Haking summed up this attitude when he advised Professor Webster on the constitution of a possible new Armistice Commission:

> the British must be the dominant Party at the next armistice; the Americans may appear to be equal partners, but they do not know enough about Europe to be really helpful. The French will do their utmost to take the leadership out of our hands; the Russians will put in

11. G.M. Bayliss, 'Introduction', in Edmonds, *The Occupation*.
12. Kettenacker, *Krieg zur Friedenssicherung*, p. 524.
13. Quoted in I. Turner, *British Policy towards German Industry 1945–1949. Reconstruction, Restriction or Exploitation?* p. 6 (a talk given to the German History Society Regional Conference, 27–28 March 1987 at St Antony's College, Oxford).
14. Sargent, quoted in Kettenacker, *Krieg zur Friedenssicherung*, p. 518.

impossible clauses; the Poles will bleat; the Americans will say 'I guess' and 'is that so' in the most aggravating manner and having little idea how to deal with any European situation.[15]

In fact, such a scenario was to turn out to be the product of wishful thinking, and in the cold light of the post-war world Britain's bluff was called on an unprecedented scale.

15. Haking to Webster, 19.9.43, CAB 45/82.

Abbreviations

AA	Auswärtiges Amt (German Foreign Office)
AN	Archives Nationales, Paris
AQMG	Assistant Quartermaster-General
BA.KO	Bundesarchiv Koblenz
BL	British Library, London
C.in.C.	Commander-in-Chief
CGS	Chief of the General Staff
CIGS	Chief of the Imperial General Staff
DBFP	Documents on British Foreign Policy
DMO & I	Director of Military Operations and Intelligence
FCO Lib.	Foreign and Commonwealth Office Library
fo(s)	Folio(s)
GOC	General Officer Commanding
GS	General Staff
HA d SK	Historisches Archiv der Stadt Köln
HLRO	House of Lords Records Office
IAACC	Inter-Allied Aeronautical Control Commission
IAMCC	Inter-Allied Military Control Commission
IANCC	Inter-Allied Naval Control Commission
IARHC	Inter-Allied Rhineland High Commission
IWM	Imperial War Museum
LG	Lloyd George Papers
LHCMA	Liddell Hart Centre for Military Archives, Kings College, London
LSE	London School of Economics
MAE	Ministère des Affaires Etrangères (French Foreign Ministry)
MICUM	Mission Interalliée du Contrôle des Usines et Mines
Min.	Minute
NLOS	National Library of Scotland
RTO	Railway Transport Officer
Sipo	Sicherheitspolizei
SWC	Supreme War Council
USFR, PPC	Papers relating to the Foreign Relations of the United States, the Paris Peace Conference, 1919
Vincennes	Service historique de l'Armée de Terre, Château de Vincennes, Paris

Glossary of German Terms
Used most frequently in Text

Abwickelungsamt	Office set up to preside over the liquidation of the war-time army
Auswärtiges Amt	German Foreign Office
Bezirk	A local government district
Betriebsrat	Works Council
Einwohnerwehr	'Home Guard'
Freikorps	Volunteer forces of demobilized officers, NCOs and students raised in the winter of 1918–19 to defend Germany from Poles and Communists
Kreis	A district or unit of local government
Kreis officer	Allied official in charge of such an area
Notenbank	Bank of Issue
Orgesch	'Organization Escherich': a Bavarian paramilitary force created by Dr G. Escherich
Polizeipräsident	Chief Constable
Reichsbahn	German State Railways
Reichsbank	German Central Bank, Berlin
Reichskanzler	The Chancellor of the German Reich
Reichsmarine	German Navy
Reichswehr	German Army
Reichswehrministerium	German War Office
Regierungspräsident	District President
Rentenmark	A new mark currency introduced on 15 November 1923 by the German government
Selbstschutz	Self-defence forces
Schutzpolizei	'Protective police' created in the autumn of 1920 to replace the Sicherheitspolizei
Sicherheitspolizei (Sipo)	'Security police' created in August 1919

Select Bibliography

ARCHIVAL SOURCES

A. British

1. Public Record Office, Kew, London

Admiralty Papers
ADM 116   Admiralty and Secretariat Cases

Board of Trade Papers
BT 60   Department of Overseas Trade, Correspondence and Papers

Cabinet Papers
CAB 23   Conclusions of the Cabinet
CAB 28   Allied War Conferences
CAB 29   Peace Conference and Other International Conferences to 1939
CAB 44   Cabinet Office Historical Section. Official War Histories: Narrative, Military
CAB 45   Cabinet Office Historical Section, Official War Histories: Correspondence and Papers

Foreign Office Papers
FO 371   General Correspondence: Political
FO 374   Peace Conference of 1919–20: Acts of Conference
FO 382   General Correspondence: Contraband
FO 608   Peace Conference of 1919–20: Correspondence
FO 852   International Plebiscite Commission in Slesvig
FO 894   Minutes of the Inter-Allied Rhineland High Commission

War Office Papers
WO 32   Registered Papers, General series
WO 95   War Diaries 1914–1922
WO 137   Papers of Lord Derby
WO 144   Inter-Allied Armistice Commission, Chief of Mission Despatches
WO 155   Allied Military Committee of Versailles
WO 158   Correspondence and Papers of Military Headquarters

WO 106	Directorate of Military Operations and Intelligence: Papers
WO 256	Haig Diaries (up to 11 November 1918)

2. *The Bank of England, London*

OV 34	Files on Germany
OV 120	Danzig

3. *The British Library, London*

The Papers of Lord D'Abernon

4. *The Foreign and Commonwealth Office Library, London*

Unpresented Ph.D. thesis on 'The British Embassy of Lord D'Abernon, 1920–26' by D.A. Holt.
10 volumes of press cuttings, etc., compiled by Sir Reginald Tower

5. *Friends House, London*

Archives of the Friends Emergency and War Victims Relief Committee, 1914–1924
Silvia Cowles Papers

6. *House of Lords' Record Office, London*

Papers of David Lloyd George

7. *Imperial War Museum, London*

The following collections were particularly useful;

(a) Archives
The papers of:
Capt. A.B. Ashby
Major C.J.P. Ball
Brigadier J.A. Barraclough
Lt C. Carter
Capt. W.G. Cook
Pte D.H. Doe
Pte J.A. Douglas
Pte J.W. Drury
Lt Col. A. Fleetwood-Wilson
G.E.R. Gedye

Lt Col. R.B. Gooden
Lt Col. N.M. Goodman
Pte G.W. Sullivan
Field Marshal Sir Henry Wilson

(b) Library
5 volumes of photos, press cuttings, etc., compiled by General Sir William Thwaites, 1927–9

8. *Liddell Hart Centre for Military Archives, Kings College, University of London*

Field Marshal Sir William Robertson Papers
Major–General Sir Sidney Clive Papers

9. *Labour Party Archives, London*

Minutes of the National Executive Committee, vols 26–30

10. *Lloyds Bank Archives, London*

The Minute Books of Lloyds Bank (France) and of the National Provincial Bank (France) Ltd

11. *The London School of Economics, London*

The papers of Violet Markham
The papers of Sir Frederick Wise
The papers of Professor Sir Charles Webster

12. *Midland Bank Archives, London*

Minute Books of Mr Buchanan and reports from the Overseas Branch

13. *National Army Museum, Chelsea, London*

Colonel Jourdain's Diary, 1921–2

14. *National Library of Scotland, Edinburgh*

Papers of Field Marshal, the Earl Haig
Papers of General Sir Aylmer Haldane

15. *Oxford University*

Select Bibliography

Christ Church: The papers of Colonel Percival
St Antony's College: The papers of General Sir Neill Malcolm

16. TUC Archives, London

Joint International and Joint Executive Minutes (T. 39)

17. Private Papers

1. Beaumont, Sir Henry Hammond Dawson: unpublished memoirs made available by his son, Mr C.A.W. Beaumont (microfilmed copy in Imperial War Museum).
2. Bourdillon, Francis Bernard: a miscellaneous collection of souvenirs and a diary for 1920 made available by his son, Dr John F. Bourdillon.
3. Marling, Sir Charles: a miscellaneous collection of letters, photos and a scrapbook on 'Slesvig' made available by his grandson, Mr D.W.M. Long.
4. Morgan, Brigadier-General John Hartman: proofs and galley slips of the second volume of *Assize of Arms* made available by Mr Barry O'Brien.
5. Robertson, Sir Malcolm Arnold: a comprehensive official and unofficial correspondence and unpublished memoirs, made available by his son, Major D.S. Robertson.
6. Tiarks, Frank Cyril: correspondence with his wife, January–April 1919 and the transcript of an interview conducted with Henry F. Tiarks (his son) by Dr R. Roberts, 11 May 1984, made available by Mr H.F. Tiarks and Dr R. Roberts.

B. French

1. Archives Nationales

The papers of the Haute Commission Interalliée Des Territoires Rhénans ('Papiers Tirard')

2. Archives Diplomatiques, Ministère des Affaires Etrangères, Paris

Série Z Europe, 1918–1929: Allemagne, Danzig, Rive Gauche Du Rhin, Pologne

3. Service historique de l'Armée de Terre, Château de Vincennes

Selected files of l'État-Major de Foch (Série 4N)
Selected files of le Deuxième Bureau (Série 7N)
Fond privé, Jacobson (IK.85)

C. Germany

1. *Bundesarchiv, Coblenz*

Selected files of the Reichskanzlei (R43 I)
Nachlaß Erich Koch-Weser
Nachlaß Paul Silverberg

2. *Historisches Archiv, Köln*

Best.83/1/16, 17, 19, 20:	Files dealing with the British Occupation, December 1918–January 1926
Abt.902, Nr. 241, Fasz 1:	Files containing Adenauer's interviews with British military officials, December 1918
Chroniken und Darstellungen Nr. 501:	The unpublished manuscript of Dr Josef Becker, 'Sieben Jahre britischer Herrschaft in Köln', 2 vols

3. *Auswärtiges Amt*

Photocopied and Microfilmed Records of the Auswärtiges Amt available at the Foreign and Commonwealth Office Library, London (references given are from the Kent Catalogue):
I. The occupied Rhineland Territories and the Ruhr: L1620, L1711, L1766, K2131, 3058, 4501–2, 9426, 9518.
II. Disarmament and the Control Commissions: L120, L128, L319, L320, L321, L334, L337, L722, 4530, 9285, 9483, 9490, 9627, 9861, 9862.
III. The Plebiscite zones: L912, K1809, K2281, K2286, K2288, K2295, 3137, 3139, 4718, 8868.
IV. Great Britain: K128, K131, K136, K138, 2368, 5742.
V. The Armistice: 4080.

PUBLISHED DOCUMENTS

Great Britain, Parliament, *Parliamentary Papers*, 1919, vol. 53. (Accounts and Papers, vol. 22), Cmnd. 153, July 1919, 'Treaty of Peace between the Allied and Associated Powers and Germany, signed at Versailles, 28th June 1919'
Morsey, R. and K. Repgen (eds), *Untersuchungen und Dokumente zur Ostpolitik und Biographie*, Veröffentlichungen der Kommission fur Zeitgeschichte, Reihe B. Forschungen, vol. 15, Adenauer-Studien III, Mainz, 1974
Parliamentary Debates, House of Commons, 5th series, vols 98–240, London, 1919–20

Parliamentary Debates, House of Lords, 5th series, vols 31–77, London, 1920–6

United States, Department of State, *Papers Relating to the Foreign Relations of the United States, the Paris Peace Conference, 1919*, 13 vols, Washington, 1942–7

Woodward, E.L. *et al.* (eds) *Documents on British Foreign Policy*, London, 1947 (continuing)

CONTEMPORARY NEWSPAPERS AND PERIODICALS

Bystander
Cologne Post and [after 1926] *Wiesbaden Times*
Daily Mail
Daily Telegraph
Deutsche Allgemeine Zeitung
Echo de Paris
Evening Standard
The Gong (University College, Nottingham, 1923)
Kölnische Zeitung
Le Temps
Manchester Guardian
Morning Post
Nation and Athenaeum
Observer
Quarterly Review
Spectator
The Economist
The Times
Vossische Zeitung

PUBLISHED LETTERS, DIARIES, MEMOIRS AND BIOGRAPHIES

Allen, H.T., *My Rhineland Journal*, Boston, 1923

Blake, R., *The Private Papers of Douglas Haig*, London, 1952

——, *The Unknown Prime Minister*, London, 1955

Callwell, Major-General Sir C.E., *Field Marshal Sir Henry Wilson: His Life and Diaries*, 2 vols, London, 1927

Cambon, Paul, *Correspondance, 1870–1924*, 3 vols, Paris, 1940–6

D'Abernon, Helen, *Red Cross and Berlin Embassy, 1915–26*, London, 1946

D'Abernon, Viscount Edgar Vincent, *An Ambassador of Peace*, 3 vols, London, 1929–30

Davenport-Hines, R.P.T., *Dudley Docker. The Life and Times of a Trade Warrior*, London, 1984

Dugdale, B.E., *Arthur James Balfour*, 2 vols, London, 1936

François-Poncet, A., *De Versailles à Potsdam*, Paris, 1948

Gilbert, M., *Winston Churchill*, vols 4 and 5, London, 1975 and 1976

Godley, Sir A., *Life of an Irish Soldier*, London, 1939

Greene, G., *A Sort of a Life*, London, 1971

Gregory, J.D., *On the Edge of Diplomacy, Rambles and Reflections, 1902–1928*, London, 1929

Harrington, General Sir C., *Lord Plumer*, London, 1935

Headlam-Morley, Sir James, *A Memoir of the Paris Peace Conference, 1919* (ed. A. Headlam-Morley, R. Bryant and A. Cienciala), London, 1972

Henniker, M.C.A., *Memoirs of a Junior Officer*, London, 1951

Jones, T., *Whitehall Diaries*, 2 vols, London, 1969

Kessler, H.G., *Tagebücher, 1918–27*, Frankfurt, 1961

Laroche, J., *Au Quai d'Orsay avec Briand et Poincaré, 1913–26*, Paris, 1957

Lloyd George, D., *War Memoirs*, 2 vols, London, 1938

——, *Memoirs of the Peace Conference*, Yale, 1939

Markham, V.R., *A Woman's Watch on the Rhine*, London, 1920

Middlemas, K. and J. Barnes, *Baldwin*, London, 1969

Morgan, J.H., *Assize of Arms*, vol. 1, London, 1945

Nicolson, H., *Curzon, The Last Phase 1919–1925*, London, 1934

——, *Peacemaking*, London, 1933

Nollet, C., *Une Expérience De Désarmement. Cinque Ans de Contrôle militaire en Allemagne*, Paris, 1932

Noske, G., *Von Kiel bis Kapp*, Berlin, 1920

Petrie, C., *The Life and Letters of the Right Honourable Sir Austen Chamberlain*, 2 vols, London, 1939–40

Prittie, T., *Konrad Adenauer*, London, 1972

Rathenau, W., *Tagebuch 1907–1922*, ed. H. Pogge von Strandmann, Düsseldorf, 1967

Reynolds, B.T., *Prelude to Hitler. A Personal Record of Ten Postwar Years in Germany*, London, 1933

Riddell, G.A., *Lord Riddell's Intimate Diary of the Peace Conference and after, 1918–23*, London, 1933

Robertson, Field-Marshal Sir William, *From Private to Field Marshal*, London, 1921

Roddie, S., *Peace Patrol*, London, 1932

Ronaldshay, Earl of, *The Life of Lord Curzon: Being the Authorized Biography of George Nathanial Marquess Curzon of Kedleston, K.G.*, 3 vols, London, 1928

Stresemann, G., *Diaries, Letters and Papers*, 3 vols, ed. E. Sutton, London, 1935–40

Tirard, P., *La France sur le Rhin: Douze années d'occupation rhénane*, Paris, 1930

Trebitsch-Lincoln, J.T., *The Autobiography of an Adventurer*, London, 1931

Temperley, J.A.C., *The Whispering Gallery of Europe*, London, 1938

CONTEMPORARY ARTICLES AND STUDIES

Allen, Major-General H.T., *The Rhineland Occupation*, Indianapolis, 1927

Anon., '1st Battalion Notes', *Regimental Annual of The Sherwood Foresters*, 1920, pp. 5–10

Anon., '3rd Battalion', *Royal Fusiliers Chronicle*, 1921, pp. 38–45

'Apex' (R.G. Coulson), *The Uneasy Triangle. Four Years of Occupation*, London, 1931

Bingham, Sir Francis, 'Work with the Allied Commission of Control in Germany, 1919–24', *Journal of the Royal United Services Institution*, vol. 69, 1924, pp. 747–63

Gedye, G.E.R, 'La justice Militaire', *Nation and Athenaeum*, vol. 40, 1924, pp. 555–6

——, *The Revolver Republic*, London, 1930

H.W.M., 'The French War on Germany', *Nation and Athenaeum*, vol. 31, 1922, pp. 644–6

Hutchison, G.S., *Silesia Revisited, 1929. An Examination of the Problems Arising from the Plebiscite and the Partitions, and the Relations between the British Coal Problem and Silesia*, London, 1929

Keynes, J.M., *The Economic Consequences of The Peace*, London, 1920

Morgan, J.H., 'The Disarmament of Germany and After', *Quarterly Review*, vol. 242, October 1924, pp. 415–57

Osborne, C., 'In Berlin', *The Gong*, December 1923, p. 475.

Repington, C., *After the War*, London, 1922

Tardieu, A., *The Truth about the Treaty*, Indianapolis, 1931

Temperley, H.W.V. (ed.), *A History of the Peace Conference of Paris*, 6 vols, published under the auspices of the Institute of International Affairs, London, 1920–4

Thwaites, Sir W. (Lt. Gen.), 'The British Legion on the Rhine', *The British Legion (the Journal for all ex-servicemen)*, November 1929

Tuohy, F., 'France's Rhineland Adventure', *Contemporary Review*, vol. 138, 1930, pp. 29–38

——, *Occupied, 1918–30: A Postscript to the Western Front*, London, 1931

Tynan, K., *Life in the Occupied Area*, London, 1925

GENERAL HISTORIES AND SPECIAL STUDIES

Abrahams, P., 'American Bankers and the Economic Tactics of Peace, 1919', *Journal of American History*, vol. 56, no. 3, 1969, pp. 572–83

Anon., *F.A. Hughes Centenary Year*, Epsom, 1968

Artaud, D., 'Le Gouvernement Américan et la question de dettes de guerre au lendemain de l'armistice de Réthondes, 1919–20', *Revue d'histoire moderne et contemporaire*, vol. 20, (April–June) 1973, pp. 201–29

Bariéty, J., *Les relations franco-allemandes après la premiere guerre mondiale,*

10 Novembre 1918–10 Janvier 1925. De l'exécution à la négociation, Paris, 1977

Barnett, C., *The Collapse of British Power*, London, 1972

Beloff, M., *Imperial Sunset*, vol. I: *Britain's Liberal Empire*, London, 1969

Bertram-Libal, G., 'Die britische Politik in der Oberschlesienfrage, 1919–22', *Vierteljahrshefte für Zeitgeschichte*, vol. 20, no. 2, 1972, pp. 105–32

Bond, B., *British Military Policy between the Two World Wars*, Oxford, 1980

Campbell, F.G., 'The Struggle for Upper Silesia, 1919–22', *Journal of Modern History*, vol. 42, no. 3, 1970, pp. 361–85

Carrington, C.E., *Soldier from the War Returning*, London, 1965

Carsten, F.L., *The Reichswehr and Politics*, Oxford, 1966

——, *Britain and the Weimar Republic*, London, 1984

Challoner, R., 'The French Foreign Office: The Era of Philippe Berthelot', in G.A. Craig and F. Gilbert (eds), *The Diplomats*, Princeton, 1953

Cienciala, A.M. and T. Komarnicki, *From Versailles to Locarno*, Kansas, 1984

Clarke, P.F., 'The Progressive Movement in England', *Transactions of the Royal Historical Society*, 5th series, no. 24 (1974), pp. 159–81.

Cobban, A., *A History of Modern France*, vol. 3: *1871–1962*, London, 1965

Craig, G.A., 'The British Foreign Office from Grey to Austen Chamberlain', in G. Craig and F. Gilbert (eds), *The Diplomats*, Princeton, 1953

——, *The Politics of the Prussian Army, 1640–1945*, London, 1955

——, *Germany, 1866–1945*, Oxford, 1978

Cumming, H.H., *Franco-British Rivalry in the Post-War Near East. The Decline of French Influence*, London, 1938 (reprinted: Westport CT, 1981)

Dawson, W.H., *Germany under The Treaty*, London, 1933

Dockrill, M.L. and J.D. Goold *Peace without Promise. Britain and the Peace Conferences, 1919–23*, London, 1981

Edmonds, J.E., *The Occupation of the Rhineland*, London, 1944 (reprinted in Facsimile Edition with Introduction by G.M. Bayliss, London, 1987)

Eliasberg, G., *Der Ruhrkrieg von 1920*, Bonn, 1974

Erdmann, K.D., *Adenauer in der Rheinlandpolitik nach dem Ersten Weltkrieg*, Stuttgart, 1966

Erger, J., *Der Kapp–Lüttwitz Putsch. Ein Beitrag zur deutschen Innenpolitik, 1919–20*, Düsseldorf, 1967

Eyck, E., *Geschichte der Weimarer Republik*, 2 vols, Zürich, 1956

Felix, D., *Walther Rathenau and the Weimar Republic*, Baltimore and London, 1971

Fink, C., *The Genoa Conference*, Chapel Hill and London, 1984

Fox, J.P., 'Britain and the Inter-Allied Military Commission of Control, 1925–26', *Journal of Contemporary History*, vol. 4, no. 2, 1969, pp. 143–64

Fraenkel, E., *Military Occupation and the Rule of Law*, London and New York, 1944

Gajda, P., *Postscript to Victory, British Policy and the German–Polish Borderland*,

1919–1925, Washington, 1982

Garston, J., 'Armies of Occupation: II', *History Today*, vol. 2, July 1961, pp. 479–89

Gatzke, H.W., *Stresemann and The Rearmament of Germany*, Baltimore, 1954

Geoghegan, S., *The Campaigns and History of the Royal Irish Regiment*, vol. 2, *1900–1922*, Edinburgh, 1927

Gilbert, M., *Britain and Germany between the Wars*, London 1964

——, *The Roots of Appeasement*, London, 1966

Heideking, J., 'Oberster Rat – Botschafterkonferenz – Völkerbund', *Historische Zeitschrift*, vol. 231, 1980, pp. 589–630

Hiden, J.W., *The Weimar Republic*, London, 1974

——, *Germany and Europe, 1919–39*, London, 1977

Hill, C.J., 'Great Britain and the Saar Plebiscite of 13 January, 1935', *Journal of Contemporary History*, vol. 9, no. 2, 1974, pp. 121–42

Holborn, H., *A History of Modern Germany, 1840–1945*, London, 1969

Howard, M., *The Continental Commitment: The Dilemma of British Defence Policy in the Era of the Two World Wars*, London, 1972

Howard, T.H., 'Tales of the E.O.T.A: The British Army of the Rhine', *Army Quarterly*, 1943–44, pp. 759–70

Jacobson, J., *Locarno Diplomacy. Germany and the West, 1925–29*, Princeton, 1972

——, 'The Conduct of Locarno Diplomacy', in W. Michalka and M. Lee (eds), *Gustav Stresemann*, Darmstadt, 1982, pp. 209–24

—— and J.T. Walker, 'The Impulse for a Franco-German Entente: The Origins of the Thoiry Conference, 1926', *Journal of Contemporary History*, vol. 10, no. 1, 1975, pp. 157–75

Jaffe, L.S., *The Decision to Disarm Germany*, London and Sydney, 1985

James, R., *The British Revolution, from Asquith to Churchill, 1793–1940*, Oxford, 1967

Jeremy, D., *Dictionary of Business Biography*, vols I and IV, London, 1985

Jordan, W.M., *Great Britain, France and the German Problem, 1918–1939* (new impression), London, 1971

Kaiser, A., 'Lord D'Abernon und die Entstehungsgeschichte der Locarno-Verträge', *Vierteljahrshefte für Zeitgeschichte*, vol. 34, January 1986, pp. 85–104

——, *Lord D'Abernon und die englische Deutschlandpolitik 1920–26*, Europäische Hochschulschriften, Reihe III, vol. 362, Frankfurt am Main, Bern, New York and Paris, 1989

Kemp, T., *The French Economy, 1913–39. The History of a Decline*, London, 1972

Kennedy, P., *Strategy and Diplomacy, 1870–1945*, London, 1983

Kettenacker, L., *Krieg zur Friedenssicherung. Die Deutschlandplanung der britischen Regierung während des zweiten Weltkrieges*, Publications of the German History Institute, London, vol. 22, Göttingen and Zürich, 1989

Kimmich, C.M., *The Free City*, New Haven and London, 1968

King, J.C., *Foch versus Clemenceau*, Cambridge MA, 1960

Knight-Patterson, W.M., *Germany from Defeat to Conquest*, London, 1945

Kochan, L., *The Struggle for Germany, 1914–45*, Edinburgh, 1963

Krüger, P., *Die Außenpolitik der Republik von Weimar*, Darmstadt, 1985

Laubach, E., *Die Politik der Kabinette Wirth, 1921/22* (Historische Studien, Heft 402) Lübeck and Hamburg, 1968

Lowe, C.J. and M.L. Dockrill, *The Mirage of Power*, vol. 2, *British Foreign Policy, 1914–22*, London, 1972

Lyman, R., *The First Labour Government of 1924*, New York, 1975

McCallum, R.B., *Public Opinion and the Last Peace*, London, 1944

McCrum, R., 'French Rhineland Policy at the Peace Conference, 1919', *Historical Journal*, vol. 21, no. 3, 1978, pp. 623–48

McDougall, W.A., *France's Rhineland Diplomacy, 1914–24*, Princeton, 1978

Maier, C.S., *Recasting Bourgeois Europe*, Princeton, 1975

Marquand, R., *Ramsay MacDonald*, London, 1977

Mason, J.B., *The Danzig Dilemma: A Study in Peacemaking by Compromise*, London, 1946

Mayer, A.J., *Politics and Diplomacy of Peacemaking. Containment and Counter-revolution at Versailles, 1918–1919*, London, 1968

Medlicott, W.N., *British Foreign Policy since Versailles, 1919–63*, London, 1968

Morgan, K., *Consensus and Disunity. The Lloyd George Coalition Government 1918–22*, Oxford, 1979

Mowat, C.L., *Britain between the Wars, 1918–1940*, London, 1955

——, *Great Britain since 1914*, London, 1971

Nelson, H.I., *Land and Power. British and Allied Policy on Germany's Frontiers, 1916–19*, London and Toronto, 1963

Nelson, K.L., 'The Black Horror on the Rhine: Race as a factor in Post-World War I Diplomacy', *Journal of Modern History*, vol. 42, December 1970, pp. 606–27

——, *Victors Divided*, Berkeley, Los Angeles and London, 1975

Néré, J., *The Foreign Policy of France from 1919 to 1945*, London and Boston, 1975

Niedhart, G., 'Die Britische Antwort auf die Krise des Weltreiches und des internationalen Systems vor dem 2. Weltkrieg', *Historische Zeitschrift*, vol. 226, 1978, pp. 67–88

——, 'Multipolares Gleichgewicht und Weltwirtschaftliche Verflechtung: Deutschland in der britischen Appeasementpolitik 1919–33', in M. Stürmer (ed.), *Die Weimarer Republik – belagerte Civitas*, Königstein, 1980, pp. 113–30

——, 'Stresemanns Außenpolitik und die Grenzen der Entspannung', in W. Michalka and M. Lee (eds), *Gustav Stresemann*, Darmstadt, 1982, pp. 416–28

Northedge, F.S., *The Troubled Giant*, London, 1966

Piggott, J., 'The Rhineland Republic', *History Today*, vols 3 and 4, December 1953 and January 1954, pp. 817–22 and 11–19

Porter, B. *Britain, Europe and the World 1850–1982, Delusions of Grandeur*, London, 1983

Recker, M-L., 'Adenauer und die englische Besatzungsmacht (1918–26)', in *Konrad Adenauer. Oberbürgermeister von Köln. Festgabe der Stadt Köln zum 100. Geburstag ihres Ehrenbürgers am 5.1.76*, Cologne, 1976, pp. 99–121

Ronde, H., *Von Versailles bis Lausanne*, Stuttgart and Cologne, 1950

Rothstein, A., *The Soldiers' Strikes of 1919*, London, 1980

Rothwell, V.H., *British War Aims and Peace Diplomacy, 1914–18*, Oxford, 1971

Salewski, M., *Entwaffnung und Militärkontrolle in Deutschland, 1919–27*, Munich, 1966

Schuker, S.A., *The End of French Predominance in Europe: The Financial Crisis of 1924 and the Adoption of the Dawes Plan*, Chapel Hill, 1976

Schwarzschild, L., *World in Trance: From Versailles to Pearl Harbour*, London, 1943

Sharp, A.J., 'The Foreign Office in Eclipse', *History*, vol. 61, no. 202, June 1976, pp. 198–218

Silverman, D.P., *Reconstructing Europe after the Great War*, Cambridge MA, 1982

Soutou, G., 'La Politique Economique de la France en Pologne (1920–24)', *Revue Historique*, vol. 251, 1974, pp. 85–116

——, 'La France et Les Marches de l'est, 1914–1919', *Revue Historique*, vol. 260, no. 2, 1978, pp. 341–88

Stambrook, F.G., 'Das Kind. Lord D'Abernon and the Origins of the Locarno Pact', *Central European History*, vol. 1, no. 3, 1968, pp. 233–63

Stevenson, D., *French War Aims*, Oxford, 1982

Taylor, A.J.P., 'The War Aims of the Allies in the First World War', in R. Pares and A.J.P. Taylor (eds), *Essays to Namier*, London, 1956

——, *English History, 1914–45*, Oxford, 1965

Terraine, J., *To Win a War*, London, 1978

Tillman, S.P., *Anglo-American Relations at the Paris Peace Conference of 1919*, Princeton, 1961

Toynbee, A.J., *Survey of International Affairs, 1920–23*, London, 1925

——, *Survey of International Affairs, 1924*, London, 1926

Trachtenberg, M., *Reparation in World Politics: France and European Diplomacy, 1916–23*, New York, 1980

——, 'Versailles after Sixty Years', *Journal of Contemporary History*, vol. 17, no. 3, 1982, pp. 487–506

Troughton, E.R., *It's Happening Again*, London, 1945

Turner, H.A., *Stresemann and the Politics of the Weimar Republic*, Princeton, 1963

Veitch, C., '"Play Up! Play Up! and Win the War!" Football, the Nation and the First World War, 1914–15', *Journal of Contemporary History*, vol. 20, no. 3, 1985, pp. 363–76

Waite, R.G.L., *Vanguard of Nazism. The Free Corps Movement in Post-War Germany*, Cambridge MA, 1952

Wandycz, P.S., *France and Her Eastern Allies, 1919–1925*, Minneapolis, 1962

Wambaugh, S., *Plebiscites since the World War*, 2 vols, Washington, 1933

Wheeler-Bennett, J., *The Nemesis of Power. The German Army in Politics*, London, 1961

White, S., 'Labour's Council of Action, 1920', *Journal of Contemporary History*, vol. 9, no. 4, 1974, pp. 99–122

Williamson, D.G., 'Cologne and The British', *History Today*, vol. 27, November 1977, pp. 695–702

——, 'Great Britain and the Ruhr Crisis, 1923–24', *British Journal of International Studies*, vol. 3, 1977, pp. 70–91

Wolfers, A., *Britain and France between Two Wars: Conflicting Strategies of Peace since Versailles*, New York, 1940

Index